Claudia Linnhoff-Popien   Heinz-Gerd Hegering (Eds.)

Trends in Distributed Systems: Towards a Universal Service Market

T0238183

Third International IFIP/GI Working Conference, USM 2000
Munich, Germany, September 12-14, 2000
Proceedings

Springer

Series Editors

Gerhard Goos, Karlsruhe University, Germany
Juris Hartmanis, Cornell University, NY, USA
Jan van Leeuwen, Utrecht University, The Netherlands

Volume Editors

Claudia Linnhoff-Popien
Heinz-Gerd Hegering
Ludwig-Maximilians-University Munich, Institute for Computer Science
Oettingenstr. 67, 80538 Munich, Germany
E-mail: {linnhoff/hegering}@informatik.uni-muenchen.de

Cataloging-in-Publication Data applied for

Die Deutsche Bibliothek - CIP-Einheitsaufnahme

Trends in distributed systems: towards a universal service market :
third international IFIP GI working conference ; proceedings / USM
2000, Munich, Germany, September 12 - 14, 2000. Claudia
Linnhoff-Popien ; Heinz-Gerd Hegering (ed.). - Berlin ; Heidelberg ;
New York ; Barcelona ; Hong Kong ; London ; Milan ; Paris ; Singapore ;
Tokyo : Springer, 2000
  (Lecture notes in computer science ; Vol. 1890)
  ISBN 3-540-41024-4

CR Subject Classification (1998): C.2, D.4.6, H.4, H.5, I.2.11, K.4.1, K.5.1-2, K.6.5

ISSN 0302-9743
ISBN 3-540-41024-4 Springer-Verlag Berlin Heidelberg New York

Springer-Verlag Berlin Heidelberg New York
a member of BertelsmannSpringer Science+Business Media GmbH
© Springer-Verlag Berlin Heidelberg 2000
Printed in Germany

Typesetting: Camera-ready by author, data conversion by PTP-Berlin, Stefan Sossna
Printed on acid-free paper   SPIN: 10722515   06/3142   5 4 3 2 1 0

Preface

USM 2000 is the third event in a series of international IFIP/GI conferences on Trends in Distributed Systems. Following the venues in Aachen, Germany (1996) and Hamburg, Germany (1998), this event in Munich considers the trend towards a Universal Service Market – USM 2000.

The trend towards a universal service market has many origins, e.g., the integration of telecom and data communications, the deregulation efforts with respect to telco markets, the globalization of information, the virtualization of companies, the requirement of a short time-to-market, the advances in network technologies, the increasing acceptance of e-commerce, and the increase in mobility. This leads to new business-to-business (B2B) and business-to-customer (B2C) environments that offer both challenges and opportunities to enterprises and end-users. There is the need for ubiquitous services, trading, brokering and information management, for service market and business models, and for flexible infrastructures for dynamic collaboration.

Researchers, service vendors, and users must cooperate to set up the appropriate requirements for a universal service market and to find solutions with respect to supporting platforms, middleware, distributed applications, and management. The basis for these solution is a common understanding of means for defining, creating, implementing, and deploying the service market. Then, service market makers, service aggregators, service auctioneers, ISP, ASP, BPO, and customers can freely interact in a dynamic, open, and universal market place.

Of course, this is still a vision and many of unsolved technical, organizational, and legal problems still need to be tackled. The goal of USM 2000 was to gain an insight into the state of the art in this area. The international call for papers resulted in the selection of the papers in these proceedings. This book is organized into a section for invited talks and a section of papers that corresponds with the sessions of the conference. Moreover, a third section consists of several papers accepted for a poster session. The regular sessions deal with electronic auctions and trading, internet-based service markets, quality-of-service, mobile and distributed services, middleware architectures, and service management. The poster sessions are dedicated to mobile agents and applications as well as to trends in data and telecommunications.

The selection of the papers followed a rigorous review process involving an international expert group. We express our gratitude to all members of the program committee for their valuable work. We also want to thank the members of the Munich Network Management Team who were responsible for the organization of the conference.

Munich, September 2000

Claudia Linnhoff-Popien
Heinz-Gerd Hegering

Organization

Conference Chairs

Claudia Linnhoff-Popien and Heinz-Gerd Hegering, LMU Munich

Program Commitee

Sebastian Abeck	University of Karlsruhe, Germany
Andrew T. Campbell	Center for Telecommunications Research, Columbia University, New York, USA
Kurt Geihs	University of Frankfurt, Germany
Bernd Heinrichs	Cisco Systems Europe, Düsseldorf, Germany
Yigal Hoffner	IBM Zurich Research Laboratory, Switzerland
Axel Küpper	RWTH Aachen, Germany
Lea Kutvonen	University of Helsinki, Finland
Winfried Lamersdorf	University of Hamburg, Germany
Luigi Logrippo	University of Ottawa, Canada
Michael Merz	Ponton, Hamburg, Germany
Zoran Milosevic	DSTC, Brisbane, Australia
Elie Najm	Ecole Nationale Superieure des Telecommunications, Paris, France
Bernhard Neumair	DeTeSystem, Darmstadt, Germany
Jerome Rolia	Carleton University, Ottawa, Canada
Alexander Schill	TU Dresden, Dresden, Germany
Doug Schmidt	ARL, St. Louis, USA
Gerd Schürmann	GMD FOKUS, Berlin, Germany
Morris Sloman	Imperial College, London, UK
Otto Spaniol	RWTH Aachen, Germany
Michael Stal	Siemens ZT, Munich, Germany
Ralf Steinmetz	TU Darmstadt & GMD IPSI, Darmstadt, Germany
Volker Tschammer	GMD FOKUS, Berlin, Germany

Organization Commitee

Helmut Reiser (chair)	Bernhard Kempter	Holger Schmidt
Christian Ensel	Annette Kostelezky	Gerald Vogt
Markus Garschhammer	Igor Radisic	
Rainer Hauck	Harald Rölle	

Referees

Sebastian Abeck
Shelby Abraham
Arnaud Bailly
Andreas Bartelt
Christian Becker
Mark Borning
Andrew T. Campbell
Cyril Carrez
Dan Chalmers
James Cole
Dan Dragan
Christian Ensel
Kazi Farooqui
Reza Farsi
Markus Garschhammer
Kurt Geihs
Frank Griffel
Andreas Guther
Rainer Hauck
Stephen Heilbronner

Klaus Herrmann
Yigal Hoffner
Stefan Kaetker
Martin Karsten
Bernhard Kempter
Axel Küpper
Lea Kutvonen
Michael Langer
Luigi Logrippo
Michael Merz
Zoran Milosevic
Michael Nerb
Bernhard Neumair
Vaggelis Ouzounis
Igor Radisic
Kerry Raymond
Helmut Reiser
Gabi Dreo Rodosek
Jerome Rolia
Michael Samulowitz

Andreas Schade
Alexander Schill
Holger Schmidt
Gerd Schürmann
André Schüppen
Morris Sloman
Otto Spaniol
Michael Stal
James Steel
Ralf Steinmetz
Alexandre Tauveron
Dirk Thißen
Volker Tschammer
Mark Tuan Tu
Gerald Vogt
Norbert Wienold
Stefan Müller Wilken
Andrew Wood
Michael Zapf
Christian Zirpins

Sponsors and Exhibitors

Ludwig-Maximilians-University (LMU)
http://www.lmu.de

International Federation for Information Processing (IFIP)
http://www.ifip.or.at

German Informatics Society (GI)
http://www.gi-ev.de

Computing Centre of the Bavarian Academy of Sciences (LRZ)
http://www.lrz.de

BMW AG
http://www.bmw.com

DG Bank
http://www.dgbank.de

Bavaria's Software Initiative
http://www.software-offensive-bayern.de

Siemens AG
http://www.siemens.com

Munich Network Management Team
http://wwwmnmteam.informatik.uni-muenchen.de

Redwood Technologies Ltd.
http://www.redwoodtech.com

Contents

Session IV: Mobile and Distributed Services

Session V: Middleware Architectures

Session VI: Service Management

Poster Session I: Mobile Agents and Applications

Poster Session II: Trends in Data- and Telecommunications

Invited Talks

Beyond the TINA Lesson: Distributed Processing for Integrated Fixed and Mobile Communications

Sebastiano Trigila

Telecommunications Network Department at Fondazione Ugo Bordoni, Rome, Italy
trigila@fub.it

Abstract. A major keyword of the Information and Communication Technology progress in the Nineties is convergence: integrated provision of telecommunications and information services, integrated management and control, provision of services above an infrastructure resulting from the interconnection of various network types, ubiquitous offering of fixed and mobile services. This paper deals with a technological enabler of convergence, namely network programmability, on a geographical scale and, eventually, on a global, worldwide level. Nowadays, the main convergence problem appears to be UMTS, defined by somebody as "the fusion of Fixed and Mobile Networking". The distributed processing paradigm of TINA as an enabler of fixed and mobile convergence is analyzed, through a timeline summarizing more than a decade of research and development. Pre-TINA solutions and post-TINA solutions are included in this timeline.

Introduction

The booming development of telecommunications and information technologies is a self-commenting reality that can be analyzed from various viewpoints: human factors, enterprise organization, regulatory aspects, economical implications, and technology. A major keyword of the developments occurred in the Nineties is *convergence*, in many senses: integrated provision of telecommunications and information services, integrated management and control, provision of services above an infrastructure resulting from the interconnection of various network types, ubiquitous offering of fixed and mobile services. This paper deals with a major technological enabler of convergence, namely what many experts agree to call *network programmability*, on a geographical scale and, eventually, on a global, worldwide level. Nowadays, the main convergence problem appears to be UMTS, defined by somebody as "the fusion of Fixed and Mobile Networking" [1]. In fact, integration of fixed and mobile communications, of course from the viewpoint of control and management, will be presented in this paper as the main challenge to be met by any solution that claims to cope with complexity of networks today.

More than ten years of scientific and technical work have elapsed in proposing, defining and experimenting what network programmability be about. The author of this paper has had a unique opportunity to observe a timeline where different solutions for network programmability have popped up, become trendy, in most cases even implemented. Some solutions, like the Intelligent Network (IN) standards and

C. Linnhoff-Popien and H.-G. Hegering (Eds.): USM 2000, LNCS 1890, pp. 2-16, 2000.

the Telecommunications Management Network (TMN) specifications, have gained enough acceptance in the industrial environment to be rolled out in the telecommunications market. Some others, like TINA, though not yet accepted (and most probably not likely to be ever adopted) as industrial standards, have brought fruit in other terms.

TINA is a major initiative that is based on distributed processing technology scaled up to global network level. Its success as a holistic solution for tomorrow's global networks, integrating telecommunications and information systems, is under debate. In fact TINA does not seem to uptake at the speed foreseen by its developers and hoped by its promoters. The trend is difficult to revert.

Nevertheless, the lesson learned from TINA and its numerous results, gained within the research and development stream related to it and available for exploitation as independent pieces of technology, are worth to be retained. This opinion is a major motivation for the writing of this paper. We focus on TINA and its derived solutions to discuss a number of lessons learned and the future prospects in applying distributed processing to the programming of telecommunications applications.

Distributed Processing in Telecommunications: A Timeline

The earliest known solution to network programmability was the Intelligent Network (IN) model, which became popular in the late Eighties with the spread of services like free-phone and telephony supplementary services, attracting a lot of intellectual and industrial investment, and attaining eventually the global telecommunications market.

The main advantage of IN was the breakage of the tight coupling between service provision and network technology. This was perceived as an impressive step towards flexible provisioning of new services (no network redesign required, only the intelligent node needed reprogramming).

Drawbacks of IN were pointed out from its very beginning by people for whom node programming was just one step towards true network programming. The lack of a strong programming paradigm in the Intelligent Network was very soon perceived as a factor hindering quick-to-market development of services.

Object-oriented modeling and programming was then identified as a challenging opportunity to improve programmability of the Intelligent Network. This idea gave rise to the Bellcore driven initiative said INA (1988-1991). Meanwhile, the European Commission (EC) started to sponsor research projects, within its RACE framework programme, namely ROSA (1989-92), SCORE (1992-94) and CASSIOPEIA (1992-94) [2], whose object-oriented approach was complemented by distributed processing models and inspired by the pioneering ANSA project and ODP standards. The term Service Architecture was coined to mean a specification, design and development paradigm to cope with integrated service engineering, that is object-oriented service creation in a network-technology independent fashion. Services were seen as applications running on a ubiquitous distributed processing platform, ideally spanning the overall telecommunications network. The TINA (Telecommunications Information Networking Architecture) initiative saw the light in 1991 in the form of annual workshop series, where corporate and academic research results would be shared. The pathway from telecommunications node programming to network programming had been started.

The TINA initiative progressed into a consortium TINA-C (1993-97) involving several telecom operators and manufacturers in the fields of telecommunications and information technology. A *core team* of researchers, contributed by the TINA-C members, was hosted in Bellcore to work on a set of specifications suitable to cope with the complexity of the converging worlds of information technology and communications. A Service Architecture and a Network Resource Architecture were defined, starting from results developed in previous projects, and the distributed object oriented technology CORBA was adopted. Other international projects and corporate projects, working with the title of TINA *auxiliary projects,* complemented, refined and consolidated, e.g. via trials, the results and the specifications produced by the core team.

In the second half of the Nineties, the EC funded, within its programme ACTS (Advanced Communications Technologies and Services), a pool of projects that assumed TINA as a reference architecture for open service provision. In particular, the project VITAL (1995-98) was established to enhance, assess and consolidate TINA specification via extensive field trials that proved quite successful and encouraging. Another ACTS project, DOLMEN (1995-98), developed OSAM [3, 4], an "Open Service Architecture for fixed and Mobile environments", as an extension of the TINA Architecture [5] to cope with requirements for provision of personal and terminal mobility in the prospects of *personal communications services.* An international technology trial, between UK and Finland, involving applications deployment and demonstration over a connectivity infrastructure made of GSM, ATM and Wireless LAN layer networks, was successfully held by DOLMEN.

In the last three years TINA has been maintained and promoted by the TINA Forum. Numerous success stories, regarding both corporate field trials and commercial solutions based on TINA have been announced and acclaimed.

Integrated Fixed and Mobile Communications

As regards work in the area of mobile communications, third-generation wireless networks are currently the focus of major technological, pre-normative and normative activities. These networks should be able to carry multimedia traffic including voice, video, images, files, data or a combination of these, and to enable communication among persons at any time, in any place.

Third-generation networks have been under intensive study by worldwide and European standardization bodies, such as the International Telecommunication Union (ITU) and ETSI, as well as the European Commission, leading to the concepts of IMT2000 [6] and UMTS respectively [7]. Laboratory trials and field trials have been taking place. After more than a decade that has seen the succession of analog and digital cellular systems such as NMT, TACS, AMPS and GSM [8], new services and new radio systems based on the UMTS standards are finally ready to enter commercial operation.

The key concepts in UMTS include terminal mobility and personal mobility. Terminal mobility is a basic feature of a mobile network and refers to "the ability of a terminal to access telecommunication services from different locations and while in motion, and the capability of the network to identify and locate that terminal" [9]. Personal mobility has been introduced as a new set of services that has had limited success in its UPT version, but is having more success within the Internet (according to the ITU-T H.323 standards and the IETF SIP protocol suite) and is expected to boom within UMTS. It refers to "the ability of a user to access telecommunication services at any terminal on the basis of a personal telecommunication identifier, and the capability of the network to provide those services according to the service profile of the user. Personal mobility involves the network capability to locate the terminal associated with the user for the purpose of addressing, routing and charging of the user's calls" [10]. The reader, for the rest of this paper is assumed to be familiar with most concepts and functions related to UMTS.

In our view, service architectures based on open distributed processing can effectively support seamless provision of multimedia services in an integrated fixed and mobile environment. The proposed vision overcomes the current trend of having mobile domains and fixed domains interwork through gateways (GW) where full protocol stacks are converted (Figure 1). The aim is towards a unified control and management service platform spanning over federated mobile and fixed network domain. This is represented in Figure 2, where NA denotes generic adaptation functionality to specific network technology.

Fig. 1. Interworking between Mobile and Fixed Network domains

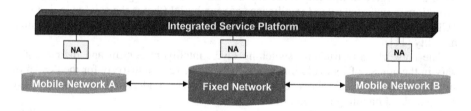

Fig. 2. Integration of Mobile and Fixed Network domains under a Service Platform

Control of mobile communications systems and networks is currently being dealt with by means of proprietary solutions, mainly inspired by the ITU-T IN Conceptual Model and extended as needed by the requirements of mobility. In fact, there is still limited practical experience with TINA, so questions of performance and stability remain open. Moreover the high investment that was already spent by operators on the existing IN infrastructure may delay or even hinder the adoption of TINA. However, UMTS is standardized for the radio access network, but is still open to solutions in the control and management of the core network. We therefore believe that TINA, though not having strong chances as a global solution, has a lot to say in the long-term solutions that will be adopted for UMTS control and management. Only time, during which extensive prototyping and experimental sub-networks will have been put on trial, will say whether telecom networks of the future will be really based on evolution of classical IN or on a new paradigm like TINA.

Fixed-Mobile Integration with IN

Classical IN is a reality for current PSTN and narrow-band ISDN. The technology has proved to work well and with acceptable performance and stability. The evolution of the IN architectural framework is being currently investigated in several directions and within different initiatives.

In the research activities and standardization work of the third generation mobile systems (UMTS and IMT2000), IN is considered the enabling technology to implement mobility functions. The application of IN to mobility is an essential element for integrating mobile access into future networks such as B-ISDN. In this integration scenario, IN takes care of user and mobility control with related data, while B-ISDN caters for the basic switching and transport mechanisms.

The main elements of IN that make it suitable for handling mobility are:

1. IN is able to provide serviceindependent functions that can be us ed as "building blocks" to construct a variety of services. This allows easy specification and design of new services.

2. IN provides services independently from the network implementation. This allows isolating the services from the way the service-independent functions are actually implemented in various physical network infrastructures. In particular, no matter whether a network is fixed or mobile, IN allows to have a universal core network regardless of means of access: from a core network point of view a fixed/mobile interworking unit and a wired terminal have the same behavior.

Following the evolution of the IN Capability Sets (CS), different steps for the modeling of mobility functions can be identified. They differ with respect to the integration degree of mobility functions into the IN service logic. Going through this evolutionary path, the role of intelligence as seen by IN (that is the service logic in the SCPs) increases gradually to embrace the system functions of user and terminal mobility [11].

The network infrastructure, switching layer, intelligent control and their relation vary in the course of IN evolution. In CS1, IN is utilized exclusively for the design of supplementary services above a mobile system. The underlying network is fully responsible of handling mobility of the users.

To find the mobile specific IN services, we must consider the successive step: CS2 standard. In this phase the scope of IN is widened to cover non-call related mobility functions themselves. IN is not only additional intelligence to a basic call or a mobility function, but an elementary technology to implement those functions. Non-call-related mobility functions, while not involved during call establishment, might occur during call progression. New functional entities and new IN state models are needed to model signaling processes that trigger IN for requesting mobility services.

The IN modeling of mobility functions can still be broadened to call-related mobility functions resulting in a situation where all mobility functions are defined in an IN way. Examples of call-related mobility functions are interrogation, paging and handover. This capability is partially covered by the IN CS2 and will be finalized in the IN CS3. Call related mobility functions imply also new state models in addition to the classical Basic Call State Model.

Long term IN is the final step for the IN view of mobility. It does not add any mobility function into the scope of IN, but brings object orientation, the new separation of services from underlying resources and the concept of distributed processing. It presumes a complete renewal of IN modeling in a way that goes very much towards the TINA concepts, which are described in the next section.

Essential Novelties of TINA

Paradigms different than IN were not only thought because of its lack of openness of the underlying software platform. There were also conceptual and functional reasons. The *IN protocol-centered approach* was criticized because the lack of open interfaces within the Service Control Point left the operators fully dependent on IN manufacturers, thus hindering really open service provision. Moreover, the *IN call-processing focused approach* (all services are variations or add-on's to the basic call service) was targeted as a weakness hindering openness in time, as it was not obvious that all services could be seen as enhancement to the basic call service. A third drawback was the neat *dichotomy between control of network resources to concur in service provision and management of those network resources.* The dichotomy was so obvious that the TMN framework spun off as a complementary technology to the IN: otherwise stated, the management network would be an overlay and distinct network seeing resources both at SSP level and at SCP level as "objects" to be monitored and managed.

The essential principles of TINA are shown in Figure 3, whose elements are explained in the next paragraphs.

To take into account a multi-player deregulated telecommunications environment where the motto is "to cooperate in order to compete", TINA proposes an open business model where *retailers*, i.e. providers of services to customers and users, collectively called *consumers*, are distinct from *connectivity providers*, i.e. owners of network resources, and from *third-party providers*, i.e. owners of specific services. Consumers deal with retailers only, that in turn resort to connectivity providers and third party providers, to make services available to their consumers as value added chains.

TINA supersedes the call processing focus of IN by introducing three level of abstraction when dealing with service provision to users: access session (where registration and authentication of users takes place), service session (application specific), communication session (association of users as perceived by the TINA system), and connectivity session (binding of network resources necessary for the communication). Access, service and communications sessions obey to a set of concepts, principles and rules known as *service architecture*. Service access and service use require interactions with a *user agent* object representing the user in the retailer domain; a user agent may be seen as the "doorway" through which services are accessed, provided and used.

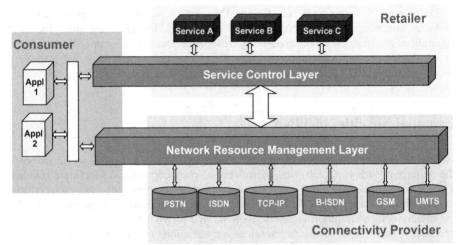

Fig. 3. Essential principles of TINA

TINA overrides the protocol-centered approach of IN and enters an API-oriented approach by the adoption of the CORBA reference model, which leads to a platform called Distributed Processing Environment (DPE). However, to meet the needs of telecommunications the CORBA specifications had to be enhanced with an event notification service, which eventually was incorporated in the OMG standards. The OMG Interface Definition Language (IDL) is the main specification technique used in the TINA documents.

TINA also resolves the dichotomy between IN and TMN by proposing a Network Resource Architecture (NRA) and a related Network Resource Information Model (NRIM). The IN connection control becomes connection management according to the principles dictated by the NRA and the TMN applications become TINA services handling resources in compliance with the NRIM.

Fixed-Mobile Integration: The DOLMEN Approach

The main objective of DOLMEN was the definition of an open service architecture for fixed-mobile integration. The TINA framework appeared as the outstanding expression of a novel approach to mobility support via distributed object-oriented platforms. For its making use of state-of-the-art provisions in software technology (distributed object-oriented computing) it seemed very promising to cope with interoperability and distribution requirements. However, the initial project phase showed that TINA did not involve enough awareness of mobility in the core network, but only in the access network. Moreover, the presence of terminal mobility and radio access modified the assumptions made in TINA-C when designing objects and operations within its Distributed Processing Environment.

In evaluating the impact of mobility on TINA, a list of mobility functions was examined at quite an abstract level, regardless of any possible system architecture or network environment configuration. A classification was made to help separation of concerns, thus facilitating identification of architectural requirements. It was determined how personal and terminal mobility functions could be decomposed into elementary components and, for each of them, which parts of TINA were significantly affected.

A reference model giving a layered view of TINA concepts was adopted in the form shown in Figure 4. The elements depicted are considered self-explanatory, once it is said that NCCE means "native computer and communications environment" and it is clear that the Kernel Transport Network (kTN) is a TCP/IP + CORBA based "signaling" network and the Transport Network (TN) is the vector for user information stream transfer.

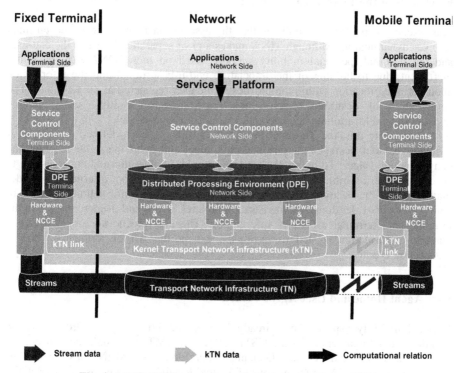

Fig. 4. A DOLMEN reference configuration compliant to TINA

DOLMEN found that personal mobility required changes in the TINA business model [1]. We found also that, with respect to Figure 4, personal mobility impacts the TINA Service Architecture definitions at all three sides: fixed terminal, network and mobile terminal. Finally, we determined that terminal mobility impacts the DPE, and the TINA Network Resource Architecture.

Some major innovations were added to TINA, without destabilizing in any way the overall TINA framework and principles. Here they are listed:
1. A new role for the TINA business model: the Terminal provider.

---

[1] The author, having served as the project manager of DOLMEN, takes the freedom to say "we" when describing DOLMEN results.

2. Splitting of the TINA User Agent object into two: User Agent Home and User Agent Visited, as a consequence of the UMTS notions of Home Domain and Visited Domain.
3. New interoperability concepts in the DPE, to cope with terminal mobility and wireless access.
4. New objects in the NRA to deal with Handover in Mobile Networks.

The above innovations are briefly described in the sequel of this section. A more detailed description is supplied in [12].

Extensions of the TINA Business Model

The essence of personal mobility is that the association between user and terminal changes dynamically. Although TINA makes a clear separation between the end-user and the terminal, personal mobility support based on mere TINA may be rather inefficient, due to holding of the association end-user/terminal and the information about terminal location within the profiles of the user registered at the terminal. The combination of desirable features like registration of multiple users, remote registration and location update becomes clumsy if not impossible.

To overcome this, the Terminal Provider concept has been defined in OSAM. A terminal provider manages the terminal equipment and owns the rights to grant and deny terminal usage. To do so, the terminal provider holds information necessary to access and use a terminal. In addition to consumer information, a terminal provider may maintain the following information: terminal location information (in terms of connectivity provider domains), registration policies, list of end-users registered at the terminal, and terminal capability information. The user profile no longer needs to maintain information related to terminals, except the list of terminals where a registration is active.

User Agent Home and User Agent Visited

Personal mobility aspects have already been covered in 2nd and 3rd generation mobile systems and services (like GSM, UPT, and UMTS) through the concepts of Visited Domain and Home Domain. Therefore, DOLMEN has based its enhancements of TINA on the notions of Visited Retailer Domain and Home Retailer Domain. A *Home Retailer Domain* is the administrative domain under the responsibility of the retailer with which the end-user has subscribed for service use. A *Visited Retailer Domain* is the administrative domain under the responsibility of a retailer different from the Home Retailer, but federated with him and closer to the current location of the roaming user.

When establishing an access session, the user has two choices: reach his home retailer via a connectivity provider or use a visited retailer as proxy of his home retailer. The choice depends on whether (1) the home retailer is contractually bound with at least one connectivity provider available in the visited region or, (2) the home retailer is federated with at least one retailer in the visited region. Federation need not be static, it can be established on-line and dynamically upon security check and feasibility of charging. The location of the service session (in terms of retailer domains) depends on the way the access session is managed, i.e. whether by the home or by the visited retailer. In case the end-user is "assigned" to the federated retailer, this could provide the service session. Of course, a federation agreement must exist for the service being used. In case the end-user access session is managed by the home retailer, this could provide the service session. However, the home retailer could also decide to delegate the service session control to a federated retailer closer to the actual location of the roaming user for the following reasons:

- The transfer of invocations and their responses over long distances may require a considerable amount of time, which decreases service performance.
- Long paths between the point at which the system is accessed and the place where invocations are processed require a significant amount of resources and increase service provision costs.
- Information transferred over long distances has a higher probability of corruption, which necessitates additional protection.

The OSAM computational model supports personal mobility in a multi-retailer environment through the creation of a new user agent each time the user accesses the system from a remote area served by a local retailer other than the home retailer. Such "hosting" retailer should be federated with the home retailer and able to offer services to the user more effectively than the home retailer. The new user agent is called User Agent Visited (UAV). The UAV is destroyed when the federation with the local retailer is terminated. Of course, in the home retailer domain a user agent exists as well, which is called User Agent Home (UAH). Such an agent is created when a subscription is made and destroyed only when the subscription is terminated. A UAH maintains the subscription information and personal user information together with references to the UAV's created in the visited retailer domains where the user is registered for different services. Information maintained in the UAH is used to initialize the UAV.

Mobility Management at DPE Level

As the DPE also encompasses the user terminal, terminal mobility becomes an additional challenge to DPE technology. In particular, *continuous terminal mobility* is seen as the most demanding requirement to satisfy. Some of the key issues in the field are: what is the impact of terminal mobility on client-server interaction? how to ensure terminal mobility management? and, how to cope with the unique performance characteristics of wireless access?

A more fundamental question underpinning those issues is whether mobility should be included within the DPE or delegated to the supporting infrastructure. A straightforward solution would leave the DPE intact and resolve mobility problems below the DPE, by exploiting Mobile IP or its equivalents. Such an approach, however, has some serious limitations. For example, handover between different connectivity providers (administrative domains) would be cumbersome, if not impossible.

The mechanism used by a client to invoke an operation offered by a server comprises two steps:

1. Retrieval of a reference to an instance of the interface that gives access to the operation.

2. Invocation of the operation across the interface, using the returned reference, provided a valid one has been obtained.

Terminal mobility in a DPE context means frequent changes of references to objects that reside in the moving terminal, as a result of change in location. The following computational requirements arise:

1. Over a wireless access network, from terminal to network and vice versa, the DPE should preserve the above basic interaction mechanism.

2. Whenever a reference changes as a result of mobility, even though pointing to the same interface instance, the DPE should be able to detect these changes, and issue a new valid reference for the interface instance transparently to the client.

3. The DPE should notify interested (client) objects of the reference change.

Regarding mobility at the DPE level, our solution is based on our novel choice of viewing the terminal as a (complete) CORBA domain of its own and an unprecedented way of using the interoperability bridging concept described in the CORBA 2.0 architecture. We have designed and implemented a prototype of two half-bridges. A Fixed DPE Half-Bridge (FDBR) at the edge of the core network serves as a DPE access point for mobile terminals. A Mobile DPE Half-Bridge (MDBR) within the terminal connects the local ORB domain to an ORB domain in the core network. The FDBR and the MDBR interact through the wireless access network. They co-operate to perform location management and handover at DPE level, as well as access control, and object reference translation between different CORBA domains. In particular, handover at DPE level is seen as the MDBR leaving its on-going association with a given FDBR and establishing an association with a new FDBR, for instance, as a result of the terminal roaming in a geographical area. We have defined a relocatable object reference structure that, together with the bridges and a special Location Register, allows us to support referencing to mobile objects, i.e., objects residing in a mobile terminal. The location register maintains the current mapping between the terminal and the bridge currently in charge of delivering object invocations from the network to the terminal and vice-versa. We found that this innovative approach can be easily applied to reliable addressing of mobile objects in a way completely transparent to the communicating objects themselves. We have also enhanced the reliability and performance of object communication in the wireless environment by introducing a Light-Weight Inter-ORB Protocol (LW-IOP) between the MDBR and FDBR, which maximizes statistical efficiency in the use of the wireless transport connections.

Impact of Mobility on the Network Resource Architecture

The need to support *handover* was the main driver for enhancements of the TINA Network Resource Architecture. Handover is the procedure of changing the radio connection devoted to an on-going established association between a network and a mobile terminal, as a result of a set of well-determined reasons. Reasons for handover include degradation of the radio link quality, requirements on the spectrum, user requirements or management reasons. If the changing of the radio connection is not noticeable to the user, a seamless handover has taken place. The type of handover may also differ, mainly depending on the capabilities of the underlying transport network.

Within TINA, handover applies to both stream and operational binding, and is referred to as *stream handover* and *kTN handover*, respectively. Stream binding is supported by computational objects in the NRA, utilising network resources to transport information. Operational binding, on the other hand, is supported by the CORBA-based DPE, extended by DOLMEN to support wireless access and terminal mobility as explained just earlier.

Stream handover occurs when the change of association between the flow end-points at the terminal, and the termination points at the Access Node, takes place while there is an active communication service session. On the other hand, kTN handover occurs when the CORBA Bridge, connecting the fixed side of the network with the mobile terminal, releases its association and must establish a new one. The TINA NRA is divided into four conceptual levels, whose synergy aims at mapping service session communication requirements into mechanisms implemented by the network resource elements. Each level corresponds to the management of connections at various grades of detail: communication, connection, layer network and sub-network level. Based on these distinct levels of management, four handover cases can be distinguished, namely (see Figure 5):

1. The mobile station leaves the current connectivity provider and enters a new one.

2. The mobile station leaves the current layer network and enters a different one.

3. The mobile station moves from one sub-network to a different one.

4. The mobile station moves within the same sub-network.

Firstly, we have upgraded the NRA to provide a computational model that is adequate for the support of handover. The NRA computational objects have been analyzed, thus widening their applicability in connection establishment in the case of terminal mobility. Slightly modification of TINA objects such as Connection Coordinator, Trail Manager, and Connection Performer has been provided.

Secondly, we have introduced additional computational objects in the Connectivity Provider domain, to fulfil the handover initiation, execution and control stages. When solving handover in a TINA context, one has to bear in mind that both kernel kTN and streams connections need to be handed over. As a matter of fact, various network connections might be active at the same time from one terminal, and all these connections may need to be handed over simultaneously.

Thirdly, we have introduced an abstraction of Resource Adaptor for wireless networks, called Mobile Network Adaptor (MNA), that hides technology dependent aspects of mobile networks and supports, to some extent, QoS and traffic classes, even if the underlying infrastructure does not offer them. Our MNA is designed to

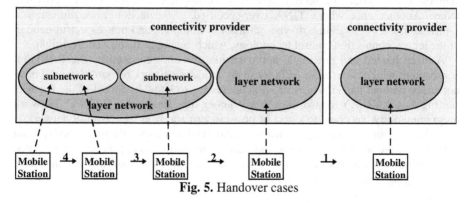

Fig. 5. Handover cases

overcome the limitations of the underlying mobile technologies, by suitable mechanisms that maximize efficiency in the use of the available resources, offering to the higher layers that kind of reliability that mobile links do not have intrinsically.

Our mobile network adaptation is based on the mediation principle as in the Mobile Network Computer Reference Specification (MNCRS) [13] and in the specifications of the Wireless Application Protocol (WAP) Forum.

New Trends for Fixed-Mobile Integration

Some problems of classical IN originally hindering its universal acceptance as an open platform are now being overcome. Its difficulty of interoperation in a multi-vendor and multi-operator environment, its lack of standardized open interfaces to service creation environments, and its lack of integration between control and management, both at network and service level, are no longer so dramatic as ten years ago. The concepts and functionality of IN are being extended (with capability sets CS2 and CS3) in order to cope with open service provision in an integrated fixed and mobile communications environments. Also the obsolete software technology so far underlying IN implementations is being replaced by state-of-the art technology. For instance, among numerous attempts to "objectify" IN we should quote the JAIN initiative, which has proposed APIs to wrap major resources like protocols and switches in Java classes and interfaces. Other attempts are quoted in the recent literature towards replacement of the SS7 protocol stack with a CORBA platform. If these attempts mean the uptake of distributed object-oriented processing technology in telecommunications, TINA marks a score.

The CORBA specifications have been improved, in particular from the version 2.0 to the version 2.3, thank to the determining contributions from OMG members also involved in TINA and to the liaisons established between TINA and OMG, through the Telecom Task Force. The DOLMEN results on mobility management at DPE level have been contributed to OMG and partially incorporated in version 2.3 of CORBA. These are two other important scores of TINA.

The limited success of TINA as a whole solution has probably one sole reason: its architects went too far and perhaps over-specified the architecture by extending its scope to the realm where competition is high: the services. No unified paradigm can synthesize the variety of services (or network applications) that can be provided today. Another area where TINA over-specified is connection management: too centralized, too constraining, maybe intrinsically complex, and not respectful enough of the legacy connection control technology, which cannot be dismissed overnight.

A disenchanted and pragmatic approach like the one proposed by the PARLAY consortium, which is defining APIs for many kinds of network resources, would have not arisen without the TINA lesson. It is interesting to know that most of the Partners starting the PARLAY consortium were among the founders of TINA! Network programmability has come to a sort of post-modern era, where the overall network is a pool of resources (protocols, switches, and services) available to anybody, from anywhere (save access restrictions and performance limitations) through their APIs. Telecommunications services can be written as network-wide applications controlling and managing objects through their APIs.

Acknowledgements

For the content of Section 6, the author owes credit to many colleagues of the DOLMEN Consortium, which was formed by the following Partners: Fondazione Ugo Bordoni (Italy), Intracom (Greece), KPN Research (The Netherlands), Lucent Technologies (The Netherlands), Orange (UK), PEP (UK), Sema Group Telecom (France), Sonera (Finland), National Technical University of Athens (Greece), University of Catania, University of Helsinki (Finland), VTT (Finland). However, the views summarized in that section may not reflect the official position of DOLMEN.

References

[1]   O'Mahony, D. "UMTS: The Fusion of Fixed and Mobile Networking". IEEE Internet Computing 2, 1 (Jan/Feb 1998), 49-56.

[2]   S.Trigila, A.Mullery, M.Campolargo, and J.Hunt, 'Service architectures and service creation for integrated broadband communication', *Computer Communications* **18**, 11 (November 1995) 838-848.

[3]   ACTS AC036 DOLMEN, "Open Services Architecture for Mobile and Fixed Network Environment (OSAM), Final Release, AC036/FUB/ASD4, August 1998.

[4]   S. Trigila, K. Raatikainen, B. Wind, P. Reynolds, "Mobility in Long Term Service Architectures and Distributed Platforms", *IEEE Personal Communications Magazine 5*, 5 (August 1998) 44-55.

[5]   H. Berndt *et al.*, *The TINA Book: A co-operative solution for a competitive world*, Prentice Hall, 1999, ISBN 013 095 4004

[6]   K.Buchanan et al., "IMT-2000: Service Provider's perspective", *IEEE Personal Commmunications*, 4 (4), August 1997, 8-13.

[7]   J.Rapeli, "UMTS: targets, system concepts, and standardisation in a global framework", *IEEE Personal Communications 2*, 1 (February 1995), 20-28.

[8]   A.Mehrotra, *Cellular radio – Analog and Digital Systems*, Artech House Publishers, 1994.

[9]   R.Pandya, "Emerging Mobile and Personal Communications Systems", *IEEE Communications Magazine*, June 1995.

[10]   M.Zaid, "Personal Mobility in PCS", *IEEE Personal Communications*, 1 (4), 1994. *IEEE Personal Communications*, 2 (1) , February 1995, 20-28.

[11]   M.M.Khan, "The Development of Personal Communication Services under the Auspices of Existing Network Technologies", *IEEE Communication Magazine*, 35 (3), March 1997, 78-82.

[12]   S.Trigila, K.Raatikainen, B.Wind, P.Reynolds, "Mobility in Long-Term Service Architectures and Distributed Platforms", *IEEE Personal Communications*, August 1998, 44-55.

[13]   Montenegro, G. "MNCRS: Industry Specification for the Mobile NC". IEEE Internet Computing 2, 2 (Jan/Feb 1998), 73-77.

[14]   Rahnema, M. "Overview of the GSM System and Protocol Architecture". IEEE Communications Magazine 31, 4 (Apr. 1993), 92-100.

Biography

Sebastiano Trigila graduated in Electronic Engineering, at the University of Rome "La Sapienza", in 1980. He started his career with a one-year fellowship at Fondazione Ugo Bordoni (FUB) and then served in the Italian Army for another year. In June 1982 he joined FUB as researcher, on the subjects of specification, validation and testing of OSI protocols and systems. In 1987 he was appointed leader of Communications Software Technology Group FUB to coordinate research on automated verification algorithms for protocol and services and studies on the applied semantics of SDL and LOTOS specification languages. He has been serving as representative of FUB in the framework of European Co-operation projects and within selected study groups of ITU and ETSI. The list of European Co-operation projects he participated to includes: WAN/CTS (Certification and Testing Services for Wide Area Networks), RACE/ROSA (RACE Open Service Architecture for long term intelligent networks with integrated control and management capabilities), RACE/ITACA (Integrated Broadband Communications: Architecture for Certification and Assessment of protocols and services), and RACE/Cassiopeia (Open Service Architecture for Integrated Service Engineering). In the last ten years his interests have focused on Service Architectures for Telecommunications and Service Creation Technologies. In 1995-98 he served as the Project Manager of ACTS/DOLMEN (definition and on-field demonstration of a service architecture for integrated control of communications over a federation of fixed and mobile network domains). He is author of several papers published in conferences and magazines. He has also been teaching and tutoring at several courses and seminars on information technology and telecommunications.

Quality of Service and Service Provisioning on a Competitive Market

Lambert J.M. Nieuwenhuis[1] and Ing Widya[2]

[1]KPN Research, the Netherlands
[2]University of Twente, the Netherlands
(L.J.M.Nieuwenhuis@kpn.com, widya@cs.utwente.nl)

Abstract. The objective of this paper is to provide an economic and commercial context for QoS research in open distributed environments. The analyses are based on a telecommunications value chain model. The model is used to define possible roles for telecommunications companies, migrating from traditional telephony network operators towards privatised ICT companies in a new economy. Based on these developments, we advocate R&D activities aiming at standardised concepts and engineering principles to establish and control QoS in open distributed environments.

1. Introduction

At the beginning of the 21st century, developments on the telecommunications services market are far from stable. The process of privatisation of the incumbent operators has not been completed yet. Almost every day, we read articles in newspapers on the world's largest mergers and acquisitions, which primarily were related to the communication industry, and recently also include the content industry. On the other hand, at national and European level, we are confronted with new regulations, e.g., preventing that companies dominate a national market. Besides these developments, the Internet has grown explosively and now governs today's developments in many aspects. It is not surprising that the Internet has a major influence on our economy on the telecommunications industry and on our ICT technologies. In this paper, we will discuss a number of these developments from a network operator's perspective in more detail to obtain a context for the technological challenges that face the service provisioning industry in the years to come. We believe that in a mature and open market, as in many other industries, the primary economic forces will be determined by customers selecting from a wide range of services and products that differ with respect to price and quality.

In the years to come, the quality of service will not primarily be determined by the available bandwidth of our networks anymore. Quality of Service (QoS) will more and more be determined by the availability of <u>all</u> the resources needed for service provisioning, e.g., the communication links, the routers, the computing devices, and data stores. From the major trends and developments from a network operator's perspective we derive research questions that in our view should be addressed by the distributed computing community in the years to come.

C. Linnhoff-Popien and H.-G. Hegering (Eds.): USM 2000, LNCS 1890, pp. 17-26, 2000.
© Springer-Verlag Berlin Heidelberg 2000

The paper is structured as follows. In Section 2, we present our telecommunications value chain model, involving multiple players in our industry. In Section 3, we compare the added value of various players in these value chains. In Section 4, we elaborate on Internet service provisioning as it is today. In Section 5, we identify new players and roles in the telecommunications value chain. In Section 6, we discuss how the industry can benefit from standards and concepts for establishing and control of QoS in an open distributed telecommunications environment. We summarise our findings in Section 7.

2. Telecommunications Value Chain Model

For many years, developments in the field of telecommunications research have been driven by an isolated and autonomous joint effort of telecommunications manufacturers and network operators. They developed standards co-ordinated by de-jure and industrial standardisation organisations comprising both manufacturers and network operators. In sharp contrast with this, Internet technologies are emerging very

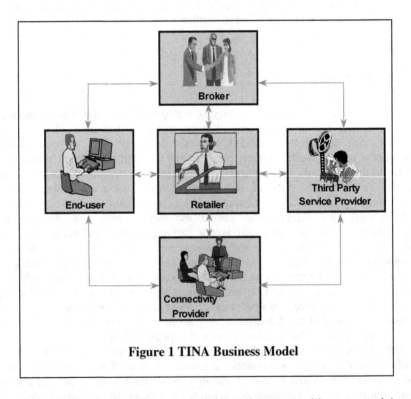

Figure 1 TINA Business Model

rapidly and in an open, collaborative, and distributed process, with many participants, originally dominated by the academic world. The Internet is now governing the entire telecommunications industry. Hence, Internet will be the basis for a universal service

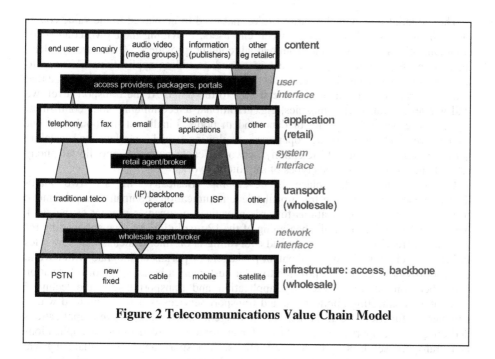

Figure 2 Telecommunications Value Chain Model

market. The Internet will continue to develop, which requires large-scale, mass-market technologies, fitted to serve the needs of the open market. Figure 1 shows the TINA Business Model [1], emerged from developments that started more than five years ago in the telecom industry. The power is that TINA has shown the world that a business model should be the basis for technological developments. The model is however very generic. We believe that in practice, a more detailed and dynamic model is needed to understand the roles, stakeholders and companies of tomorrow's world.

In Figure 2, we present a picture of our model that describe the developments in the telecommunications industry in Europe. The model represents the value chains of both, the 'traditional' telecommunication and media content industries, as well as the newly emerging Internet industries. This model in fact depicts various value chains, which can be constructed using elements from four layers, i.e., content, applications, transport, and infrastructures.

Content can be multimedia data generated by end users, in case of one-to-one or one-to-many communication. Content may be any type of multimedia data, e.g., enquiry, advertisement, e-commerce information, news, traffic or stock exchange information, and multimedia data related to entertainment. Applications are tailored end-user services, which encode content into a form suitable for transport. Traditionally, we see telephony and fax services, but also Internet services like email and web, which will develop into more complex business applications needed for various E-commerce applications. The transport layer encompasses all transmission and routing of packaged and encoded content. Finally, fixed and wireless networks are needed to carry the information across the world.

The model also depicts the various roles that need to be played in the value chains of the industry. We distinguish between end-users, providing their own content for communications purposes and commercial content providers. There are retailers, maintaining the relationship with customers and providing applications offerings to the end-users. For example, an end-user subscribes to a mobile telephony service that is used to transfer content from one end-user to the other. At the transport level, we find wholesale transport companies, e.g., traditional telecommunications companies, selling voice network capacity or data modem pools. Finally, at the bottom of our model, we find the network operators, exploiting fixed, wireless and satellite networks, e.g., the plain old telephony networks, cable networks, mobile telephony and data networks and various types of satellite networks.

Currently, the market place is developing. Basically, we see two major developments. First, we see traditional telecommunications companies on the move from governmental organisations towards privatised companies present at the stock markets. Second, we are at the beginning of the IP revolution, i.e., we are heading for a world where virtually everybody and everything is on line. It means that new roles in the value chain will emerge. Content packagers or portals collaborate with several content providers, creating a position to offer customers a broad range of information and other content. In between the application and transport layers, the technical function of connecting applications and transport services is being combined with a commercial function. Retail brokers or retail agents are linking different applications and different transport services. They offer customers a broad range of applications and transport services, provided by others. Transport and the actual physical infrastructure are sometimes linked through wholesale agents or wholesale brokers, buying and selling (backbone) network capacity.

3. Generating Added Value

In the previous section, we have presented a telecommunications value chain model. In fact, all parties are needed in order to deliver a service to the end-user. Economical and technological forces suggest that parties in the top rows of the model add more value than parties in the bottom rows. In order to determine which roles in the model are more favourable, it is relevant to determine who has direct access to the customers. We can distinguish between physical, commercial and perceptual access to the customers.

- Physical access to the customer is a crucial factor. For the residential market, owning the public telephony network is an extremely important asset. Currently, narrow band technologies like PSTN and ISDN are currently provided. In Europe, broadband technologies like ADSL are currently being rolled out. Cable networks extent their original TV distribution services with telephony and IP services. They also create added value from their physical access to residential customers. Additionally, wireless and satellite networks play an increasingly important role. In the business markets, newcomers start connecting customers with own networks, in order to decrease their dependency on national, public network operators. A strong position could be obtained, when a company includes one or more elements of each layer of the telecommunications value chain model shown in Figure 2.

- Commercial access to customers seems to be even of more importance than having physical access. Companies that posses this type of access set the brand in the market, determines the customer interface and can tailor the customer interface to provide marketing information of other players in the value chain.
- Finally, perceptual access to customers relates to the chase of eyeballs. The number of people that can be reached through various media creates value. We generally want to maximise the number of people actually reading newspapers and magazines, watching programs on TV channels, or hitting Web pages on the net. The number of eyeballs directly relates to the way players make money in the telecommunications value chain.

In general, a position at the top of the telecommunication value chain model (see Figure 2) is more favourable than a position on the bottom. Perceptual access can be obtained through interesting and preferable unique content. Applications create value for end-users and create a commercial relationship. Transport and infrastructures are anonymous. It is difficult to generate more revenues than cost price with a fair margin. As infrastructures become cheaper and cheaper, the margins will decrease proportionally.

4. Internet Service Provisioning

In this section, as an example, we elaborate the model that is currently being used in Europe to provide Internet services to end-users. We show that it is complicated from both, the end-user's perspective and an economic perspective.

Figure 3 shows a picture of the current Internet model, which for a comparison can be related to Figure 1, the TINA model. In general we need to subscribe to a service to obtain a PSTN or ISDN line for setting up a connection to an Internet Service Provider (ISP). This service is in most cases provided by a traditional telephony company. These types of connections can also be set-up through a mobile telephony company using on GSM or GPRS and in the future UMTS. An IP dial tone can be obtained from an ISP. In Europe some ISPs provide these and other basic Internet services for free, others demand subscription fees. The Internet services are used to access content of a content provider. Currently, much content on the Internet can be accessed for free. A limited set of content can only be accessed after paying a certain amount of money, either in the form of a subscription fee or on a pay per view basis. In a number of cases, security support or payment services require yet another party. Hence, for current Internet service provisioning multiple roles need to be fulfilled. In the current situation different companies fulfil these roles. Consequently, the consumers and end-users have to deal with a number of different companies. In order to improve the Customer Relationship Management (CRM), we may expect that retailers and brokers will provide end-users with one stop shopping concepts. Obviously, this puts requirements on the technologies that are needed to actually make this happen.

One of the most challenging developments with Internet service provisioning relates to the business model. Using Figure 3, we also see which companies may send a bill to users of Internet service providers. First, a public network operator can send a bill for setting up a connection between the end-user and the ISP. In Europe, in most

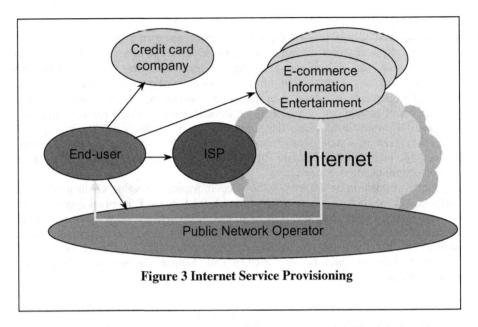

Figure 3 Internet Service Provisioning

cases users are charged on a connect time basis. In the US, usually users pay a flat fee, i.e., they are charged independent of the connect time. Second, ISPs charge users for the services they provide, e.g., mail and web hosting, and the interconnection to the Internet. Various models exist. Due to increased competition, we see a rapidly growing number of ISPs that provide their services for free. In Europe, ISPs make traffic revenue-sharing agreements with public network operators in order to survive. It is unclear, whether regulators in Europe will allow this type of interconnections between ISPs and public network operators. Besides this type of revenue sharing with network operators, ISPs expect to generate revenues from advertisements and revenue sharing models in E-commerce transactions. It is still unclear, whether these business models are strong enough to let ISPs survive.

As the number of ISPs is growing, in both the residential and business segments, as in any other industry, Quality of Service (QoS) starts to become a critical success factor in the ISP business. In the past, ISPs have been unable to offer QoS agreements as because of problems with infrastructure reliability and availability. In the business segment, customer attitudes to QoS are changing, because IP connections are becoming a key factor for delivering business applications, and users are increasingly dissatisfied with the 'best effort' level of service that ISPs provide today.

In this section, we have shown that Internet Service Provisioning is maturing. Consequently, we expect that such issues as customer care, costs and revenues, and Quality of Service will play an increasingly important role.

5. Open Services Market

Currently, in the middle of the year 2000, the telecommunications industry is in a process of what is called unbundling. Traditional telecommunications companies are followed by investors and compared to their competitors. The stock market demands transparency of telecom operators, and rewards increased transparency with a higher share price. At the same time we see new companies entering the market place, playing only a few or even a single role in our telecommunications value chain model. Definitely, unbundling enables these companies to become a specialist in their element of the value chain. On the other hand, for users and customers, the service provisioning becomes more complicated, as we have seen in our Internet Service Provisioning example in the previous section. Therefore, we may expect that brokers will play more and more important role in telecommunications value chain model. Examples of brokers are content packagers, retail and wholesale brokers. A growing customer base will strengthen their position in the telecommunications value chain.

In fact, the vertical and horizontal unbundling in the telecommunications value chain model creates a number of interesting win-win positions. A content provider benefits if the number of outlets increase. An application provider benefits if more content becomes available from a variety of content providers. An ISP benefits from an increase of applications, and a network operator benefits from more traffic on its network. In fact, this was also the idea behind the 3rd party service-provisioning role as indicated by the TINA business model (see Figure 1).

Obviously, the co-operation between different parties in the market needs to be enabled by technological developments. Standards are needed. The development of standards has undergone a major change. The IETF and OMG and a number of other similar organisations have shown how fast standards can be developed compared to the traditional bodies like ITU-T and ISO. However, what remained the same through the years are the huge commercial interests related to standardization. Strong players in the market try to establish and keep market shares through de-facto standardisation of their products.

At this place, we would like to underline the major differences and commonalties between such telecommunications standardisation activities as TINA and other developments like IETF, W3C, or OMG.

Due to our experience gained with TINA [11], we believe that the Service Architecture concepts are a valid vehicle to obtain standards for services that are much more complicated than the services we encounter today on the Internet. Setting up a multimedia, multiparty, multi-domain service, which guarantees secure and reliable connections in a closed user group, definitely requires some standards. It is also likely, that such high quality connections can only be provided when users are prepared to pay for it. We also believe that such open standards for distributed object technologies as CORBA can provide the infrastructure to create such open services market.

6. Quality of Service Research Activities

In previous sections, we have presented the telecommunications value chain model and discussed some of the commercial forces that determine the developments in the telecommunications arena. The development of an unbundled open services market implies more competition with multiple players in various areas. As the market matures, we believe that a variety of product-market combinations will create differentiation on basis of Quality of Service (QoS) in particular and Service Level Agreements (SLAs) in general. In this section, we propose to combine the results of the telecommunications value chain model and integrate the need for standards, open services market, and the need to control the end-user QoS.

The notion of QoS is very broad and applies to many areas of service provisioning. The bottom line is of course the QoS as perceived by the end-user. However, the perceived QoS depends on the QoS of the constituting components of the system that deliver the service. Accordingly, the QoS is determined by the QoS of the content, the application, the transport systems and the underlying networks. From a technological point of view, we believe that the end-user perceived QoS of multimedia services is determined by the way distributed systems are capable of handling such things as availability and reliability of bandwidth, jitter, delay of audio and video signals. But, from an end-user perspective, we have to translate QoS in user oriented terms to increase their awareness of the delivered QoS.

There are typically two ways to have a distributed system deliver a certain QoS. One is to over-dimension the system to easily support peak usage. This approach is widely used in practice, in particular in the Internet. However, over-dimensioning is generally inefficient and often unattractive because a lot of system capacity remains unused when the system is lightly loaded. In general, the system usage is determined by at least three factors, which are nondeterministic in practice:

- The number of users that need to be served at a certain point in time
- The amount of resources that each user needs at a certain point in time
- The number of faults disturbing the system at a certain point in time

The alternative approach to deliver QoS is to dimension the system more conservatively and make system's components QoS aware. This means that the system has a notion of the QoS of information streams and distributed processing, and that it can use its resources accordingly. These resources comprise not only network elements but also the software infrastructure, e.g., the web servers in today's systems and multimedia servers capable of storage and retrieval of audio and video information.

There are a number of QoS standardisation and research activities going on in organisations like ISO, IETF, ITU-T, TINA, OMG and various research groups, like GMD Fokus in Berlin, COMET group at Columbia University, Distributed Multimedia Research Group in Lancaster. Overviews of the activities of these groups can be found in [2], [3], [4].

At the University of Twente, we participate in several projects of the Telematics Institute on QoS research. In the AMIDST project [5], we focus on end-to-end QoS control in open distributed environments, like for example CORBA. We believe that QoS control is also needed for the software infrastructures that are used to control QoS of underlying networks and of processes that stream multimedia information. We search for a generic QoS control framework for establishment of QoS, for both operational and multimedia streaming control loops, and for which a diversity of QoS control mechanisms can be developed, for example, mechanisms for QoS (re)negotiation, QoS computation, QoS monitoring and QoS re-enforcing. In fact we would like to complement CORBA's functional specifications with QoS specifications, and generate code for QoS control [6], [7], [8].[9], [10]. We are currently focussing our research on the following issues:

♦ A challenging question is how to relate the end-user QoS to the QoS of the subsystems, constituting the entire system. This includes investigation on QoS specification, mapping of QoS characteristics to capability of underlying resources in local sites and mechanisms for peer to peer mapping and control of QoS, both in the establishment and operational phases of services[6].

♦ We are considering telematics services, engineered in such open distributed object environments as CORBA. The challenge is to establish and control the QoS of these telematics services at the level of the distributed environment rather than the applications itself. In this way, we can design and develop the telematics services independent of applications. We looking for CORBA extensions to create QoS awareness. This research also relates to current activities within the OMG on replication and fault tolerance. Here, we look at the management of component and object based systems.

♦ In the field of audio and video streams, we try to overcome heterogeneity in a multi provider environment (e.g. an environment with fixed and mobile network providers). We are investigating solutions for which dynamically connected piecewise homogeneous parts model heterogeneity. Topics that are in study are, for example, mechanisms to support multimedia scaling and transcoding, mechanisms for smooth (i.e. QoS preserving) hand-over when end-users move across homogeneous parts or providers management domains. We also look at the influence of SLAs between the end-user and provider but also between the providers on the choice of previously mentioned mechanism.

7. Conclusions

In this paper, we have presented a telecommunications value chain model. We have used this model to describe how horizontal and vertical unbundling progresses in the telecommunications industry. We have shown that the telecommunications industry is developing towards a real open and competitive market. QoS provisioning delivers an import contribution to these developments. We have identified a number of interesting subjects for further research, focusing on concepts and engineering principles on the establishment and control of QoS in distributed open environments.

8. References

[1]   TINA Business Model and Reference Points, Version 4.0, May 1997, TINA C Deliverable

[2]   C. Aurrecoechea, T. Campbell, and L. Hauw, A Survey of QoS Architectures 1998.Center for Telecommunications Research Columbia University.

[3]   De Meer, J. and Hadif, A. "*The Enterprise of QoS*". 98.

[4]   F.A. Aagesen, QoS Frameworks for open distributed processing systems, *Telektronik*, vol. 1.97, no. magazine on Quality of Service in Telecommunications, pp. 26-41, 1997.

[5]   AMIDST project, http://amidst.ctit.utwente.nl/

[6]   C. Hesselman, I. Widya, A.T. van Halteren, L.J.M. Nieuwenhuis *Middleware support for media streaming establishment*, accepted for IDMS2000, October 2000

[7]   M. Wegdam, D.J. Plas, A.T. van Halteren, L.J.M. Nieuwenhuis, *ORB Instrumentation for Management of Corba,* accepted for PDPTA2000, Las Vegas, June 26-29, 2000

[8]   L. Bergmans, A.T. van Halteren, L. Pires, M. van Sinderen, M. Aksit, *A QoS-Control Architecture for Object Middleware,* accepted for IDMS2000, October 2000

[9]   M. Wegdam, A.T. van Halteren, *Experiences with CORBA interceptors*, Position paper for the Workshop on Reflective Middleware (RM 2000), co-located with the IFIP/ACM International Conference on Distributed Systems Platforms and Open Distributed Processing (Middleware'2000), April 2000

[10] A.T. van Halteren, A. Noutash , L.J.M. Nieuwenhuis, M. Wegdam, Extending CORBA with specialised protocols for QoS provisioning, Proceedings of International Symposium on Distributed Objects and Applications (DOA'99), September 1999.

[11] L. J.M. Nieuwenhuis, A. T. van Halteren, EURESCOM Services Platform, Proceedings of Telecommunications Information Networking Architecture Conference 1999 (TINA '99), Apr. 1999.

About the Speaker Lambert J.M. Nieuwenhuis

In 1980, Lambert J.M. Nieuwenhuis joined KPN Research, the innovation centre of KPN in The Netherlands. His interest in the area of Information and Communication Technology includes fault tolerant, parallel, and distributed computing. Within KPN Research, he had several positions including project manager, seicientific advisor and Head of Strategy. He was also leader of European projects on distributed object technologies. Currently, Lambert J.M. Nieuwenhuis is heading the department of Middleware. He is also parttime professor at the Computer Science and Electrical Engineering Faculty of the University of Twente. He has a BSc and MSc in electrical engineering and a PhD in Computer Science.

The TAO of Patterns - Understanding Middleware and Component Architectures

Michael Stal

Siemens AG, Corporate Technology
Dept. ZT SE 2
Otto-Hahn-Ring 6
81739 Muenchen Germany
Michael.Stal@mchp.siemens.de

1 Abstract

Nowadays, most architects and developers have to cope with networked infrastructures when they build new software systems. E-Business is one of the main reasons for this trend, the wide-spread availability of network operating systems is another reason. Instead of using low-level communication mechanisms for plumbing distributed functionality together, standardized middleware and component technologies have become common place. The most notable examples are Microsoft COM+, Enterprise JavaBeans and CORBA Components. However, most of these technologies evolve over time. Moreover, the applications themselves must inevitably evolve due to changing requirements or the necessity to modify or extend their functionality. To cope with such a fast moving target, at least the core parts of the software architecture should remain stable and well-documented. Thus, architectural issues are very important when we are going to build complex software. The emerging discipline of software patterns helps to develop such systems by documenting good programming practice in a well-defined style. Patterns do not only help to build such systems, but also to understand existing software systems. In order to leverage middleware and component technologies, basic knowledge of the underlying design principles is essential. It is the goal of the talk to introduce basic elements of middleware and component infrastructures by using patterns. This helps to understand and compare such infrastructures, as well as to apply the extracted patterns in other software applications.

2 Biography

Michael Stal is the head of the Middleware & Application Integration group at Siemens Corporate Technology. He is co-author of the bookd "Pattern-Oriented Software Architecture - A System of Patterns", Wiley & Sons, 1996 and *Pattern-Oriented Software Architecture - Patterns for Networked and Concurrent Objects*, Wiley & Sons, 2000. In addition, he is editor-in-chief of the Java Spektrum Magazine, Siemens Primary Contact at the OMG, and former member of the ANSI C++ standardization working group.

C. Linnhoff-Popien and H.-G. Hegering (Eds.): USM 2000, LNCS 1890, p. 27, 2000.
© Springer-Verlag Berlin Heidelberg 2000

Electronic Auctions and Trading

Chair: Lea Kutvonen, University of Helsinki, Finland

Market-Skilled Agents for Automating the Bandwidth Commerce

Monique Calisti[1], Boi Faltings[1], and Sandro Mazziotta[2]

[1] Laboratoire d'Intelligence Artificielle
Swiss Federal Institute of Technology (EPFL)
CH-1015 Lausanne, Switzerland.
{calisti,faltings}@lia.di.epfl.ch
[2] Swisscom AG Corporate Technology
Ostermundigenstrasse 99
CH-3050 Bern, Switzerland.
sandro.mazziotta@swisscom.com

Abstract. In the current deregulated Telecom scenario the number of network operators and service providers is rapidly increasing. The resulting competition generates the need for a flexible resource management. In parallel, the fast growth of electronic commerce opens a new market where operators can offer network bandwidth commodities. In this dynamic context, the traditional architecture of Telecom networks needs to be evolved. The integration of economic principles with software technology is a strategic contribution to this evolution. In particular, market-skilled software agents seem to be one of the most promising paradigms. In this paper we describe an agent-based system for the e-commerce of "IP bandwidth", and we discuss how the integration of this system within a network management platform would automate the advertisement of *Telecom goods*, the monitoring of market trends, the pricing and the configuration of network resources.

1 Introduction

The idea of deploying economic mechanisms for a variety of applications has been actively deployed in several fields. With the Internet providing a powerful and worldwide accessible medium for communicating and advertising business information, Internet-based commerce is flourishing. Virtual market-places facilitate in fact commerce transactions by bringing together buyers and sellers [8]. Many service and network providers are therefore considering, and in some cases already deploying [1], electronic market places to offer services. These services include for instance fiber and satellite bandwidth, IP telephony minutes, etc. Even though this kind of business is more and more popular, the risk of failing or not being effective is not negligible. Several researchers believe that a smart generation of *e-commerce* would reduce these risks by integrating market-based

---

[1] As reported by *Makris* at least seven bandwidth brokers are already active on the Web [10].

C. Linnhoff-Popien and H.-G. Hegering (Eds.): USM 2000, LNCS 1890, pp. 30–41, 2000.
© Springer-Verlag Berlin Heidelberg 2000

techniques within agent technology (see [14], [4] for good examples). Automated agents can follow more efficient and more flexible specific strategies, and can evaluate and optimise the utility of specific actions (such as bidding, offering, etc.). However, the integration of economic principles in electronic environments reveals the limitations of software instruments and the need to modify some economic mechanisms from their original formulation.

This paper reports the experience gained by developing a multi-agent auction house, the *IP-market*, for trading *IP-bandwidth goods*. The architecture of this auction house is not dependent on the specific type of goods offered in the market. For this reason, the lesson we report has a general validity that can be useful for the development of electronic market places selling a variety of goods. The novelty of our approach is in the automatic integration of an Intelligent Resource Manager (IRM) within the auction house on one side and within the network management platform on the other. While, some existing Internet-based auction houses allows human network operators to enter offers, our paradigm aims to automate the overall negotiation process. From the good offering phase to the end of trading transactions, software entities autonomously act on behalf of humans. This is possible because of the integration of the IRM within the network resources management and because of the agent communication structure supported by the IP-market. The description of the architecture of the auction house shows how the integration of this system within a network management platform has the potential of automating the advertisement of Telecom goods, the negotiation, the monitoring of market trends, the pricing and the configuration of network resources, as it is depicted in Figure 1. Another major contribution of this work is on the use of standard agent-to-agent communication facilities. This renders the IP-market open and very easy to access, which is essential to encourage several potential buyers and sellers to enter the electronic IP commerce. Finally, authors hope to stimulate and contribute to a productive discussion about the concrete challenges for the success of the e-commerce of Telecom services.

Section 2 gives some background on market-based approach to QoS and bandwidth allocation in the networking field and briefly reviews auctioning principles. Section 3 describes the *IP-market simulator* architecture. More focus on agent interactions and on the lessons learned is given in Section 3.4, with additional comments on the potential of integrating negotiating agents with a network management platform. Section 5 concludes the paper with final comments on the major contributions.

2   Background

There have been several efforts to exploit markets for distributed applications that need to coordinate a set of autonomous entities [9], [14]. The main motivations come from extensive studies done by economists about the problem of coordinating multiple agents in a societal structure [6]. The key advantage is that economics offers mechanisms that produce globally desirable results, avoid central coordination, and impose minimal communication requirements [18].

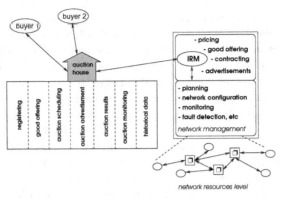

Fig. 1. *The IRM integrates e-commerce with network management functionalities.*

The auction model is a major paradigm which nowadays has been more and more deployed. In particular, many different types of auctions are appearing on the Internet, where electronic *auction houses* allow the sale of a large variety of products. These institutions are environments where certain kinds of goods are traded under explicit trading conventions. *Gibney et al.* are exploring the use of a two-levels auctioning mechanism for routing service demands in Telecom networks [9]. However, their main assumption is that a negotiation, namely a double auction, can only be started by a request coming from an end-user. Furthermore, the research is more focused on efficiently distributing the control of network resources, than on automating the potential of selling Telecom services through the use virtual market-places. *Kubawara, et al.* developed a market model for multi-agent resource allocation [7]. In their market, Activity-Agents (the buyers) and Resource-Agents (the sellers) of the network resources trade bandwidth on physical ATM links, i.e., ATM channels. An 'equilibratory' approach is investigated: the market calculates the supply and demand volume equilibrium (no auctions take place). An interesting part of this work is the definition of sellers' and buyers' strategies. In this market model a fundamental assumption is that "sellers do not know the prices of the resources at other locations when they determine the prices". This is not always the case in a real market, but it is a realistic assumption for participants that first enter the market. *Semret et al.* deployed an auction-based pricing approach for differentiated Internet services [16] and they identified the best strategies for end-users and brokers. However, despite the very interesting conceptual results and the relative simulation evaluations, it is not easy to estimate if such mechanisms could be implemented in real networks.

In the MACH project [2], we developed the *IP-market simulator*, a virtual market place for selling IP bandwidth with given Quality of Service, QoS. In this environment, IP Network Operators are the sellers and all potential customers, i.e., final end-users, IP brokers and all kind of Value Added Service Providers

---

[2] More information about MACH, *MArket meCHanism* for selling on-demand IP bandwidth, are available at: http://liawww.epfl.ch/~calisti/MACH

(voice, video, multimedia), are the buyers. The integration of seller agents within the underlying network infrastructure eliminates the need of human intervention for offering goods to a virtual market-place and allows the automation of network resources' negotiation and pricing. Furthermore, the use of a standard agent communication language and of standard interaction protocols guarantee an open and accessible auction house.

2.1 Electronic Auctions

The concept of auction is very common and almost everybody is familiar with this trading paradigm, but the simplicity is only superficial. Smart auction principles and bidding strategies have being analysed and studied in various ways, in order to maximise the revenue. The work ranges from more theoretical and general principles [2], to very specific studies related to auctions for selling specific products, such as wine and art [1], second hand automobiles [11], etc. Electronic auctions are becoming more and more popular due to basically three main factors. First, they represent an alternative way to implement negotiation and to establish prices. Second, auction mechanisms are more and more known: deep studies of how to optimise auction protocols and strategies promise efficient results [14]. Finally, the success of the Internet and the development of the e-commerce give to auctions a natural environment, where a larger number of potential customers and suppliers can settle business transactions in a shorter time.

There are qualitatively different auction settings depending on how bidders evaluate a good. In *private auctions* the evaluation is not dependent on external factors and is based on private bidder's information. Auctions are *non-private* if the valuation of bids is decided upon private considerations and valuations of others' bids. If the value is partly dependent on other's values the auction is called *correlated value* auction. Whether the value is completely dependent on other's bid valuations the process is called a *common value* auction. Considering the IP-bandwidth market, the auction setting depends on whether the bidder is a final end-user or a potential re-seller. Auction protocols establish the order in which prices are quoted and the manner in which bids are tendered. There are basically 4 major one-sided auction protocols: *English, First-price sealed-bid, Vickrey* and *Dutch*. A good list of references is given in [15] and good reviews are given in [8] and [14]. The IP-market uses the first three types of protocols. Several considerations are important when defining an auction strategy: first, a seller has to choose an auction protocol, which means he has to predict the behaviour of bidders. A buyer makes an estimation of his own value of the good and evaluates what other bidders are likely offer. A seller can influence auction results by revealing information about the good. An optimal strategy from a seller's perspective is to reveal information, since in general the more information a bidder has, the more a price moderation effect of winner's curse is reduced [14]. The *revenue-equivalence theorem* [12] demonstrates that, under the assumption of private value, all four basic auction types produce the same expected value to the auctioneer when bidders are risk-neutral and symmetric.

However, this theoretical results do not apply in many real situations. From the bidder's perspective the kind of auction protocol has the effect of revealing more or less information in the course of the auction. Bidders must decide the maximum amount they will bid, based on their own valuation of the good and their prior beliefs about the valuations of other bidders. If useful information is revealed during the auction, bidding strategies can take into account this additional input. In the IP-market a negotiation strategy is coded into agents using a set of rules specifying how and when they should bargain and/or accept a deal (rule-based approach).

3   The IP-Market Architecture

In the IP-market it is not a network operator that directly offers IP bandwidth goods, but an intermediary, the *auctioneer*, who calls for tenders and adjudicates the purchase to the highest bid. The IP-market is designed to be fair and neutral in respect to both sellers and buyers: it is a third trusted party that guarantees standard and known trading mechanisms to all participants in the same way.

In order to cast the IP bandwidth commerce in terms of a computational market, it is necessary to specify: the goods traded, the buyer and the seller agents' characteristics and the markets structure.

3.1   Modelling the Goods

At a very abstract level, the type of good offered in our market is a *certain amount of bandwidth with some QoS guarantees*. Referring to the Differentiated Service framework [5], the complexity of QoS specification is abstracted by three levels: *gold, silver* and *bronze*. *Gold* stands for virtual leased lines, *silver* for better than best-effort and *bronze* symbolises the classical best-effort. Different entities in the market can have different internal representations of the market's goods, however, for a common global understanding, a minimal agreement on a common model is needed. This implies the need of abstracting from specific internal representations and of defining a common ontology to refer to. The common representation of the good expresses an agreement between the buyer and the seller that the service which the customer bids for corresponds to what the seller is committing to provide. This is formalised by the Service Level Agreements (SLAs [17]). Since SLAs depend on the nature of services provided by a network operator, and since we are far from having a standard and common way of expressing SLAs, the big challenge for software developers willing to implement agents reasoning about SLAs, is how to represent them (the SLA representation is not covered in this paper). In the following we describe the good's representation that is valid in the IP-market .

Network provider's good representation. The IP network has been modelled as a set of nodes interconnected by links. The nodes represent routers and/or switches in the network and the links represent connections existing between nodes.

Every link can be characterised by several parameters, such as price, available bandwidth, end-to-end delay, etc. Figure 2 shows two different levels of abstractions: link-level (e.g., *a-a1*) and path-level (e.g., *a-e*).

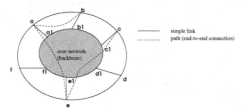

Fig. 2. *The abstract network model.*

Market's good representation. Every good offered to the IP-market must be described in terms of: *end-points*, i.e., termination points of the end-to-end path, *asking-price* that is the starting price of the good, *resale-price* that expresses the demand for the good on the IP-market, i.e., the value at which the good could be eventually re-sold. This value is fixed for the duration of an auction, is known before the auction starts, it can be defined according to the market history or it may be defined in terms of external supply considerations. The resale price can be either set by the seller, or defined as a function of other market-variables or set according to other conventions. The *offer timeout* is the time the offer will be valid for and *time* states when the service will start and stop to be available. The *amount of bandwidth* and the *QoS level*, i.e., bronze, silver or gold, characterise the connection type.

The buyer's view of the goods is built upon the information that the IP-market makes publicly available, which are usually the same described above.

3.2   The Market Actors

Several entities populate the IP-market. *Seller Agents* (SA) represent network and/or service providers and send IP-bandwidth offers to the market house. *Buyer or Bidder Agents* (BA) represent all potential customers and send bids to the market in order to purchase a specific good. For every auction process that takes place in the market, an *auctioneer agent* (AA) is responsible to manage it. An AA receives bids from buyers, evaluates them and determines the winner. At the end of an auction an AA notifies both the winner and the seller about the results of the transaction. Two different kinds of potential buyers can access the IP-market: *end-customers* or final and *re-sellers customers*, or non-final. A *private value* auction model is valid for end-customers that are willing to buy IP-bandwidth for private usage and do not intend to re-sell the IP-good to the market. Re-seller or broker customers are willing to re-sell the IP-bandwidth to other end-customers. In this last case the bidder's value of a good depends partly on its own preferences and partly on others' values, i.e., *non-private* value settings. For this reason, under the same auction protocol end-customers and re-sellers may deploy different strategies.

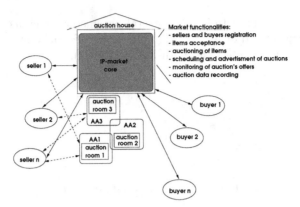

Fig. 3. *The IP-market architecture. Buyer and seller agents directly interact with the IP-market core. Buyers participate in specific auctions by interacting with an Auctioneer Agent in an auction room.*

Every BA is assumed to know the preferences of the user is acting on behalf of. The set of *preferences* is specified at the creation of every BA, so that a *user profile* is generated. Whenever an auction is started, a BA evaluates whether to take part in the auction or not by comparing the user profile and the goods' characteristics. If the BA enters a specific auction, the bidding strategy will be based on a set of rules that take into account the user profile, other user's preferences parameters, when available, and historical data about past auctions. The BA is also responsible for dynamic updates of the user profile.

3.3   The IP-Market Core

The IP-Market core is the central brain of the overall simulator, see Figure 3, by supplying the mechanisms required for managing individual auction process and for coordinating parallel auctions with other market activities.

In the IP-market simulator several auctions can take place in parallel. Every auction process runs in a separate virtual *auction room* managed by a different AA. Dedicated entities for managing distinct auctions increase the scalability and the efficiency of the market. All communications concerning a specific auction process are handled transparently to all other market activities. While an auction is going on, the market can for instance accept new incoming goods, register new buyers, etc. In order to access the market-place and to be able to participate to trading transactions, seller and buyer agents need to register within the market. A registered SA can then offer items to the market, and a registered BA can then participate in one or more auctions. The identity of every auction's participants is kept confidential. The auctioneer determines the winner and notifies participants about the auction results. After this notification, the winner and the seller can directly contact each other in order to fix the contract details [3]. More precisely, the core functionalities offered by the IP-market are:

---

[3] The current IP-market implementation does not support automatic contract definition routines.

- Registration of incoming sellers and buyers for identifying all potential trading participants. The market creates and records a profile for each registered entity that is then used for controlling market's access and trading activities. At the registration, every agent has to declare the name of the seller or of the buyer that is acting on behalf of, an address, an e-mail, a password that will be used to verify future accesses, a phone number, etc.
- Registration of IP-bandwidth offers. During this phase, a registered seller offers a specific item o the IP-market . The IP-market creates an auctioneer agent and informs the seller about the auctioneer agent's name and the auction identifier.
- Scheduling auctions and notification of potential bidders (i.e., all registered buyers) about the current active auctions. Different mechanisms can be used for auction scheduling: *regular* schedule when fixed appointments are established during the day, and *asynchronous* schedule when the good is made available (an auction is activated) as soon as the good registration succeeds. Registered buyers can either receive advertisements from the market, or proactively ask which auctions are currently active.
- Displaying all active auctions, registered buyers and sellers.
- Creation of auctioneer agents, one for every auction that is activated. In order to deploy historical results, every auctioneer records auction's data that the market will maintain and manage. From these data structures it is possible to extract information that agents will use for future speculations.
- Routing of all messages to and from agents that have been registered with the market.
- Winner computation and notification of all auction participants about the final results (these tasks are performed by the auctioneer agent). If a single item is sold within every auction, the winner computation is not a very difficult task (it takes $O(am)$ where a is the number of bidders and m is the number of items sold per auction). If multiple items are offered during the same auction process the complexity of the winner determination increases. If the goal is to maximise the revenue the *optimal* winner determination becomes NP-complete [13]. The combinatorial auction infrastructure is currently under construction.
- *Closing auction* phase. The auction is successful when a winner has been selected and the bid is compliant to the seller requirements. Both winner and seller are expected to confirm that they accept auction's results.

Security issues represent a common open problem for many e-commerce applications, that is even more crucial for agent-based systems, where distributed and autonomous software entities increase the number of possible attacks points. The current IP-market implementation needs more work on security aspects: while a *login-name* and a *password* can be enough for a simulator, a real market would need to verify the truthfulness of the information supplied by buyers and sellers. On the other hand, buyers and sellers would need to verify the market's behaviour and the fairness of auctioneer agents. For a real implementation specific agreements among all potential participants would be required.

3.4   An Open and Inter-operable Market

A preliminary and fundamental feature of an open and inter-operable market-place is the capability of supporting *standard communications*. Two main issues need to be solved: messages have to be physically delivered to the right destination and delivered messages need to be understood.

The first task, common to all distributed systems, requires that the IP-market is capable of addressing and routing messages to remote and distributed entities. For this purpose, every agent has a unique identifier and a unique address that the Agent Communication Router, (ACR) processes to forward messages. The ACR is part of the IP-market and is a sub-component devoted to message routing. Once a message has been delivered, full inter-operability can be reached only if the message can be conveniently processed. Figure 4 visualises different levels of understanding. This is first reached through the use of standard agent interaction protocols, which means standard sequences of messages. For every communication phase, i.e., *starting auction, bidding, closing auction*, etc., a specific protocol is selected. Some standard FIPA protocols have been adopted and some new ones have been defined. FIPA [3] is a non-profit standardisation group that aims to promote inter-operability of emerging agent-based applications, service and equipment. In particular FIPA defined standard communication facilities. Inter-operability is also achieved by the usage of a common

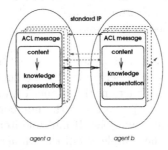

Fig. 4. *In order to achieve full inter-operability a common understanding is needed at different level: standard interaction protocols, a common ACL, a common content representation and the same ontology.*

agent communication language, which allows to parse and process delivered messages in a standard and common way. The official market-place language is FIPA ACL [3]. The first element of an ACL message is the name of the performative, the following part is a sequence of parameters that can occur in any order in the message. In particular the *:protocol* field specifies the expected sequence of messages during a specific agents' conversation. The *:content* field of a refers to whatever the communicative acts apply to. In the IP-market an ad hoc common content language capable to express actions, objects, and propositions has been developed and deployed. An *action* is an activity that can be performed by some agent, e.g., *activate-auction*. An *object* in the language defines an identifiable thing (with a name), e.g., a *good*. A *proposition* states that a sentence in a language is true or false, e.g., *auction-successful*. By convention, agents accessing the IP-market use this common language. Finally, a common ontology has been referred. An *ontology* is an explicit specification of the structure of a certain domain. This includes a vocabulary for referring to the subject area, and a set of logical statements expressing the constraints existing in the domain and restricting the implementation of the vocabulary. The IP-market ontology provides a vocabulary for representing and communicating knowledge about IP-bandwidth goods and about auctioning mechanisms. Furthermore, a set of relationships and properties that hold for the entities denoted by this vocabulary has been fixed.

The IP-market and all its auxiliary components, such as ACL parsers, ACR, bidder, seller and auctioneer agents, etc. have been implemented in Java. Successful tests have proved the inter-operability between the IP-market, developed at the LIA Laboratory in Lausanne, and seller agents developed by Swisscom. In particular, seller agents running in machines located in Bern (at Swisscom), have successfully registered with the IP-market running remotely at in Lausanne (at LIA). The connection has been established through the use of Java messages over TCP-IP sockets. Swisscom seller agents offered IP-services between different cities in Switzerland with different amount of available bandwidth and various QoS characteristics. Buyers agents, previously created and registered with the IP-market, registered for active auctions matching their preferences. The pre-designed and standard interaction protocols and the common terms used during all agent conversations have guaranteed full interconnectivity, so that auctions have successfully been run.

4   Integrating E-Commerce Capabilities within a Network

The Intelligent Resource Manager (IRM) automates all interactions between the IP-market and the network infrastructure. The interaction with the network management platform on one side and with the IP-market on the other side allows the integration of the e-commerce activity with traditional network management functionalities such as *planning, configuration, resource allocation, monitoring,* etc. This kind of architecture leads to advantages for both customers and providers. There are advantages for customers, since there is a third trusted party controlling all trading transactions: the IP-market auction house supplies in fact standard and fair mechanisms for all potential participants. The providers' advantages come from the fact that such an architecture would:

- Automate the advertisement of Telecom and/or Internet goods, according to network resources availability.
- Accelerate various steps of the service provisioning process
- Provide an alternative way to sell *bandwidth surplus*
- Support an automatic pricing mechanism through the auction paradigm.

The IP-market is *open* and *inter-operable* since standard communication techniques have been adopted. The common ontology that has been defined and deployed contains terms and definitions for the e-commerce of IP-goods. This ontology can be enriched and eventually modified to enable agent negotiations to address more specific markets, such as IP telephony, video on demand, etc. Furthermore, agents can simply refer to a different ontology in order to deploy the same IP-market structure for the e-commerce of books, flowers, wine or any other kind of good.

Flexibility is given by IP-market structure that is able to support transactions independently on the type of good that is offered and on the type of trading paradigm that is deployed. The IP-market can currently run auctions, but it is possible to integrate supports for other trading paradigms, such as automatic contract-net mechanisms . Furthermore, focusing on auctioning capabilities, several protocols are available: *Vickrey, English* and *First-Price Sealed-Bid.* In addition, for auction scheduling two different mechanisms have been implemented: *regular* and *asynchronous.* The auction advertisement can be either automatic, i.e., once an agent register with the market a notification of active auctions is received, or pro-actively triggered by an agent request.

Scalability is mainly achieved thanks to the modular structure of the market, which makes it possible to satisfy an high number of participants. Different market's sub-modules are in fact devoted to solve specific tasks such us users' registration, message routing, auctions' advertisement, etc. Furthermore, the creation of dedicated auctioneers for every distinct auction process allows more efficient management of agent communications and auction timing thereby increasing the potential scalability.

5   Conclusion

This paper reports the experience learnt during the implementation of the IP-market, an electronic auction house for selling 'IP-bandwidth goods'. Particular attention was devoted to concrete issues faced for developing an *open, interoperable, flexible* and *scalable* virtual market.

The authors believe that the major contribution of this work is in showing the feasibility of an automated interaction between buyers and sellers for the e-commerce of Telecom services. Furthermore, it shows the potential of deploying auctions for pricing IP services. Secondly, as stated above, the deployment of standard agent interaction instruments enables this system to be open and easy to access. Finally, the IP-market formalism abstracts networking complexity by providing a 'customer-friendly' view of IP end-to-end connections with QoS guarantees. Future work on the IP-market simulator includes transferring the platform over the Web, enhancing the system with XML-based descriptions of the goods traded, and integrating multi-items auctions facilities.

Acknowledgements. Many thanks to the other participants of the MACH project, especially to Sankalp Upadhyay and Thomas Fayet for their fundamental work and to Steven Willmott for his precious suggestions.

References

1. O. Ashenfelter, "How auction work for wine and art". Journal of Economic Perspectives, Vol. 3, No. 3 (Summer 1989) pp. 23-36.
2. R. Cassady, "Auction and Auctioneering". Reading, Univ. California Press, Ont. 1979, ISBN 0520002164.
3. FIPA'97 Specifications. Available on line at: http://www.fipa.org
4. R. Guttman, A. G. Moukas and P. Maes, "Agent-mediated Electronic Commerce: A Survey". Knowledge Engineering Review, 1998.
5. T. Li and Y. Rekhter. "RFC 2430: RA Provider Architecture for Differentiated Services and Traffic Engineering" (PASTE), October 1998.
6. T.C. Koopmans, "Uses of prices". *Scientific Papers of Tjalling C. Koopmans*, Springer-Verlag, 1970. pp. 243-257.
7. K. Kuwabara, T. Ishida, Y. Nishibe and T. Suda, "An Equilibratory Market-Based approach for distributed resource allocation and its application to communication Network Control". In *Market-Based Control*, Worl Scientific, Editor Scott H. Clearwater, 1996.
8. M. Kumar and S. I. Feldman, "Internet Auctions". Technical report, November 1998. http://www.ibm.com/iac/tech-paper.html
9. Gibney M.A. and Jennings N.R., "Dynamic Resource Allocation by Market-Based Routing in Telecommunications Networks". In *Proceedings of the 2nd International Workshop on Intelligent Agents for Telecommunication Applications (IATA'98)*, LNAI, Vol. 1437, pp. 102-117, Springer, July 4-7 1998.
10. J. Makris, "Not Exactly Nasdaq". http://www.eocenter.com/internetwk/
11. Lee, H.G., "Do electronic marketplaces lower the price of goods?", Comm. of the ACM, Vol. 41 No. 1, Jan. 1998, pp. 73-80.
12. A. Mas-Colell, M. Whinston, J.,R. Green, "Microeconomic Theory". Oxford University Press, 1995.
13. T. Sandholm, "An Algorithm for Optimal Winner Determination in Combinatorial Auctions". In *Proceedings of the 16th International Joint Conference on Artificial Intelligence (IJCAI'99)*, Stockholm, Sweden, 1999.
14. T. Sandholm, "Automated Negotiation". Communications of the ACM 42(3), 84-85, 1999. Special issue on Agents in E-commerce.
15. T. Sandholm, "Issues in Computational Vickrey Auctions". International Journal of Electronic Commerce, 1999.
16. Semret, Liao, Campbell, Lazar, "Market Pricing of Differentiated Internet Services", 7th IWQoS, London, May 31 - June 4, 1999.
17. D. Verma. "Supporting Service Level Agreements on IP Networks". Macmillan Technical Publisher, September 1999.
18. M.P. Wellmann, "A computational market model for distributed configuration design". In *Proceedings of 12th conference of the American Association on Artificial Intelligence (AAAI'94)*, p. 401-409, Seattle, WA, 1994.

Integrating Trading and Load Balancing for Efficient Management of Services in Distributed Systems[*]

Dirk Thißen[1] and Helmut Neukirchen[2]

[1]Aachen University of Technology, Department of Computer Science, Informatik IV
Ahornstr. 55, D-52074 Aachen, Germany
thissen@i4.informatik.rwth-aachen.de
[2]Medical University of Lübeck, Institute for Telematics
Ratzeburger Allee 160, D-23538 Lübeck, Germany
neukirchen@itm.mu-luebeck.de

Abstract. Due to the requirements of open service markets, the structure of networks and application systems is changing. To handle the evolving complex distributed systems, new concepts for an efficient management of such systems have to be developed. Focussing on the service level, examples for existing concepts are trading, to find services in a distributed environment, and load balancing, to avoid performance bottlenecks in service provision. This paper deals with the integration of a trader and a load balancer. The allocation of client requests to suitable servers is adaptable depending on the current system usage and thus the quality of the services used is increased in terms of performance. The approach used is independent of the servers' characteristics, as no provision of additional service properties to cover load aspects is necessary for the servers involved. Furthermore, it may be flexibly enhanced, as the concept of 'load' used can be varied without modification of trader or load balancer. This approach was implemented and evaluated in several scenarios.

1 Introduction

The integration of small isolated networks into bigger ones, distributed all over the world, caused a change in the design of application systems. Single applications are increasingly becoming distributed, thus can use resources more efficient and enable more flexible team work. The distribution of subtasks to different nodes enables an increase in a system's performance. By using middleware concepts, e.g. the *Common Object Request Broker Architecture (CORBA)*, it is possible to create an open service market. Different application objects, which provide services with known service types, can be used to compose the functionality of a new application. A trader supports the search for objects providing a required service. If the same service can be provided by several objects, it is possible to distribute the requests among them. Nevertheless, a system can by partly overloaded, if one resource is used intensively. Here, the concept of load balancing can be used to distribute tasks uniformly to available servers.

---

[*] This work has been funded by the German Research Council (DFG) under SFB 476.

C. Linnhoff-Popien and H.-G. Hegering (Eds.): USM 2000, LNCS 1890, pp. 42-53, 2000.
© Springer-Verlag Berlin Heidelberg 2000

This paper addresses the integration of a load balancing component into a trader. This enhancement enables the trader to consider performance aspects when selecting a server. The enhanced trader selects a service which is optimal in two aspects. First, the service quality determined by the service properties is taken into account. Second, the load of the corresponding server is considered. The concept was implemented and evaluated on a CORBA basis. The concepts of trading, load balancing, and a combination of both are briefly explained in chapter two, and related work is presented. Chapter three introduces our approach. In chapter four, some analyses show the usefulness of our approach. Finally, chapter five concludes the paper and addresses some perspectives for further work.

2 Trading and Load Balancing

If the same service is offered by several servers, a client will have to be supported in choosing one of them. Two powerful mechanisms are *trading* and *load balancing*. Whereas in trading the choice is driven by a client's requirements, the load balancing approach applies on the server side.

2.1 Trading

The trading service can be seen as an enhancement of the naming service, which gives a client more flexibility in specifying the service it needs. Whereas with the naming service a server and the service this server offers, respectively, must be assigned a unique name, the trading concept describes a service by a service type and service properties. The *service type* defines the functionality of a service. This type contains the *interface type* definition of a service, thus enabling an open service market. Yet, the interface type is not sufficient to describe a particular service. Therefore, the service type also includes a set of *service properties* which can be used to describe non-computational aspects of a service. A server which wants to make a service available in a distributed system passes a description of this service in terms of a service type instance, i.e. the object reference and the corresponding service property values, to the trader. Such a server is called exporter. It has to be considered that some service properties are dynamic, i.e. their values are varying over time. For these properties, the values are not registered at service export time, but when a service is requested. If an importer, i.e. a client searching for a service, contacts the trader it has to specify the service type, too. It can formulate restrictions on the service properties to express its needs, as well as criteria to determine an order on the services found, for example a minimisation of a property's value. The trader matches the importer's description against all recorded services and returns a list of server references. Traders were implemented in various environments [4], but they never became very popular. However, with the adoption of trading as a CORBAservice it became of general interest. Today, many trader implementations exist for CORBA platforms.

2.2 Load Balancing

Load balancing aims at a uniform utilisation of all available resources in a system by distributing tasks according to a given strategy. An optimal strategy would achieve a minimal response time of the system and the servers involved. Simple strategies are *static*; usually, such strategies are referred to as load sharing. New tasks are distributed to the available servers using a fixed schema. Strategies of this category include the cyclic assignment of tasks to the given servers or random server choice. They are easy to implement, but cannot adapt to special situations. The more promising strategies adapt to a system's load, and can react on changes in the system. Tasks are distributed according to the load of the available servers. Such d*ynamic* load balancing strategies have to consider the fact that measured load values only reflect the past. By updating the load values more often this problem could be minimised, but the network load for transmitting load information to the load balancer would increase too much. A compromise between communication overhead and relevance of the data has to be made. Furthermore, *semi-dynamic* strategies are possible, which use the load balancer's knowledge about the past distributions, but not the current servers' states. Much work has been done mostly on homogeneous systems. For example, [2] came to the result that simple strategies with small communication effort are most suitable. Strategies which were based on a threshold showed the best results. In these strategies servers are randomly chosen for the next task if their load is lower than the threshold. More recent strategies use more complex techniques, for example fuzzy decision theory [1]. These works contradict the advantage of simple strategies. On the other hand, [3] affirms the earlier results on simple strategies.

2.3 Combining a Trader and a Load Balancer

Trading is a good concept to support the binding between clients and servers in large open systems. But if one service type is searched for frequently, and each client wants the 'best' service instance, single servers can be overloaded. On the other hand, a load balancer tries to realise a perfect distribution of the clients' requests to the available servers. Yet, it can only select one server in a particular group; in large open systems, where many services with different types exist, the load balancer would have to know the type of the service to select a server. Additionally, the load balancer can only select a server by its load, not by considering service properties. Thus, a combination of trader and load balancer seems to be a suitable solution for a load-oriented assignment of clients to servers in a distributed environment. The direct approach would be the usage of *load values* as *dynamic service properties*. The trader could do a load distribution based on these attributes. Yet, it could be hard or even impossible for a service provider to provide an additional interface where the trader could request the information for dynamic attributes, especially in cases where legacy applications are used. Furthermore, this concept is inflexible, as a more differentiated interpretation of the 'load' value, also taking into account other load information aspects, would be hard.

Although both trading and load balancing are current research topics in distributed systems, only little work has gone into combining these approaches. The first were [8] and [11], which did simulations for the usage of a fair service selection strategy which considers global system aspects when mediating a service. Such a strategy does not guarantee an optimal selection for each client, but tries to optimise the global behaviour of a system. They confirm the results of earlier work regarding the usage of simple strategies. Additionally, [11] mention the risk of an oscillating overload of single servers. As a solution, a dynamic strategy with a random component is proposed. A main topic in [11] is the use of the knowledge of a server's load a trader has from past service mediation. It was shown that a cyclic assignment of clients to the servers, and using load balancing, are similar with respect to the quality of load distribution. Yet, this approach is based on knowledge of the service time for each task. An approximation of this time, considering the server performance and the service type, is not feasible in heterogeneous and open systems. Furthermore, it has to be considered that not every service utilisation is arranged by the trader; on each host, there will be a load independent from the trader's activities.

In [5], the co-operation of a trader and a management system is discussed. On each host a management agent gets management information from the components hosted locally. A trader is implemented on top of the management system and uses its functions to request the values of dynamic attributes or a server's load. Dynamic attributes are obtained by mapping management attributes onto service properties. By specifying complex selection and optimisation criteria for a service selection, a load distribution can be made. Disadvantages of this approach include the dependency on the management system and the lack of a special load balancing component. Furthermore, a load distribution is not transparent for a user, who must specify special optimisation criteria. In [10], an integration of load balancing for middleware platforms with an interface definition language is proposed for the distribution of load in a heterogeneous distributed system. The stub generated from the interface definition is enhanced by a sensor component. This sensor transmits load information to a local load balancer, which propagates all information to the other local balancing components to achieve an overall view of the system load. A naming service uses a local load balancer if a client requests a service. This concept has some disadvantages, too. A naming service, as opposed to a trader, is used here, which is a less powerful approach. The stub manipulation is inadequate because the source code must be known, and no transparent integration into servers is achieved.

3   Architecture of the Enhanced Trading System

For our enhancement of a trader with a load balancing mechanism we specified some design issues [9]. It must be possible to *use the trader in the normal way*, without making a load distribution, as well as to *combine the ordering of the services made by the client's constraints with the ordering of servers with respect to their load*. The load distribution process has to be *transparent for the user*, but he should have the option to *influence the process*, e.g. by defining special service properties. Such properties could refer to the information if load balancing should be performed at all, or which influence the load parameter should have compared to the service quality. The load balancer should be integrated into the trader to achieve a *synergy effect* by exchanging knowledge between trader and load balancer. Furthermore, the load balancer should be flexible to enable the use of *several load balancing strategies and load meanings*.

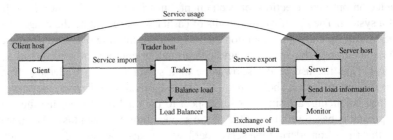

Fig. 1. Architecture of the trader-load balancer system

The architecture of the enhanced trading system is shown in figure 1. On each server host a monitor is installed to observe all local servers. The monitor is connected to the load balancer, which is located on the trader host. A client imports a service from the trader and uses the selected server. The work described in the following is based on a trader implementation done in our department using IONA's middleware platform Orbix 2.3.

3.1 Sensors

Service usage can be determined using a variety of metrics, e.g. the CPU load, the network load, or the load caused by i/o operations. Initially, we only considered the CPU load. To determine this load, the servers' queue length, the service time, and the request arrival rate can be used. Each participating server is enhanced by a sensor which collects these information and sends them to a monitor. As most applications used in our scenario are legacy applications, management wrappers were constructed to enhance an application with the necessary functionality [7]. As load information we use the service time in real time, the service time in process time, the usable CPU performance, and the queue length. The load information is passed to the monitor as a struct `LoadType`, see figure 2. This format is used to transfer load information in the whole system.

```
interface loadbalancing_types {

    enum LoadmetricType {SERVICETIME_REALTIME, SERVICE-
            TIME_PROCESSTIME,
                PROCESSTIME_REALTIME_RATIO, QUEUELENGTH,
                ESTIMATED_TIME_TO_WORK, ON_IDLE, REQUEST_RATE,
                USAGE_COUNT, HOST_LOAD, UNVALID };

    struct LoadType {LoadmetricType loadmetric; float loadvalue };

};
```

Fig. 2. Structure for covering load information

3.2 Monitor

A monitor manages a local management information base of load information and enables the load balancer to access it. It has a list containing all hosted servers together with their load. As the usage of different load metrics should be possible, all load information, which are transmitted by a sensor, are stored. The monitor not only stores the received load values, but also calculates additional, more "intelligent" values. This includes the computation of a floating average value for the load values mentioned above as well as an estimation of the time to process all requests in a server's queue. This estimation uses the mean service time of the past service usages and the time for the current request to estimate the time the server has to work on all of its requests. As no outdated load information should be used by the load balancer, a monitor uses a caching strategy to update the load balancer's information at the end of each service usage. Some values, e.g. the queue length and the estimation of the time to work, are also sent upon each start of a service use. Based on the access and change rates for load values, a dynamic switch between caching and polling is possible. This mechanism is shared by load balancer and monitor. In case of the polling strategy, the monitor knows about access and change rates, thus it can switch to the caching mechanism. On the other hand, if caching is used, the load balancer has both information, and can switch to the polling mechanism.

3.3 Trader

Based on a client's service specification, the trader searches its service directory. Services fulfilling the specification are stored in a result list. In a common trader, this list is sorted relating to the constraints the client has defined, i.e. the most suitable service is the first in the list. This process can be interpreted as a sorting of the services according to the degree of meeting the client's quality demands. For the integration of a load balancer this sorting is not sufficient, because the servers' load must also have an influence on this order. Thus, we had to introduce some modifications to our trader. When a new entry is added to the result list, the trader informs the load balancer about the corresponding server. Yet, the load balancer only knows about load aspects, thus it can not do the sorting relating to the client's constraints. To enable the consideration of both the trader's sorting and load aspects, the trader must assign a score characterising the degree to which the client's requirements are met by each service offer. To obtain such a score, a method as that proposed in [6] can be used. When the trader informs the load balancer about a server the quality score for its service offer is computed and also passed to the load balancer. After searching the whole service directory, the trader calls the load balancer to evaluate the most suitable service offer instead of sorting the result list relating to the client's constraints. To influence the evaluation, information about the client's weights regarding quality score and load is passed to the load balancer as well as the metric to combine both values. The trader is returned an index identifying a service offer in its list. The object reference identifying this offer is returned to the client.

In addition to the load balancer's mechanisms the trader implements a *random strategy* to determine an order for the services found. This can be seen as a static load balancing strategy.

3.4 Load Balancer

As shown in figure 3, the load balancer manages two tables. The first table contains the management information for the known servers (ServerMonitorTable). In this table, each server in the system is listed together with the monitor responsible for measuring the load, and the load itself. The other table, ScoreTable, is created when the trader receives a service request. Each service offer found by the trader for this request is recorded in the table together with the trader-computed quality score.

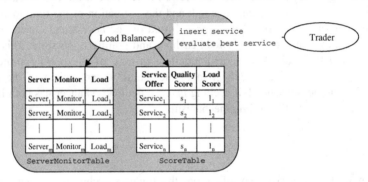

Fig. 3. Structure of the load balancer

After the trader has searched the whole service directory, the load balancing process begins. The approach chosen here consists of two steps. First, the load for all recorded servers is obtained from the ServerMonitorTable and inserted into the ScoreTable. Getting the load for all service offers at this time implies that no old load information is used. It also has to be mentioned that the 'load' field in the ServerMonitorTable does not contain a single value, but a set of load values for all different load balancing strategies. At this time, three strategies which try to minimise the system's load regarding to a particular load metric are implemented:

- *Usage_Count* only counts the number of requests mediated by the trader to a server in the past.
- *Queuelength* considers the current number of requests in a server's queue.
- *Estimated_Time_to_Work* calculates the estimated time a server has to work on the requests currently in its queue.

The load value given by theses strategies is seen as a score for a server, that is, the server with the lowest score has the lowest load. The load values corresponding to the chosen load balancing strategy are copied into the ScoreTable. The second step combines the score obtained by the load balancer with the quality score calculated by the trader. Metrics like the euclidean metric are used to calculate an overall score for each service offer, see figure 4.

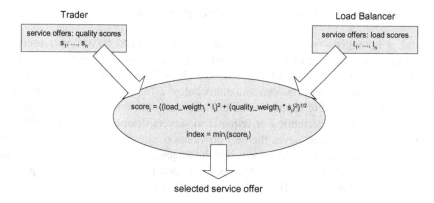

Fig. 4. Combination of quality score and load score

The client can influence the combination by specifying weights for quality and load score. For each service in the `ScoreTable`, an overall score is computed and registered in the `ScoreTable`. After all scores have been computed, a minimisation of these values gives the best suited service offer. The load balancer passes an index back to the trader, which identifies the corresponding entry in its result list.

4   Evaluating the Enhanced Trading Approach

To evaluate our approach, measurements were performed to analyse the effects on server utilisation, response times, and service selection time. To approximate a real scenario, a request sequence was generated by using a random number generator to place requests in a given interval. One restriction was the avoidance of a system overload, but temporary overload situations were desirable. Thus, the request sequence contains request bursts and intervals of silence. This sequence was used in all measurements. The service time for the requests varied from 1.1 to 16 seconds. For load balancing, the strategies *Random, Usage_Count (UC), Queuelength (QL)* and *Estimated_Time_to_Work (ETTW)*, as described above, were used. To evaluate the new component, the mean response time of the servers as well as the service selection time of the trader were measured at the client. The measurements were made in a local network (10/100 Mb/s-Ethernet). As a sample for a homogeneous system, four Sun UltraSPARCs with 167 MHz and 128 MB RAM were used. For measurements in a heterogeneous environment, four different Suns with clock rate between 110 and 167 MHz and RAM between 32 and 128 MB were used. Restrictions to a caching strategy to avoid communication overhead was made. To evaluate the benefit of the implemented load balancing strategies, the order determined by the trader computing a quality score, was not considered in the first measurements.

4.1 Homogeneous vs. Heterogeneous Server Performance

At first, a homogeneous system with four equally equipped servers was used. All servers had a service time of 1.1 seconds. In figure 5a, the mean response times of the servers are shown. The usage of the strategies UC, QL and ETTW lead to relatively equal response times, and for load situations below 50% they almost reach the optimum of 1.1 seconds. For higher load situations, response times go up only slightly, whereas the random distribution of requests to servers deteriorates dramatically. For the given scenario, UC achieves the best distribution, since all servers need the same time to process a request. For a system with homogeneous computer performance and no server usage without contacting the trader, a good load balancing is only possible with the trader's knowledge. This is the same result as in [11].

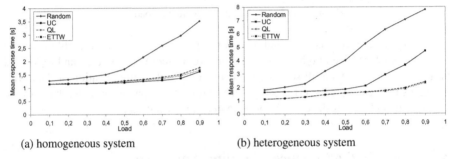

(a) homogeneous system   (b) heterogeneous system

Fig. 5. Mean server response times

The behaviour of the load balancing strategies changes in a heterogeneous environment. As a result of the varying computer performance, the servers had service times of 1.1 to 2.2 seconds. In figure 5b, the mean response times of the servers are shown. In this case as well the random strategy yields the worst behaviour. However, in contrast to the homogeneous case, the UC strategy performs poorer than the dynamic strategies. This behaviour was to be expected, as in this case, servers with less performance receive the same number of requests than more powerful ones. The dynamic strategies achieve equal request distributions, that is, even in situations of high load the mean response time for both strategies is only as high as the service time of the slowest server. To improve the quality of the static strategies, it would be possible to weight the distribution with regard to the servers' performance. However, in this case, the trader would have to know the performance characteristic of all servers in the system, and this might be impossible in a real open environment.

4.2 Using Different Request Classes

Considering different service request classes, i.e. requests to servers with different service times, represents a more interesting example of a real environment. In our analysis, we used four request classes with service times from 0.4 to 8 seconds. The requests were randomly chosen from these classes. This analysis covered two different situations. First, the request classes could be considered as requests for different service types with varying service times. Second, requests could be made for the same service type, but the service time is temporarily delayed by a background load on the server nodes. The mean response times for all request classes can be seen in figure 6. In case of a homogeneous system, the random strategy yielded the worst request distribution as could be expected, see figure 6a. Looking at the other strategies, UC is the worst in high load situations, because it does not consider the service times for the incoming requests. For lower system loads, UC is more suitable than ETTW. As the service times vary heavily, errors may occur in the estimation of that strategy, which than causes a wrong decision for the next request distributions. Only for high load situations this error is smaller than the misdistribution caused by UC. The error in estimation is also the reason for ETTW performing poorer than QL. QL only counts the number of outstanding requests; in this case, doing the distribution without more information about the requests is better than using potentially wrong information.

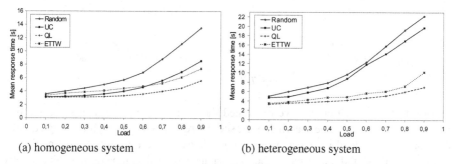

(a) homogeneous system   (b) heterogeneous system

Fig. 6. Mean response time using different request classes

The most interesting scenario is the combination of the other ones, i.e., the usage of heterogeneous server performance and different request classes. The measured response times are shown in figure 6b. In this analysis, the static and the dynamic strategies can be clearly distinguished. With the exception of the random strategy, the results are the exact opposite of those in the first examination. UC is almost as bad as the random strategy, because to many factors influence the response time of a server, but none is considered. For the same reasons as above, the results of the dynamic strategies are equal to the results in the homogeneous case with different request classes.

4.3 Analysing the Trader

The trader's order of the service offers based on a client's constraints was ignored in the presented analyses to examine only the benefit of the load balancing strategies. As in a real situation this order denotes the user's requirements on a service, it cannot be neglected; both, the service quality described by the trader's ordering, and the server load have to be considered. We found that the behaviour of the load balancing strategies is similar to the case without considering the trader's ranking. Weighting the load with 75% and the trader's ranking with 25%, yields hardly any difference to the former measurements; the ranking was influenced mostly by the load situation. In case of reversing the weights, the load was almost neglected, and for load situations of more than around 20% the mean response time increased heavily, as nearly all requests were sent to the server which was valued best by the trader. The best result was achieved with a weighting of 50% for both, load and quality score. In figure 7a, the mean response time for the homogeneous case without different request classes is shown as an example. Yet, weighting the load influence in comparison with the service quality must be a choice of the user.

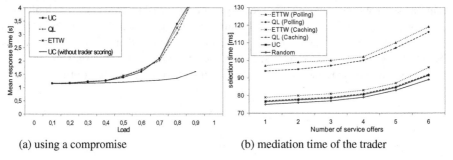

(a) using a compromise   (b) mediation time of the trader

Fig. 7. Trader analysis

In a further measurement, we examined the influence on the trader's service mediation time caused by the load balancer, see figure 7b. When using a caching strategy for obtaining the load values as well as for using UC, the time for service mediation increased only slightly, as most of the load balancer's work can be done independently from the trader. The load scores only have to be copied into the ScoreTable and the whole list has to be searched for the minimal value. When using a polling strategy, additionally all load values are obtained from the monitors. This adds a significant overhead to the mediation time, and should be avoided in most cases. By using the dynamic switching between caching and polling described in chapter 3, this overhead can be adapted to a given scenario.

5   Conclusions

In this paper, a combination of a trader and a load balancer was presented. Instead of using the trader's dynamic service properties, a load balancer was added to the trader as an additional component. Thus, the approach is independent of the servers' characteristics, and is flexible to enhance. Several load balancing strategies, and a concept for combining the trader's and the load balancer's results, were implemented on a CORBA platform. The implementation was evaluated in several scenarios.

The optimisation of service selection with respect to the servers' load seems to be a worthwhile enhancement of the trader. The response times of servers offering a service which is available in several places can be significantly reduced. The cost for this advantage is an increased service mediation time, but this overhead is very small. The usage of trader-internal knowledge like the number of mediations of a server is only useful in idealised scenarios. In a heterogeneous environment, it does not help to improve the load situation significantly. For such environments, dynamic strategies are more suitable. A simple strategy like the trader's queue length is best for most situations. The weighting of the load influence in comparison to the service quality must be the user's choice, but an equal consideration of both seems to be the best.

In addition to an evaluation of our trader in a bigger and more realistic scale, the next steps will be to realise a load balancing in a larger system in which trader federations are used. Obtaining load information and the co-ordinated interworking of traders in the load balancing process adds new, additional tasks. Additionally, the load concept has to be enhanced to consider more aspects influencing a server's performance. Furthermore, a usage of the load balancer component for other trader types or existing traders would be interesting. In such a case, the load balancer would need to encapsulate the trader. As in our approach trader and load balancer are largely independent, this approach is a candidate for these studies.

References

1. Dierkes, S.: *Load Balancing with a Fuzzy-Decision Algorithm.* Informatics and Computer Science, Vol. 97, No. 1/2, Elsevier/North-Holland, 1997.
2. Eager, D. L.; Lazowska, E. D.; Zahorjan, J.: *Adaptive Load Sharing in Homogeneous Distributed Systems.* IEEE Transactions on Software Engineering, Vol. 12, No. 5, 1986.
3. Golubski, W.; Lammers, D.; Lippe, W.: *Theoretical and Empirical Results on Dynamic Load Balancing in an Object-Based Distributed Environment.* Proc. 16th International Conference on Distributed Computing Systems, Wanchai, Hong Kong, 1996.
4. Keller, L.: *From Name-Server to the Trader: an Overview about Trading in Distributed Systems* (in German). Praxis der Informationsverarbeitung und Kommunikation, Vol. 16, Saur Verlag, München, 1993.
5. Kovacs, E.; Burger, C.: *MELODY – Management Environment for Large Open Distributed Systems.* Institute for Parallel and Distributed High-Performance Computers, University of Stuttgart, 1995.
6. Linnhoff-Popien, C.; Thißen, D.: *Integrating QoS Restrictions into the Process of Service Selection.* In: Campbell, A.; Nahrstedt, K.: Building QoS into Distributed Systems. Chapman & Hall, 1997.
7. Lipperts, S.; Thißen, D.: *CORBA Wrappers for A-posteriori Management.* Proc. 2nd International Working Conference on Distributed Applications and Interoperable Systems, Helsinki, 1999.
8. Milosevic, Z.; Phillips, M.: *Some new performance considerations in open distributed environments.* IEEE International Conference on Communications, New York, 1993.
9. Neukirchen, H.: *Optimising the Set of Selected Services in a CORBA Trader by Integrating Dynamic Load Balancing* (in German). Diploma thesis at the Department of Computer Science, Informatik IV, Aachen University of Technology, 1999.
10. Schiemann, B.: *A New Approach for Load Balancing in Heterogeneous Distributed Systems.* Proc. Workshop on Trends in Distributed Systems, Aachen, Germany, 1996.
11. Wolisz, A.; Tschammer, V.: *Performance aspects of trading in open distributed systems.* Computer Communications, Vol. 16, Butterworth-Heinemann, 1993.

Mapping Enterprise Roles to CORBA Objects Using Trader

Alistair Barros, Keith Duddy, Michael Lawley, Zoran Milosevic,
Kerry Raymond, and Andrew Wood

CRC for Enterprise Distributed Systems Technology (DSTC)
University of Queensland, Brisbane, Queensland 4072, Australia
{abarros, dud, lawley, zoran, kerry, woody}@dstc.edu.au

Abstract. The ODP Enterprise Language concept of Role provides a
useful abstraction for behaviour in a context that is independent of how
the behaviour is enacted in a run time system. In CORBA implementations of ODP systems a client object reference variable is analogous
to a Role - it is a placeholder for an object whose behaviour is specified by an IDL type. The DSTC UML Profile for Enterprise Distributed
Object Computing expresses the Role concept as a UML Action, which
is a placeholder for behaviour in UML, and has an attribute representing constraints on the objects that may perform the behaviour (fill the
Role). CORBA Object reference variables are assigned to object references using some "bootstrapping mechanism", implemented by a programmer, perhaps using a Trader or Naming Service to locate suitable
objects. For the first time in UML, the DSTC EDOC Profile allows designers to specify Roles independent of the class of objects that may perform the Roles. Designers also specify which objects are appropriate for
filling which Roles. Furthermore the mapping of this Profile to CORBA
technology allows automatic generation of Trader query code to bootstrap the object references of a distributed application according to the
high-level design, not the whims of the programmer.

1 Overview

As distributed object technologies mature and become more widely deployed,
there is an increasing need for rich modelling languages to be able to describe
the kinds of enterprise-wide applications that these technologies facilitate. In
particular, it is no longer sufficient to provide just an information or computational specification of a system. Rather, for such enterprise systems, there is a
recognised need to be able to describe such enterprise-level aspects of the system
as the business processes, entities, roles, and events that are involved.

In addition, it is not sufficient to simply be able to describe such aspects
of a system. It is important that there be a clear mapping from such enterprise
models to distributed object technologies that will be used in the implementation
of systems.

C. Linnhoff-Popien and H.-G. Hegering (Eds.): USM 2000, LNCS 1890, pp. 54–66, 2000.

Our approach to providing this support is based on the introduction of modelling concepts that represent dynamic, structural and policy aspects of enterprises. The goals we have in producing such a modelling language are to provide: a small but powerful set of enterprise modelling concepts; an expressive graphical notation; and a basis for automatic generation of component-based enterprise systems.

This paper focuses on how some of our enterprise modelling concepts can be used to specify aspects of a system implementation involving CORBA and CORBA services. In particular we discuss how the CORBA Trader can be used to bind implementations of business roles and business entities.

This paper begins by introducing the Object Management Group (OMG) activity to standardise a UML Profile for Enterprise Distributed Object Computing (EDOC)[5], and DSTC's submission to this process. Section 2 describes our notions of business process, business roles and business events. It outlines what is seen as the key relationship between the use of business processes and business roles in describing aspects of an enterprise system. Section 3 then provides details of the Role and Entity Model within the DSTC's UML Profile for EDOC submission. Section 4 explores the mapping from these design-level models into CORBA implementations using Trader. Section 6 gives an example of a role-based specification of an enterprise system and how that system would be implemented making use of the OMG Trader. Finally in section 7 we discuss the benefits of this novel approach to raising the bootstrapping of distributed applications into the design of applications.

2   Key EDOC Modelling Concepts

This section introduces the key models we use to describe various aspects of Enterprise Distributed Object Computing (EDOC) systems. These models provide direct support for describing business processes, business roles, business entities, and business events. As such, they are well suited for forming the basis of extensions to the UML so as to meet the EDOC requirements specified in the OMG UML Profile for EDOC RFP [5].

In order to provide a set of self-contained concepts suitable for practical enterprise modelling, we have integrated ideas from areas such as workflow systems, requirements engineering, and the ODP Enterprise Language Standard [1]. Our submission to the OMG and the work described in [?] focuses heavily on the expression of the modelling constructs in UML. This paper is a companion to [?] as it focuses on how Enterprise models can be mapped to technologies to support implementations of systems.

While this section introduces and positions our definitions of business processes and business events, the main focus of this section, and indeed this paper, is the specification of business roles and business entities and the relationship between them.

2.1   Process Modelling for Enterprises

In our approach, a business process is represented as a dependency graph of business tasks linked in a specific way to achieve some particular objective. A business process can be control-driven or data-driven, or both, and our model provides a rich semantics for expressions of these task dependencies. Our model also supports the composition of business tasks in a way that is suitable for implementation as off-the-shelf components. We also make provision for an association of business tasks with business roles to execute them.

Although our business process model uses concepts found in many workflow systems, nonetheless we view workflow as an IT solution to automating and managing business processes, mostly focusing on the execution semantics. Instead, in our approach, we have attempted to create a succinct business process model that encompasses different workflow execution semantics. We also consider business processes in the context of other business determinants, such as business roles, business entities and business events resulting in an emphasis on business semantics over computational semantics. Our submission to the OMG [6] describes a number of ways of implementing these business process concepts using CORBA interfaces, only one of which includes the OMG's Workflow Management Facility specification [7].

2.2   Business Processes and Business Roles Are Dual Concepts

We believe that business process modelling is only one (though frequent) approach to modelling some aspect of a business. There are other possible ways of modelling business systems. In particular, we argue that business role modelling represents an alternative or possibly complementary way of modelling the enterprise. We provide a separation of process-based and role-based modelling concepts as a way of offering different modelling choices. We also separate the notion of business role and business entity, as this separation provides a powerful mechanism for distinguishing between required behaviour and the business entities that can satisfy this behaviour.

2.3   Business Roles and Their Support

We believe that Business Roles should be described as fragments of behaviour of the enterprise - those that can then be fulfilled by specific business entities. The separation of the concepts of business entities and business roles enables the specification of the enterprise in terms of behaviour and not in terms of business entities. This modelling approach provides flexibility in assigning business entities to business roles; one business entity can fill more than one role and one role can be filled by different entities, as long as the behaviour of such an entity is compatible with the behaviour of that business role. This allows flexibility in changing the assignment of business entities to business roles as new policy or resource requirements may demand. This is possible because of the way we partition the behaviour of business roles onto business entities.

Such treatment of business roles also provides a basis for flexible assignment of the performers of actions in a dependency graph of business tasks forming a business process. In fact, a business role can be regarded as a collection of actions that are involved in performing one or more business task. The grouping of these actions corresponds to the definition of business roles. This business task versus business roles separation gives an additional power of expression to the business roles versus business entities separation already described. In this respect, our notion of Role is similar to the OORAM concept of Role [13].

2.4   Business Events Are Related to Business Processes and Business Roles

In both, process-based and role-based approaches, it is important to expose business events of significance to the enterprise. These events are associated with the modelling elements that can be their sources or sinks and our approach allows for flexible mapping of business event parameters onto the business process elements as well as business roles.

Although we find the use of business events in the description of an enterprise system to be of great interest, they are not of major significance to the intent of this particular paper and little more about them is discussed.

2.5   Example

A very brief illustration of the kind of enterprise model that we are describing here is shown in Figure 1. This is a fragment of a model describing the business processes, business roles and business events in a system for managing the technical support for an enterprises that releases software. The fragment shown describes how requests for support are received and serviced.

Figure 1 shows the business process for receiving and processing requests for support realised as a compound task labelled Receive/Process Support Request. This compound task is composed of three simple tasks - Process Support Request, Service Request, and Recursive Invocation.

The Process Support Request task can begin when the enclosing compound task has started and when it has received an event: sup_req of type support_event. This event delivers as payload the data_input that this task requires to begin, indicated by the open circle in the figure. When this task has completed, it enables the Service Request task, and the Recursive Invocation task to proceed in parallel.

The Service Request task has an associated business role - Software Support which will be the role performing the task. The rest of this paper is dedicated to business roles and their implementation and further examples will illustrate our modelling of roles in more detail.

The Recursive Invocation task invokes a new instance of this task at run-time allowing another sup_req event to be received and processed. This kind of recursion is how iteration is modelled in our system.

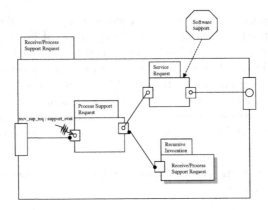

Fig. 1. Example fragment of an Enterprise Model

Much detail in this example has been left undescribed due space limitations. However more information and illustrative examples on our approach can be found in [6], [10], and [11].

3   Business Roles and Business Entities

In this section we describe how business entities relate to other entities in the business entity model, and to constructs in the business process model. The business entity model is concerned with the descriptions of the behaviour of roles that will, as a collection, describe the behaviour of the enterprise system.

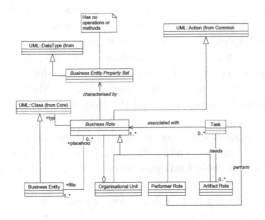

Fig. 2. Our Business Entity Model in UML

Central to our Business Entity Model are the abstraction of Business Roles, as illustrated in Figure 2. A Business Role represents a characterisation of some part of the behaviour of the system being described. Performer and Artifact Roles are specialisations of Business Roles. Performer Roles describe active behaviour while Artifact Roles characterise those things that are needed for the actions of Performer Roles (i.e. Artifact Roles do not initiate behaviour). A Business Entity can be said to fill a Business Role if it is capable of enacting the behaviour described by the role being filled. Organisational Units are a composition of Business Roles, enabling the collective behaviour of a set of roles to be another (larger) role. This gives us the ability to describe behaviours at different levels of abstraction.

3.1   Business Role

Business Role defines a placeholder for behaviour in a context. This context is an organisational unit (established with some objective in mind) and the behaviour of the role becomes part of the behaviour of the organisational unit as a whole. A business role is defined by its behaviour, its structure and a context in which it exists. For example, a Programme Committee Chair is a role in the context of a Programme Committee (an Organisational Unit).

Business Role inherits from the UML concept of Action, which enables a generic description of behaviour. The behaviour can be expressed using different languages, varying from a program code to English statements. Each Business Role is associated with a UML Class to provide it with a structural description. Finally, each Business Role is defined within the context of an Organisational Unit, which is itself a specialisation of a Business Role that is composed of other Business Roles. Thus Organisational Units (as Business Roles) can be composed into larger Organisational Units, and so on, until the enterprise has been modelled.

Business Role has two subtypes: Performer Role and Artifact Role. Performer Role describes behaviour for carrying out tasks in the enterprise - those that will be assigned to the Business Entities fulfilling the Performer Role. These entities will be responsible for the execution of some aspects of the tasks specified in the business process model described in section 2.1. Artifact Roles have behaviour, however the behaviour described is in some sense passive in that Artifact Roles do not initiate the execution of any action. Artifact Roles are used to represent inanimate things in the system such as resources. For example, a Programme Committee member (Performer Role) performs the review task using a paper (Artifact Role).

In a process-based description, the behaviour of a Business Process is specified in terms of causally-ordered Tasks. There is a correspondence between actions of Tasks and behaviour described by Business Roles. The behaviour of a Task can be composed from (some subset of) the behaviour of one or more Business Roles. Thus a Task is associated with one or more Business Roles (i.e. performed by the Performer Roles and using the Artifact Roles). Each Business Role can be associated with zero or more tasks.

3.2   Business Entity

A Business Entity describes an actual object that can carry out (some part of) a Business Role. A Business Role may be filled by one Business Entity or by a collection of them. Similarly, a Business Entity can fill more than one Business Role. For example, Prof. Smith (business entity) can fill the Performer Role of Programme Committee Chair and the paper "O-O for Fun and Profit" can fill the Artifact Role of Submitted Paper.

A Business Entity Property Set is used for specifying non-functional requirements of the behaviour of the Business Role. For a Business Entity to fill a Business Role, the Business Entity object must match the properties specified in the Business Entity Property Set.

Instantiation of a Business Role is achieved by binding to a Business Entity that is able to fulfill the behaviour specified by Business Role. This binding is possible when the Business Entity type is compatible with the Business Role type. However, binding of a Business Entity will commonly be based on more than just type compatibility. Some non-functional characteristics of a Business Role (e.g. QoS) may be specified as a Business Entity Property Set. Hence, Business Entities to be bound to a Business Role can also meet some additional criteria defined by the Business Entity Properties Set. Bindings between roles and objects can be statically defined in the Business Entity model or by Yellow Pages services. In particular, the OMG Trader service [8] can be used to automate the selection of object instances to fill roles, allowing run-time binding. Section 4 details just how Trader can be used for automating this binding.

4   Mapping of EDOC Roles to CORBA and Services

While our work describing how it is possible to model Business Entities and Business Roles is useful, this work is of only limited value if there is no clear mapping between the model and some concrete implementation of a system implementing the model. The modelling constructs presented are implementation independent and so can be mapped to a range of suitable technologies including Microsoft COM/DCOM, Java RMI and EJB, and OMG technologies. This paper presents a possible mapping of Roles and Entities to the OMG's CORBA and CORBA Services.

A Business Role is mapped in CORBA as a set of object reference variables in use in some context. This is a novel modelling concept in the Object Management Architecture (OMA) [2], as specifications of clients of CORBA objects, and the binding process by which client code comes to refer to the "right" objects, has been impossible until now.

In order to model a Role we must choose functional characteristics of Objects that will implement the behaviour we are modelling. This is done using a UML Class which is associated with the Role using its "type" metaassociation. The non-functional characteristics of the Role can be specified using a Business Entity Property Set, which is associated with the Role using its "characterised_by" metaassociation. The Business Entity Property Set is also a UML

Class, but one that contains only Attributes, which have names and data types, and may even have specific values given. The Role draws these functional and non-functional descriptions together using its metaattribute called "target" of type ObjectSetExpression, which it inherits from UML Action. This target specification describes (using any appropriate concrete syntax) which Objects it is appropriate for the Role to bind to at runtime.

At the highest level of abstraction, the target expression will probably be a natural language statement of requirements. As the model is refined, technology choices will be made and the target expression can be refined so as to use appropriate concrete syntax.

The type of a Role is mapped from UML Class to IDL Interface.

The mapping for filling a Role is as follows.

As we refine the model by choosing appropriate CORBA Services to implement the binding between object reference variables and CORBA Objects, the "target" expression in the Role's inherited UML Action may provide

- a key for use with a factory/finder (type manager) in order to locate or create an appropriate object.
- an Interoperable Naming iiopname or iioploc URL which nominates a specific object,
- a Naming Context or hierarchy of Contexts which contain appropriate objects.
- a Trader Service Request containing Service Type and Constraint expression which can be used to match appropriate objects through the Trader service.

The mapping for Business Entity Property set will depend on the technology choice made above.

A Business Entity will of course be a CORBA Object instance.

5   Mapping Role Binding to Trader

The CORBA Trader allows objects to advertise themselves by submitting a Service Offer in a category of service, called a Service Type. Clients of objects then make Service Requests of the Trader which specify a Service Type and a Constraint expression, which result in a set of appropriate Service Offers being returned to the Client.

The Service Type specifies the CORBA interface type of the objects being advertised, and gives a set of property names and types which will be given values in Service Offers. The Constraint given in a Service Request is a boolean expression over the properties of the Service Type, which the Trader uses to match appropriate Service Offers.

Figure 3 shows a Role with its associated Business Entity Property Set and Type, querying a Trader for matching Service Offers (SO's).

When mapping an abstract Role specification to a Role that will use Trader to bind its entities, the modeller will first design or choose a Service Type. The Business Entity Property Set will then be refined to include property types and

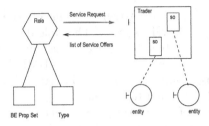

Fig. 3. Binding Roles to Entities Using Trader

names that: match the specific properties available in the Service Type; are an element type of a sequence-typed property in the Service Type; and are a structured type representing a high/low range of acceptable values for a property in the Service Type

Naming conventions are established to allow the Business Entity Property Set properties to be related to the Service Type properties.

Finally the Role's natural language target expression must be refined to nominate a Service Type and to formulate a Trader constraint expression that uses the names of the Business Entity Property Set properties as variables to be instantiated when a Service Request is made.

This refinement process is demonstrated in Section 6.

6 Example

6.1 Scenario

Fnord is a software development organisation that produces a number of software products that are used by clients in many countries around the world. Fnord provides a 24 hour, worldwide support service for clients using Fnord's software products. As part of Fnord's commitment to its clients, Fnord promises to attend to service requests within 24 hours of them being filed. Service requests are made through a web-based online system. For each request, data about the software package concerned, the nature of the problem, the time the request was lodged, as well as the the preferred language of correspondence of the requester is recorded by the service request system.

Based on the data in the service request, the system determines the service representative who is most suitable to handle the request. Because Fnord is a global organisation, this process involves choosing someone who is working in a location in an appropriate time zone, who is able to communicate in the language of choice, and who has the time and expertise to handle the service request.

Figure 4 presents a conceptual overview of the way that Software Support Requests from Clients are assigned by the Software Support Service to Service Representatives. Service representatives may service more than one client at a time, and, as with Client 4, it is possible that Service Representatives cannot be

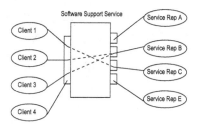

Fig. 4. Relating Clients to Service Representatives

assigned to Clients due to some lack of necessary properties such as expertise or availability.

6.2   Enterprise Model

Figure 5 is a UML diagram which shows the definition of a Role called `Software Support`. Notationally, we have chosen to represent the Performer Role stereotype with hexagonal boxes. The overlapping box with the two attributes: `lang` and `pkgs` indicates that this Role is a Template Role. This templating is explained in more detail below.

Associated with the `SoftwareSupport` Role are the class `SoftwareSupport Req` which is in the `type` association with the Role. `SoftwareSupportReq` is a class whose operations and attributes are used to specify the functional behaviour for the Role.

The Business Entity Property Set is populated by values from the web-based online `Service Support Request` system. In figure 5 the Role is templated by the required fields from the Business Entity Property Set, namely `<lang>` and `<pkgs>`.

The `SoftwareSupport` Role contains an expression of the required behaviour that the objects filling this Role must exhibit. This behaviour is expressed in terms of a Trader Service Request. The Trader Service Request is composed from the Role target expression parameterised by properties from the Business Entity Property Set.

The Type `SoftwareSupportReq` defines the computational interface that objects filling this role must support. This type information will be included in the Trader Service Request so that only the Service Offers of Business Entity objects with appropriate functionality will be returned as candidates for instantiating the Role. The `SoftwareSupportReq` interface inherits the Traders DynamicPropEval interface so that it may provide dynamic service offer property values to the Trader. In this case, to indicate the time remaining at work for a given support person.

Figure 6 depicts the refinement of the Role. On choosing to use CORBA and Trader, the first stage shows the refinement of the natural language expression of behaviour into the parameterised Trader Service Request. The final

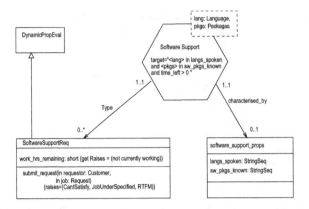

Fig. 5. Role, Type and Property Definitions

stage shows the binding that will occur at runtime of the `SoftwareSupport` Role Template with concrete parameters from a Property Set to produce the concrete `SoftwareSupport` Role. At this stage, the Trader Service Request can be completed.

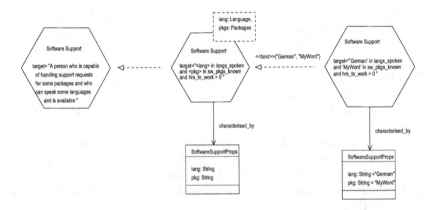

Fig. 6. Parameterising a Template Role

Figure 7 depicts a trader with a number of service offers. Corresponding to each service offer is the Business Entity object publishing the service offer. So, the objects `Woody`, `Zoran`, `Kerry` and `Keith` are all objects advertising services in this Trader. In this figure, all these service offers are of the same service type.

The Service Offer for the object Keith has been blown-up to expose the some of the details of the Service Offer. The service offer includes details of the attribute/values of the properties of the object such as `langs_spoken =`

[''English'', ''German'', ''Japanese'']. It also includes a reference to
the object to query to resolve the dynamic property: time_left which in this
case is the object offering the service.

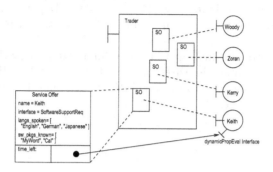

Fig. 7. Trader Service Offers

Given the specification of a Software Support Role from figure 6, and the
Trader populated with the service offers of objects representing software support
personnel who are able to provide support for a range of software products in a
range of languages and who are currently working, it is possible to use Trader
find appropriate staff to satisfy software support requests in a timely fashion.
In this example, the object Keith can fill the Software Support Role. That is,
given an Enterprise-level description of a Role in the system, it is possible to
find objects to fill these roles at runtime using Trader.

7 Conclusion

The DSTC UML Profile for Enterprise Distributed Object Computing introduces
small but powerful set of enterprise modelling concepts that represent a suitable
basis for the automatic generation of component-based infrastructure to support
enterprise systems. In this paper we have introduced our notions of Business
Process, Role, Entity and Event. The paper has described in some detail our
notion of Business Roles and their relationship with Business Entites.

In our model, we expresses the Role concept as a UML Action, which is a
placeholder for a behaviour specification in UML. We give this role a computational type by associating it with a class, and non-functional characteristics
through an association with a property set.

The mapping to an appropriate binding technology is achieved by refining
the behavioural specification into an appropriate concrete syntax. In this paper
we show how this is done for CORBA Trader.

The mapping of the DSTC EDOC Profile to CORBA technology allows automatic generation of Trader query code to bootstrap the assignment of object
references to objects in a distributed application according to the high-level design, not the whims of the programmer.

8   Acknowledgements

Our views on enterprise modelling have been influenced by involvement in the standardisation of the ODP Enterprise Language within ISO [1]. Our Business Process Model has a basis in work [12] done at the Department of Computer Science, University of Newcastle upon Tyne, UK, sponsored in part by Nortel Corporation.

The work reported in this paper has been funded in part by the Co-operative Research Centre for Enterprise Distributed Systems Technology (DSTC) through the Federal Government's AusIndustry CRC Programme (Department of Industry, Science & Resources)

References

1. ISO, Open Distributed Processing - Enterprise Language, ISO/IEC JTC1/SC7/SC17 N0080, July 1999.
2. Object Management Group, "The Object Management Architecture (OMA)" OMG http://www.omg.org/library/oma1.html,
3. Object Management Group, "Unified Modelling Language v1.3", OMG ad/99-06-08, June 1999.
4. Object Management Group, CORBA Components - Volume 1, OMG orbos/99-07-01, August 1999.
5. Object Management Group, "Request for Proposal: UML Profile for Enterprise Distributed Object Computing" OMG ad/99-03-10, March 1999.
6. DSTC, "UML Profile for Enterprise Distributed Object Computing", OMG ad/99-10-07, October 1999.
7. Object Management Group, Workflow Management Facility, OMG bom/98-06-07, July 1998.
8. Object Management Group, Trading Object Service, OMG formal/97-12-23, 1997.
9. Object Management Group, "Request for Proposal: Action Semantics for UML" OMG ad/98-11-01 Nov 1998
10. A. Barros, K. Duddy, M. Lawley, Z. Milosevic, K. Raymond, A. Woody, "Processes, Roles, and Events: UML Concepts for Enterprise Architecture", submitted to the Third International Conference on the Unified Modeling Language (UML2000), October, 2000.
11. S. Abraham, K. Duddy, M. Lawley, Z. Milosevic, K. Raymond, A. Woody, "Mapping Enterprise Events to the CORBA Notification Service", submitted to the Fourth Enterprise Distributed Object Computing Conference (EDOC 2000), September, 2000.
12. J.J. Halliday, S.K. Shrivastava, S.M. Wheater, Implementing Support for Work Activity Coordination within a Distributed Workflow System, Proc. 3rd International Enterprise Distributed Object Computing Conference, Sept 1999, pp 116-123.
13. T. Reenskaug, P. Wold, and O. A. Lehne, Working with Objects - The OOram Software Engineering Method, Manning Publications, ISBN 1-884777-10-4, 1996

Internet-Based Service Markets

Chair: Winfried Lammersdorf, University of Hamburg, Germany

A Scheme for Component Based Service Deployment

Steve Rudkin and Alan Smith

Distributed Systems Group, BT Laboratories,
Adastral Park, Martlesham Heath,
Ipswich, IP5 3RE, England
{srudkin, asmith} @jungle.bt.co.uk

Abstract. A dynamic and open service market should be characterised by the frequent appearance of new and diverse services. But in the internet environment, where a significant proportion of the functionality of new services is supported by Customer Premises Equipment (CPE), deployment can be an issue. How can such a diverse range of new services be easily deployed - particularly in a heterogeneous environment, like the internet, where different users have different terminal capabilities, and access bandwidths. This paper describes how the delivery, to the CPE device, of a recipe for dynamically building an application on the CPE device may be used to simplify the deployment of new services. In particular it shows how IBM's Bean Mark Up Language, an XML-based scripting language for describing a configuration of JavaBeans, can be used.

Keywords: Component, service creation, service deployment, session description, XML, BML.

1 Introduction

The ever increasing growth of the Internet is rapidly realising the most basic requirement of a universal service market – namely universal connectivity. At the same time, the end to end design principle of the Internet [1] is driving service intelligence to the edge of the network, and often to the customer premises equipment (CPE). As the capabilities of CPE devices (e.g. PCs, mobiles, set-top boxes) grow, we can expect a significant proportion of the functionality of new services to be supported by the CPE device.

In this paper, we regard a *service* as a function delivered to users through the execution of software components on one or more CPE devices, on an IP network and on a number of servers. We refer to the configuration of components on a particular machine (especially the CPE device) as an *application*. As our focus is on realtime services, we use the term *session* to refer to a particular instance of some real-time service (such as a conference, game, or TV program).

Many services share a great deal of functionality in common – both on the CPE device and on remote servers. For a number of years there has been increasing interest in

C. Linnhoff-Popien and H.-G. Hegering (Eds.): USM 2000, LNCS 1890, pp. 68-80, 2000.

the application of Component Based Software Engineering techniques to support the reuse of common software components in the development of new applications [2]. We are interested in the application of these techniques in the creation of new services. The creation of services should be a matter of describing the relationships between pre-existing components and adding session specific information such as: Internet addresses and media content. The creation of service instances should not be in the hands of specialist programmers, but rather the domain of service providers.

In a dynamic and open service market, we would expect to see the frequent appearance of new and diverse services. But, each new service may bring with it a deployment problem – how to distribute the necessary functionality to each CPE device? Whilst the new services would typically share some functionality with previously deployed services, we can also expect many differences. The heterogeneity of the Internet further complicates deployment. With varying terminal capabilities, access bandwidths, and intermittent connectivity, different service capabilities may be needed to suit the circumstances of different users.

This paper describes how the delivery, to the CPE device, of a recipe for dynamically building an application on the CPE device may be used to simplify the deployment of new services.

Previous work [3] describes how the Session Description Protocol (SDP) [4] can be used as a simple recipe for building a real-time application. For example it shows how the media fields could be used to select appropriate media processing components for configuration within the overall application. In this paper we extend this idea in a number of ways.

Our first extension is conceptual. We now consider a session description to be a description of an instance of a real-time service used by a service provider to advertise the associated service. For example an on-line training company might advertise a particular training session using a session description. The result is that a service creation environment can be split into a service definition environment (at the service provider) and a service instantiation environment (on the CPE device). The session description generated by the service definition environment is passed to the service instantiation environment, where it is used as a recipe for building the application.

Our second extension concerns the introduction of remote component services. Component services may be server-based (e.g. payment gateways, key distribution servers and media servers) or network-based (e.g. multicast or network QoS). We assume that a service may be composed from a number of component services as well as some functionality that resides on the CPE device (which partly acts to pull the various component services together into the overall service). Each component service may be offered by any service provider. In this way we seek to go beyond the retailer model [5] developed for TINA in order to produce a more open market place.

Our third extension, and main topic of this paper, concerns implementation. We show how we can use IBM's Bean Mark Up Language [6,7] as a way of defining the configuration of components that make up the application on the CPE device.

The paper is structured as follows. Section 2 discusses session descriptions. Section 3 sets the context for the work described in this paper by outlining the process we expect to see for creating and deploying new real-time services in an open market. Section 4 outlines the approach we have taken for dynamically building applications on the CPE device. Section 5 describes an example. Section 6 describes future work and section 7 concludes the paper.

2 Session Descriptions

On the Internet Mbone[1], a session directory tool (e.g. *Session Directory Rendezvous* (SDR) [8]) is used to advertise and discover multimedia sessions. The sessions are described using the Session Description Protocol (SDP). An SDP session description is entirely textual and consists of a number of lines of text of the form <type>=<value>. The type is always exactly one character and is case-significant, the value is a structured text string whose format depends on the type. An example of an SDP session description is given below. Note that the text in brackets are meant as explanations and should not appear in the actual description.

```
v=0 (protocol version)
o=srudkin  2890844526 0 IN IP4 132.146.107.67 (owner,
session identifier, version, network type, address
type, address)
s=SDP Seminar (session name)
i=A Seminar on the session description protocol (ses-
sion information)
u=http://www.labs.bt.com/people/rudkins (URI of de-
scription)
e=srudkin@jungle.bt.co.uk(email address)
c=IN IP4 224.2.17.12/127 (network type, network ad-
dress/TTL)
t=2873397496 2873404696 (start and stop time)
a=recvonly (media attributes set to receive only)
m=audio 3456 RTP/AVP 0 (media type, port number, trans-
port, media format)
m=video 2232 RTP/AVP 31
```

It can be seen that an SDP session description both identifies the application and defines the session specific parameters such as IP addresses to be used by the application. SDP uses the media field to declare the relevant media types and formats, and thereby implicitly identifies the application that should be used to participate in the associated session. In the case of the above example, SDR would launch the Mbone applications vat (for audio conferencing) and vic (for video conferencing). SDR can do this since it knows they support the specified formats.

---

[1] The Mbone is the part of the Internet that supports IP multicast which permits efficient many-to-many communication.

We are investigating replacing SDP with an XML [9] based session description framework. We believe that XML can be used to define a wider range of session specific parameters including QoS, charging and security policies. Moreover we show, in this paper, how the media fields of a session description can be replaced by a BML specification of the application(s) that are to be dynamically configured. BML is an XML-based scripting language developed by IBM for describing structures of nested and interconnected JavaBeans [10]. BML is directly executable, that is to say, processing a BML script results in an application program configured according to the script.

3. The Service Creation and Deployment Process

This section briefly describes the process of creating and deploying a new service. Figure 1 illustrates the main elements and their role in this process.

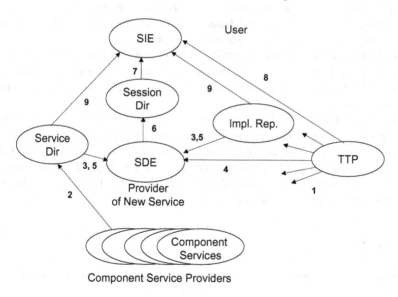

Figure 1: The process of creating and deploying a service

3.1   The Main Elements

Service Directory: A service directory is used by component service providers to advertise their component services to other service providers. It also allows users to download any client components which are needed as part of a third party service to interact with the component service. The service directory is outside the scope of this paper.

Implementation Repository: The implementation repository is a store of components that may be used in the implementation of applications that reside on the CPE device. These are components that are not part of an actual service, but which offer functionality in their own right (e.g. codecs, GUI elements, etc.). The implementation repository is outside the scope of this paper.

Service Definition Environment (SDE): This comprises an Application Development tool (for example supporting drag and drop development of components) combined with a tool for adding session specific characteristics (such as title of the session, purpose of the session, details of the session owner, IP addresses of the different media channels etc.) The practical use of the approach described in this paper depends on the existence of an Application Development tool that generates a suitable application description based on BML. In the absence of such a tool we have simply hand-written the BML for a number of component-based applications we have previously developed.

Session Directory: The session directory allows users to view details of current and future sessions and allows users and service providers to announce sessions. Currently we have implemented a complete multicast session directory that handles SDP session descriptions, and a very basic web-based session directory that handles the simple XML-based session descriptions described in this paper.

Service Instantiation Environment (SIE): This is resident on the User's CPE device. It is used by the Third Party Service Provider to build the required application and to launch it with the specified session parameters. The Service Instantiation Environment is the subject of section 4.

Trusted Third Party (TTP): It is the role of a Trusted Third Party to dynamically establish sufficient trust between two or more parties to give them the confidence to transact business. The Trusted Third Party issues and revokes certificates which are statements signed by the TTP about the certificate subject. Typically these statements include the subject's public key and identity, but they may also include higher value statements such as the subject's credit rating [11].

3.2   The Process

The process of creating and deploying a new service involves the following steps:

Bootstrap

1.   The various parties obtain certificates from the Trusted Third Party.
2.   The component service providers register their services with the Service Directory. This involves generating service offers describing the service itself, and any obligations on the users of the service (including for example payment details). The client components are passed to the Service Directory. It is a decision of the component service provider as to how much functionality is implemented in the client component and how much should be accessed remotely.

Service Definition

3. The Third Party Service Provider uses the Service Directory to find appropriate component services that may be used to support a new service they wish to offer. It also uses the Implementation Repository to find any functionality which will reside solely on the CPE device (e.g. codecs).
4. The Third Party Service Provider verifies, that the component service providers and the providers of components found in the implementation repository can be trusted, by obtaining the relevant certificates from the TTP.
5. The Third Party Service Provider downloads the client components for the component services, downloads any required components for the implementation repository and checks they are all correctly signed (using the public keys from the certificates that have just been obtained from the TTP).
6. The Third Party Service Provider builds an appropriate CPE application (using a suitable application development environment) and generates a BML application description (currently we are using conventional development and test to ensure the components work together). The Third Party Service Provider defines the necessary session specific parameters and advertises the whole session description (including the application description and session specific parameters) in the session directory.

Service Instantiation

7. The Customer downloads a session description from the Session Directory.
8. The Customer verifies with the TTP that the component service providers can be trusted.
9. The Customer downloads the relevant client components from the Service Directory and any other components from the Implementation Repository, checking they are correctly signed. The application can then be built on the CPE device and the relevant session specific parameters are instantiated. Service Instantiation is discussed in detail in the next section.

4 Service Instantiation Environment

Figure 2 shows the process for building applications dynamically on the CPE device; this is the Service Instantiation Environment. It also shows the inputs into the process. The inputs and the process are discussed in turn below.

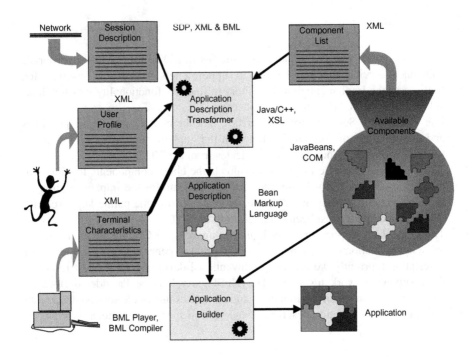

Figure 2: Dynamic application building process

4.1 Inputs into Application Building

There are several inputs into the application building process. All of these can be implemented in XML.

Session Description: The base input is the Session Description. A session description comprises user directed information (e.g. session owner, purpose of the session), session parameters (e.g. IP addresses) and an application description (in BML).

User Profile: This contains user preferences. For example, in the case of an aurally impaired user a preference may be to omit the audio component from an application and instead receive sub-titles. Whilst someone with unimpaired hearing might elect to receive the audio, but ignore sub-titles.

Available Components: Components can be stored on a user's own machine, or they can be downloaded from the network. Using components stored locally could offer the benefit of reducing time to start the application. Also, a local component may already have been paid for, whereas one to be downloaded may have to be rented (how components are charged for has not yet been addressed).

Terminal Characteristics: This has a critical influence on the application building process. A low resourced device is less able to show certain media-types. A mobile device will probably not be capable of displaying high resolution video. In the case of a session containing audio and video the mobile device could still join the session, but would only instantiate an audio component.

Network Characteristics: This has a very similar effect to the terminal characteristics. For example, a GSM network is not capable of relaying high resolution video

4.2 Dynamic Application Building Process

The process starts with a user browsing a list of available sessions using a Session Directory tool. Once the user has decided to join the session the session is passed to the Application Description Transformer for the application building to start.

Application Description Transformer: This takes the Session Description as primary input. As described above the Session Description will contain details of the media-types that make up the session, connection information, QoS data, charging data, etc. In order to adapt the application, this process may also use the other inputs described in section 4.1 namely user profile, available components and terminal (and network) characteristics. There are currently a number of different options for implementing this process. The choice is basically between XSL transformations or code written in a conventional programming language. Currently implementations have been tried using XSL and Java. The output of this process is an **Application Description**.

The application description uses IBM's Bean Markup Language (BML) from IBM's Alphaworks programme. BML is itself an instance of XML. It is used to describe the structure of a set of nested and interconnected beans. It is a language whose only functions are to describe how components relate to one another and how each of those components is configured. In fact Bean Markup Language is a bit of a misnomer as any Java classes can be included in the BML. It is just that special consideration is given to JavaBeans.

Application Builder: Once an application description has been produced it must be turned into a running application. For this stage we have used IBM's BML Player and compiler. The BML Player takes a BML script and produces a running program from it. The BML Compiler will compile a BML file into a class file which can then be run like a normal Java program.

4.3 Adaptation

Section 4.1 detailed the inputs to the application building process. The simplest form of adaptation will be to include or exclude particular media-types from the session and which components are selected in order to display those media-types. Examples include not selecting a media-type because of user preference or because of the type of terminal being used. Here the media-type will be removed from the BML. Presentation characteristics such as style of window objects used are also determined by the user profile. The session description could be extended to include alternative sources for data such as video at different bandwidths. A low resourced machine would select the video at the lower bandwidth.

5   An Example Implementation

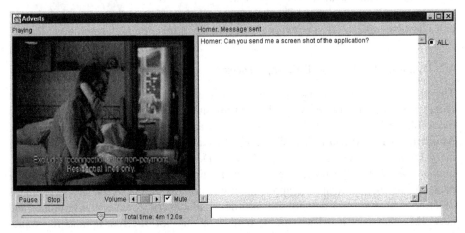

Figure 3 Audio-video-chat Application

As an example application we will describe an integrated chat and audio-video application (Figure 3).

This example combines two major components, namely chat and a JMF (Java Media Framework) implementation of Real Player. The Real Player component is used to access a remote component service streaming audio and video. There are a number of smaller scale components representing the GUI components, e.g. buttons and frames. The chat and the audio-video components have been used in other applications where they provide the sole functionality.

In the example implementation the only input to the Application Description Transformer is the Session Description; the other inputs remain to be implemented.

5.1 Session Description

```
<?xml version="1.0"?>

<session>

<title>Adverts</title>
<media-type id="audio-video">
<address>sherekhan.jungle.bt.co.uk</address>
<port>1545</port>
</media-type>
<media-type id="chat">
<address>ferao.jungle.bt.co.uk</address>
<port>1546</port>
</media-type>
<application-description>
<url>http://www.jungle.bt.co.uk/projects/internet-
```

middleware/bml/audio-video-chat.bml</url>
                     </application-description>
      </session>

In this example a session description consists of two media-types audio-video and chat. Each media-type information includes the address of the server and the port number (other location information such as a URL could be provided instead). The media-type tags serve to scope the address data so that they can be matched with the appropriate placeholders in the BML. In practice the media-type information would include other data such as QoS parameters and user directed information. QoS parameters would be used in order to adapt a session, e.g. by excluding a particular media-type because the terminal is incapable of meeting the QoS requirements. The user directed information would include such things as the owner of the content or comments, e.g. that the audio-video is the directors cut.

The application-description tag includes an address where a BML file representing a description of the application can be found. Note that the BML file is generic description for a class of applications that implement a combined real player and chat. It does not include session specific information. These generic BML files can be stored in a cache so that they only need to be downloaded when first needed.

We have produced a Session Description Parser in Java. The parser takes the input session description in XML and creates a session description object. This is used to display user oriented content to the user. This parsing is done using the XML for Java parser from IBM. A DOM (Document Object Model) tree is created then a separate Java object is instantiated to handle each tag and transfers the data from the tag to the session description object. The user is then presented with the title of the session and a list of media-types in the session.

5.2 BML

The BML represents a class of application. The BML produced at application creation time includes place-holders for the session parameters. Rather than show the entire BML script, excerpts will be used to illustrate key points

```
        <?xml version="1.0"?>

    <bean class="java.util.Vector">
            <add>
    <bean class="java.awt.Frame" id="mainFrame">
                                        <property name="title">
    <SD-session-name/>
        </property>
        <property name="background">
    <field target="class:java.awt.Color"
    name="lightGray"/>
                                        </property>
```

At the topmost level of BML there is a Java Vector which contains all the JavaBean components in the application. The first of these is a Java Frame class. There follow a number of property setters. The second of these is standard BML; the background colour of the frame is set to light grey. The first property setter has a place holder for the session name; identified by the tag <SD-session-name>. This must be filled in with details taken from the session description.

BML Bindings

```
<bean source="chatFrame">
        <event-binding name="window" filter="windowClosing">
<script>
                                        <call-method          tar-
                                get="chatClient" name="quit"/>
</script>
        </event-binding></bean>
```

JavaBeans in BML are connected together via event-bindings. An event from one component is mapped to call a method or set a property on another. In this simple example the chatClient component responds to a windowClosing event from the chat-Frame component by closing.

5.3   Application Description Transformation

If the user elects to join the session, then the BML is retrieved from either the cache or from the address specified in the session description. The BML is then parsed and the place-holder tags replaced by the session specific data. This is again achieved using XML for Java. The "Element Handler" event based parser is used. An element handler is associated with each placeholder tag in the BML. Each time the placeholder is encountered the element handler is called. The placeholder tag is replaced by data from the session description object.

A local component cache is checked to see if the components are already loaded onto the user's terminal. If not, they are downloaded over the network. Currently the version is not checked. In the future a scheme such as COM GUIDs could be used.

The initial three applications (chat, audio-video and the combined application) have been extended to include a payment component. If the session creator specifies that payment is required, then a payment component will be included by the application transformer. The amount to be charged for the session and the location of the payment gateway is taken from the session description and passed to the payment component. The user is then presented with the amount to pay and requested to provide credit card details. The payment component contacts a payment server for authorisation. Only when payment has been authorised will the other application components start.

We have also implemented an Application Writer using an XSL (XML Style Language) style sheet. The XSL processor (Lotus XSL) takes the session description XML file and XSL style sheet as inputs and outputs the complete BML file. The XSL style sheet contains snippets of BML which are output to the final BML file.

6 Future Work

Probably the most important task to complete is the definition of a session description DTD that is flexible enough to address a range of application types and service policies. The session directory will need to be adapted to handle these new session types. We are seeking to broaden the approaches to wiring giving alternative methods to BML.

On the server side, service creation would be improved if existing application development tools were securely coupled with the service directory, and implementation repository. Application developers should be able to securely drag and drop client components from the service directory and implementation repository and automatically generate BML describing the CPE application. It should be a simple further step for service providers to add session parameters and advertise the session description .

In the longer term we wish to explore the possibility of selecting and configuring components based on high level declarations of requirements of the kind described in a Taxonomy of Communication Requirements [12].

7 Conclusion

The use of a session description containing a recipe to dynamically build the CPE part of a new service offers a number of benefits.

- By using a session announcement to "deploy" a recipe for building the application, barriers to deployment are reduced.
- By overcoming deployment barriers, it becomes easier for service providers to offer innovative new services.
- By dynamically building the application from components on the client, only those components that are not available locally need to be downloaded.
- During dynamic construction, the application can be adapted to suit the local environment.

Acknowledgements

The authors would like to thank Ian Fairman for the contribution of his ideas to this work. We would also like to thank Kashaf Khan and Luca Tavanti for their implementation of components (under Eurescom project P925: Internet Middleware).

References

[1]   B. Carpenter, Editor, Architectural Principles of the Internet, IETF Network Working Group RFC1958, June 1996, ftp://ftp.isi.edu/in-notes/rfc1958.txt

[2]   Clemens Szyperski, Component Software - Beyond Object-Oriented Programming, Addison-Wesley; ISBN: 0201178885

[3]   Sarom Ing, Steve Rudkin. Simplifying Real-Time Multimedia Application Develop ment Using Session Descriptions, IS&N 99, Barcelona, Spain, April 1999

[4]   M. Handley. and M. Jacobson, SDP: Session Description Protocol. IETF MMUSIC Working Group RFC 2327 (1998). ftp://ftp.isi.edu/in-notes/rfc2327.txt .

[5]   M. Bagley, I. Marshal, et al, The Information Services Supermarket - a trial TINA-C Design, TINA Conference, Melbourne Australia. Feb 1995

[6]   Mark   Johnson,   "Cover   Story: Bean   Markup   Language,   Part   1", http://www.javaworld.com/javaworld/jw-08-1999/jw-08-beans.html .

[7]   Mark   Johnson,   "Cover   Story: Bean   Markup   Language,   Part   2", http://www.javaworld.com/javaworld/jw-10-1999/jw-10-beans.html .

[8]   M. Handley, The Session Directory Tool (SDR) http://mice.ed.ac.uk/archive.srd/html

[9]   Extensible Markup Language (XML) 1.0. W3C Recomm. http://www.w3.org/XML/

[10]   JavaBeans, http://web2.java.sun.com/beans/docs/beans.101.pdf .

[11]   T. Rea, High Value certification - trust services for complex eCommerce transactions, BT Technology Journal Vol 17 No.3 July 1999.

[12]   P. Bagnall, R. Briscoe, A. Poppitt, A Taxonomy of Communication Requirements for Large Scale Multicast Applications, IETF Large Scale Multicast Applications Working Group RFC2729, December 1999, ftp://ftp.isi.edu/in-notes/rfc2729.txt .

Performance Modeling of a Service Provisioning Design

Mohamed El-Darieby and Jerome Rolia

Systems and Computer Engineering Department
Carleton University, Ottawa, ON, K1S 5B6, Canada
{mdarieby, jar}@sce.carleton.ca

Abstract. The convergence of the telecommunications and computer industries is nearing a reality leading to service-based business models. The ability to provision services efficiently and quickly will be a competitive differentiator between service providers. This paper describes recent efforts to evaluate performance and predict the scalability of software architectures for provisioning services to end-users. We focus on network services that require the establishment of a Virtual Private Network. An analytical performance model for the service creation process is described. It expresses the high-level performance characteristics of the different subsystems involved in service provisioning. We study the effects of increasing numbers of network elements, end users, and autonomous systems on service provisioning infrastructure.

1. Introduction

The convergence of the telecommunications and computer industries [13] is nearing a reality. Service providers are able to use, rent or trade each other's resources and services. In such an environment, the competitive differentiator between service providers will be determined by the ability to provision well-performing services efficiently and quickly [11]. Service level management requires technical (e.g. performance) models [6] of the infrastructure of computer networks. This paper presents a modeling approach for such systems.

Service provisioning is of growing importance. For example, in 1998, the CMI corporation projected that the revenues from the provisioning of Virtual Private Network (VPN) services will be US$3 billion in 1999, US$10 billion in 2004, and US$47 billion in 2010. Corresponding provisioning systems must be designed to support increasing user loads and the growth in networks in general.

Service provisioning has two main functions:

1. **Service creation:** allocating network resources, establishing network connections, adding QoS features, and linking the service logic to control data flows.
2. **Service management:** operational support for accounting, billing, and managing Service Level Agreements (SLA).

This paper focuses on service creation. A model is developed and used to study how a service provisioning system performs as its managed network evolves. Network evolution is characterized by the number of autonomous systems, the

C. Linnhoff-Popien and H.-G. Hegering (Eds.): USM 2000, LNCS 1890, pp. 81-92, 2000.
© Springer-Verlag Berlin Heidelberg 2000

number of network elements per each autonomous system and the rate of requests for services.

We consider the following questions: a) How will the increase in demand for the standardized broadband network services affect the performance of the service provisioning system? b) What is the impact of increasing the number of autonomous systems and the network elements they manage on performance?

We are not aware of similar work to study the scalability of service provisioning systems. However references are made to related scalability studies in the distributed system and software performance engineering literature.

Section 2 describes network services in more detail and the ITU effort to standardize their performance measures. A performance modeling approach is introduced that is used to model and predict the service provisioning system's performance measures. Its relevant features are described. Section 3 describes the service-provisioning environment considered in this paper and an example network topology. A scenario for service provisioning is introduced. Section 4 describes the corresponding predictive model. Section 5 gives results from the study along with concluding remarks.

2. Network Services and Their Performance Metrics and Models

Standardization bodies, for example the IEEE and ITU, have set standards for measuring and evaluating the performance of network services. Sections 2.1 and 2.2 explain the relationship between these efforts and our work. This is followed by a brief description of the method and tool we used to model the performance of creating a service.

2.1 Network Services

The word *service* is often used as a synonym for the word function and consequently is used differently in different contexts [9]. The following taxonomy for services is provided by the IEEE Project 1520 for standardizing programming interfaces for network resources.

1. **Application services** that are *provisioned* in response to a request from application services by Service Providers (SP). These services include services that are defined in ITU recommendation I.211 [1] and are categorized into two main categories: a) *Interactive services* such as retrieval, messaging and conversational services; and b) *Distribution services* that include distribution services with or without user individual presentation control. Other types of these services include value-added VPN services such Intranet, Extranet, and remote dial-in VPNs.
2. **Value-added communication** *services* that are used by a service provider to enable the provisioning of broadband services. Examples of such services include policy, Service Level Agreement (SLA) management, security, location and mobility management, and Virtual Private Networks (VPN) services. They also include operational support services such as billing and reporting.

3. **Basic communication services** that are provided by the network provider (i.e. the carrier). These services span:
- Access networks: such as dial-in, cable, wireless, and TDM access services.
- Backbone network: such as optical networks, Frame Relay, ATM, and VPN services.

Our focus is on provisioning application services to end-users. Of these services we will study services that require the establishment of a Virtual Private Network (VPN) between end users. We call such services VPN-based Application Services. Such services include: media on demand services, video/audio conferencing, tele-education, and Intranet and Extranet services.

2.2 Performance Metrics

The levels of Quality of Service (QoS) are defined in the ITU recommendations E.800 [2]. Basically, they are categorized into service support, operability, serviceability, and security performance metrics. Serviceability is our focus in this paper. We are concerned with the mean response time of the service creation process as a performance measure. The response time of the process belongs to the service accessibility performance metrics that is a subset of the service serviceability metrics. The response time includes the response time of the network and of the software processes that participate in the service.

2.3 Performance Models

There are two widely applied approaches to predict a system's behavior: a) use performance measurements from a controlled testbed, or b) use predictive models. Measurements techniques usually consume more time and costs, and presume that the system or a substantial prototype exists. Estimates from performance models can often reveal performance blunders [15] and provide feedback for making system design decisions even before prototypes exist. We follow the latter approach.

To study the system we develop a Layered Queuing Model (LQM) [4], [8], [7], [10]. LQMs describe the request scenarios submitted to a system and the resources they consume. Requests pass through layers of software processes, consuming network, processor, and disk resources. The layered model is decomposed into a series of queuing network models that are solved iteratively, using Mean Value Analysis (MVA), to provide performance measures for the system as a whole [10].

An LQM is characterized by the:

- The mix and rate of request scenarios by end users
- The resource demands of requests (CPU, disk, network) as they pass through processes
- The nature of interactions between processes: for example whether they are synchronous or asynchronous
- The number of instances of each process and their maximum permitted level of concurrency (they are queuing centers)

- The allocation of software processes to server nodes and the resulting loads on the networks connecting them

The MoL tool implements the Method of Layers algorithm [7], [10]. It has a system description language that defines server nodes and their CPU and I/O rates, the underlying network infrastructure, software processes, their objects, methods, and concurrency characteristics, sequences for the flow of control of scenarios, and workload intensity and mixes of the sequences. It also supports the design of full-factorial experiments through the definition of factors and levels for different parameters in the model. The tool provides fast analytic performance estimates including: estimates for the utilization, mean response time, and average queue length of software processes and for the mean response time of requests. These predictions include contention for both device and logical software process resources.

3. Service Provisioning

Typical service provisioning environments consists of a carrier's core network, an access network and service provider systems. Such an environment is shown in Figure 1.

Users use an access network to dial in and get connected to the service provider. Usually, users dial in to a Point of Presence (PoP) of the service provider. Access networks deploy technologies such as Subscriber Digital Lines (SDL). The service provider systems consist of policy and service management servers. These servers are responsible for enforcing the policies of the service provider, creating service instances in response to user requests, maintaining service levels as agreed upon with users in accordance to the Service Level Agreements (SLA), and billing the users.

The carrier's network consists of many Autonomous Systems (AS). Each of them embraces a number of network elements (i.e. routers or switches). An AS usually uses a specific technology to transport packets for example IP, ATM, or Frame Relay.

The number of AS and the number of network elements each embraces characterize the number of network elements that participate in service provisioning.

3.1 Service Provisioning Scenario

This paper describes an example scenario for creating a broadband service for a hypothetical service provisioning system. The scenario considers the fundamental features of such a scenario and system and is used to guide the development of the corresponding performance model. The scenario is a best-case scenario that assumes no faults or exceptions. The scenario, shown in Figure 2, is as follows:

1. A user logs in to the Access Server, using his login name and password.
2. The Access server consults the Remote Access Dial In User Service (RADIUS) server for Authorization & Authentication.
3. The user ID is returned to the Access Server.

4. The Access Server issues a login event that is load balanced across a pool of servers capable of servicing the event. The event is then directed to the appropriate Policy Server (manager). In the example system presented in this paper, a layer-4 router acts as a load balancer dividing requests equally across pools of identical policy and service processes.
5. The Policy Manager consults the policy directory for policies assigned to the user.
6. The SLA corresponding to the user-application combination is returned to the Policy Manager that invokes the Service Manager.
7. The Service Manager gets the requested service template from a service model database (DB), and determines the network resource requirements of the service.
8. The Service Manager allocates the required network resources by invoking Bandwidth Brokers (BB).
9. The BB discovers resource availability via Topology and resource DB's.

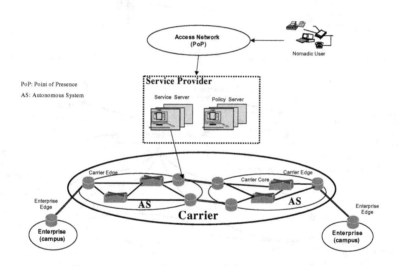

Fig. 1. A typical service provisioning environment.

10. If the service requires resources that span many Autonomous Systems (AS), Intra-BB negotiation takes place.
11. The service Manager is notified as the resource allocation process is completed to admit the service request and start administrative processing.
12. The service Manager downloads any required software components (a.k.a. filters) from a repository.
13. The controlling software components are uploaded to the different Edge Routers; enforcing the policies of the service provider.
14. Data packets flow and billing starts.

4. System Modeling for Performance

The MoL tool was used to document that scenario and obtain performance estimates for the scenario/service provisioning system documented in Figure 2. The tool has two distinctive characteristics. First, it is *representationaly efficient*. It permits the organization of system components (hardware and software) into hierarchical packages. These packages can be replicated. For example a policy server and its underlying hardware can be a package. As the workload for a system increases we can increase the number of replicates of this server's package. The visits to the server are divided equally across the replicates. This reflects the behavior of a load balancing

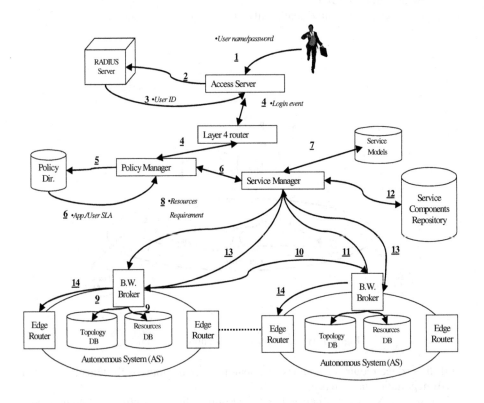

Fig. 2. Service provisioning scenario.

router in the model. The tool is also *computationally efficient*. Increasing the number of replicates does not increase the size of the model to be solved [7].

Figure 3 shows how the service provisioning system is modeled as a set of packages for the LQM. The figure shows also the number of requests for services each process issues for services offered by other processes. These are the processes involved in the scenario described in Section 3.

The model consists a parent package, *service_package* that groups all other packages. It contains the *service_server_package* for modeling the service provider environment, the *carrier_network_package* for modeling the network of autonomous systems, *and user_node* for modeling the behavior of the users and the rate they request services.

The *service_server_package* contains the *policy_servers* package that manages service policies and the *service_mgmt_node* package that creates a service instance and *vpn_mgmt_node* that instantiates a VPN. The policy and service servers communicate through a network that is modeled by the *net1* network component. The Replication Factor (RF) represents the number of each of the nodes.

The *carrier_network_package* consists of many *autonomous_system_package* communicating with each other via the *WAN2* network component. Within an autonomous system, there is the *b_w_broker_node*, *resource_db* and *the net_element_nodes* packages that represent the different components of physical autonomous systems. The interaction among the *user, service_server_package,* and *carrier_network_package* is carried via Wide Area Network represented by the *WAN1* component of the model.

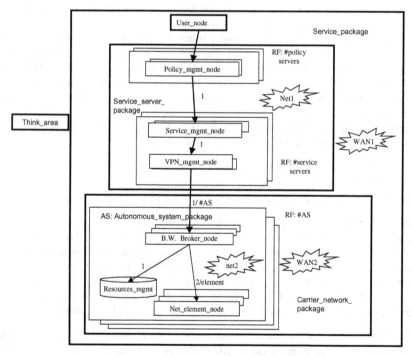

Fig. 3. A layered-queuing performance model.

Each of nodes contains processing entities that are characterized in terms of the CPU processing speed and the speed of Input/Output operations. Also, each one contains a running process that carries out the function of the package. The process has an average service demand for the scenario. The CPU and IO demands are estimates.

They express the relative costs of different processes and requests and permit us to present the proposed modeling approach.

Visits between processes are synchronous, except for calls from the *vpn_mgmt_node* to different bandwidth *brokers* and calls from a bandwidth *broker* to the different *elements_mgmt* processes within the same autonomous system. These are represented in the model using asynchronous interactions followed by a join operation. For example, the *broker* issues asynchronous resource allocation calls to all network elements that will be traversed in VPN connections within that autonomous system. Consequently, as the number of network elements increases, the number of methods the broker waits for increases.

The performance modeling experiments estimate performance and predict the scalability [14] of the system as the network evolves. As mentioned above the two parameters characterizing that evolution are: the number of network elements and the number and type of user requests for services. The average total number of network elements is the product of the average number of autonomous systems traversed by a VPN and the number of network elements per autonomous system. For the sake of simplicity we assume that all autonomous systems have the same number of network elements and statistically identical behavior.

Each experiment provides an estimate for the mean time taken by the system as a whole to create a service instance. This is known as the service creation response time and it is the sum of the (blocking) response times of each of the different subsystems; namely, the policy servers, the service management servers, the VPN management servers, and the processing that takes place within an autonomous system. The results also help to identify system bottlenecks. A bottleneck, software or hardware, is the resource that limits throughput and contributes most to increases in service creation response time. The effect of the delays caused by network latencies for communication among the subsystems is also taken into consideration.

The following factors and their levels are considered:

- The number of autonomous systems (AS): 3, 6, and 9
- The number of elements per AS: 20, 30, and 40
- The average number of end user requests per unit time: 10, 50, and 100

The MoL tool conducts a full-factorial experiment to calculate the effect of the experiment factors on different parts of the model. These changing factors reflect the evolution of the network. In our experiment, we assumed an autonomous system to be a domain for Open Shortest Path First (OSPF) protocol. The OSPF specification does not recommend an OSPF domain to embrace more than 50 network elements.

The resource demands of the various subsystems depend on the above factor levels. We assumed and reflected the following relationships in the model:

- The response time of the *policy_mgmt_node* depends on number of users, amount of data per user representing the profile of the user, service level agreements with a user, and number of service provider's policies. Only the arrival rate of requests affects response times at this node in our experimental design.
- The response time of the *service_mgmt_node* depends on the response time of the service model database that is a function of the product of the number of services and the number of templates for each service. Another component that contributes to this time is the service instance database that maintains a list of the instances in

operation. Only the arrival rate of requests affects response times at this node in our experimental design.

- The response time of the *vpn_mgmt_node* is the solution time needed to discover tentative paths across all autonomous systems to establish a VPN. This depends on Dijkstra's shortest path algorithm. Its solution time is of order $O(N^2)$ where N is the number of AS in the system. A multiplier of N^2 is used to inflate service demands on this node as the number of AS increases. The solution time also depends on the topology of the network and the IP addresses of source/destination nodes that will be connected via the VPN to use the service. However we do not yet reflect these aspects in this high level model and consequently we've assumed that the average number of autonomous systems spanned for each requests is equal 3.

- The response time of the *broker_node* is the summation of the time taken to find the shortest path within an AS, the time taken to allocate and reserve resources of different elements, and the time taken to enforce the policies of the server provider along that path. The time to find a shortest path is of $O(N^2)$ where N is the number of network elements per autonomous system. A multiplier of N^2 is used to inflate service demands on this node as the network topology changes. The time taken to allocate resources and enforce policies depend on the number of network elements within an autonomous system and the performance of the network connecting the broker and the elements within an autonomous system

5. Results and Conclusions

The mean response time estimates for the four main sub-systems are shown in Figures 4, 5 and 6.

Figures 4, and 5 show the response time for 20, and 100 requests/ unit time for services issued by end user, respectively. The mean response time for the service creation process as a whole is dominated by the response time of the VPN manager process. As we increase the request rate to 200 requests/ unit time, the number of elements to 40, and the number of AS from 3 to 9, the VPN process gets fully utilized (utilization of 0.98, 0.96, and 0.97 as number of AS changes from 3, to 6, and 9). This is shown in Figure 6 and illustrates the high response times for the service creation process. Consequently, the VPN manager process is the main performance bottleneck in the system.

The other processes do not contribute much to the service creation response time. Their response times are almost constant with respect to our factors levels. In the model, they are only sensitive to the end user requests rate.

The response time of the VPN process depends a great deal on the number of network elements in the network. This is not a big surprise since its resource demands is a function of the square of the number of network resources considered (due to Dijkstra's algorithm). As the resource demands grow, increasing arrival rates of requests cause dramatic increases in queuing for physical and logical resources leading to very large response times (e.g. Figure 6). The performance models help to illustrate how catastrophic such combinations can be for service performance.

Moreover, performance models allow us to study how we can solve the problems arising from software bottlenecks. An obvious solution is to increase the number of the software processes/nodes causing the bottleneck. We have increased the number of VPN and bandwidth brokers nodes from 1 to 10 and studied the impact on the response time of service creation. We have assumed these 10 processes operate independently and consequently we have not included overhead for synchronization; such overheads may be included in the future. Table 1 shows the results. There is little impact under low loads. For the case with 20 requests per unit time, 9 AS and 40 elements/AS, the mean response time decreases slightly as we increase the number of bandwidth broker and VPN management nodes. The response times decrease by half.

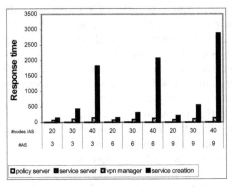

Fig. 4. Response time for 20 requests/unit time

However, the effect of replication is more significant as we increase the load on the system. For example, for 200 requests per unit time, 9 autonomous systems and 40 elements/AS, the response time decreases by a factor of 20. This motivates the need for the parallel processing of requests.

This study demonstrates that it is important for a corresponding implementation of this design to support replication of processes and their corresponding nodes. Such replication is more important for the bandwidth broker and VPN management nodes than for other nodes.

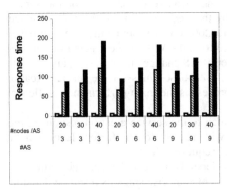

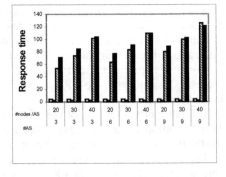

Fig. 5. Response time for 100 request/unit time

Fig. 6. Response time for 200 requests/unit time

Performance modeling is an important tool for those designing such systems. In our future work we plan to introduce further detail into the models and investigate the performance of the different techniques for creating and deploying VPNs. This will help to determine which methods are best for various workload mixes and network configurations.

Furthermore, we believe this work complements programmable network research. It offers a framework that could be used to reflect and predict the impact of programmed network changes on a system as a whole.

Table 1. Response Time (based on units) for processes at different replication levels

#users	#AS	#elements per AS	1 VPN_mgmt and 1 broker processes		1 VPN_mgmt and 10 brokers processes		10 VPN_mgmt and 10 brokers processes	
			VPN mgmt.	Service creation	VPN mgmt.	Service creation	VPN mgmt	Service creation
20	3	20	53	71	52	70	52	69
20	3	30	74	84	72	83	72	80
20	3	40	101	103	97	101	97	96
20	6	20	63	77	62	77	62	75
20	6	30	83	90	82	90	82	87
20	6	40	109	109	107	108	107	102
20	9	20	80	88	79	88	79	85
20	9	30	99	102	99	101	99	97
20	**9**	**40**	**125**	**121**	**124**	**120**	**124**	**112**
100	3	20	59	87	53	80	53	72.
100	3	30	84	118	73	102	73	84
100	3	40	123	191	99	142	99	101
100	6	20	66	94	63	91	63	78
100	6	30	87	123	82	115	82	90
100	6	40	118	181	108	159	108	107
100	9	20	81	114	79	111	79	89
100	9	30	102	147	99	141	99	101
100	9	40	131	215	125	197	125	118
200	3	20	69	140	54	100	54	74
200	3	30	101	426	74	159	74	88
200	3	40	145	3823	101	423	101	107
200	6	20	70	143	63	122	63	80
200	6	30	94	308	83	206	83	94
200	6	40	129	2072	109	654	109	113
200	9	20	84	213	80	188	80.	92
200	9	30	106	550	99	387	99	106
200	**9**	**40**	**137**	**2876**	**125**	**1717**	**125**	**125**

References

1. "B-ISDN Service Aspects." ITU-T recommendations I.211
2. "Terms and Definitions relate to the Quality of Telecommunications Services." ITU-T recommendation E.800
3. Umar, A.: "Distributed Computing: A Practical Synthesis." Englewood Cliffs, Prentice Hall, N.J. 1993
4. Woodside, C.M.: "Performability Modeling for Multi-Layered Service Systems", Third International Workshop on Performability of Computer and Communications Systems, Bloomingdale, Illinois, USA, Sept. 7-8, 1996
5. Caswell, D., Ramanathan, S.: "Using Service Models for Management of Internet Services." HP Labs, HPL-1999-43, CA, 1999.
6. Wetherall, D., Legedza, U., Guttag, J.: "Introducing New Internet Services: Why and How." IEEE Network, May/June, 1998
7. Sheihk, F., Rolia, J., Garg, P., Frolund, S., Shepherd, A.: "Layered Modeling of Large Scale Distributed Applications," Appears in the proceedings of the 1st World Congress on Systems Simulation, Quality of Service Modeling, Singapore, September 1-3, 1997, pages 247-254
8. Franks G., Woodside, C.M.: "Performance of Multi-level Client-Server Systems with Parallel Service Operations", Proc. First Int. Workshop on Software and Performance (WOSP98), pp. 120-130, Santa Fe, October 1998
9. Vicente, J., Miki, J.: "Designing IP Router L-Interfaces." IP Sub Working Group, IEEE P1520, http://www.ieee-pin.org/
10. Rolia, J.A., Sevcik, K.C.: "The Method of Layers," IEEE Transactions on Software Engineering, Vol. 21, No. 8, pp. 689-700, August 1995
11. Lazar, A.: "Programming Telecommunication Networks." IEEE Network, September/October 1997
12. Asawa, M.: "Measuring and Analyzing Service Levels: A Scalable Passive Approach." HP labs, HPL-97-138, Palo Alto, CA, 1997. http://fog.hpl.external.hp.com/techreports/
13. Decina, M., Trecordi, V.: "Convergence of Telecommunications and Computing to Networking Models for Integrated Services and Applications." Proceedings of the IEEE, vol. 85, No. 12, December 1997
14. Jogalekar, P., Woodside, C. M.: "Evaluating the Scalability of Distributed Systems", Proc. of Hawaii Int. Conference on Systems Sciences, January 1998
15. Smith, C.: "Performance Engineering of Software Systems", Addison-Wesley, 1990

Acknowledgments

The authors would like to thank Ferass El-Rayess, Anant Jalnapurkar, and Greg Franks for the help they provided during this research. This work was supported by grants from the Ontario Centers of Excellence CITO program and Nortel Networks.

Correlation DialTone—Building Internet-Based Distributed Event Correlation Services

Gabriel Jakobson and Girish Pathak
GTE Laboratories Incorporated
40 Sylvan Road, Waltham, MA 02541-1128, USA
{gjakobson, gpathak}@gte.com

Abstract. In this paper, we propose an Internet-based information correlation service called *Correlation DialTone* that is designed to increase the utility of event-based information. This service concept opens new business opportunities for Internet-based information services, such as Stock Market Correlation DialTone, Health Care Correlation DialTone, and Home Security Correlation DialTone. We present the component-based architecture of the distributed event correlation service and its component services: correlation subscription, data mediation, event parsing, event correlation, event delivery, and event notification services. We describe process/knowledge representation models and implementation of the distributed correlation service using CORBA, XML, Java, and model-based reasoning technologies. In addition to discussing the concept, the proposed service architecture, and the candidate applications, we also describe an implementation of a distributed event correlation system supporting the Correlation DialTone service.

1 Introduction

The Internet is becoming a universal information transport and service medium. It will soon be possible to connect any business, home, device, process, transportation vehicle, living body, or any other object (in any pragmatic information-producing sense) to any information consumer, human or machine.

While the amount of information flowing over the Internet is enormous and increasing exponentially, the utility of the information is growing much more slowly. This situation presents two related problems: "information flood" and low information utility. Simply stated, how does one effectively process the huge volume of information and extract, fuse, and interpret information in a way that is truly useful? In this paper, we propose partial solutions to these problems that focus on *events* and their *correlation*.

Depending on the way information is generally handled, one can see an evolutionary path in the use of the Internet:

- Information transportation
- Transaction processing
- Dynamic information change management

C. Linnhoff-Popien and H.-G. Hegering (Eds.): USM 2000, LNCS 1890, pp. 93-104, 2000.
© Springer-Verlag Berlin Heidelberg 2000

The majority of Internet applications today provide basic information transportation utility. Good examples include sending e-mail, transferring files, retrieving HTML documents, etc. New opportunities for utilization of the Internet are related to conducting business, such as banking, trading, commerce, and other transactions. In the future, we will see rapid expansion of the Internet for *dynamic information change management – event management*. The dynamic information change includes events such as notifications of physical processes, system status changes, fault alarms, changes in sensor measurement data, changing news items, surveillance information changes, etc. The Internet will become the predominate medium for generating, notifying, transporting, analyzing, correlating, and presenting all forms of dynamic information change. Important applications in dynamic information change management include automatic process control, network fault and performance management (system, device, and home), security management, location management, workforce mobility management, etc. All of these require collection and correlation of events.

In this paper, we propose an Internet-based information correlation service that we call Correlation DialTone (CDT). The CDT service, based on real-time, distributed event correlation technology, is designed to increase the utility of event-based information and is expected to have applicability to several new business opportunities, such as Stock Market CDT, Personal News CDT, and Home Security CDT. We will present the concept of CDT, the distributed service architecture of CDT, and the underlying real-time event correlation technology that will be utilized to correlate Internet events; and, finally, we will describe the components of a distributed event correlation system developed at GTE Laboratories.

As applied to Internet-based services, ideas similar to CDT have been expressed in the Keryx system from HP [1].

Event correlation technology that will be used for CDT is a widely accepted solution for managing the complexity of modern telecommunication and data networks. It has been used for various network management tasks, but the majority of its applications have been for network fault management. Specific correlation applications have been developed to manage switched, SS7, wireless, ATM, SONET, IP, and other networks. All major players in the network management arena either have developed their own, usually embedded, event correlation procedures or have used event correlation products such as InCharge [2], NerveCenter [3], ILOG [4], ART-Enterprise [5], NetExpert [6], and NetCool [7]. Various approaches to event correlation exist, including rule-, case-, and model-based reasoning, finite-state machines, petri nets, and binary coding methods. Several general issues for future directions in event correlations, including distributed event correlation and global correlation, have been discussed in [8].

2   Correlation DialTone—Concept and Applications

Real-time event correlation has been used for well over a decade with applications in various fields, not the least of which is network management. The Internet is creating a plethora of new opportunities for event correlation while also presenting new challenges. This evolving landscape has given rise to the Correlation DialTone concept. Correlation DialTone is an Internet-based event correlation service that allows real-time analysis of various information sources and managed systems/devices connected to the Internet (Figure 1). At its core it is an intelligent, knowledge-based information processing service, capable of recognizing correlations between events using application domain knowledge and data about the internal structure (topology) of the managed sources and objects. Subscribers to CDT will be able to identify the information sources of interest, specify event filtering and correlation conditions, select how they want to be notified about the correlation discoveries, and determine the information notification presentation media and form

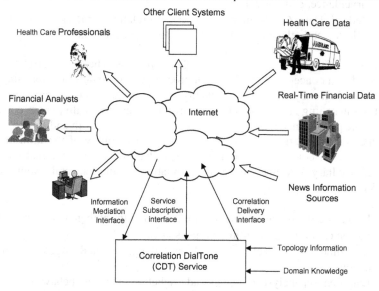

Figure 1. Correlation DialTone Conceptual Architecture

CDT is a distributed system with different component services for correlation subscription, event mediation, parsing, correlation, correlation delivery, system administration, and other component services. The correlation subscription service allows the clients to define their requests for CDT, such as the information sources, the managed objects, the type of correlation, the way the client will be notified, etc. The event mediation service provides connectivity to information sources and managed objects. It also performs the tasks of communication protocol and data adaptation. The event correlation service performs real-time event correlation. This service will be described in more detail in the following sections. The message parsing service performs event analysis functions that may include steps of different complexity of syntactic and semantic processing, depending on the nature of the event sources to be correlated. The event delivery service returns the CDT results to the client, while the administration service performs such tasks as billing, security, and the CDT internal management tasks.

One example of CDT applications is the Stock Market CDT—a system for real-time stock portfolio margin management. The system gets real-time feeds of predefined stock quotes and correlates them to determine adjusted and federal margin calls. The system will be able to perform single stock, diversified portfolio, or full portfolio volatility calculations, and may contain an expert system advisory component to provide buy/sell recommendations.

Other examples of CDT applications include:

- Personalized News CDT—customizable, real-time filtering and correlation of structured news data.
- Home Security CDT—correlation of data from home fire and intrusion detection, surveillance, and other devices.
- Medical Data CDT—monitoring and correlation analysis of bodily statistics, collected and relayed in real-time back to a medical center.

The heart of the CDT is the event correlation process. The event correlation process is defined as a conceptual interpretation procedure that assigns new meaning to a set of events [9]. It may range in complexity from simple event compression to complex pattern matching across asynchronous events. Algorithmically, event correlation is a dynamic pattern-matching process over a stream of events. In addition to the real-time events, the correlation patterns may include the topology of the information source (e.g. network connectivity), diagnostic test data, data from external databases, and other ancillary information. Event correlation enables several event management tasks:

- Increasing the semantic content of information through generalization of events.
- Fusion of information from multiple sources.
- Real-time fault detection, causal fault diagnosis, and suggestion of corrective actions.
- Ramification analysis of events and prediction of system behavior.
- Long-term trending of historic events.

3   Distributed CDT System Architecture

One of the most fundamental changes in the architecture of telecommunication and enterprise network management systems is the move from embedded, monolithic, and loosely coupled architectures toward distributed, open, component-based architectures. The use of standard services (components) with well-defined functionality and standard intercomponent communication protocols allows the building of open, scalable, and customizable systems. The encapsulation of the idiosyncrasies of components and the easy addition, replication, and replacement of components provide an effective environment for developing multiparadigm, fault-tolerant, and high-performance systems. Various technologies can be used for building the infrastructure of distributed network management systems, including CORBA [10], DCOM [11], and Java RMI [12]. Figure 2 shows a general overview of the CDT system architecture. The architecture is based on the following principles:

- Encapsulation of implementation idiosyncrasies of the different components (in our case, CORBA objects).
- Use of a standard event presentation (CORBA structured events).
- Use of a common knowledge/data transportation format (XML).

Thanks to these features, one can build customized management systems of different functionality, scale, and complexity. Different instances of the domain level services can be used, as long as they all satisfy overall functional and data semantic constraints. For performance or functional reasons, multiple processes of the same service could be launched. For example, a hierarchy of event correlation processes could be created. This hierarchy could be used to implement a multilevel system management paradigm, e.g., to implement local and global correlation functions.

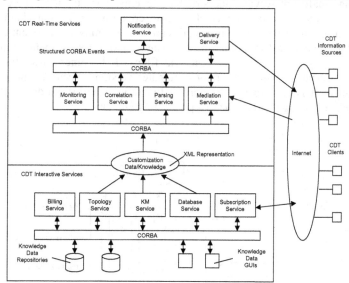

Figure 2. Distributed CDT System Architecture

In this CDT architecture, we divided the services into Real-Time Services (Mediation, Parsing, Correlation, and Event Notification Services) and Interactive Services. The latter ones are grouped into Support (Security, Billing, Subscription) and Customization (Topology, Knowledge Base, Modeling, Database) Services. This division supports our desire to provide fast channels of real-time event processing, and to make available interactive services, on an on-call basis, to provide required knowledge, models, procedures, and data in support of the real-time processes. The real-time services are sensitive to performance, and require a certain level of fault tolerance.

The Mediation Service provides Internet connectivity to CDT information sources. The incoming raw events (messages) are parsed by the Parsing Service. This might involve procedures stretching from analysis of simple structured data or text to complex semantic analysis of (near) natural language expressions, e.g., processing of news items. The Correlation Service performs the functions of real-time event pattern matching; processes event objects, topology, and other data; and executes actions predescribed by the correlation rules.

The Event Notification Service plays a special role in the architecture. It facilitates communication between the real-time components of the architecture. It enables sophisticated event passing interfaces between distributed objects—the producers and consumers of events. The interfaces are mediated via event channels that allow decoupling of producers and consumers in the sense that they possess no knowledge about each other. The CORBA standard for the Notification Service, the OMG's COSNotification Service, defines several important features of the Notification Service, including asynchrony, event subscription, multicast event routing, event filtering, quality of service, and structured events. The output of one channel can be chained to the input of another channel to create a notification chain as shown in Figure 3. Each of the nodes in a notification chain may cache events, take actions, perform some transformation on the events, and forward them along the chain. Services may select relevant events via filters. It becomes easier to replace these chained services with newer or alternate versions because the interaction is decoupled. It is easy to add supporting functions, such as validation, by creating a service and having it subscribe to a preexisting channel.

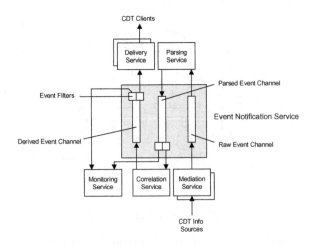

Figure 3. Chaining Services for CDT

4   The Event Correlation Model

We will follow the event correlation model described in [9], where event correlation is broadly defined as a conceptual interpretation procedure of assigning a new meaning to a set of events that happen within a predefined time interval. This conceptual interpretation procedure could stretch from a trivial task of event compression to a complex dynamic pattern-matching task.

The event itself is a time-stamped dynamic piece of information, which represents a manifestation of a change in the state of an object, system, or process. Relative to the correlation process, we make a distinction between the raw (base) events and the derived (correlated) events. The raw events are external events originated outside the correlation process, while the derived events are results of a correlation process. Depending on the nature of the operations performed on events, different types of event correlation could be defined, including event compression, filtering, suppression, generalization, specialization, temporal relations, and event clustering [9].

Each event correlation process has an assigned correlation time window, a maximum time interval during which the component events should happen. The correlation process will be started upon the arrival of the first component event and stopped as the last component event arrives. As any other event, correlation has its time of origination, time of termination, and lifespan. By definition, the time of origination of the correlation is equal to the time of origination of the last component event. Event correlation is a dynamic process, so the arrival of any component event instantiates a new correlation time window for some correlation.

The adopted approach to event correlation uses the principles of model-based reasoning originally proposed for troubleshooting electronic circuit boards. The idea of the model-based approach is to reason about the system based on its structure and functional behavior. The structural representation captures the specifications of the components that the system is built upon and the relations between the components, such as class, containment, and connectivity relations. The behavioral representation describes the dynamic processes of event propagation and correlation. These processes are described using correlation rules. Each rule activates a new event (correlation), which in its turn may be used in the firing condition of the next correlation rule.

On a phenomenological level, a correlation is a statement about the events happening on the network. On a system internal level, a correlation is an object-oriented data structure that contains its component objects and attributes. All correlations are organized into a correlation class hierarchy. The root node of the correlation class hierarchy describes the basic correlation class. The terminal nodes represent correlation classes, which will be instantiated each time particular conditions are met in the stream of incoming events. A correlation rule defines the conditions under which correlations are asserted. Different correlation rules may lead to the assertion of one and the same correlation. The subsequent application of correlation rules, instantiation of correlations, and consumption of produced correlations by the next rule describe the event propagation process.

5   Correlation Service

The Correlation Service (see Figure 4) runs all of the processes required for real-time event correlation. It contains the following subcomponents:

- Correlation Engine—performs the functions of real-time event correlation; processes event objects, topology, and other data; and interprets the state of the network. The Correlation Engine uses CLIPS [15] as the underlying real-time inferencing tool.
- RT (Real-Time) Event Export Module—caches, in real time, the state of the Correlation Engine (including the input events passed to the Correlation Engine and the resulting derived events) and passes it to the Event Database for further use by the Explanation Engine.
- RT Topology Export Module—handles the real-time interface to the Network Topology service using asynchronous CORBA calls.
- Action Service—application-specific services that provide asynchronous scripting (Tcl, Perl, Java), external function calls (e.g., in C), database queries, access to test equipment, and other functions to the Correlation Engine.

By subscribing to the Event Notification Service, the Correlation Engine receives a variety of input events, such as parsed base events from the Message Parsing Service, results from database queries or other external actions, and derived events generated by other correlation processes. All real-time events are presented as CORBA structured events. To proceed with the correlation process, the Correlation Engine gets required correlation knowledge from the Knowledge Management Service. This information is transported in XML. The output of the Correlation Engine is derived structured events pushed to the Event Notification Service. Information in the derived structured events may be used to filter and select items of interest to other components. Specific information in the derived structured events may include:

- Requests to other services to take actions or fetch data.
- Messages that should be added to event lists.
- Messages that should be removed or modified in event lists.
- Input to other correlation processes performing global correlation.
- Status information, which may be logged or ignored.

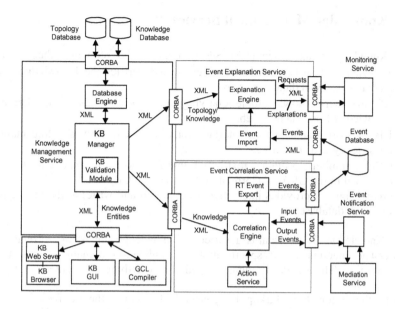

Figure 4. Correlation, Explanation, and Knowledge Management Services of CDT

6   Explanation Service

The Explanation Service (Figure 4) is used to analyze conclusions or situations recognized by the Correlation Engine. Some of the things this component is responsible for are:

- Finding events subsumed by a selected event.
- Finding independent events.
- Performing detailed non-real-time analysis of the cause of an event.
- Displaying a causal tree of a derived event.
- Displaying rules, messages, and other information related to the derived event.
- Displaying advisory text associated with derived events.

The Explanation Service gets requests for explanations from CDT customers via the Monitoring Service. The Explanation Engine has access to the Event Database, and, in the same manner as the Correlation Engine, it is provided with the required knowledge and topology information. As shown in Figure 4, the event explanation and correlation processes are separated and run by different engines. They only share access to the common event database, and to the correlation knowledge and the topology information. This solution better accommodates the real-time nature of the correlation process and the interactive (on-call) service of the Explanation Engine.

7   Knowledge Management Service

The Knowledge Management (KM) Service contains the following subcomponents:
- Knowledge Base (KB) Manager—serves and verifies the Knowledge Base and mediates physical database access.
- KB Browser—allows simple querying and reporting about GRACE and the Knowledge Base via the Web.
- KB GUI—a graphical user interface for editing KB entities, while maintaining consistency and correctness.
- GCL Compiler—provides text-based interface to define and edit KB entities described in the GRACE Correlation Language (GCL).

Database Engine—provides interactive access (read and write) to the knowledge and topology databases.

The Knowledge Base contains a variety of knowledge, including correlation rules, finite-state machines, and specification of application domain entities and their relationships. The standard language used for describing the content of the KB is XML.

XML, the Extensible Markup Language, is becoming the de facto standard for transporting data and knowledge between distributed components. XML represents arbitrary semantics as strings. It is not necessary to predefine the contents of these strings for the sake of the transport medium, making XML ideal for transferring data of arbitrary semantics over CORBA. While the distributed systems will define their framework in CORBA IDL, they will define much of the data semantics in XML. This approach will allow components of the system to be decoupled supporting a consistent knowledge and data transport mechanism. A sample of this transportation schema based on XML as an intermediary data/knowledge representation language and implemented in the CDT system is shown in Figure 5.

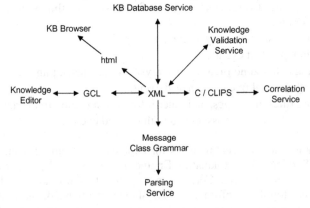

Figure 5. Data/Knowledge Transportation via XML Representation

8   CDT—Implementation

CDT is built from distributed CORBA components that communicate via IIOP (Internet Inter-ORB Protocol). OmniORB [13] is used for ORB programming, while the CORBA COSNotification (with a few small exceptions) was implemented at GTE Laboratories. The rest of the components were programmed in C/C++, Java, XML, and CLIPS. The system runs on Solaris, Linux, and AIX.

As events are passed from the Internet-based information sources or transported from managed systems via the Internet, the incoming stream of events is handled by the Mediation Service. The Mediation Service performs low-level protocol conversions and data adaptation functions, and turns events into a standard CORBA structured event format. Following the event notification chain discussed in Section 3, incoming events are then processed by the Parsing Service. In principle, many different parsing algorithms may be used; in the CDT implementation, however, a declarative knowledge-based method for event parsing was used [14]. At the core of this approach is a declarative message parsing knowledge called Message Class Grammar (MCG). MCG drives a universal parsing engine, allowing it to be customized to the messages of different active elements. The proposed method unifies message processing. It allows easy specification of different message processing tasks such as generalization, classification, specialization, transliteration, and others.

The event correlation model discussed in Section 5 is implemented in the Correlation Service component, which in its core uses an enhanced RETE network-based dynamic rule engine [15].

The Mediation, Parsing, Correlation, Topology, and possible other CDT component services are customized to specific CDT applications by utilization of the customization knowledge base. The content of the customization knowledge base is diverse. For the particular CDT implementation, discussed in this paper, it includes domain element classes, objects, message classes, correlation rules correlations (objects), relations, and finite-state machines. This content of the knowledge base (KB) is developed by CDT domain experts (engineers) using KB development GUIs. The Knowledge Management Component serves and verifies the Knowledge Base and mediates physical database access. It provides the Event Explanation and Event Correlation components with online access to the correlation knowledge and topology. The Knowledge Base editors are used for creating and modifying Knowledge Base entities, while maintaining consistency and correctness of the Knowledge Base.

9   Conclusion

Penetration of the Internet into all segments of the economy, including public and private institutions, the government, and the home, creates real business needs for online information correlation services. In this paper, we introduced the notion of Correlation DialTone—an Internet-based information correlation service. We described the concept, architectural framework, potential applications, and some key technologies for implementing real-time event correlation procedures.

Several research and implementation issues are still open, e.g., efficient processing of unstructured source information (natural language news events), discovery of new correlation rules from large bodies of data (data mining), understanding and incorporation of nontextual information, etc. The market size and the benefits of Internet-based correlation services are hard to overestimate. A deeper study of the full potential of Internet-based correlation services is in the works.

References

[1]   Keryx, http://keryxsoft.hpl.hp.com/.HYPERLINK
[2]   Yemini, S., Kliger, S., Yemini, Y., Ohsie, D., High Speed and Robust Event Correlation, IEEE Communication Magazine, May 1996.
[3]   VERITAS NerveCenter 3.5, http://www.veritas.com/products/nervectr/.
[4]   ILOG Rules, http://www.ilog.com/products/rules/whitepaper.pdf.HYPERLINK
[5]   ART*Enterprise™, http://www.brightware.com.
[6]   NetExpert, http://www.osi.com/.
[7]   NetCool, http://www.micromuse.com/index.html.HYPERLINK
[8]   Jakobson, G., Weissman, M., Brenner, L., Lafond, C., Matheus, C., GRACE: Building Next Generation Event Correlation Services, NOMS 2000, April 2000, Honolulu, Hawaii.HYPERLINK
[9]   Jakobson, G., Weissman, M., Real-Time Telecommunication Network Management: Extending Event Correlation with Temporal Constraints, Proceedings of the Fourth IFIP/IEEE International Symposium on Integrated Network Management, May 1995, Santa Barbara, CA.
[10] Siegel, J., CORBA Fundamentals and Programming, John Wiley & Sons, 1996.
[11] Pinnock, J., Professional DCOM Application Development, Wrox Press Inc., 1998.
[12] Downing, T. B., Java RMI: Remote Method Invocation, IDG Books Worldwide, 1998.
[13] OmniORB, http://www.uk.research.att.com/omniORB/omniORB.html
[14] Jakobson, G., Weissman, M., A New Approach to Message Processing in Distributed TMN, Fourth IFIP/IEEE International Workshop on Distributed Systems, October 5–6, 1993, Long Branch, NJ.
[15] Jackson, P., Introduction to Expert Systems, Addison Wesley, 1999.

Quality of Service

Chair: Gerd Schürmann, GMD FOKUS, Berlin, Germany

Programming Internet Quality of Service

John Vicente[1,2], Michael Kounavis[1], Daniel Villela[1],
Michah Lerner[3], and Andrew Campbell[1]

[1] Center for Telecommunications Research, Columbia University, NY, USA
{mk, dvillela, jvicente, campbell}@comet.columbia.edu

[2]Intel Corporation, USA
john.vicente@intel.com

[3]AT&T Labs, USA
michah@att.com

Abstract. The deployment for new Internet services is limited by existing service creation platforms which can be characterized as closed, vertical and best effort in nature. We believe there is a need to develop a programmable Internet built on a foundation of open service interfaces and middleware technologies. To help speed the introduction of value-added services, we propose a unified, programmable Quality of Service (QoS) API framework based on the IEEE P1520 Reference Model fostering open, standard interfaces for networks. We argue that this is a necessary evolutionary step towards a QoS-flexible, Internet service platform. We propose the design of APIs for upper level network QoS be based on service-dependent and service-independent abstractions, supporting alternative styles of QoS specifications and provisioning. Additionally, we propose the design of low-level network element APIs be based on the notion of a building block hierarchy and the separation of service-specific and resource abstractions for the creation and deployment of network services.

1   Introduction

The increasing value of e-business, seen for example in home markets and personal financing, impels the Internet toward universal connectivity supporting diverse end-user requirements.   Businesses compete for improved customer access and greater productivity. This fuels the development of personalized services and interactive environments including "virtual offices". Reliable and pervasive services may leverage the competitive innovations of multiple providers, and this requires flexibility, service differentiation, isolation, privacy, and manageability. The basic IP infrastructure provides, however, a limited service-delivery platform for the introduction of new scalable network services.   More than "best effort" data transport, these services increasingly require guaranteed Quality of Service (QoS) with pervasive security. Some customers may require Service Level Agreements (SLA) as well. Reliable and simple realization of such goals may soon leverage ubiquitous directory technologies placing identities and information on an open network. The control and usage of such information is essential as the Internet supports increasingly complex activities. In turn, this creates demand for policy-based management at multiple layers from transport to content.   Coordination of authentication, authorization and accounting appears

C. Linnhoff-Popien and H.-G. Hegering (Eds.): USM 2000, LNCS 1890, pp. 106-123, 2000.

mandatory, and these need to function over diverse standards and technologies. This guides the Internet towards a service-delivery platform, thus satisfying the increasingly diverse and demanding customer requirements.

The commercial success of the scalable Internet infrastructure may be limited unless the constituent entities support interoperability while preserving differentiation of service quality; this may exploit dynamic configuration as well as management of fluctuating demands. Convergent solutions of these challenges occur within the baseline of "stateless best effort" IP (ISO layer three). This may leverage recent protocols (DiffServ [1], IntServ/RSVP [2,3] and draw upon diverse transport capabilities. Existing solutions for IP-based service quality utilize alternative transport composed of multiple layers (e.g., ATM, frame relay, MPLS [4]).

These vertically deployed technologies may induce an unintended and dangerous partitioning of the Internet into multiple and incompatible network domains. This occurs as an artifact of using proprietary architectures with distinct QoS semantics. Thus, various solutions are being proposed which deal with traffic class translation [5], network integration, and virtualization techniques [6]. Indeed, the diverse protocols reflect the multiple transport requirements. Interoperability between these protocols may occur through Application Programming Interfaces (APIs) as adaptation layers.

While progress has been made toward network QoS programmability [7], [8], [9], there has been little work to unify QoS programmability across architectural platforms and distinct network QoS domains. In this paper, we propose a set of QoS APIs spanning multiple network programmability layers to support application, network service and device-level QoS programmability essential to the formation of an Internet servicedelivery platform. Such uniform APIs define the essential *protocol invariant* specification of QoS. We propose a unified QoS API framework for programming Internet QoS based on the IEEE P1520 Reference Model [10]. Rather than assume a single API can satisfy the diverse requirements at multiple transport layers, P1520 describes interactions between standard building blocks.

This unified QoS framework provides sets of low-level APIs. These comprise the resource-specific and service-centric QoS abstractions. Each level encapsulates the notion of building blocks that enable network device programmability. At the platform level, these APIs act as layered services that insulate the end-user from the complexity of network algorithms (e.g., admission control, reservations, or service level agreements). These support programming interfaces suitable to a network-domain's specific QoS characteristics. In addition, a higher-level and architecture-independent interface establishes the QoS of Internet sessions. New Internet applications leverage this interface without need for detailed resource-provisioning knowledge of the network domains. The adapter objects convert architecture-independent interfaces to architecture-dependent interfaces. These adapters may also maintain policies for provisioning, accounting, charging and billing.

The paper proceeds as follows. In Section 2 we discuss the emergence of programmable networks. We introduce our programmable QoS API framework in Section 3. In Section 4 and 5, we present and discuss the QoS API design forming the lower and upper QoS interfaces, respectively. Following this, we discuss related work in Section 6. Finally, in Section 7, we present some concluding remarks.

2   Programmable Networks

2.1   Open Signaling and Active Networking

The current developments in network programmability have mainly sourced from the OpenSig (Open signaling) [11] and DARPA Active Networks [12] communities. The OpenSig approach argues for a set of open, programmable network interfaces, enabling access to internal state and control of network devices (e.g., switches, routers). Thus independent software vendors (ISV) and service providers can enter the telecommunications software market, thereby fostering the development of new and distinct architectures and services.   Alternatively, the DARPA Active Network community, operating mainly within the IP communication model has offered a more radical approach to network programmability by advocating dynamic deployment of new services at runtime. While both communities have made good progress towards the development of programmable networks, much of this progress has taken on a research for "new architectures" motivation. The Internet industry, on the other hand, has been slow in adopting programmable networks within the commercial marketplace. Moreover, current network systems consist of vertical, proprietary architectures, duplicating the mainframe orientation of bundled OS, hardware and underlying services. Therefore, we believe a necessary step to achieving success or evolution in the Internet is the "horizontalism" of network systems through standardization of common, open APIs.

2.2   Programming Interfaces for Networks

The IEEE P1520 standardization effort is leading industry initiatives for standard programming interfaces for networks (PIN) to enable rapid service creation and open signaling. The scope of P1520 activities covers technology from ATM switches to IP routers and media gateways. The P1520 Reference Model (RM), illustrated in Figure 1, is a generalized model for network programmability structured without architectural or technology context. The interfaces, as shown, support a layered design offering services to the layers above it while abstracting the components below it for customization or programming. Each level comprises a number of *entities* in the form of algorithms or objects representing logical or physical resources depending on the level's scope and functionality.

More specifically, we distinguish the interfaces as follows:

- User level programming interfaces, collectively called the *V interface*, provide access to the value-added services level. This interface provides a rich set of APIs supporting highly personalized end user applications through value added services.
- *U interfaces* exist between the value-added services level and network generic services level (NGSL). The U interface deals with generic network services. The power of this interface comes from its generality, creating a separation between the actual interface and vendor implementations, allowing multiple network-level schemes to coexist in a single network.

- The *L interface* provides programming interfaces between the network generic services level and the virtual network devices level (VNDL). The L interface defines the API to directly access and manipulate local device network resource states.
- Open protocols to access the state of physical elements. Collectively called the Connection Control and Management interface, the *CCM interface* is a collection of protocols that enable the exchange of state and control information at a very low level between a device and an external agent.

P1520 Reference Model

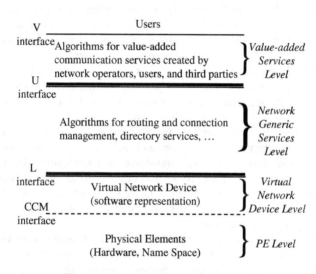

Fig. 1. IEEE P1520 Reference Model

2.3   Internet Service Platform

The P1520 RM provides a framework for positioning programming interfaces and operations of networks over a specific networking technology. A contribution of this paper is a proposed mapping of current Internet-based QoS technologies and their corresponding functionality to the P1520 RM. This enables customization to support valued-added services by use of the underlying network infrastructure for the delivery of diverse services and QoS requirements. This customization is essential to a malleable service environment that adapts to new services or requirements. Ensuring this customization is the assumption that the network does not impose *a priori* limits upon the diversity of providers of networks, services, content or other functions.

The deployment of QoS on the scalable Internet is inherently complex due to the range of traffic classifications, numerous providers, and service levels. This complexity should not burden the network, nor induce network partitions due to loading variations. Sustained reliability, scalability and capacity should not become vulnerable to mandatory access and migration of state information, and should remain relatively insensitive to temporary outages or unannounced reconfiguration. While one approach push substantial state information to the network edges, such an approach may also be perceived as shifting the state management to less informed or capable exterior elements. Such evolving issues present somewhat of a challenge to the ongoing Internet growth. Thus, simplification through common and open APIs is an essential element of the solution. Deployments of such standard interfaces may either manage or delegate the state information as the technologies allow. This applies the well-understood software engineering principle of standard interfaces to common components. Various API implementations are largely interchangeable provided they satisfy the interface and functional requirements.

API deployments often exploit adaptive middleware technologies. In particular, a service-oriented middleware structure supports the highest layer of the QoS framework, through definition of services and QoS at the points of service definition and service invocation. Although few practical examples are available in the literature, the AT&T GeoPlex project [13] established the concept of an open, service-oriented platform operating over IP supporting a multitude of complex and heterogeneous Internet services [14]. The GeoPlex adhered to unifying design principles thereby imbuing services with a stable behavior. It demonstrated sophisticated facilities such as coordination through usage recording and asynchronous event processing; administration through account and profile management; managed security including firewall-enforced authentication, sign-on and access control; as well as network integration including proxies, protocol translation and mediation. Using middleware and middleware services, GeoPlex provided a common management structure including global account hierarchy (with reference to network directories as available) with uniform APIs. These APIs allow adaptation to multiple system management solutions, each with their particular advantages.

These common APIs isolate functionalities and avoid unnecessary implementation constraints. Control and functionality may therefore move to the most effective locations. In particular, this migrates network control (often called "intelligence") closer to the core networking resources, and enables effective use of high bandwidth resources. This is compatible with emerging network architectures. We view the integration of QoS with the provisioning infrastructure without such as a middleware platform, analogous to having resource APIs within an computer platform architecture without the operating system services necessary to manage, isolate or protect critical resources. Few people would argue that the OS services are unnecessary complexity. However, within the context of a "networked" platform the complexity extends to include network protocol heterogeneity, mobility, address management, security policy integration and finally, inter-domain SLA coordination. To illustrate appropriate alignment, we anticipate the integration of QoS APIs with an open service platform, e.g., [13], [14] at the equivalent V interface of the P1520 Reference Model.

3   A Framework for Programming Internet QoS

The motivation for network QoS includes optimal service delivery, service differentiation and network bandwidth efficiency. The motivation for network programmability includes flexibility, customization, reconfigurability and portability.

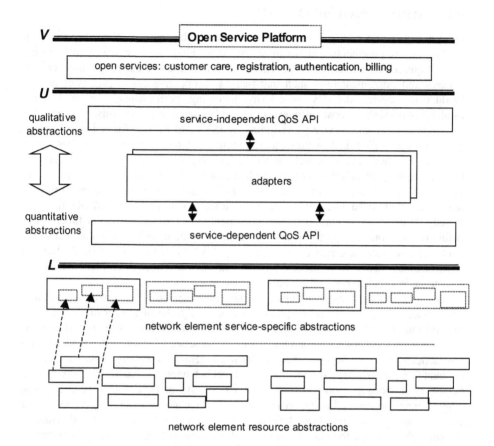

Fig. 2. Programmable Internet QoS Model

As we define programmable QoS, it is the notion of having network systems that enable customization and flexible integration of QoS over multiple layers of the communication model. Whether it is the seamless integration across application layers, or network devices, we advocate open interfaces that would minimize complexity and heterogeneity of network infrastructures to an appropriate higher layer abstraction. The P1520 Reference Model inherits the architectural hierarchy of value-added services, network services and algorithms, device and protocol implementations in its layered structure.

We propose a unified QoS API framework to support application, network service and device-level QoS programmability essential to the formation of an Internet *service-delivery* platform. More specifically, our contribution focuses on U (upper) and L (lower) interfaces of the P1520 Reference Model as a unified approach to deliver programmable QoS. Figure 2 depicts a conceptual view of the QoS API framework integrated with a general open platform API structure and superimposed onto the P1520 RM. We describe the architectural perspective of our proposal in the next sections, and provide specific detail in Section 4 and 5, corresponding to the design of the L and U interfaces, respectively.

3.1   Network Element QoS API

In pursuing a common design of QoS interfaces for network elements, there are fundamental requirements that we must adhere to. First, we recognize that there is a clear requirement for network providers to differentiate their proprietary product features and implementation, such that market competitiveness is preserved through product or service delivery superiority including performance, design features, availability/reliability, cost efficiency, etc. Complementary to this, is the clear requirement to enable service provisioning by ISVs and ISPs to foster innovation and rapid service deployment within the spectrum of Internet network services. So, a necessary balance must be struck, as we design network element APIs such that both requirements are satisfied. Secondly, with increasing intelligence being designed into network elements, we anticipate traditional packet and flow processing becoming the default network behavior, while emerging devices will perform multiple functions thereby defining a new class of network elements that extend behavioral functionality within the network transport. Thus, the traditional routers and switches are subsumed with multi-service aggregation devices (e.g., VPN) with explicit multi-function requirements.   This will include address translation, firewall enforcement, proxy activation, load balancing, and advanced monitoring.

Therefore, to meet these challenges, we have proposed an API structure that is based on abstraction granularity and scope. More specifically, the first order of abstraction is the separation of the *service-specific* and *resource abstractions*. The second order of abstraction is the notion of "building block" abstractions, which are course resource abstractions that can be combined to form *i.)* default behaviors within a network element (e.g., scheduling); *ii.)* new resource-level behaviors; or finally, *iii.)* service-level behaviors supporting service-specific abstractions. As in [15], we propose exposing control, management and transport functionality associated with the objects by way of the semantics of the interface definition. This includes the discovery of available resource abstractions, their composition, configuration, policies and state. In summary, the proposed L interface is formed from fundamental object-oriented design principles with the goal towards the development of open, extensible network element APIs.

3.2   Network Services QoS API

There are many commonalities which exist between alternative approaches for guaranteeing QoS in multimedia networks today. For example, the Differentiated Services Framework defines the notion of a 'leased line emulation' service, a service closely associated with flows in the Integrated Services Architecture, and virtual circuits in ATM networks. However, the QoS, requirements associated with each - leased line emulation services, flows and virtual circuits - are widely disparate. For example, the quantitative descriptions for QoS of multimedia sessions differ significantly between alternative networking technologies. Although all descriptions attempt to codify the predictable statistical characteristics of multimedia streams, the traffic assumptions associated with these descriptions are not the same.

The QoS mechanisms (i.e., admission control, scheduling, reservations) used by a particular network domain to support service differentiation and resource control are reflected in the service model characterizing that domain. While appropriate U interfaces should capture the granularity in which service models allow the specification of QoS for multimedia sessions (e.g., the flowspec in the IntServ model), alternatively U interfaces must be generalized in a manner that allows seamless development and integration of Internet applications and middleware platforms. These two design requirements contradict each other. To satisfy both, we separated the quantitative from the qualitative descriptions of QoS requirements in the U interfaces, as illustrated in Figure 2.

Therefore, what we propose is to have a *service-dependent* layer that is open and extensible offering quantitative and network-specific abstractions for multimedia services, and a *service-independent* layer of abstractions offering more qualitative and application-specific abstractions for multimedia applications. The lower-level abstractions are rigidly defined for different technologies and hide the complexity of different network algorithms. The upper-level abstractions are loosely defined and span multiple service-specific technologies, hiding the heterogeneity of the service models associated with the different network domains. By 'loosely defined', we mean that some information, necessary to establish sessions with QoS, is concealed at this level. Such information is handled by an 'adapter' object, which also performs the necessary conversion and mediation between the layers to meet the requirements of each. Adapter objects can be introduced dynamically into end-systems and in the network using a variety of methods. Adapter objects are specific to user preferences, network domain characteristics, and the types of services offered. Under an open service platform, as described earlier, QoS services can dynamically generate adapter objects on behalf of their clients, when the clients register with the platform. The design of the U interfaces and the role of adapter objects is further explained in the Section 5, where we also present the design of service-dependent interfaces for the Integrated Services and Differentiated Services architectures.

4   Open Network Elements

4.1   Virtual Network Device Level Interfaces

As illustrated in Figure 3 below, the proposed L interface is formed of three models of abstraction. This is an architectural extension from our previous work on the two-layer model [15]. Similar to [15], our approach enables network device programmability from two complementary perspectives, corresponding to an association with the layers of the L abstraction model, primarily service-specific and resource. This allows, for example, upper level interfaces to create or program completely new network services using resource abstractions or modify existing services using service-specific abstractions, which are themselves built on resource abstractions. The third layer is introduced to facilitate common device programmability via a standard set of base building block abstractions, which both the service-specific and resource layers are built.

Furthermore, the abstractions within these three layers differ in form to the previous work [15], as we propose an aggregation model based on building blocks. The upper part of the L interface is the service-specific abstraction layer of the network-element. The *service-specific building block* abstractions at this layer expose "sub"-interfaces associated with underlying behaviors or functions, state or policies on the local node that have concrete meaning within the context of a particular supported service (e.g. Differentiated Services). The idea here is that an administrator or ISV need only program the device within the context of the service rather than deal with low-level abstractions associated with generic resources (e.g. scheduler, dropper) of the network device. Therefore, in order to deliver the required service-specific behavior, the programmer need only modify or provision the service abstraction at the level that they understand or have a need (or privilege) to supplement.

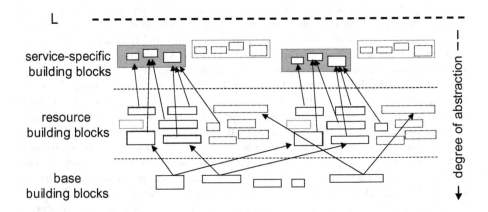

Fig. 3. P1520 L interface abstraction model

Alternatively, the middle part of the L interface abstraction model is the resource abstraction layer of the network element. The abstractions here are termed *resource building blocks*, from which default behaviors (e.g., Diffserv PHB) or new behaviors can be built. We envision the programmer as a sophisticated ISV developer or network software architect, who is knowledgeable of underlying resource abstractions of a network element[1] (e.g., router) and can construct new behaviors or functions, and can change state or policies within the context of the abstraction without knowledge of the underlying vendor device implementation.

The maximum degree of abstraction is achieved at the lowest layer of the abstraction model. This new layer is fundamental to the design of the proposed L interface. The idea behind the *base building blocks* are to have abstractions that have no service or resource significance from a network element behavioral or packet processing perspective. These base blocks serve the needs of the programmer, only in an inheritance fashion such that abstractions above the base layer (namely resource or service-specific) can be designed appropriately to create new functional service behaviors or resources or modify (enhance) existing ones in a consistent, standard object-oriented manner.

---

[1] We use the term 'network element' loosely here, as we position L interfaces such that resource building block or service-specific abstractions need not be associated with just a router device, but any network device that processes network flows or IP packets.

4.2   Designing Network Element QoS Interfaces

Rather than trying to align standardization across proprietary resource or service implementations, we propose a model for API development and standardization that can be built on common building blocks. Furthermore, the building block concept allows varying degrees of abstractions for network element programmability. For example, one can support either a "queue" building block or "traffic conditioner" building block that can be a collection of subcomponents including shapers, droppers, etc, which form the traffic conditioner. The API standardization discussion becomes a matter of resources or services that are deemed sufficiently common and open for service provisioning and do not compromise any compliant (e.g., P1520) vendor's proprietary features. The proposed model makes the L interface truly open, flexible, reusable, extensible and dynamic.

Table 1. Base building blocks

Building block	Vari able	Methods	Description
Action	ID, priority, type	discover () actionmethod () target () raises (exception)	Performs a specific function on the directed path from which the processing unit traverses within the network element.
Component	ID, status, type	discover (target()) get(target()), set(target()), delete(target()), add(target()), modify(target()) target () internal-block(target()) raises (exception)	A resource or component entity on the router. This may be a singular component (e.g., queue), or an aggregate component consisting of several building blocks.
Condition	ID type	predicate () target () raises(exception)	A decision point, possibly pre-staging an action or component.
Target	ID, type	reference(nextblock) raises(exception)	Provides a reference to the next building block, from which the previous entity directs the network element processing.
Processing Unit (PU)	ID, state, size		This is the unit of processing through the router, i.e. a packet.

4.2.1   Base Building Blocks

As listed in Table 1, the base building blocks provide the foundation to the building block concept, and have architectural significance in serving the needs of the programmer through inheritance of these base classes. Thus, as new resource or service-specific abstractions are created, they may leverage the inherited characteristics offered by the base classes. Building of new service-specific behaviors, resources or resource functions can be accomplished through the inheritance of base classes, and the concatenation or chaining of one or more service-specific or resource building blocks and their corresponding methods. The programming and deployment models are considered out of scope of this document, but can range from rule-based approaches (e.g., policy-based management), active networks language-based techniques to quasi-static techniques (e.g. CORBA).

4.2.2   Resource Building Blocks

The resource building blocks represent the functional entities of the network element that either perform action (e.g., mark packet) or function; exist as generic resources (e.g, buffer or queue) or guide decisions (e.g., route table) based on some criteria. The granularity of abstraction is a key question with regard to standardization; as exposed control or manipulation of critical network element resources may compromise the vendor's proprietary features that allow the vendor to differentiate itself in terms of scalability, performance or service availability.

Table 2. Example resource abstractions

Abstraction	Methods	Description	Derived from
TrafficClass	SetTrafficClass() GetTrafficClass() GetTrafficClassID()	It contains the traffic classes defined for the programmable element. Traffic classed are defined by QoS and traffic description.	Component
Filter	SetType() GetType()	Implements a packet filter. More complex filters are derived based on the type of filter. Examples are the BA filter and the MF filter.	Action
Classifier	SetFilter() GetFilterInfo()	Classifiers map traffic based on a set of filters to different streams in a 1:N relationship. More complex classifiers can be defined as well.	Action
Meter	SetType() AddProfileEntry() ChangeProfileEntry() DeleteProfileEntry() SetNonConforming() GetMeterStatus ()	Measures the level of conformance of the traffic to specified profiles.	Action
Scheduler	GetAlgorithm() SetAlgorithm()	Implements the scheduling function and can be defined upon a queuing discipline.	Action
Queue	SetPriority() GetPriority() SetMaxProfile () GetMaxProfile()	Stores the packets at some stage on the programmable element. It can receive different parameters such as priority, guaranteed rate etc.	Component
Profile	Set(AvgRate, Delta, Gain, BurstSize) Get(AvgRate, Delta, Gain, BurstSize)	The profile is defined in terms of rate, burstiness, the amount of traffic (in bytes) in a small fixed sampling interval (delta) etc.	Component

Thus, a degree of granularity and the proper selection of resources, which necessitate ubiquitous operation are key to the question of API standardization. Table 2 below provides some typical examples of resource building blocks within a router or network element, along with their associated base abstractions from which they inherit fundamental building block characteristics.

4.2.3   Service-Specific Building Blocks

The level of abstraction achieved at this layer serves the needs of the ISP, ISV or application developer by facilitating service provisioning, service control and management from a pre-defined service perspective. For example, under DiffServ, a DSProvision class can be created as a DiffServ service-specific building block. It may be formed on underlying resource building blocks (e.g., traffic class, profile, meter, queue, scheduler) or it may inherit the component and condition building blocks and their characteristics to form a simple output port (e.g. on DSCP=xx, *set(target(local))*). Therefore it is possible to build services over existing resources building blocks or directly from the base abstractions.   The flexibility provides the programmer more or less control of the resources that it depends on to accomplish the task.

Table 3. *Example* - Diffserv service-specific abstractions

Abstraction	Methods	Description	Derived from
DSTrafficClass	setType() getType() setDSTrafficClass() getDSTrafficClass()	Implements a Differentiated Service traffic class based on traffic description and QoS description.	TrafficClass
DSProfile	SetDSProfile() modifyDSProfile() deleteDSProfile()	Contains specification of a Differentiated Service profile.	Profile
DSMonitor	getStats()	Collects measurement information on the DiffServRouter	Monitor
DSProvision	getQoS() setQoS()	Receives information about desired QoS, e.g., average delay, packet loss rate etc.	Provision

5   Open Network Services

5.1   Network Generic Service Level Interfaces

Programmable networks enable the composition of distributed network algorithms over network element interfaces. Programmable networks should also enable the deployment of higher-level middleware platforms without exposing the complexity of the distributed algorithms characterizing their architectures. Moreover, developers should be provided with simple, open interfaces for programming and controlling network services. In response to these requirements, the P1520 reference model specifies the U interface as a Network Generic Service Level interface for modeling the functionality of the network. Communication algorithms can control open programmable routers/switches by invoking methods supported at the L interfaces, while exposing U interfaces to higher-level entities. The U interface captures the functionality of resource allocation, admission control, routing, and network management algorithms, providing standard means for using any network architecture. As illustrated in Figure 4 below, U interfaces are grouped into three categories:

- *Transport interfaces* are used for controlling the transport protocol stacks, which are operational within a network domain. Examples of transport interfaces include monitoring and protocol stack management interfaces. Monitoring interfaces are used for obtaining feedback about the quality of established sessions within a network domain (e.g., a video conferencing session). Protocol stack management interfaces can be used for dynamically composing or modifying transport protocol stacks on behalf of middleware users.

- *Network control interfaces* are used for managing communication resources among competing parties in the system, as well as for accessing or modifying routing information. Network control interfaces support higher level communication services with Quality of Service guarantees. Resources can be allocated to support point-to-point, point-to-multipoint sessions, or they can be used for dynamically creating virtual private networks.
- *Network management interfaces* support open management functions such as policy-based management, network monitoring, event management or capacity planning.

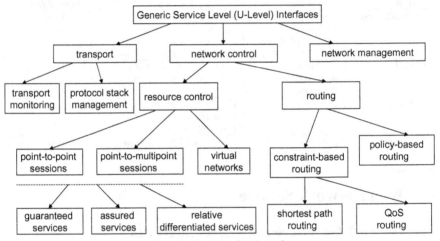

Fig. 4. Family of U interface

5.2   Designing Service-Level QoS Interfaces

U-level interfaces represent the macroscopic counterparts of functions supported by network elements through their L interfaces. The main difference between the L and the U interfaces is that L interfaces have local significance only (i.e., abstract the operations of a single network node), whereas the U interfaces abstract distributed services operating across one or multiple network domains. We believe that there is a need to understand the level of abstractions and scope characterizing the U interfaces to develop more flexible, efficient and customizable service platforms in the next generation Internet. Among the family of the U interfaces, discussed above, resource control interfaces are the least understood. While different network architectures support alternative mechanisms for providing QoS to their users, it is difficult to specify a generic QoS API which can characterize the underlying QoS architecture and semantics of every network domain.

5.2.1   Service-Independent Interfaces

The design of the service-independent abstraction layer is motivated by the commonalities, which exist between traffic classes of different network architectures. Most network architectures support some type of service with very low or bounded queuing delay. Examples of such service include the guaranteed service in Integrated Service networks and the leased line emulation service in Differentiated Service networks. In addition these architectures support the notion of a service that is better than best effort, but does not provide explicit delay guarantees. Controlled load and assured forwarding-based services belong to this category. A third group of services comprises relative differentiated services.

Table 4. Service-level QoS interfaces

Abstraction	Methods	Description
GenericResourceController	ReqGuaranteedService() RemQuaranteedService() ReqAssuredService() RemAssuredService() ReqRelativeService() RemRelativeService()	A generic QoS abstraction that allows the establishment or removal of multimedia sessions between a pair or group of end-systems with some QoS assurances.
IntServResourceController	ReqGuaranteedService() RemGuaranteedService() ReqControlledLoad() RemControlledLoad()	A QoS abstraction layer specific to the Integrated Service (IntServ) resource model. This layer allows the establishment or removal of multimedia sessions, which are characterized by the guaranteed service and controlled load classes of the IntServ model.
DiffServResourceController	ReqLeasedLineService() RemLeasedLineService() ReqAssuredService() RemAssuredService() ReqOlympicService() RemOlympicService()	A QoS abtraction layer specific to the Differentiated Service (DiffServ) resource model. The DiffSDerv architecture aims in the standardization of per hop behaviors, not end-to-end traffic classes.

The service-independent layer supports the division of services among guaranteed, assured, and relative differentiated services. This distinction is qualitative, not quantitative. The quantitative characteristics of different traffic classes are concealed at this level. Table 4 lists the `GenericResourceController` interface with corresponding methods that support the generic QoS specifications. Methods supported at this service-independent layer accept two generic abstraction parameters - namely `rate` and `application_type`. These parameters are passed into adapter objects, which convert the service-independent interfaces to appropriate QoS 'service-specific' interfaces. As described earlier, adapters capture QoS provisioning intelligence including user preferences and service provider policies.

5.2.2   Service-Dependent Interfaces

As shown in Table 4, the `IntServResourceController` interface abstracts the QoS provisioning characteristics of Integrated Service networks. Integrated Service networks support two traffic classes with QoS assurances: guaranteed service and controlled load service. The guaranteed service ensures that datagrams associated with an Internet session arrive within some specified delay bound. To support guaranteed service, routers need to schedule link capacity among competing flows. In addition, resource reservations need to be setup along the path which datagrams follow. A controlled load service tightly approximates the behavior visible to applications receiving best-effort service under unloaded conditions. Network elements support controlled load service by allocating service rate and buffer space, which are larger than the token bucket rate and size characterizing the multimedia source. The difference between the guaranteed and controlled load services is that in the controlled load case no explicit rate allocations are requested. The rate allocated to multimedia flows depends on the implementation of network elements and it is not always high enough to guarantee that queuing delays are below a deterministic bound.

Integrated Services networks have been associated with scalability problems, due to the requirement for maintaining per-flow state in network elements. To overcome this deficiency the IETF is currently pursuing stateless resource management using a differentiated service model. In differentiated services networks user flows are compared against negotiated traffic profiles before entering a network domain. Packets are marked with code-points corresponding to specific forwarding functions. A small group of standardized forwarding functions, called Per-Hop Behaviors (PHBs), are used for realizing higher level services that do not require per-flow state management.

As described in Table 4, the `DiffServResourceController` interface abstracts the QoS provisioning characteristics of Differentiated Service networks. Three distinct types of differentiated service are supported. *Leased line emulation* service ensures the delivery of customer traffic with very low latency and very low drop probability. Leased line emulation service uses an 'expedited forwarding' per hop behavior. *Expedited forwarding* per hop behavior has the highest priority. *Assured service* is used for carrying data traffic at higher priority than competing best effort traffic. Supporting the corresponding methods in Table 4, the sustained traffic rate characterizing a leased line emulation service and the offered rate which characterizes an assured service are specified in a `LeasedLineSpec` and `AssuredServiceSpec` data structures (not shown), respectively.

Both the leased line emulation service and the assured service support absolute traffic profiles. A fundamentally different approach in the differentiated service framework is the relative differentiated services. In this approach the quality spacing between different traffic classes is not defined deterministically. Relative service differentiation does not require admission control for the establishment of service level agreements. Relative differentiation can be based on strict prioritization, price differentiation, or capacity differentiation. To accommodate this, we specify corresponding methods in the interface for an 'olympic' service, a generic relative differentiated service. In this case, user traffic and differentiation (e.g., cost or otherwise) is handled according to a `traffic_class` parameter.

6   Related Work

New developments in the area of open networks or network programmability have emerged with a sense of realization. This has been motivated by research progress[2] founded mostly from the DARPA formed Active Networks community and OPENSIG initiatives. Several projects [16], [17][3], [9], [18], [19] have demonstrated unique contributions towards the development of programmable network control and QoS. Alternatively, very little activity from the IETF has focused on standardizing APIs. However, we are encouraged by the following recent developments:

- The formation of the Multiservice Switching Forum [20] is committed to an open, standardized control interface that will support multiple control planes.
- The Parlay [21] consortium, paralleling similar ideas of an open service platform, provides an extensible API specification that includes a framework and service interface for customer care (e.g., registration, security, billing, management, etc) and value-added services (e.g., call control, messaging), respectively.
- Complementary to Parlay, the Java Advanced Intelligent Networks [22} effort, focusing on the convergence of the telephony and data networks, provides a middleware framework to enable service creation and service execution. This is achieved by way of a specification of component abstractions for call control, coordination and transaction models that are independent of implementation specific call models, protocols and underlying infrastructure.

In general, there has been very little published material from these initiatives that address open programmability for Internet QoS -- addressing flexible QoS service creation, provisioning and SLA delivery across heterogeneous network domains and infrastructure equipment. Alternatively, consider the several recent IETF initiatives that have similar motivations to the above and been proposed towards interoperability and/or the development of management-based QoS:

- The IETF has established a GSMP [23] Working Group that is focused on developing a general switch management and control protocol for switching devices.
- In [24], the authors propose a SNMP MIB-based interface standard for Differentiated Services QoS. Similar to our work on the L interface, the work here is heavily influenced by [25] and takes a rigorous approach to modeling lower level resources of the router to support slow timescale control, provisioning, monitoring and event management.
- Similarly, the authors in [26] provide a management interface model (i.e., to [23]) to support the provisioning of QoS, using policy and policy-based semantics through COPS (Common Open Policy Services) [27]. The QoS Policy Information Base (PIB) also abstracts network devices providing the means to set policies for resource definition and configuration, provisioning, and discovery of underlying QoS resource abstractions.

---

[2] See [29] for a more complete survey of the activities here.

[3] Both xbind and Tempest initiatives have spun off new companies -- xbind Inc. and Cplane, respectively.

- A contribution by Hitachi, LTD [28] leverages the SNMP protocol to create a programming interface MIB for routers. Here, the work is close to ours as QoS programmability is introduced through the concept of a "virtual flow labels" (VFL) to form modular policy rules, and extending static conditional semantics such as those used in [24].

While the industry and research communities have very different agenda and timelines, we view our contribution addressing a middle ground and practical step towards the evolution of the Internet agenda for open networks and flexible, unified QoS control and delivery

7   Conclusion

In this paper we have presented a programmable QoS API framework based on the IEEE P1520 Reference Model. We have discussed the QoS API framework in the context of network service and network element quality of service deployment, and suggested its integration with a open service platform which provides the necessary infrastructure to support QoS inter-workings over the complex and evolving Internet. We have discussed the design of APIs for upper level network QoS, which is based on a service-dependent and service independent model; supporting alternative styles of QoS specifications and provisioning. Similarly, we presented an abstraction for designing underlying network elements based on the notion of building blocks and the separation of service-specific and resource context for network element programmability.

References

[1] Y. Bernet, S. Blake, J. Binder, M. Carlson, S. Keshav, E. Davies, B. Ohlman, D. Verma, Z. Wang, W. Weiss, "A Framework for Differentiated Services," Internet-Draft draft-ietf-diffserv-framework-01.txt, work in progress, Feb. 1999.

[2] R. Braden, L. Zhang, S. Berson, S. Herzog, and S. Jamin, "Resource ReSerVation Protocol (RSVP)," Version 1 Functional Specification, RFC 2205, Sept. 1997.

[3] R. Braden, D. Clark, S. Shenker, "Integrated Services in the Internet Architecture: an Overview," RFC 1633, June 1994.

[4] Xiao Z, Ni L.M., "Internet QoS: Big Picture," Dept of CS, Michigan State University.

[5] Andrikopoulos I., Pavlou G., "Supporting Differentiated Services in MPLS Networks," Proc. 7th International Workshop on Quality of Service (IWQOS'99), London, May 1999.

[6] Session on "Enabling Virtual Networking", Organizer and Chair: Andrew T. Campbell, OPENSIG '98Workshop on Open Signaling for ATM, Internet and Mobile Networks, Toronto, October 5-6 1998.

[7] Adam, C. .M., et al., "The Binding Interface Base Specification Revision 2.0", OPENSIG Workshop, Cambridge, UK, April 1997.

[8] Angin,O., Campbell,A.T., Kounavis,M.E. and Liao,R.R.-F., "The Mobiware Toolkit: Programmable Support for Adaptive Mobile Networking", IEEE Personal Communications Magazine, Special Issue on Adaptive Mobile Systems, August 1998.

[9] Chandra, P. et al., "Darwin: Customizable Resource Management for Value-added Network Services", Sixth IEEE International Conference on Network Protocols (ICNP'98), Austin, October 1998.

[10] Biswas, J., et al., "Application Programming Interfaces for Networks", IEEE P1520 Working Group Draft White Paper, http://www.ieee-pin.org/

[11] OPENSIG Working Group http://comet.columbia.edu/opensig/

[12] DARPA Active Network Program, http://www.darpa.mil/ito/research/anets /projects.html,

[13] Vanecek, G., Mihai, N., Vidovic, N., and Vrsalovic, D., Enabling Hybrid Services in Emerging Data Networks, IEEE Communications Magazine, July 1999.

[14] Lerner, M., Vanecek, G., Vidovic, N., and Vrsalovic, D., Middleware Networks: Concept, Design and Deployment of Internet Infrastructure; Kluwer Academic Press, April 2000 (ISBN 07923-78490-7)

[15] Denazis, S., Vicente J., Miki K., Campbell A., "Designing Interfaces for Open Programmable Routers", July. 1999.

[16] Lazar, A.A., Lim, K.S. and Marconcini, F., ``Realizing a Foundation for Programmability of ATM Networks with the Binding Architecture," IEEE Journal on Selected Areas in Communications, Special Issue on Distributed Multimedia Systems, No. 7, September 1996.

[17] Van der Merwe,J.E. and Leslie,I.M., "Switchlets and Dynamic Virtual ATM Networks", Proc Integrated Network Management V, May 1997.

[18] Raguparan, M., Biswas, J., Weiguo, W., L + Interface for routers that support Differentiated Services, May 1999.

[19] Vicente, J., Biswas, J., Kounavis, M., Villela, D., Lerner, M., Yoshizawa, S., Denazis S., A Proposal for IP L Interface Architecture, January 2000.

[20] Multiservice Switching Forum (MSF), http://www.msforum.org/

[21] The Parlay Group, http://www.parlay.org/

[22]Java Advanced Intelligent Network (JAIN)
http://java.sun.com/aboutJava/communityprocess/jsr/jsr_018_oam.html

[23] General Switch Management Protocol from Peter Newman (Netsim Inc www.ensim.com/) find the specification at http://www.iprg.nokia.com/protocols/rfc1987.htm

[24] Baker, F. et al, "Management Information Base for the Differentiated Services Architecture" Internet Draft, draft-ietf-diffserv-mib-01.txt. Oct. 1999.

[25] Bernet, Y., Smith, A., Blake, S., A Conceptual Model for Diffserv Routers, October 1999, INTERNET DRAFT.

[26] Fine M., McCloghrie K., Hahn S., Chan K., Smith A., "An Initial Quality of Service Policy Information Base", draft-mfine-cops-pib-01.txt, Internet Draft, June 1999.

[27] Boyle J., Cohen R., Durham D., Herzog S., Rajan R., Sastry A., "The COPS (Common Open Policy Service) Protocol," Internet Draft draft- ietf-rap-cops-07.txt. Aug. 1999.

[28] Kanada Y. et al, "SNMP-based QoS Programming Interface MIB for Routers" Internet Draft, draft-kanada-diffserv-qospifmib-00.txt., Oct. 1999.

[29] Campbell, A.T., De Meer, H., Kounavis, M.E., Miki, K., and Vicente, J., "A Review of Programmable Networks", ACM Computer Communications Review, April 1999.

Monitoring Quality of Service across Organizational Boundaries

Rainer Hauck and Helmut Reiser

Munich Network Management Team,
University of Munich, Dept. of CS, Oettingenstr. 67, D-80538 Munich, Germany
{hauck|reiser}@informatik.uni-muenchen.de

Abstract *In a customer/provider relationship a provider offers services to a customer who pays for using them. To control service delivery certain Quality of Service (QoS) parameters have to be agreed through so called Service Level Agreements (SLAs). Monitoring of some of these QoS parameters only makes sense when done from a customer perspective. Therefore, the data collection has to take place at the customer site, which means at least one organizational boundary has to be crossed. In a cooperation project we developed a flexible and extensible agent for that purpose using the Java Dynamic Management Kit (JDMK) and the Application Response Measurement API (ARM). Based on our experiences with the prototype implementation this paper analyses the suitability of JDMK and ARM for the monitoring of QoS parameters and SLAs and for building scalable and flexible management systems in large–scale enterprise networks.*

Keywords:
Quality of Service, Intra-/Extranet, Application Response Measurement, Service Level Agreement, Application Management, JDMK, JMX

1 Introduction

In a typical customer/provider scenario a customer demands - and pays for - a certain Quality of Service (QoS) laid down in so-called Service Level Agreements (SLAs). In recent years growing demand from customers to monitor the performance of their network services can be realized. Poor performance is no longer tolerated. Instead customers now can receive discounts or even have the right to cancel the contract and choose a different provider. But network parameters like numbers of IP packets dropped or the available bandwidth at a certain point in time are not very meaningful to the vast majority of customers. So it seems preferable not to monitor network performance but service performance instead. In order to observe the quality of delivered services it is necessary to negotiate Quality of Service (QoS) parameters as well as means for the measurement and evaluation of these parameters. The monitoring of the QoS parameters has to be done by an agent running at the customer site, because this is the only way to monitor actual service usage of the customer. The fact that an agent belonging to a provider must be running at the site of a customer implies strong security requirements. Due to numerous changes to SLAs in course of time, the agent has to be flexible and extensible in order to allow easy updating.

C. Linnhoff-Popien and H.-G. Hegering (Eds.): USM 2000, LNCS 1890, pp. 124–137, 2000.
© Springer-Verlag Berlin Heidelberg 2000

The paper shows how concepts and services of the Java Dynamic Management Kit (JDMK) can be used for building such an architecture. It also points out weaknesses and deficiencies JDMK still has to deal with. As an example of how monitoring of QoS parameters can be done, a web browser was instrumented using the Application Response Measurement (ARM) API to deliver information about the actual response times a customer is experiencing.

The paper is structured as follows: Section 2 gives an overview about the scenario the paper deals with and shows the requirements a management solution for this scenario has to fulfill. In section 3 JDMK and the ARM API which are both used in building our solution are introduced. Section 4 describes how we applied JDMK and ARM to the problem domain. An example how actual QoS parameters can be obtained is shown. Section 5 summarizes our experiences and evaluates how JDMK and ARM are suitable for monitoring QoS parameters in large enterprise environments. The *Java Management Extensions (JMX)* specification is intended as a replacement for the *Java Management API (JMAPI)* and relies to a large extent on JDMK. We will therefore contrast JMX with JDMK in section 6 and discuss to what degree JMX alleviates the shortcomings of JDMK. Section 7 concludes the paper.

2   Scenario: Outsourcing of Extranets

An exemplary scenario – which this paper is based on – is a car manufacturer (customer) which enables all its dealers (more than 1000) to use special applications within its corporate network (CN) (e.g., Online Ordering of cars). The dealers build a so called extranet (EN). Besides the specific applications the EN enables connections to the worldwide Internet. The provider implements the EN infrastructure with all the demanded services on the customers behalf. It is also responsible for the management of the extranet with all services it offers. It has to be remarked that the provider is not responsible for applications offered by the customer.

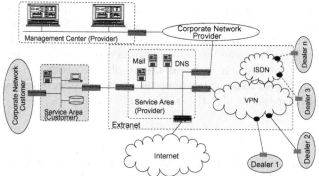

The corresponding infrastructure is presented in figure 1. Dealers are connected with a Point of Presence (PoP) of the provider over leased lines or ISDN dial-up lines. They form a virtual private network (VPN) on top of the infrastructure of the provider, which is also used by

Figure 1. Extranet Solution for a Car Manufacturer

other customers. In the Service Area (SA) of the provider reside servers for the services rendered by the provider (e.g. Mail, DNS, Authentication Service, ...) and a well defined access point to the Internet. If a dealer wants to use a service of the manufacturer it will be routed into the SA of the car manufacturer. In this configuration dealers use services both in the SA of the provider and in the SA of the customer.

2.1 Management Requirements for Monitoring Quality of Service

In order to observe the quality of delivered services it is necessary to negotiate QoS parameters between customer and provider. As mentioned before, it is important that these parameters are meaningful to the customer and reflect its expectations. They are part of Service Level Agreements which essentially are a contractual relationship between a customer and a provider. SLAs are used – among other things – for billing purposes. If a service is not delivered with the quality that was agreed in the SLA the customer may get a discount. Therefore the SLA (and therefore the QoS parameters) have to be supervised by the management system of the provider. Further the provider is obliged by the SLA to report compliance with agreed QoS parameters. Examples for such QoS parameters are the response time, the connectivity or the availability not of a network connection but of a certain service from a customer's point of view. Thus these parameters have to be measured and valued in the customer environment. Most of the QoS parameters (e.g. the connectivity or the availability) of a service are only defined if the customer actually tries to use this certain service. For the monitoring of such parameters it is necessary for the management system of the provider to be able to measure from the side of the customer. In our scenario that means an agent which performs the monitoring of QoS parameters must be installed at a dealer's host. Thus the agent has to cross the organizational boundary between the customer and the provider. The customer will allow the provider to do so only if high security requirements are met. Additionally a customer will only accept such a solution if no additional or only minimal costs are caused. This especially causes problems for customers which are connected via dial-up lines, because the initiation of a connection solely for management purposes cannot be tolerated in this case. Furthermore it means the agent has to do its measures locally as far as possible and transfered results should be as small as possible. As requirements for services, QoS parameters and SLAs could change in course of time the architecture has to be flexible and must be able to react on such changes quickly. In large–scale corporate networks as described in the scenario, well–scaling management systems are absolutely necessary. In addition, a lot of different hardware and software at the customer side, requires a high degree of platform independence for the corresponding agent.

2.2 Related Work

Distributed network, systems and application management is an active field of research motivated – among others – by the experiences with deploying centralized management systems in large-scale corporate networks. To overcome deficiencies of centralized management systems a lot of research has been done.

Management by Delegation (MbD) [5,15,14] defines a concept for delegating functionality from managing systems to agents in order to enhance them at runtime. The decision when this delegation should happen and which kind of functionality should be transferred to the agents is taken by the managing system, thus preventing autonomous decisions by the agents. **Flexible agents** [11] rely on MbD and exhibit a certain degree of autonomy; they are able to receive event notifications from peers and can be grouped together in order to jointly achieve a task. In recent years **mobile agents** [12,13] which add the concept of mobility to flexible agents or MbD have been investigated. Their roaming capabilities allow them to move across networks in order to achieve specific, predefined tasks. However, the applicability of mobile agents is bound by security concerns; [6] and [23] discuss these aspects. **Mobile management agents** are designed to achieve administrative tasks on systems and software; while [1] discusses the advantages of applying mobile agents to management, [4] presents a Java-based environment for configurable and downloadable lightweight management applications.

The following approaches for the monitoring of application response times are commonly used today: First **network monitors** like the *Tivoli Netview Performance Monitor*[1] can be used to monitor traffic on the network. However the packets must be correlated to actual user transactions in order to calculate response times, which is quite a complex task [16]. Moreover, it is very unlikely that a customer will allow a provider to place a network monitor in his corporate network. A different approach is by using **active probes** like done by *Geyer & Weinig's GW-TEL INFRA-XS*[2]. Here an agent at the remote site actively initiates transactions and measures the response time. The problem with this solution is that it does not monitor the actual transactions of the user but some test transactions and that it increases network and server load.

3   Framework and Development Tools

The Java Dynamic Management Kit (JDMK)[3], developed by Sun Microsystems [18,19], promises to overcome many of the problems mentioned and supports some new requirements. Application Response Measurement API (ARM) is a valuable standard for the application perfomance instrumentation. In the next sections, we will introduce the architecture and services of JDMK and the concepts and use of ARM.

3.1   Architecture and Services of JDMK

JDMK represents a framework with corresponding tools, based on the JavaBeans specification [17], for the development of management applications and management agents. The base components of the architecture are shown in figure 2.

M–Beans (Managed Beans) are Java objects implementing the intelligence and the functionality of an agent.

---

[1] http://www.tivoli.com/products/index/netview_perfmon/

[2] http://www.gwtel.de/

[3] http://www.sun.com/software/java-dynamic/

They act as a representative for one or more managed objects (MOs). In order to use JDMK services or communication resources M–Beans have to be registered at the so called Core Management Framework (CMF) . Only registered Beans can be accessed from outside the CMF. The CMF together with its M–Beans represents the management agent.   C–Beans (Client Beans)   can be generated from M–Beans using a special compiler. C–Beans are proxy objects

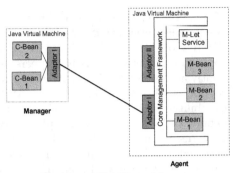

Figure 2. JDMK Architecture

for remote M–Beans. Together with their adaptors and additional management functionality they form the manager. An agent is also able to register C–Beans with its CMF. By doing this, the agent becomes a manager for that agent which implements the corresponding M–Beans. The strict separation between the manager and the agent role in protocol-based management architectures is therefore abolished in JDMK. An Adaptor implements a special kind of a protocol, it is an interface for the CMF and hence for the agent. At present RMI, HTTP, HTTPS (HTTP over SSL), IIOP, SNMP and a so called HTML adaptor, which represents a web server, are available. This concept allows to communicate with the same JDMK agent by means of different protocols. It is not necessary to change the functionality or the code of the agent, the only thing to do is to register a different adaptor. Of course it is possible to use more than one adaptor at the same time.

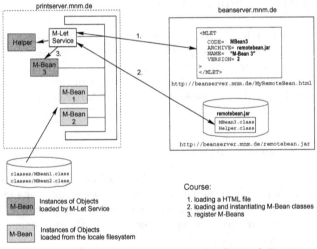

Figure 3. JDMK Management Applet (M-Let) Service

Besides the base components of JDMK several services and tools exist to simplify the development of management applications and agents. Services relevant for the project are briefly explained in the following paragraphs.

Beans may be registered with the aid of Repository Service either as volatile or persistent within the CMF. The Discovery Service is used to detect all active CMFs. To determine the properties and methods which are supported by an M–Bean the Metadata Service, can be used. The Class and Library Server serves as a local or remote repository for class files and libraries. M-Let, Launcher and Bootstrap Service are used for dynamic extension of agents, for update mechanisms and for bootstrapping. The M–Let Service (Management Applet Service) offers the possibility to download and configure M–Beans dynamically (cf. figure 3). For this purpose a new HTML tag (`<MLET>`) is defined. First M–Let Service loads a HTML page from an URL from which it can obtain all the necessary information about the Beans to load. Then M–Let Service is able to download the implementation classes of the M–Beans and to instantiate them. Afterwards, the M–Let Service must register them with the CMF. It is also possible to put version information inside an (`<MLET>`) tag and thus use the M–Let Service for versioning. The Bootstrap Service simplifies the distribution and instantiation of JDMK agents. This service is used to download implementation classes. Therefore the Bootstrap Service initializes the CMF, starts the M–Let Service, loads the necessary classes, initializes, registers and starts all required M–Beans and services of the agent.

Besides `mogen` compiler which is used to create C–Beans there is `mibgen` compiler for developing a JDMK based SNMP agent for a device. If SNMP–MIB files are available for a managed device, `mibgen` is able to use them to create M–Beans representing the MIB. The M–Beans have to be enlarged with functions e.g., implementing access to resources of the managed system.

3.2   The Application Response Measurement API (ARM)

The Application Response Measurement API (ARM) [2] has been developed in 1996 in a joint initiative of Tivoli Systems and Hewlett-Packard. Later that year HP, Tivoli and 13 more companies established the ARM Working Group of the Computer Measurement Group (CMG)[4] to continue development and promotion of the API. It promises to allow transaction based monitoring of response times in a distributed and heterogeneous environment. Work on version 2.0 of the API was finished in November 1997. In January 1999 the ARM API version 2.0 was adopted by the Open Group as its technical standard for application performance instrumentation.

To achieve the goals mentioned above a simple API was defined that is supposed to be implemented by management tools. The applications to be monitored have to be instrumented to call the API whenever a transaction starts or stops. Actual performance monitoring is done

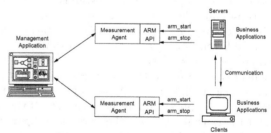

Figure 4. Using the ARM API

by using management tools that provide measurement agents implementing the API. These are linked against the application to be monitored and thus are called whenever a transaction is initiated or ended. (see figure 4). An important feature added with version 2.0 of the API is correlation of transactions. Often one transaction visible to the user consists of a number of subtransactions. When indicating the start of a new transaction, a data structure called a correlator can

---

[4] http://www.cmg.org/regions/cmgarmw/index.html

be requested from the measurement agent. When indicating the start of a sub-transaction, this correlator can be used to inform the measurement agent about the existence and identity of a parent transaction.

4   Monitoring of QoS Using JDMK and ARM

In an industrial cooperation project with DeTeSystem [8] a prototypical manage-ment solution was developed that fulfills the requirements mentioned in chapter 2.1. In this project JDMK (version 3.0 beta 2) and ARM (version 2.0) were used for the monitoring of QoS parameters.

4.1   Architecture

As seen before there is a strong requirement for Service Level Monitoring to be considered from a customer's perspective. QoS parameters of SLAs are only reasonable if the user actually tries to use a service. If it does not try to use a special service there cannot be a violation of an SLA caused by the provider. Through the use of Flexible Management Agents (FMA) positioned in the cor-porate network of the customer, our solution enables the measurement of the actual Service Levels provided to the customer.

In order to avoid additional costs for a customer connected by a dial-up link the following solution was examined: The agent transmits the collected informa-tion to the manager only when the link is up and free. In addition packets from the agent do not affect the idle timer responsible for the disconnection of the link if it was unused for a predefined period of time. That would mean that only the (otherwise useless) timeout intervals are used for management traffic. However, the needed functionality is not available in ISDN routers commonly used today, as there is no way to distinguish between packets that should affect the idle timer and packets that should not. As a trade-off the following solution was chosen: Management traffic is created only when the link is up. Although being sub-optimal this approach avoids establishing a connection solely for management purposes and thus reduces the additional cost to a minimum. To check whether the link is up or down, some kind of status information needs to be available. Two different solutions have been examined. Many routers send SNMP traps whenever a link is established or goes down. The router can be configured to deliver these traps to the agent. So the agent gets informed immediately about any change in link status. As not all routers send traps concerning the link status the second approach might be necessary: If the agent has management informa-tion to transmit, it polls the variable `ifOperStatus` (operational state of the interface) from MIB-II [10] on a regularly basis. Both variants mean that from the perspective of the router, the agent acts in the role of a SNMP manager. As a relatively high polling interval can be chosen (about half of the idle timeout value for the link) the additional load induced by polling is minimal.

Every time the SLAs change or new means of measurement are needed, new functionality must be installed in the corporate network of the customer. As the customer network is typically located far from the management center of the provider a solution is necessary that allows dynamic download of new function-ality. This requirement is one of the main reasons why the presented solution is based on JDMK. The CMF has to be installed only once at the customer site and from then on all the functionality needed can easily be downloaded as an M-Bean using e.g., the M-Let Service. To prevent data from being accidentally destroyed, the agent can regularly be serialized to local disk. When the system comes up – for example recovering from a system crash – the JDMK Bootstrap Service tries to load the local copy of the agent before it contacts the central repository. Of course this does not prevent a customer from explicitly deleting the information collected by the agent before it is transmitted to the manager. Another benefit of using the JDMK was its ability to use different adaptors. The provider uses a management platform and also wants to use web browsers to configure the agents. By using JDMK's SNMP and HTML adaptors this could be achieved easily. A manager application was built to receive the performance data sent by the agents using the RMI adaptor. In the current version it writes the data to a database where management tools can access it.

4.2   Quality of Service Measurement

There are many different ways Service Level Agreements might be defined. Typical representatives are the availability of IP connectivity and the time needed by a server to fulfill a user request. In the given scenario there is the need to measure the response times of web servers in the service areas of both the provider and the customer. The transactions of interest are the download of web pages by the dealers. In order to learn about the actual re-

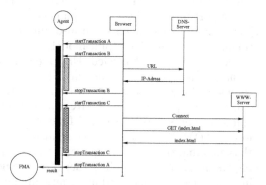

Figure 5. ARM instrumentation of a web browser

sponse times the user experiences, a web client (Lynx) was instrumented with calls to the ARM API. Figure 5 shows the transactions to be monitored.

Most important is transaction A which spans the whole process of loading the page. To allow the manager the localization of failures or bottlenecks two subtransactions are defined. Subtransaction B covers the part of contacting the DNS for hostname resolution and subtransaction C covers the actual download of the page. The measurement agent forwards the results to the FMA which can do some preprocessing on the data and transmits it to the manager whenever the link is up. If the FMA receives information about timed-out connections or if the reported response times exceed given thresholds, it can take some further action to identify the problem. In our example it does a ping to the local router, to the PoP and to the server that the user tried to contact. The results can be used to determine if the problem is located in the dealer's LAN or in the service area of the customer. Both would mean that the provider cannot be held responsible for the malfunction. Through an ARM instrumentation of the servers and a correlation of server transactions with client transactions even more accurate information can be collected. Lynx was chosen as an example because it is a simple browser and the source code is available, so an instrumentation could be done in the course of the project. Of course, typical dealers will not be using Lynx but as ARM is gaining more and more momentum many browsers might come instrumented in the near future.

5   Evaluation of JDMK and ARM

This section evaluates JDMK and ARM with respect to their applicability to large enterprise management environments. We will thereby focus on the major problem domains which are of critical importance for a successful deployment and address the requirements identified in section 2.1.

5.1   Rapid Prototyping of Flexible, Dynamic Management Systems

As outlined in the previous sections, the primary strength of JDMK is its capability of realizing flexible and highly distributed management systems. Agents developed with JDMK can be enhanced and modified at runtime, thus yielding the opportunity of delegating management tasks to them via the push model. Furthermore, these agents can also initiate the download of management functionality by themselves (pull model). These additional services are only transferred to the agent if needed. Under regular conditions, particular tasks of the management system may be carried out by the agent, thus preventing the exchange of large amounts of data between the managing system and the agent. The services provided by JDMK enable distribution and update mechanisms to enhance agents with additional functionality residing in centralized code repositories. JDMK also provides mechanisms for the persistent storage of M-Beans, thus enabling the agent components to remain close to the resource and eliminating the need of downloading them from remote servers. Simple web-based user interfaces can be generated automatically by using the HTML-Adaptor. JDMK-administered resources can be easily accessed from systems in other management architectures because several adaptors for different management protocols are provided. It is thus possible to administer JDMK-based agents from SNMP management platforms through the SNMP adaptor. The toolkit also enables the development of adaptors for new protocols not yet supported. The adaptor concept is helpful if agents should support multiple management protocols simultaneously e.g., information provided by a specific agent should be accessible not only from an SNMP-based management platform but also from a web browser via HTTP.

In summary, we believe that JDMK has a strong potential for the rapid development of highly distributed management environments and providing several protocol adaptors is a good basis for today's heterogeneous management environments.

5.2   Scalability

JDMK does neither provide standardized directory nor naming services. Features for achieving location transparency (like the CORBA Interoperable Object

References) are also not available: An M–Bean is identified by a protocol identificator, the host address and port number, and its object name. These parameters and some knowledge about the registered beans in a given CMF must be present in order to make use of the M–Beans. The scope of the Metadata Service that can be used to retrieve information on registered M–Beans is limited to *a single* CMF, i.e., there is no global Metadata Service. Consequently, the only way of finding the currently active CMFs is the JDMK Discovery Service which sends a broadcast message that is answered by all running agents. The establishment of domains and the structuring of the agents in functional groups is not supported by the development environment and has to be done by the developer.

The conceptual weaknesses mentioned above impede the development of management applications for large IT infrastructures where a high number of different JDMK-based agents is needed. The JDMK services are useful for small, local environments where the amount and the degree of diversity of the agents are restricted. Due to the absence of focus on large systems, the scalability of JDMK-based solutions may be critical at the current stage of the toolkit.

5.3   Security Aspects

JDMK does not have a homogeneous security concept; instead, developers need to be aware of the different security mechanisms to implement comprehensive security for agents that support different protocol adaptors. The SNMP adaptor relies on a file containing access control lists to determine which management systems have the right to read or modify specific parts of the MIB. Although this can be considered as an enhancement compared to the (password-based) mechanism of the early SNMP, modern fine-grained SNMP security mechanisms like VACM [24] are not supported yet. As the authentication of remote systems is based on their IP address, the agent is vulnerable with respect to IP-spoofing attacks. The authentication method of the HTTP/HTML adaptors are login/password combinations. As sensitive data is exchanged unencrypted, it is not possible to implement secure HTTP-based management solutions. The RMI and IIOP adaptors do not support authentication and access control. The only way of enabling secure authentication is based on the HTTPS (HTTP over SSL) adaptor which allows the exchange of cryptographically secure certificates. The appropriate access control system must then be implemented by the developer.

We believe that the current security mechanisms of JDMK are insufficient because developers still have to implement a large part of the security mechanisms themselves. Furthermore, the large differences between the various security mechanisms are not yet shielded behind a comprehensive security architecture.

5.4   ARM

The ARM API offers many benefits to a manager who needs to monitor the response times of applications: The most important factor is its openness. Resulting from a joint initiative of 15 companies, it offers a well defined interface that can be used either by application developers or by management tool vendors. Applications instrumented with the API calls will work seamlessly with management tools from various manufacturers (e.g. *Tivoli Application Performance Management (TAPM)*[5] or *HP MeasureWare/PerfView*[6]). However, it is also general enough to allow sufficient differentiation between management solutions from different vendors. Its adoption as a standard by the Open Group further strengthens its position as the predominant standard for response time measurement. Another important fact is its simplicity and efficiency. There are not more than six calls to be used. Technically it is very easy to instrument an application using these calls and it is also relatively easy to provide a measurement agent that implements the calls. Depending on the amount of processing the measurement agent does, it affects system performance only to a minimal level. A further benefit is the way transactions are defined. Even in a highly distributed environment it is easy to monitor the transactions a user is aware of. Users are not interested in certain parts of the transactions but in the total amount of time from their request to the reception of the response. Through the concept of subtransactions, managers still have the chance to find out which part of the transaction is responsible when performance problems occur.

However, the ARM API still comes with a lot of problems: Obviously, the first to mention is the need for instrumented applications. Today most commercially available applications are not instrumented. As normally no source code is available it is also impossible to instrument these applications on your own. Even if the source code is provided it is a difficult and time consuming task because the business transactions seen by the user must be identified in the code, which requires expert knowledge of the implementation. When using transaction correlation, the correlator received by the measurement agent must be known to the subtransactions. In a distributed environment this requires changes to the applications because the correlators have to be passed explicitly as parameters when calling the server component.

6   Java Management Extensions

In the middle of 1999 the draft version of the new Java Management Extensions (JMX) specification [20] has been released for public review. JMX integrates the former developments within the scope of the Java Management API (JMAPI) and JDMK into a Java-based management framework. The specification does not only focus on the agent part of the management system (as it was the case with JDMK) but will also specify the manager part. However, in the current version of the specification the JMX manager is left blank. As JDMK can be considered an integral part of JMX, we will provide a short overview over the most recent developments and address the question whether the critical issues of JDMK also apply to JMX. However, please note that the JMX specification is not yet in a final state.

JMX architecture is very similar to JDMK as depicted in figure 2. JMX distinguishes between manager, agent and instrumentation levels: Within an agent, M–Beans responsible for making a resource manageable reside at the instrumentation level. A manageable resource in JMX can be an application, a service

---

[5] http://www.tivoli.com/products/index/app_per_mgt/

[6] http://www.openview.hp.com/

implementation or a device. The instrumentation is made accessible to JMX managers (forming the manager level) through the agent level which provides a communications interface, a set of standard services and a run-time environment. The Core Management Framework of JDMK has been renamed to MBean Server. JMX MBeans[7] have been categorized into four distinct classes: standard MBean, dynamic MBeans, open MBean and model MBean. The adaptor concept of JDMK is now divided up into protocol adaptors and connectors. Protocol adaptors are used to link an JMX agent with non-JMX compliant management applications (i.e., SNMP, Common Information Model (CIM) [3] or proprietary). The connector – in contrast – is used by a remote JMX-enabled management application (i.e., developed using JMX manager services) to connect to a JMX agent. For integration with existing management solutions JMX offers additional management protocol APIs and includes an open interface that any vendor can use. Currently, an SNMP API [22] and CIM/WBEM APIs [21] are defined and implemented. The final JMX specification will provide both a reference implementation and a compatibility test suite. However, only an early access version of the reference implementation is available yet.

Based on the current draft of the JMX specification, we have to state that shortcomings of JDMK identified in section 5 also apply to JMX. To which degree the review process of the specification will eliminate the weaknesses of the current JMX version has to remain an open question. This particularly applies to the manager side of JMX, which is yet unspecified.

7 Conclusion and Outlook

The paper described a case study for the dynamic management and monitoring of QoS parameters and SLAs based on JDMK and ARM. We have discussed our implementation concept with flexible and extensible agents which operate at the customer site. Our work was motivated by the increasing demand for scalable and reliable solutions which allow the extension of management agents at runtime. The experiences gained in this project allowed an evaluation of the applicability of JDMK for managing large-scale enterprise networks and can be summarized as follows: The development environment permits rapid prototyping and is easy to use; the transfer of lightweight applications (implemented as JavaBeans) to management agents at runtime works very well: JDMK supports both push and pull models and enables agents to acquire additional functionality, thus improving their (albeit limited) autonomy. JDMK is best described as a development framework for Java-based *Management by Delegation*. At its current stage, JDMK is a powerful toolkit for the development of management agents that can be accessed and modified through several different communication mechanisms.

The usability of management systems – especially in an enterprise-wide context – depends to a high degree on the security features of the underlying middleware. However, the JDMK security mechanisms are yet unsatisfactory because the different mechanisms of the underlying communication protocols/infrastructures have not yet been integrated into a common security archi-

---

[7] The dash in the word "M–Bean" has been removed in JMX.

tecture. It therefore depends on the type of the underlying protocol whether e.g., encryption is available and how access control is handled. Another critical issue is the absence of services to obtain meta-information on the deployed agents (like a "global" interface repository and naming services): The services to obtain information regarding the whole set of agents in a JDMK environment lack scalability because they can only be applied to *a single* Core Management Framework, thus preventing a global view on the agents.

The experiences of the project further allowed an evaluation of how ARM can be used for the monitoring of service levels of client/server applications. As the benefits of ARM outweigh the disadvantages by far there is hope that it will increasingly be adopted by vendors. Recently the CMG has released a preliminary version of ARM 3.0 SDK for public review (for a short overview see [9]). The most important topic of this release is the new Java binding. With this feature Java programs can use the ARM API directly and the indirection via Java Native Interface is not necessary any longer. However, until now the formal specification of ARM 3.0 is not available. Growing customer demand for applications ready for management will lead to a growing number of instrumented applications. A number of management tool vendors already offer solutions that implement the ARM API.

Acknowledgment. The authors wish to thank the members of the Munich Network Management (MNM) Team for helpful discussions and valuable comments on previous versions of the paper. The MNM Team directed by Prof. Dr. Heinz-Gerd Hegering is a group of researchers of the University of Munich, the Munich University of Technology, and the Leibniz Supercomputing Center of the Bavarian Academy of Sciences. Its webserver is located at http://wwwmnmteam.informatik.uni-muenchen.de.

References

1. Andrzej Bieszczad, Bernard Pagurek, and Tony White. Mobile Agents for Network Management. *IEEE Communication Surveys*, 1(1), 1998. http://www.comsoc.org/pubs/surveys/4q98issue/bies.html.

2. Application Response Measurement (ARM) API . Technical Standard C807, The Open Group, July 1998.

3. Common Information Model (CIM) Specification Version 2.2. Specification, June 1999.

4. M. Feridun, W. Kasteleijn, and J. Krause. Distributed Management with Mobile Components. In M. Sloman, S. Mazumdar, and E. Lupo, editors, *Integrated Network Management VI (IM'99)*, pages 857–870, Boston, MA, May 1999. IEEE Publishing.

5. G. Goldszmit and Y. Yemini. Distributed Managment by Delegation. In *Proceedings of the 15th International Conference on Distributed Computing Systems*, June 1995.

6. Michael S. Greenberg and Jennifer C. Byington. Mobile Agents and Security. *IEEE Communications Magazine*, 36(7):76–85, July 1998.

7. H.-G. Hegering, S. Abeck, and B. Neumair. *Integrated Management of Networked Systems – Concepts, Architectures and their Operational Application*. Morgan Kaufmann Publishers, ISBN 1-55860-571-1, 1999. 651 p.

8. M. Hojnacki. Einsatz des Java Dynamic Management Kit (JDMK) zur Antwortzeitüberwachung bei der DeTeSystem . Master's thesis, Technische Universität München, May 1999.

9. M. W. Johnson. ARM 3.0 — Enabling Wider Use of ARM in the Enterprise. In *Computer Measurement Group's 1999 International Conference (CMG99)*, Reno, Nevada, USA, December, 5–10 1999. http://www.cmg.org/regions/cmgarmw/arm30enhancements.pdf.

10. K. McCloghrie and M. T. Rose. RFC 1213: Management information base for network management of TCP/IP-based internets:MIB-II. RFC, IETF, March 1991.

11. M.-A. Mountzia. *Flexible Agents in Integrated Network and Systems Management.* Dissertation, Technische Universität München, December 1997.

12. A. Pham and A. Karmouch. Mobile Software Agents: An Overview. *IEEE Communications Magazine*, 36(7):26–37, July 1998.

13. K. Rothermel and F. Hohl, editors. *Mobile Agents (MA '98)*, volume 1477 of *LNCS*, Berlin; Heidelberg, 1998. Springer.

14. J. Schönwälder. Network Management by Delegation - From Research Prototypes Towards Standards. In *8th Joint European Networking Conf. (JENC8)*, Edinburgh, May 1997.

15. Jürgen Schönwälder. *Netzwerkmanagement mit programmierbaren, kooperierenden Agenten.* PhD thesis, Technische Universität Braunschweig, March 1996.

16. R. Sturm and W. Bumpus. *Foundations of Application Management.* Wiley Computer Publishing, 1998.

17. Sun Microsystems, Inc. JavaBeans, Version 1.01. Technical report, Sun Microsystems, Inc., Palo Alto, CA, July 1997. http://www.javasoft.com/beans/docs/spec.html.

18. Sun Microsystems, Inc. Java Dynamic Management Kit – A Whitepaper. Technical report, Sun Microsystems, Inc., Palo Alto, CA, 1998. http://www.sun.com/software/java-dynamic/wp-jdmk/.

19. Sun Microsystems, Inc. Java Dynamic Managment Kit 3.0 (beta) – Programming Guide. Technical report, Sun Microsystems, Inc., Palo Alto, CA, August 1998.

20. Sun Microsystems, Inc. Java Management Extensions Instrumentation and Agent Specification, v1.0. Technical report, Sun Microsystems, Inc., Palo Alto, CA, December 1999.

21. Sun Microsystems, Inc. Java Mangement Extensions CIM/WBEM APIs. Preliminary Specification Draft 1.9, Sun Microsystems, Inc., Palo Alto, CA, June 1999.

22. Sun Microsystems, Inc. Java Mangement Extensions SNMP Manager API. Preliminary Specification Draft 1.9, Sun Microsystems, Inc., Palo Alto, CA, June 1999.

23. Giovanni Vigna, editor. *Mobile Agents and Security*, number 1419 in LNCS, Berlin, Heidelberg, 1998. Springer.

24. B. Wijnen, R. Presuhn, and K. McCloghrie. RFC 2275: View-based Access Control Model (VACM) for the Simple Network Management Protocol (SNMP). RFC, IETF, January 1998.

Automated Allocation of Multi-provider Service Demands

Monique Calisti[1] and Boi Faltings[1]

Laboratoire d'Intelligence Artificielle
Swiss Federal Institute of Technology (EPFL)
CH-1015 Lausanne, Switzerland.
{calisti,faltings}@lia.di.epfl.ch

Abstract. The increasing number of competitors and the growing traffic demand are the main factors pushing for a more dynamic and flexible service demand allocation mechanism. Software tools are becoming fundamental for supporting human decisions and/or for reducing the need of human intervention. Agent technology promises support for *pro-active* and *autonomous* network control that would enable the automation of many network provider tasks. In order to prove the feasibility of such automation, a multi-agent simulator for the allocation of service demands has been developed. This paper describes the simulator and aims to give a useful feedback for agent developers.

1 Introduction

For many distributed applications requiring intelligent, autonomous and communicating software entities the multi-agent technology seems to be on of the most promising answers. Among others, the networking community is also investigating the deployment of autonomous agents for different purposes: network control, network management, resource allocation, etc. (see [8] for a good collection of papers). In particular, in a multi-provider environment the distribution and the heterogeneity of actors, resources and technologies suggests a management solution based on static and/or mobile distributed software entities. Such autonomous entities would have the ability to directly invoke effective changes to switch and router controllers, without the intervention of human operators [12]. For evolving the interaction between distinct network providers the *Network Provider Interoperability-multi agent system* (NPI-mas) has been developed [2]. The basic idea is to provide an efficient and flexible mechanism for self-interested agents representing different network operators for the allocation of service demands spanning distinct networks. The overall service provisioning process has been modelled has a *Distributed Constrained Satisfaction problem* (DCSP). Constraint satisfaction is a powerful and extensively used Artificial Intelligence paradigm [11] that involves finding values for problem variables subject to restrictions (constraints) on which combinations of values are acceptable. The multi-provider service demand allocation can be considered as a DCSP [14], since the variables

C. Linnhoff-Popien and H.-G. Hegering (Eds.): USM 2000, LNCS 1890, pp. 138–149, 2000.

are distributed among agents and since constraints exist among them. This paper focuses on the development of the NPI-mas simulator, on the description of its software components and on first simulation results with the purpose of:

- Evaluating the feasibility of the DCSP algorithms developed for supporting the automatic allocation of multi-domain service demands. The simulations aim not only to validate the algorithms, but also to quantitatively estimate the performance that could be obtained in specific network scenarios.
- Sharing with the readers the experience gained by programming distributed, autonomous and communicating software entities.
- Discussing the potential of this multi-agent paradigm and the major limits for its integration in a real network.

Section 2 describes the architecture of the NPI-mas simulator its main structural components. Quantitative results about the NPI-mas algorithms and an evaluation of the simulator are presented in Section 3. Section 4 comments on future work and concludes the paper.

2 An Agent-Based Simulator for Service Provisioning

NPI-mas has been conceived and developed as a virtual place that allows the simulation of multi-domain service demands allocations. A service demand is defined as $d_k ::= (x_k, y_k, qos_{req,k})$, where x_k is the source node, y_k the destination node, and $qos_{req,k}$ the required Quality of Service (QoS). A demand may be anything from a video-conference to a virtual link in a Virtual Private Network. In our framework, the QoS requirements correspond to *bandwidth* and *end-to-end delay*. The 3 types of agents populating NPI-mas are End User Agents

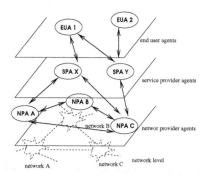

Fig. 1. *The agents' tribe populating the NPI-mas simulator.*

(EUAs), Service Provider Agents (SPAs) and Network Provider Agents (NPAs) (Figure 1). An EUA acts on behalf of a final end user, expressing his needs and formulating service demands. An SPA processes service demands and contacts

NPAs that own or directly control specific network resources. An NPA contacts peer-operators, whenever interactions are needed, e.g., when a service demand spans several networks.

2.1   The NPI-Mas Architecture

The NPI-mas simulator is entirely implemented in Java. JATLite [1] has been adopted as the main framework for the agent development. The main components of the simulator are:

- The *router* that receives messages from all registered agents and routes them to the correct recipient.
- The *Agent Management Interface* (AMI) that is a graphical interface which allows the selection of a multi-domain scenario, the creation of agents, and the visualisation of simulations' outputs.
- The *agents' community*. Several EUAs and SPAs can be created. A distinct NPA is associated with every network provider in the simulated scenario.

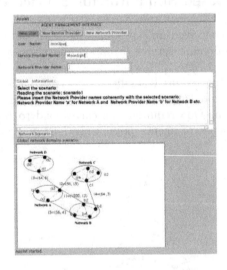

Fig. 2. *The Agent Management Interface.*

First of all, the AMI (Figure 2) enables the selection of a randomly generated network environment and the creation of all the agents populating it. Each agent automatically registers its identity with the *router*. In addition, every NPA recovers the data describing the network topology from dedicated *management information databases*. From the AMI, a text window displays the simulation

---

[1] JATLite is a set of packages that facilitate the agent framework development using Java. On-line documentation can be found at: http://piano.stanford.edu/

outputs such as the computed end-to-end paths from the source to the destination network, the results of intermediate steps of the demand allocation process and final negotiation outcomes.

Every NPI-mas agent is associated with a graphical interface that displays all messages that are sent and received by the agent. Furthermore, from the interface associated with an EUA, it is possible to enter a specific service demand in terms of source and destination nodes, required amount of bandwidth, available budget, required end-to-end delay and temporal constraints. Next, the EUA sends a *call-for-proposal* message to a selected SPA. An SPA represents both the *client* of the network services offered by the NPAs and the *provider* of a variety of telecommunications services to customers (EUAs). The SPA acts as a (currently very simple) *matchmaker*, finding suitable agents (NPAs), and accessing them on behalf of the requesting agent (EUA). In the future, this entity will be enhanced by introducing more sophisticated *brokering* and *recruiting* capabilities.

2.2 Communication Infrastructure

All NPI-mas agents communications rely upon the use of TCP/IP sockets. The first level of inter-operability is achieved through the use of standard interaction protocols, i.e., standard sequences of messages. FIPA[7] is a non-profit standardisation group that aims to promote inter-operability of emerging agent-based applications, service and equipment. Among others, FIPA specifies a set of standard communication facilities. Some standard FIPA protocols have been adopted and some new ones have been defined. Standard protocols enable a semantics interpretation of a messages' sequence in the context of a conversation, however this is not enough to guarantee full inter-operability.

Once messages are delivered and properly received, it is necessary to understand and interpret them. For this purpose, agents need to agree upon a common Agent Communication Language (ACL) and about a common way of representing common knowledge, i.e., the content language. The first version of NPI-mas makes use of the *Knowledge Query and Manipulation Language* [5] (KQML), since KQML facilities are provided within the JATLite platform. In order to increase the potential of the NPI-mas paradigm, we developed communication facilities for FIPA ACL to be used within JATLite [2]. FIPA ACL is in fact gaining more and more consensus in the agent community since it has a stronger semantic basis than KQML.

Concerning the knowledge representation, we have focused on Virtual Private Network (VPN) services and a content language that allows the representation of objects, propositions and actions has been developed: the VPN-cl. For portability and re-usability reasons, the syntax of the VPN-cl language has been defined in XML [3]. Agents deploying the VPN-cl are able to:

- Process information about objects such as services, physical connections, offers and Service Level Agreements (SLAs).

---

[2] More details can be found at http://liawww.epfl.ch/~calisti/ACL-LITE/

[3] More details can be found at http://liawww.epfl.ch/~calisti/ACL-LITE/VPN/

- Specify actions such as new service configuration, new connection activation, reservation of a connection, definition of a specific SLA, etc.
- Formulate propositions to motivate refusals or inform other agents about the results of an operation. Propositions are used for instance to inform that the end-to-end delay between two end-points is too high for a certain class of services that a given offer is too expensive that a service has been established, etc.

Finally, a common ontology has been defined and deployed. An *ontology* is an explicit specification of the structure of a certain domain. This includes a vocabulary for referring to the subject area, and a set of logical statements expressing the constraints existing in the domain and restricting the implementation of the vocabulary. The NPI-mas ontology provides a vocabulary for representing and communicating knowledge about VPN service provisioning. Furthermore, a set of relationships and properties that hold for the entities denoted by this vocabulary has been fixed.

2.3   The Network Provider Agents' Structure

Since the main goal of our simulator is to make use of algorithms and techniques designed for the inter-domain QoS-based routing, the focus is on the development of Network Provider Agents. The internal structure of a NPA is shown in

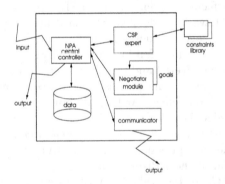

Fig. 3. *The internal NPA structure.*

Figure 3. The *perceptions* or *input* can be either messages coming from other agents or human user commands. The *central controller* is responsible for the coordination of several parallel activities, for processing inputs, for interfacing the agent world with human operators, for getting data characterising the network state. In our simulated scenario, the data is stored in a database that is dynamically updated during the simulation. In a real network, the data would be retrieved directly from the network management platform through the use of ad hoc wrappers. The NPA *communicator module* parses agents' messages, maintains communication channels, controls and manages all ongoing conversations.

The NPA *CSP expert* is a specialised sub-structure that is responsible for DCSP modelling and for applying typical DCSP consistency and searching techniques. The NPA *negotiator module* generates strategies for the controller. Considering the current state of the network, the various constraints, the utility function, and the interaction protocol, this module produces the strategy to be followed at every step of the negotiation process. Possible outputs of the NPA activity are either ACL messages to other agents, or internal actions, such as changes in the data configuration, or presentation of options to human operators.

2.4   NPA-to-NPA Interactions

Every NPA has an aggregated view of the multi-domain network topology that is deployed for computing the abstract paths to other networks in the environment. An *abstract path* is an ordered list of distinct providers' networks between the source and the destination nodes. The *initiator* is the NPA that first receives a service demand d_k and computes one or several abstract paths along which the service negotiation is started. The choice of an abstract path P is based on the following heuristics: (1) Eliminate all the paths that do not guarantee enough bandwidth. (2) Among the paths left select the cheapest (minimum cost). (3) If still more than one path exists, chose the path which has, after having accepted the incoming demand, the largest bandwidth left.

Next, the *initiator* contacts all the NPAs along P requesting them to locally determine the set S_k of possible internal routes for allocating d_k.

If all providers are locally consistent, i.e., S_k is not empty, the *arc consistency* phase is started. The NPAs exchange information about inter-domain constraints. All incompatible network access points are discarded, so that every NPA reduces the set S_k. This phase involves a propagation of messages among neighbours, in order to revise the set S_k for every access point that is discarded.

If arc consistency is successful (i.e, all NPAs have a non empty set S_k consistent with inter-domain constraints) the negotiation for selecting a specific end-to-end route is started. The initiator broadcasts a *call-for-proposal* to all NPAs along P. A NPA's offer consists of a specific local route at a certain price. The *initiator* evaluates all received offers and elaborates possible global offers for the EUA, which involves pricing mechanisms and profit maximisation. The negotiation is successful whether the EUA accepts the offer. The initiator confirms to the NPAs the results of the transition. If the negotiation fails and the end-user does not modify its requirements the demand request is rejected and the initiator notifies all other NPAs.

3   The Lessons Learned

The availability of an increasing number of agent platforms, many of which are compliant to the FIPA standards [4], facilitates the work of developers of

---

[4] FIPA-OS is an open-source agent platform developed by Nortel Networks available at: http://www.nortelnetworks.com/fipa-os. JADE is an open-source software

agent-based applications that aim to be open and inter-operable with agent so-lutions implemented and managed by others. Nevertheless, even when deploying pre-existing tools, developers should be aware of a certain number of concrete technical issues that it is important to solve in an efficient way for not affecting the applications performance.

Naming and addressing issues. No matter what kind of platform is deployed, an agent needs to be uniquely identified. This obvious requirement, common to all distributed systems and usually solved by all the most common agent tool-kits, can become a more complex issue when considering the need of supporting directory services, i.e., *yellow pages*. A FIPA compliant platform usually imple-ments an Agent Communication Router (ACR) that is responsible for registering names and verifying their uniqueness. In addition, a *Directory Facilitator* (DF) entity records which services the registered agents can supply. In that case, the ability of an agent developer consists of creating standard, concise, but effec-tive *identity cards* that the system, namely the DF, can flexibly and efficiently handle. Since JATLite does not supply any DF, an auxiliary entity devoted to 'yellow-paging' has been developed. The identity card of an NPI-mas agent con-sists of three major fields: the name, the profession and the address. The agent *name* is automatically checked by the NPI-mas Router whenever a new agent is created (the name must be unique). The *profession* identifies which kind of services the agent can support, namely if it is an EUA, a SPA or a NPA. Finally, the *address* includes the agent name, the host-name (i.e., the machine the agent is running in), and a time-stamp corresponding to the moment at which the agent has been created.

Handling multiple conversations. Every agent can be involved in parallel con-versations. For this reason, an identifier, i.e., the *conv id*, is used to identify a conversation for every non isolated communicative act. Therefore, vectors of *con-versation* objects have to be dynamically maintained by every agent. At the same time, every agent needs to manage vectors of data structures, since different ob-jects are instantiated for different and parallel allocation demands. The dynamic update of such vectors is the most delicate part of the data management, since several messages coming in parallel from different agents can concern the same data structure. To face this concurrency problem we adopted a FIFO policy, serialising the access to those data structures.

Detection of a global state. During the 'arc consistency' phase (see Sec-tion 2.4) there is a propagation of messages among agents in order to revise the set of all possible local routes S_k for a demand d_k. This phase ends when all agents are consistent (or eventually as soon as one of them is inconsistent) and when no messages are pending in the system, i.e., when the *global state* is sta-ble [3]. In order to detect that this state is reached a control mechanism, namely a Java thread instantiated by the NPA *initiator*, is used. The initiator receives notifications about the state of every single agent involved in the arc consistency and about the messages that are spread around in the system. This allows it to

---

framework that simplifies the implementation of multiagent systems developed by CSELT S.p.A. and available at: http://sharon.cselt.it/projects/jade

maintain and update a global state that is periodically checked by the control thread. However, this kind of mechanism has potential scalability problems due to the number of messages that are exchanged with the initiator NPA. For this reason, a pre-selection of intra-domain routes is important to reduce the number of updates in the set of possible local routes and therefore of messages exchanged in the system.

Integration of JATLite with 'external' Java code. The modularity of the JAT-Lite's architecture enables developers to build agent-based systems that deploy only specific packages of such a tool. The on-line documentation of both JATLite and Java were sufficient for the integration of all the NPI-mas components. The development and the integration of new software components with the original JATLite structure enables FIPA ACL based communications and DF services. In addition, an auxiliary software package allows the usage of the VPN-cl language for facilitating agents negotiating about VPN service provisioning.

3.1   Evaluation of the NPI-Mas Paradigm

The performance metrics that have been observed for evaluating the NPI-mas paradigm and the DCSP-based techniques are the average demand allocation time, T_{tot}, and the allocation rate, $A_r := nbsuccess/nbdemands$, with $nbsuccess$ the number of demands successfully allocated, and $nbdemands$ the total number of service demands generated by the EUAs.

Simulations with a variable number N_D of networks (Figure 4), and therefore of NPAs [5], have been run in order to check the scalability of our algorithms and in parallel the usability of communicating agents for the multi-provider service allocation purpose. The average values that has been obtained for T_{tot}, i.e.,

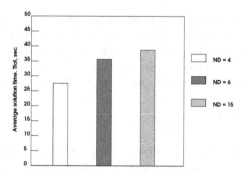

Fig. 4. *Three different simulated scenarios have been considered. T_{tot} has been computed over a set of 300 randomly generated demands.*

$[25, 40]$ seconds, can be considered a positive result when compared to the current

---

[5] In our simulations $N_D \in [4, 15]$, which correspond to a realistic multi-provider environment. However, we are testing the NPI paradigm for greater values of N_D.

delays required by human operators to negotiate solutions and topology changes. Given a fixed number N_D of providers' networks, we then tested the influence of a different number $|L|$ of inter-domain links. Increasing $|L|$ has a double effect: (1) The complexity of the solving process increases by augmenting the number of possible access points combinations between neighbour networks, therefore T_{tot} increases, see Figure 5. However, the increment of T_{tot} is smaller than $1/3$, since the addition of new links does necessarily increases the search space for all service demand allocations. (2) The probability that at least one end-to-end path satisfying the QoS requirements of demands to be allocated exists augments so that A_r increases, see Figure 6. Adding $1/3$ of $|L|$ does not lead to an equivalent increment of A_r, since new links do not always facilitate the allocation for all possible service demands. Similar results have been obtained when varying the

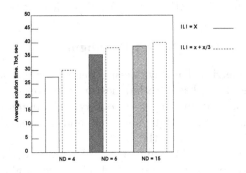

Fig. 5. T_{tot} *increases when increasing the number of inter-domain links, since the search space become larger.*

complexity of the internal topology of every network. A greater number of network nodes and intra-domain links can augment the search space and introduce an additional computational overhead. However, similarly to the augmentation of $|L|$, if the topological changes correspond to an increment of available network resources, the number of demands successfully allocated increases.

3.2   Evaluation of the Simulator

The service demand allocation problem represents a complex and articulated process becomes even more complicated for networks that aim to provide QoS guarantees [4]. This is especially true in a multi-provider context where every provider tries to maximise his own utility and knowledge about the network topology is restricted by the network providers for strategic reasons. Although multi-domain QoS routing has been tackled from many viewpoints (ATM and SDH network [9], billing [1], multi-domain management in the MISA [6] project, agent interactions for routing multimedia traffic over distributed networks, see [6]

---

[6] http://www.misa.ch

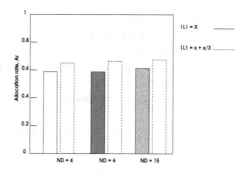

Fig. 6. *The graphic shows the increment of demands successfully allocated, when increasing the inter-domain capacity.*

and the FACTS project [7]) no previous work has addressed the possibility of dynamic negotiations about more than one path at a time.

Before starting the implementation of the NPI-mas system, an evaluation of different existing agent platforms were completed. Many multi-agent systems are available and the most common and traditional classifications distinguish between architectures for *reactive agents*, *deliberative agents* and *interacting agents* (see [10] and [13] for good overviews). Hybrid architectures have also been developed for integrating reaction and deliberation. However, some platforms are very specific to the traditional mentalistic approach, some are not freely available, and more in general no pre-existing agent platform was offering a support for any kind of CSP technique. Furthermore, when the NPI-mas project started, no FIPA compliant agent platform was publicly available. For these reasons, an ad hoc simulator has been developed from the scratch by deploying part of the JATLite architecture (the most general part) and adding new and more specific components.

In NPI-mas the use of Distributed Constraint Satisfaction techniques and the deployment of autonomous agents making use of a compact aggregated representation of network resources availability offer the capability of:

- Accelerating the allocation of multi-provider service demands, by automating many steps currently performed by humans.
- Supplying standard solutions that abstract from technical details, by using a common and standard agent communication language and a standard ontology. Standard agent communications, either via KQML or FIPA, facilitate the access to electronic service negotiations to a larger number of potential customers or sellers of Telecom services. The usage of agent communication languages instead of low levels languages such as SNMP (Simple Network Management Protocol) primitives or CMIP (Common Management Information Protocol) routines allows the abstraction from technical details and enhance agents' conversations by means of a semantics foundation behind the messages' sequence.

---

[7] http://www.labs.bt.com/profsoc/facts

- Supplying consistent solutions without the need for every participants to reveal internal and confidential data, such as network topologies, negotiation strategies, pricing mechanisms, etc.
- Supporting human decisions, or, in a more future scenario, of replacing human operators. Software entities can in fact accelerate the utility computation, optimise over different possible choices, follow more easily complex negotiation strategies, etc.
- Integrating economic principles within *self-interested* agents, in order to optimise the revenue.

NPI-mas agents could be integrated within a real network by providing ad hoc *wrappers* in order to interface the agent with the non-agent world, i.e., the network management and control level. These wrappers would take into account the low level characteristics of specific underlying network technologies. Although, it is not easy to perfectly map between the agents' understanding and the management's details, the abstraction provided by those wrappers would allows a more understandable and natural approach to many networking aspects otherwise very difficult to understand. The difficulty is related to the very low levels terms currently used for managing and controlling a network.

4   Conclusion

Currently many aspects of interworking are statically fixed using contracts and many steps of the interaction are carried out by human operators by fax, e-mail etc. The NPI-mas paradigm can be considered as a high level service which could be deployed in two different ways: in a short term period as a smart support for human operators, in a long term perspective as an autonomous system acting on behalf of humans and working at the connection management level. The first version would offer a valid support for human operators: it could compute local routes guaranteeing the QoS required and automatically verify which ones are not consistent with the inter-domain constraints (which are for instance the routes fixed in the currently used contracts). In a future scenario NPI-mas agents could supply an automated mechanism to route and negotiate the allocation of demands across distinct networks without the need for human intervention.

Implementing the NPI-mas system has been essential to validate theoretical concepts previously defined. The results obtained through the simulation prove the potential of our paradigm and estimate the performance.

Beyond more realistic simulations and more exhaustive data analysis, there are several directions that the authors are considering for the future development of NPI-mas.

- The introduction of more sophisticated negotiation techniques. This implies the definition of new protocols and/or new negotiation strategies. The gap between economic principles and software entities requires may force us to accept a "good" solution instead of looking for the optimal one.
- The development of alternative pricing mechanisms, such as auctions.

- The introduction of more complete and realistic representations of networking data and multi-provider service demands. For that purpose, more focus on current the service level agreements definitions is needed. Since there is no a standard and common way of expressing SLAs, it is non trivial to define a uniform representation that agents can use.
- The possibility of creating *coalitions* among NPAs, in order to take advantage of a higher degree of coordination.
- More work on the *service provider* level, i.e., more sophisticated brokering capabilities need to be added to the SPAs agents.

References

1. C. Bleakley, W. Donnelly, A. Lindgren, and H. Vuorela. TMN specifications to support inter-domain exchange of accounting, billing and charging information. *Lecture Notes in Computer Science*, 1238, 1997.
2. M. Calisti and B. Faltings. A multi-agent paradigm for the Inter-domain Demand Allocation process. *DSOM'99, Tenth IFIP/IEEE International Workshop on Distributed Systems: Operations and Management*, 1999.
3. K. Mani Chandy and Leslie Lamport. Distributed snapshots: Determining global states of distributed systems. *TOCS*, 3(1):63–75, February 1985.
4. Shigang Chen and Klara Nahrstedt. An Overview of Quality of Service Routing for Next-Generation High-Speed Networks: Problems and Solutions. *IEEE Network*, pages 64–79, November/December 1998.
5. Tim Finin et al. Specification of the KQML Agent-Communication Language – plus example agent policies and architectures, 1993.
6. Fipa. Fipa spec. 97 v2.0. *Foundation for Intelligent Physical Agents*, 1997.
7. Foundation for Intelligent Physical Agents. FIPA Specifications, October 1997. http://www.fipa.org/spec/.
8. Alex L. G. Hayzelden and John Bigham, editors. *Software Agents for Future Communication Systems: Agent Based Digital Communication*. Springer-Verlag, Berlin Germany, 1999.
9. D. Karali, F. Karayannis, K. Berdekas, and J. Reilly. Qos based multi-domain routing in public broadband networks. *Lecture Notes in Computer Science*, 1430, 1998.
10. J. P. Muller. The design of intelligent agents: a layered approach. *Lecture Notes in Artificial Intelligence and Lecture Notes in Computer Science*, 1177, 1996.
11. Edward Tsang. *Foundations of Constraint Satisfaction*. Academic Press, London, UK, 1993.
12. S. N. Willmott and B. Faltings. Active Organisations for Routing. In S. Covaci, editor, *Proceedings of the First International Working Conference on Active Networks.*, pages 262–273. Springer Verlag, Lecture Notes in Computer Science Series, number 1653, 1999.
13. M. Wooldridge and N.R. Jennings. Intelligent agents: Theory and practice. *The Knowledge Engineering Review*, 10(2):115–152, 1995.
14. M. Yokoo, E. H. Durfee, T. Ishida, and K. Kuwabara. Distributed Constraint Satisfaction for Formalising Distributed Problem Solving. *Proceedings 12th IEEE International Conference on Distributed Computing Systems.*, pages 614–621, 1992.

Mobile and Distributed Services

Chair: Axel Küpper, RWTH Aachen, Germany

A Vehicular Software Architecture Enabling Dynamic Alterability of Services Sets

Volker Feil[1], Ulrich Gemkow[1], and Matthias Stümpfle[2]

[1] University of Stuttgart, Institute of Communication Networks and Computer Engineering,
Pfaffenwaldring 47, 70569 Stuttgart, Germany
{feil,gemkow}@ind.uni-stuttgart.de

[2] DaimlerChrysler AG, Research and Technology 3, Vehicle IT-Architecture, HPC T728,
70546 Stuttgart, Germany
matthias.stuempfle@daimlerchrysler.com

Abstract. In this paper we present the software architecture DANA based on components for distributed systems in vehicles. Components use and provide services. Since they are binary codes that are deployable and configurable at system's runtime, it is possible to alter the set of services during the life cycle of a vehicle. Due to the flexibility of this architecture emerging new application services for drivers and passengers can be added at any time. In order to enable the offering of such application services there is a need for services collaboration inside the distributed system which meets QoS requirements. Because the existence of many small control units in future vehicles is expected, an architecture must regard also the services provided by them. We show that the presented architecture is suitable for such an automotive environment.

1 Introduction

Recent evolution of information and communications technology increasingly change our everyday life. Also, inside vehicles new services for drivers and passengers arise. For instance, typical driver supporting services (e.g. providing traffic information or navigation) become more and more familiar. Furthermore, services that are well established in the home and office area (e.g. video, or Internet based services like WWW [4]) become available in vehicles.

Until now, there are mainly proprietary software solutions in the telematics area. However, because of the spreading of software solutions the interaction of service functions becomes more and more interesting even with respect to economical constraints.

Such tendencies are visible in the success of universal technologies for distributed computing with its main representatives Java RMI [3] and CORBA [17]. New developments like UPnP [16] or Jini [20] make distributed computing even more powerful. It is foreseeable that a similar evolution will take place in the automotive environment, especially as the vehicle itself will become a node of a global network.

The approach presented in this paper regards software architectures in future

C. Linnhoff-Popien and H.-G. Hegering (Eds.): USM 2000, LNCS 1890, pp. 152–163, 2000.
© Springer-Verlag Berlin Heidelberg 2000

vehicles. In the next section special automotive requirements on a vehicular software architecture are listed. In section 3 the basic elements of the presented architecture are described. The management tasks of this architecture and how they are achieved are shown in section 4. Finally, a classification of the architecture is presented in section 5. This classification implies a comparison to universal technologies like UPnP and Jini, and the discussion of implementation aspects.

2 Requirements on a Vehicular Software Architecture

The first step of designing the architecture is to recognize the special automotive requirements.

2.1 Requirements – User's View

Manifold Set of Services. We define a set of services as a combination of user oriented application services. Within vehicles a manifold set of services will be offered. Table 1 shows a selection of application services that will be available for drivers and passengers in future.

Table 1. Application services in future vehicles

Mobile Office Services	Entertainment Services	Information Services	Transaction Services	Vehicular Services
e.g. telephone, fax, notebook access, Internet services (WWW [4], E-Mail)	e.g. digital broadcast and TV [8], audio / video sources (DVD), games	e.g. traffic information, countryside/ city informa-tion, parking information	e.g. bookings (e.g. hotel reservation), banking	e.g. navigation, car diagnosis, emergency call

The services require data exchange with different qualities: Speech data with delays of more than 200 ms or jitter effects are troubling [13]. Audio and video transmissions require large data rates. Data of Internet applications like WWW and E-Mail must be exchanged without losses.

Alterability of the Services Set. It is obvious that nobody can give accurate predictions regarding future needed services. Because a vehicle's life cycle is much larger than an usual life cycle of an application service, it is necessary to be able to update the set of services during a vehicle's life time.

Easy Handling and Easy Maintenance. It can not be expected that vehicle holders have software knowledge. Furthermore, it is unlikely that they would accept additional stops in a garage just for software updates. Therefore, easy handling and maintenance is required to achieve a dynamic changeable services set in a vehicle.

Integration in a Global Network Infrastructure. Most services shown in Table 1 are communication oriented and this communication is not limited to within the vehicle. The vehicle itself is no longer isolated, but becomes a part of a globally distributed system. Access to services provided anywhere must be possible.

2.2   Requirements – Manufacturer's View

Consideration of a Heterogeneous Environment. A distributed system with control units (devices) comprising of a processor and local memory is expected to be part of future vehicles. Even today a vehicle of the comfort class contains between 40 and 80 control units [11]. These control units are loosely coupled by communication systems. Currently, there are still rather seperate systems in a vehicle that can be roughly divided in an engine, a comfort, and a telematics area. A typical bus for the engine area is CAN (Controller Area Network) [18], and a typical communication system for the telematics area is the optical D2B [2]. D2B allows to exchange audio streams. There will be even more powerful communication systems like IEEE 1394 [14] or MOST (Media Oriented Systems Transport) [5] in the telematics area that will also provide handling of video streams. It is expected that there will be a total distributed system with very heterogenous control units and communication systems that differ in their capabilities. A vehicular software architecture has to consider this heterogeneity.

Support of Small Control Units. One result of the expected heterogeneity is the existence of a lot of small control units per vehicle. Today, usual vehicular control units do not contain sophisticated networking protocol entities. It is conceivable that lots of them will still not contain an IP stack even in next future.

Support of Standard Technologies. It is expected that besides the small control units some units will have the power to support popular, and more universal IP-based technologies, e.g. UPnP and Jini.

Integration in a Global Network Infrastructure. It is the manufacturer's interest to integrate the vehicle as a node in a global network. With respect to economical constraints it can be worthwhile to provide vehicle's functionality outside instead of inside the vehicle.

Consideration of Manufacturer/Supplier Relationships. One aim is to preserve familiar, proven, and automotive typical structures of manufacturers/supplier relationships also by introducing a new software development process.

3   Basic Elements of the Architecture

3.1   Service and Component Concept

In this paper software *components* are defined as *binary units of independent production, acquisition, and deployment that interact to form a functioning system* [10]. Interacting means that components use and provide services mutually (see Fig. 1).

Therefore, a component can be regarded as a container for services.

The usage of component software technology is meaningful to automotive manufacturers. First, components are produceable on the producer's own authority and acquirable on the vehicle manufacturer's own authority. Therefore, automotive industry suppliers can be integrated in the software development process in a familiar way. Second, components are deployable under the own control of the deploying entity. Consequently, the dynamic alterability of a services set is achieved by enabling the facility to deploy components in an existing vehicle.

There are already efforts to bring the software component idea into vehicles. For instance, in [6] a Java Beans [19] based approach is presented. In this paper we describe the component concept of DANA *(D*istributed Systems *A*rchitecture for *Net*works in *A*utomotive Environments). DANA components are binary codes, that are deployable and configurable at system's runtime (see also [9]). In Fig. 1 the component layering model of DANA is shown.

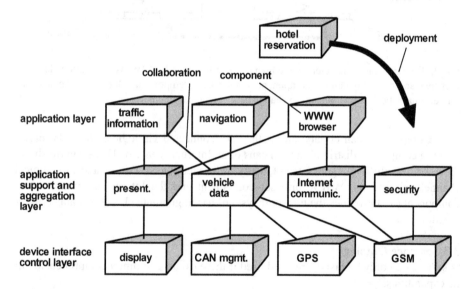

Fig. 1. The collaboration of vehicle specific components is shown exemplary. The components are put in a layered structure. Application components use application support and aggregation components, which itself use device interface control components. The latter allow the access to the attached hardware. Furthermore, the example depicts the deployment of a new hotel reservation component.

In order to enable the proper collaboration of the components, there is a need for constraints and rules that are imposed by the architecture. These rules consist of well defined interfaces, and in a management for component deployment, service discovery and enabling service utilization. As the system complexity should be transparent to the user, manual interventions and interaction with the user cannot be allowed for configuration purposes.

There are two ways considered in order to get a management for service discovery and for enabling service utilization without manual intervention. The first way is to apply standard building blocks (e. g. Java RMI, and Jini) in order to create a rapid prototype. The second way is to design a new architecture that respects the special automotive constraints (mainly the existence of small control units). The emphasis of this paper is to present that second way.

3.2   DANA Elements

In this section, the structure of a DANA component is described. In Fig. 2 the ingredients of such a component, a worker and a management, are depicted.

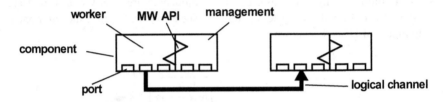

Fig. 2. Both parts are connected by the management/worker API (MW API). To allow data exchange among components, a component contains so called ports, at which logical channels can terminate. DANA components exchange data via logical channels.

Components can collaborate, if they are connected via logical channels. Fig. 3 shows a component distribution by means of an Internet scenario. This scenario shows the need for fulfilling a guaranteed Quality of Service (QoS). For instance, the logical channel between the WWW browser component and the Internet communications component (that provides the transport system) has to guarantee loss free data communication.

3.3   Service Ontology

A service can only be discovered and used if there exists a common comprehension of its capabilities.

The service that is provided by a DANA component is denoted non-ambiguously by a name (string). Several components representing the same service may exist. These components do not differ by their service name, but by their DANA standardized address. A service comprises also of a bit mask in order to denote its capabilities. A trading service is intended additionally in order to enable more complex queries.

For instance, one component in Fig. 3 provides a GSM service. It has capabilities to provide a signalling interface (E.164 numbering) for establishing and releasing connections, access to the traffic channel of an established connection, and access to a PPP entity. The traffic channel access supports a data rate up to 9,6 kbps, and a speech rate up to 13,2 kbps.

If a component looks for a GSM service explicitly by name, it knows all about the GSM service capabilities. However, if the component just looks for a signalling interface to establish a telephone connection to an outside device, it can discover the service by analyzing the bitmasks of all available services for a suitable pattern. Therefore, an UMTS [15] service which may be available in future can also be discovered, even if the component does not know that service's name. Furthermore, a component can make use of a trading service. The result of a query to a trading service may depend on the combination of the input data and vehicle specific data (e.g. position data). Thus, the result of a query on the road may be still the GSM service, whereas the result of a query at home may be a cheaper and more powerful DECT [12] service.

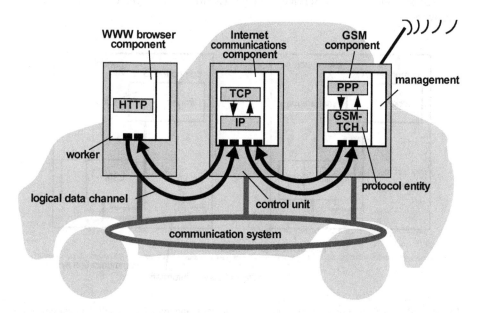

Fig. 3. An example for the component deployment is shown by a simplified Internet scenario. In this scenario only one component of the vehicle offers the service of a TCP/IP layer. This Internet communications component can even represent the car with one IP-address in the global Internet by having routing and masquerading functionality. The location of the TCP/IP-layer service users (e.g. the WWW browser component) does not matter as the existence of logical channels provides location transparency. Furthermore, Internet access for notebooks or PDAs is available by this constellation. Access to the external Internet is available through the GSM component that owns the PPP entity (OSI layer 2) and the GSM traffic channel (GSM-TCH, OSI layer 1). This component is assigned to the device interface control layer and enables access to the installed GSM hardware.

4 Management Tasks

The collaboration of the components needs to be managed. The tasks of this management are to realize discovery of components and their services, utilization of a discovered service, and deployment of components to a control unit or to the external infrastructure.

Each component contains a management (see also Fig. 2) that is connected via so called logical management channels to so called managers. Managers, which are components themselves, are also interconnected by logical management channels in order to collaborate. Only standardized messages of the DANA management can be exchanged through logical management channels.

4.1   Service Discovery

Three types of managers, Local Service Manager (LSM), System Service Manager (SSM), and External Service Manager (XSM), work together to realize service discovery.

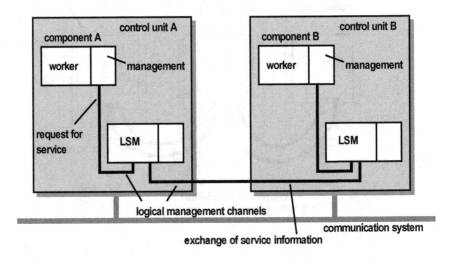

Fig. 4. LSMs exchange service information via logical management channels. They are responsible for all components of their unit. Therefore, the management of the components must communicate with them via local management channels.

Service Announce Mode. The basic mode of service discovery is based on the collaboration of Local Service Managers (LSMs) that are located in each control unit (see also Fig. 4). A LSM represents the components of its control unit and stores information about these in a local service table. After unit initialization, the LSM works in the announcing state. In this state the LSM broadcasts *service announce* messages. The content of the message consists of the representation of all services inside the unit. By evaluation of the message content each LSM builds its local system service table with all available services that are relevant for this unit. An entry of this table consists of a service name, the service capabilities, and the DANA address.

Service Polling Mode. If a System Service Manager (SSM) becomes active, it takes the registration task on. A SSM discovers all existing LSMs by receiving their service announce messages. It informs the LSMs about its existence and asks for terminating the broadcasting of the service announce messages. A SSM builds its system service table by a polling process. It cyclically asks all LSMs for service information. Therefore, each LSM that is ready for working together with the SSM needs no local system service table, and changes to a polling state.

Request for Services. By collaboration of the managers service discovery becomes available. A component can discover the location of another component by calling the service name or some service capabilities. Thus, the service management part of a component must contact its responsible LSM (see also Fig. 4).

Integration of External Services. There is a distinction between the vehicular internal management and the overall operating management. The vehicular internal discovery management is based on a broadcasting concept (service announce mode) whereas the vehicular external discovery management additionally rests on a portal concept. This is due to the inefficiency of the broadcasting concept for large networks. If a LSM even by interacting with the SSM does not posses service information for a requested component the manager can interwork with the External Service Manager (XSM) additionally. The XSM clarifies whether a service is available outside the vehicle or not. The external counterpart of the XSM is a global service center (portal) that can return a global address of an externally deployed component.

4.2   Enabling Service Utilization

In the simplest case all components can exchange data by permanent data channels that are established during the initialization phase of a service. Such a system is static because no new services can be integrated. To achieve a dynamic system with a modifiable components set, the management must enable the establishment of logical data channels to the new deployed components.

The channel management is controlled by another set of managers: The Local Channel Manager (LCM), Range Channel Manager (RCM), System Channel Manager (SCM), and External Channel Manager (XCM) are responsible for the channel management. On each unit a LCM is deployed. It appears in two roles – the requesting role and the requested role. The requesting LCM accepts an instruction to modify (e.g. establish or release) a channel from a management of a component placed on its unit. By usage of a three-way-handshake protocol the requesting LCM negotiates the channel modification with the requested LCM (see Fig. 5). Within this interaction the requested LCM is responsible for the component of its unit that is affected by the channel modification.

Furthermore, a RCM is involved if the modified channel spans over different control units. The RCM represents the communication system at the QoS negotiation. If a channel modification affects more than one communication system, the System Channel Manager (SCM) representing the total vehicle system must be involved. If a channel modification affects the communication infrastructure outside the vehicle, the External Channel Manager (XCM) must be involved.

After establishing a new data channel, components can use it for data exchange regarding the required QoS. After releasing an existing data channel, the needed resources are deallocated.

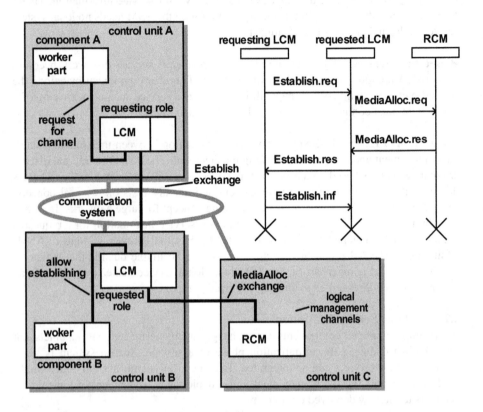

Fig. 5. Channel establishing example: After determining the DANA address of the suitable component B by requesting the service discovering LSM, the management of component A wants to establish a channel to that component B. Therefore, it requests the LCM of its control unit for establishing a channel with the suitable QoS features. This manager takes the requesting role and initiates a three way handshake exchange of *Establish* messages with the requested LCM that is responsible for component B. During this messages exchange, the management of component B is asked by the requested LCM for granting the channel establishing. Furthermore, the RCM is involved by exchange of *MediaAlloc* messages to clarify whether the communication system (bus) can guarantee the QoS requirements. For this reason a RCM may contain a table to manage the bandwidth resources of the bus. After the agreement of all manager parties, the channel can be established, and data between components A and B can be exchanged.

4.3   Component Deployment

One of the main features of the envisioned software architecture is the possibility to dynamically reconfigure the system, allowing new services to enter it. Due to the possible various configurations for the system a configuration management is needed. Configuration management knows all available components by accessing the System Service Manager (SSM) and External Service Manager (XSM) and has to decide where to run the component. This allows to dynamically adapt the system's behavior to different external requirements like available processing power, memory constraints, and cost issues related to the wireless connection between vehicle and the external infrastructure. Technically speaking this results in an optimization problem that has to be solved continuously during system life time.

Due to the remote accessibility of component interfaces, they may also be placed on infrastructure machines if the wireless connection into the infrastructure permits, and thus using the potentially higher computing power of such a device.

5   Classification of the Architecture

5.1   Consideration of Hardware Requirements
The described architecture is specified on different levels. It is possible to develop units that follow the architectural specification for service discovery and utilization with their external behavior. As a result, the internal implementation remains proprietary. Therefore, software of any unit can be developed regarding the given constraints. For instance, if developing software for embedded units enforces the usage of little RAM, it is impossible to implement the sophisticated concepts of component deployment. However, by implementing the LSM and LCM functionality, the software in a simple control unit can participate on the communication system and interact with the software of other units.

A more detailed component level specification exists besides that unit level specification. At this level, the architecture of components inside a unit is described. Software that follows this specification level allows full use of DANA's management.

Due to this approach the application of the management functionality is scalable.

5.2   Comparison to and Interaction with Other Technologies
A comparison of the presented architecture to more universal solutions like UPnP and Jini is necessary to classify the presented architecture.

A manifold and alterable set of services can be handled by universal technologies due to the existence of service discovery protocols. By using these protocols the complexity of the technologies becomes transparent to the user. Furthermore, the heterogeneity problem is solved, because all interacting parties agree in common to the IP standard to solve the addressing problems, and concerning Jini also to the Java standard to achieve platform independency.

However, in vehicles support of small control units is also required. Today, typical control units in vehicles are equipped with 60 kbyte ROM and 2 kbyte RAM [7]. Even a HTTP/TCP/IP stack in a UPnP supporting smart device according to [1] needs 60 kbyte of code. Furthermore, Jini needs additional RAM due to the capability to exchange Java objects and the realization of the Java class loading concept [3]. Today, Jini works only in a universal Java 2 environment.

DANA considers the existence of small control units in vehicles, because the application of the management functionality is scalable (see also section 5). Furthermore, in opposite to the compared technologies it explicitly regards resource management (e.g. bandwidth assignment, see also section 4.2). It is designed especially for the vehicular environment and more convenient for that specific application area than universal technologies.

Because a coexistence of DANA and universal technologies in a vehicle is conceivable, the existence of an interlinking concept is necessary. An interlinking entity is both a component in the DANA managed part of the network and e.g. a Java server object in the Jini part of the network. This entity can represent one part of the network as a proxy on the opposite side. Thereby it is possible to bring the small control units to the universal technologies.

5.3   Implementation Aspects

The presented architecture allows a large freedom in its realization. Programming paradigms, programming languages, platforms and communication protocols are not enforced by the architecture but are exchangeable technologies.

We use Java as implementation language of our prototype, because with Java a uniform component platform is given. It is important to mention that Java is not inevitably greedy of memory and performance. For instance, there exist some promising approaches that apply the Personal Java Standard. JBed [11] with its minimal memory need of 10 kbyte is one representative. A compiler that compiles Java byte code to object code and a linker produce a binary that is stored in a boot ROM. Furthermore, the possible existence of a compiler and linker inside the control unit enables classloading and thereby component deployment at run time.

Currently, our prototype hardware consists of Linux PCs. We regard to use a minimal set of libraries (e.g. no IP networking) and a minimal set of operating system services. Channels are realized by applying communication services of the IEEE 1394 bus directly. We consider several QoS aspects of the communication between components. Synchronous A/V streams as well as asynchronous data can be transferred via the IEEE 1394 bus. A shift from applying PCs to applying small control units is currently underway.

6   Conclusions

A variety of application services in future vehicles is expected. However, it is obviously not possible to predict the kind of services that will emerge. Because of the long life cycle of a vehicle we need a software architecture that allows the alterability of the offered services sets. The presented architecture DANA enables to add new functionality by the deployment of new components.

In order to achieve updateable sets of services, management functionality is needed. This management consists of service discovery, enabling service utilization with respecting QoS requirements and the deployment of components.

The architecture satisfies the specific automotive requirements. In contrast to universal service discovering technologies, also control units with small CPU power and memory can be supported due to the scalability of the architecture. Therefore, software in small control units can interact with software in high capacity control units. The functioning of the system is achieved by an uniform architecture.

References

1. B. Christensson, O. Larson: Universal Plug and Play Connects Smart Devices. WinHec 99 White Paper (2000)

2. C. Ciocan: The Domestic Digital Bus System (D2B). IEEE Transactions on Consumer Electronics, vol. 36, no. 3, (1990) 619-622

3. P. Clip: Java's Object-Oriented Communications. Byte, McGraw-Hill, Febr. (1998) 53-54

4. A. Jameel, M. Stümpfle, D. Jiang, A. Fuchs: Web on Wheels: Toward Internet-Enabled Cars. IEEE Computer, vol. 31 (1998) 69 -71

5. R. König, C. Thiel: Media Oriented Systems Transport (MOST) – Standard für Multimedia Networking im Fahrzeug. it + ti – Informationstechnik und Technische Informatik, vol. 5 (1999) 36-42

6. M. Bathelt: Komponententechnologie für verteilte Embedded Systems. In: B. Hindel (ed.): Technologie Forum Embedded Software, 3Soft GmbH, Erlangen (1999) 153-160

7. J. Schoof: Der OSEK/VDX-Standard. In: B. Hindel (ed.): Technologie Forum Embedded Software, 3Soft GmbH, Erlangen (1999) 7-19

8. G. Sigle: Digital Multimedia Broadcasting. Electronic Systems For Vehicles, VDI Berichte 1287 (1996) 373-380

9. M. Stümpfle, A. Jameel: Eine Internet basierte Komponentenarchitektur für Fahrzeug Client- und Serversysteme. In: R. Steinmetz (ed.): Kommunikation in Verteilten Systemen (KiVS), 11. ITG/GI-Fachtagung (1999) 6 - 19

10. C. Szyperski: Component-Software. Addison-Wesley, New York (1997)

11. J. Tryggvesson, T. Mattsson, H. Heeb: JBED: Java for Real-Time Systems. Dr. Dobb's Journal (1999)

12. W.H.W. Tuttlebee: Cordless Telecommunications Worldwide. Springer-Verlag, Berlin Heidelberg New York (1997) 372-412

13. D. Wright: Broadband: Business Services, Technologies and Stratetic Impact. Artech House, Norwood(1993)

14. IEEE: Standard for a High Performance Serial Bus. IEEE Std. 1394-1995 (1996)

15. IEEE: Personal Communications. The Magazine of Nomadic Communications and Computing, vol. 4 no. 4 (1997)

16. Microsoft Corporation: Universal Plug and Play Device Architecture Reference Specification. Version 0.90 (1999)

17. OMG: CORBA 2.3.1 Specification (1999)

18. Robert Bosch GmbH: CAN Specification 2.0 (1991)

19. Sun Microsystems. Inc.: Java Beans Specification, V. 1.01 (1997)

20. Sun Microsystems. Inc.: Jini Architecture Specification, V 1.0.1 (1999)

JBSA: An Infrastructure for Seamless Mobile Systems Integration

Stefan Müller-Wilken and Winfried Lamersdorf

University of Hamburg, Vogt-Kölln-Str. 30, 22527 Hamburg, Germany,
Phone: +49-40-42883-2327 Fax: +49-40-42883-2328
{smueller,lamersd}@informatik.uni-hamburg.de,
http://vsys-www.informatik.uni-hamburg.de

Abstract. While the desire to gain full access to stationary information sources (e.g. the company´s backoffice database) when in transit is only natural, inherent design limitations such as a lack of computational power, very limited resources and closed architectures, let mobile system integration still be a difficult issue. In contrast to other approaches to the field, the "Java Border Service Architecture" introduced in this article doesn't require modifications to the mobile device´s system software or the application environment to give access existing applications from the mobile system. It features a new way of generating user interface snapshots in an XML–based description format "on the fly", translating them to a light–weight format suitable for the device and sending UI snapshots to the device in real time. This article gives an overview of the architecture and its functionality and presents an application scenario that has been implemented on top of it.

1 Introduction

The demand for seamless mobile system integration and optimal access to existing information systems has been identified in its relevance to distributed systems research several years ago. Various publications have stated arising problems (e.g. [8],[9],[17]) and several approaches on how to integrate mobile devices into existing system infrastructures have been proposed over the time (e.g. [2], [11], [13], [16]). While approaches differ from one another, most of them have in common, that they are based on modifications to the mobile device and/or require special system support on the application side. Especially due to the fact that mobile systems are very often of "closed" design and resist any modification to the device itself, such integration platforms will not suffice as an universal approach to the problem. They will rather be restricted to just a few device types open for third party modifications or extensions. In addition, it will not be acceptable for numerous application contexts to make use of specialized software libraries when realizing mobile system integration. Consequently, one does have to offer an integration platform that will not have such an impact on system design on the one hand and mobile devices to be integrated on the other.

C. Linnhoff-Popien and H.-G. Hegering (Eds.): USM 2000, LNCS 1890, pp. 164–175, 2000.

This article introduces the "Java Border Service Architecture", a flexible infrastructure to support integration of arbitrary mobile devices into distributed system environments. In contrast to other approaches to the problem, the integration platform described here is based on the introduction of an abstract format used to analyze and describe an application's user interface in real time and allows for its transformation into a concrete representation *on the fly*. As the platform uses runtime analysis rather than code modification, no changes to the application involved will be necessary. Using this technique, it is possible to support the ever increasing number of device types by just changing the set of transformation rules to apply to the abstract representation for a certain class. As the application code remains unchanged, it is also possible to integrate applications where a modification is impossible due to design aspects or because the source code is not available for modification.

The article is organized as follows: section 2 describes the principles underlying the JBSA. Section 3 gives an overview on the infrastructure itself and its core components. An example is introduced in section 4 and finally, section 5 concludes with a summary and outlook on future work.

2   Integration through Abstraction

Various approaches to the problem of finding better means to seamlessly integrate mobile systems into distributed system environments were proposed in recent years. In accordance to a taxonomy proposed by M. Satyanarayanan ([18], see also [10]), one can classify mobile system integration strategies with respect to their level of adaptivity or "application awareness" in a spectrum ranging from "laissez faire" (integration without any system support to the application) to one extreme and "application–transparent" (full integration responsibility at the underlying system with no modification to the application) to the other. Adding another dimension to this taxonomy and measuring the level of "mobile device awareness", that is, the extent of modifications necessary to the mobile device, one will get the taxonomy shown in fig. 1. Most existing integration approaches have in common that they at least partly rely on modifications to the mobile client. In some cases, a special viewer has to be installed (e.g. a VNC viewer for the "Virtual Network Computing" environment [15], etc.) to enable an interaction from the mobile device to be integrated. Other approaches are based on design time modification to the application environment and thus require changes to the application itself (e.g. UIML [1], XFDL [4], etc.). Accordingly, existing mobile device integration platforms can be assigned to quadrant I or II of the taxonomy depicted in fig. 1.

In contrast to that, one of the main aims of the integration principle underlying the JBSA is to completely avoid changes to both the mobile device and the application. Consequently, the following aspects were identified as its primary design goals. *Platform indepencency:* the integration platform is not to be restricted to certain device classes but should valid for arbitrary devices. *Device transparency:* modifications are not to be made to the mobile device but rather

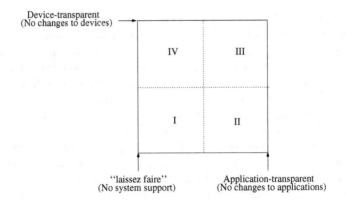

Fig. 1. A taxonomy for mobile adaption and integration strategies

to network nodes and within the infrastructure. *Application transparency:* modifications are not to be made at design time and changes to the application code are to be avoided. With respect to these goals, the integration principle can be assigned to quadrant III of fig. 1.

Separating User Interfaces

Applications can generally be subdivided into multiple layers, each one offering a certain functionality to adjacent ones. Most of the time, a *presentation layer* will be responsible for user interaction (data presentation and visualisation, interception of user commands, etc.); an *application logic* will be responsible for data creation and processing and, where applicable, a *data storage layer* is used to hold all local data the application is handling (see [14]). Application logic and presentation are commonly grouped together to coordinate all access to stored or processed application data.

The solution chosen by the JBSA is based on a runtime analysis of an application's presentation layer and its description in an abstract data representation, a specially designed XML [5] dialect. By means of a set of device–dependent transformation rules expressed in XSL [3] and processed by an XSLT processor [6], the abstract description can be transferred into a concrete format as required for a proper presentation on the target device (a technique sometimes described as "rendering" [12]). In a similar way, interaction on the device is transferred into an abstract representation, routed to the application and retranslated into events as if caused by local user interaction. All steps are performed in real time and without significant change from a user's point of view. As part of the analysis, all user interface primitives such as text fields, lists, etc., are identified at an operating system level by means of GUI object hierarchy inspection. No *semantic* analysis is performed and thus no "valence" will be added to identified elements. Type and a unique identifier of each user interface primitive is derived and registered to allow for later access to each GUI element. All results

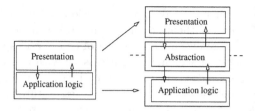

Fig. 2. An abstraction layer between presentation and application logic

of the runtime analysis are assembled and form a "snapshot" in a well defined descriptive language.

The snapshot together with a stylesheet corresponding to the target platform will then be routed to a XSLT processor. The processor in turn will translate all elements from the snapshot to a concrete representation as defined in the stylesheet. In addition to a basic transformation of user interface elements into a target language (e.g. WML), the stylesheet can contain rules on how to adapt (or even substitute) certain GUI elements to the target device where necessary[1]. New devices can be introduced at any time by providing a rule set for their respective device class and mapping each GUI element from the source platform to corresponding elements as indicated by their expressive power. The results of the transformation are finally routed through a communication adapter and to the target device itself. As part of this process, necessary adaptions to the basic communication mechanism can take place (e.g. retranslation into SMS messages, or even speech synthesis) as required by the device.

In the opposite direction, reactions on the target device will be intercepted by the communication adapter, translated into an internal representation and forwarded to an application adapter that will "replay" each event to the application itself. It is an important design feature that the application will *not* be able to distinguish between local user interaction and interaction "remote controlled" through the integration infrastructure.

3   The Java Border Service Architecture

The *Java Border Service Architecture* (JBSA) realizes a supporting framework to provide remote access to running Java applications. The JBSA can continuously inspect applications, generate "snapshot" information of their user interface in an abstract data representation and transform this abstract representation into a concrete format as required by the target platform. Generated information can be presented to the device using any transport mechanism as indicated by its communication capabilities. In addition to mere inspection, analysis, transformation and transport, the JBSA framework will aid the mobile user in locating

---

[1] Substitution can be necessary with WAP devices, for example, where horizontal scrolling is not possible and tables sometimes can only be displayed when remapping columns of a row to a vertical orientation.

optimal applications for her needs, provide session control for multiple application access and offer user authentication and authorization for enhanced security.

The requirement to realize a complete set of core services (e.g. RPC or event queueing) on the mobile device itself, as necessary with many other integration architectures, can be avoided when using the JBSA. As the application itself is not relocated to the mobile device but rather accessed through a remote copy of its *presentation layer* (i.e. its user interface), the only requirement arising will be to provide enough functionality to view that copy — and using the JBSA´s flexible mechanism of generating an abstract representation first, the copy can be presented in a way that will best suit the viewing environment offered by the device. No functionality has to be provided for any aspects concerning *application logic*, since all parts dealing with data manipulation as well as the application itself remain within the connected network. And as no libraries, or supporting services have to run on mobile devices, the JBSA will be a preferable solution for "closed" systems such as mobile phones, where modifications are hardly possible.

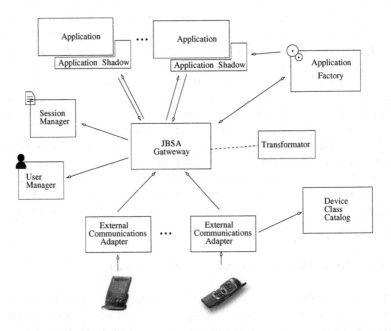

Fig. 3. The *Java Border Service Architecture* and its components

3.1   The JBSA and Its Components

A modular design was chosen for the JBSA, in which functional components are grouped into independent services. The following section will give an overview on each of the services currently realized.

External Communications Adapter. Any interaction of a mobile device with the infrastructure will take place through one of the *External Communications Adapters*. ECAs are responsible for providing a communication channel as necessary to meet the capabilities of a device class and mapping internal JBSA communication to external communication with the device. Possible examples: translation to a WAP transport protocol, translation to SMS messages, etc. ECAs will additionally provide basic session control capability to the mobile device. They will decide which ECA instance to route certain events to, when to declare a particular communication channel as interrupted, and the like.

JBSA Gateway. The JBSA gateway is responsible for routing events as intercepted by a certain *ECA* (e.g. with a button being pressed or a list item being selected) to a corresponding application. Additionally, the gateway controls the various XSLT processors used to translate user interface "snapshots" into concrete representation formats. The gateway will finally realize a higher session semantics. Supported by a session manager (see below), it will assign running applications to certain users on the one side and certain ECA instances (and hereby certain devices) on the other.

Application Shadow. *Application Shadows* are "chained" into the Java/ SWING user interface event queue mechanism of a running application and continuously monitor its state. Each application shadow is responsible for exactly one application instance and can analyze its user interface to generate "snapshots" in the "Java Swing Markup Language" (JSML), an XML–dialect specially designed to describe graphical user interfaces. Each application shadow instance offers a network interface used by the JBSA gateway to trigger snapshot creation, to fetch generated JSML documents and to "inject" user interaction back into the running application´s event queue.

Application Factory. The *Application Factory* is responsible for the management of applications registered with the JBSA infrastructure and available for remote control from mobile devices. The application factory offers necessary functionality to add applications and their respective startup parameters into a central database and it is the factory´s duty to start applications and their corresponding application shadow when triggered by the JBSA gateway.

Session Manager. The *Session Manager* realizes a session control at the application layer within the JBSA infrastructure. While *External Communications Adapters* form a *device session* that assigns a communication channel to a certain device, the *Session Manager* realizes an *application session* to assign an application context to a certain user. The *Session Manager* is responsible for temporary suspension of a running session, e.g. when changing the device used to access the application, and its subsequent reactivation after the user has reconnected to the infrastructure at a later moment.

User Manager. The *User Manager* serves to personalize the JBSA infrastructure. The User Manager organizes the user accounts known to the system and is responsible for user authentication issues. In conjunction with the Session Manager described above, the User Manager serves to provide unique reference keys for running application sessions as required to identify applications started by a certain user and for a certain communication channel. In addition to that, the User Manager will be used within the JBSA to store all user–specific information such as lately used applications, preferences, etc.

Device Class Catalog. The *Device Class Catalog* (DCC) realizes a type management system for all device classes known to the JBSA infrastructure. For each device class, the DCC holds a description on its unique characteristics and the stylesheet necessary to create contents to be displayed by a device of that class. Relations between arbitrary device classes can be stored in nets and will be utilized whenever a stylesheet for a certain device class could not be found but similarities to a known class were noticed. The DCC is used by both ECAs and XSLT processors to find optimum stylesheets for devices they are generating output for.

3.2   Functionality of the JBSA

This section gives a detailed description of a typical access cycle between application and a mobile device integrated through the JBSA. Going through the various steps that take place as part of the cycle, participating components of the infrastructure are identified in their responsibilities and illustrated in their interaction with other components.

Making Contact — Step 1

 - The device accesses an external communication adapter through a suitable access point (e.g. an HTTP–address or a dialup phone line). The ECA sends a request to the Device Class Catalog to determine the class the target device belongs, initializes a channel to the JBSA gateway and stores both in a freshly generated device session.
 - In a second substep, the ECA sends a request to the JBSA gateway to create an application session for the device session generated in the previous step.

Initialization of an Application Session — Step 2

 - The JBSA gateway creates a login dialog, translates it to a format indicated by the device type reported from the external communcation adapter, and sends the dialog to the ECA. The ECA forwards the request to the device to query the necessary authentication information and retransmits its result back to the gateway for further processing.

- The gateway sends a call to the user manager to check the validity of the user identity. As part of a positive response the user manager will send all information relevant to the starting phase (e.g. the user's default application, personal default parameters for the device class, etc.) back to the JBSA gateway.
- The gateway makes a call to the session manager to check for the availability of application sessions suspended on behalf of the user. The session manager will look through its local database and report all application sessions carrying th users identifier back to the JBSA gateway.
- If suspended sessions belonging to the user could be identified, the JBSA gateway will generate an appropriate selection dialog, asking the user if to resume, cancel a suspended session or create a new session. The dialog data will be sent to the ECA and on to the target device and the user choice back to the gateway.
- If no session belonging to the user could be identified or if the user chose not to pick up an existing one, the identifier for the newly created application session in combination with the device session identifier reported from the ECA in step one will be registered at the session manager.

Starting the Application — Step 3. Now, with a session between the target device and the Border Service Architecture instantiated, the application has to be started.

- The JBSA gateway sends the factory–identifier of the default application assigned to the user profile, the device class or the application scenario together with a unique startup identifier to the Application Factory.
- The Application Factory scans its database for the factory–identifier coming from the gateway to find the application path and startup parameters registered with it. Both, together with a unique startup identifier, are forwared to a new Application Shadow which the factory has initialized for the application session.
- The Application Shadow starts the selected application within its runtime environment, "hooks" up with the application's event queue and initializes a communication channel to allow for further access through the JBSA gateway. Information about this channel together with the startup identifier is sent back to the JBSA gateway.
- The JBSA gateway uses the startup identifier reported back by the freshly created Application Shadow togeher with the Shadows's communication channel to assign the latter to the application session as generated in step two.

Using the Application — Step 4. As the application is running and the Application Shadow is ready to generate user interface snapshots in JSML, the actual interaction between target device and application instance sets in.

- After registering the application as part of the application session with the Session Manager, a request for a first user interface status is sent from the JBSA gateway to the Application Shadow. To accomplish this, a connection between the gateway and the Shadow registered with the application session is opened and a JSML snapshot is fetched from it.
- The JSML snapshot is sent to the XSLT processor initialized with the stylesheet identified by the Device Class Catalog for the target device. The processor translates it into an appropriate representation and hands it back to the gateway.
- The user interface snapshot, now in a representation suitable for a presentation on the target device is sent forward to the External Communication Adapter responsible for the target device.
- The user interface snapshot is presented to the user through some browser installed on the device. The user can begin her interaction with the application, e.g click a button of edit a text field.
- The browser reports any user interaction back to the External Communication Adapter. Considering the channel the interaction was reported through (e.g. the phone line used for the interaction), the ECA assigns the incoming interaction to a certain device session. The ECA transforms the reported interaction event (e.g. pressing a button) into a form useable within the JBSA infrastructure, combines it with the device session identifier and forwards both to the JBSA gateway.
- Using the device session identifier, the JBSA gateway identifies the corresponding application session. It extracts the Application Shadow assigned to the session from the session record and forwards the event on to the Application Shadow.
- The Application Shadow generates valid Java SWING events from the request coming from the JBSA gateway and "injects" them into the application's event queue for further processing. The application can not tell the difference of an event generated by the Shadow to an event caused by local interaction.
- The application reacts to the event as it would have done to a local user interaction and changes its user interface according to changed status within its application logic.
- After a short break (but still not noticeable to the user), the whole process is reinitiated by the JBSA gateway and starts with another update request to the Application Shadow.

4   Application Example

An office communication context was chosen as one application scenario for the JBSA[2]. In this scenario, field workers need access to a central group calendar held at a company's back office. Modifications should be possible from *any* location using a desktop PC as well as a PDAs or a mobile phone. The application

---

[2] The application is limited in its functionality and thus meant as an example and not a real time management software.

Termin Manager	▼ 🗗 ⊠

Anlegen	Bearbeiten	Löschen

Leitung	Ort	Betreff	Beginn	Ende
Stefan Müller-W...	Raum F530	Projektmeeting ...	20.01.2000 09:15	20.01.2000 11:45
Winfried Lamers...	Mitarbeiterbespr...	Raum F530	20.01.2000 04:00	20.01.2000 05:15
Jan Hauberg	MAZ Harburg	Projektdemo	21.01.2000 11:30	20.01.2000 01:00

Filters: ● Alle   ○ Heute   ○ Diese Woche   ○   von: 20.01.2000   bis: 20.01.2000

Fig. 4. A simple datebook application

offers basic functionality such as adding, modifying or removing dates (see fig. 4). It is implemented in a client/server design with a front end Java/SWING user interface accessing a backend database via RMI. Multiple users interfaces can access a single backend at a time and changes to the database will be propagated to all registered user interfaces at once. The application backend will serialize incoming requests and keep the database consistent when processing concurrent tasks. Stylesheets were designed for various target device classes such

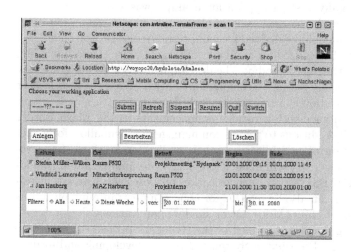
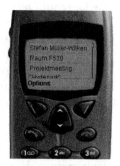

Fig. 5. The datebook shown in different target representation formats

as 3Com PDAs, WAP phones (espec. Nokia 7110, Ericsson R380) and HTML browsers (Netscape Communicator, Internet Explorer). Fig. 5 shows access to the application from a WAP phone and a terminal using Netscape Communicatior. Even though actual *handling* differs sometimes significantly between two device classes (and even among various WAP phones), all application functionality remains available for remote access. Changing from one device to another is possible anytime and without losses at runtime using the JBSA. Support for new device classes can be integrated even with applications being actively accessed.

5 Conclusions and Future Work

Integrating mobile devices into existing system infrastructures represents one important issue in distributed systems research today. Various approaches exist but most of them show the drawback of being based on modifications to the mobile device, the application to be accessed while on transit, or both.

This article proposes a new approach to the field based on the introduction of an abstract layer between presentation layer and application logic of an application. By means of a mechanism of generating user interface "snapshots" on the fly and transforming generated descriptions through a flexible stylesheet processor, all integration related problems can be hidden away from both the application and the target device. This is of particular importance for mobile devices, where a "closed" design renders modifications on the device itself hardly possible most of the times, and resource limitations make porting of application clients a difficult task even where third party code *can* be installed on the device (e.g. for Java applications to be used from an average PDA). The principles described were implemented in the "Java Border Service Architecture", a modular integration framework for mobile devices. This article gave an overview on the architecture, its main components and their functionality. The actual operation was described and, finally, a short application example was given.

Early experiences with the prototype implementation were very promising, and a proof–of–concept could be derived from our tests. Access to Java client/server applications could be realized for a number of target device classes including first WAP phones on the market today. The development cycle to integrate new devices could be drastically reduced as changes are only necessary to a stylesheet while device and application can remain untouched.

We are currently implementing various enhancements to the "Java Border Service Architecture". Additions to the session management will allow for a user transparent reactivation of multiple suspended application sessions. Improvements to the user management will make it possible to use unique mobile device identifiers (such as GSM SIMs) for authentication purposes. And we are invesigating if JBSA support can also be realized for non-Java programming platforms such as native Win32 or Unix (Motif, Qt or similar) applications.

The JBSA is being developed as part of the Hydepark project, in which the University of Hamburg's Distributed Systems Group is developing and evaluating new methods on how to integrate mobile devices into distributed system infrastructures. Another subproject within the Hydepark context is currently working on ways to integrate non–Java devices into SUN´s "Java Intelligent Network Infrastructure" (JINI) [7] using the JBSA. JINI itself features an approach comparable to JBSA with so called "service proxies" acting as loosely coupled front end interfaces to corresponding service instances. The JINI framework is thoroughly done in Java and consequently not accessible from non–Java devices at this time. A combination with the JBSA will eliminate this drawback and give access to JINI–enabled services from any location and with arbitrary devices, making JINI even more appealing as a platform for distributed systems design.

References

1. ABRAMS, M., PHANOURIOU, C., BATONGBACAL, A., WILLIAMS, S., AND SHUSTER, J. UIML: An Appliance Independant XML User Interface Language. In *Proc. 8th International World Wide Web Conference* (Toronto, Canada, May 1999).
2. ADAMS, N., GOLD, R., SCHILIT, W., TSO, M., AND WANT, R. An infrared network for mobile computers. In *Proc. of USENIX Symposium on Mobile Location-Independant Computing* (Cambridge, Mass., 1993), pp. 41–52.
3. ADLER, S., BERGLUND, A., CARUSO, J., DEACH, S., GROSSO, P., GUTENTAG, E., MILOWSKI, A., PARNELL, S., RICHMAN, J., AND ZILLES, S. Extensible Stylesheet Language (XSL) 1.0. Tech. Rep. WD-xsl-20000327, W3C, March 2000.
4. BOYER, J., BRAY, T., AND GORDON, M. Extensible Forms Description Language (XFDL) 4.0. Draft Specification NOTE-XFDL-19980902, W3C, September 1998.
5. BRAY, T., PAOLI, J., AND SPERBERG-MCQUEEN, C. Extensible Markup Language (XML) 1.0. W3C Recommendation REC-xml-19980210, W3C, Feb 1998.
6. CLARK, J. XSL Transformations (XSLT) 1.0. W3C Recommendation REC-xslt-19991116, W3C, November 1999.
7. EDWARDS, W. K. *Core JINI*. The SUN Microsystems Press Java Series. Prentice Hall PTR, Upper Saddle River, NJ, 1999.
8. FORMAN, G., AND ZAHORJAN, J. The challenges of mobile computing. *IEEE Computer* (April 1994), pp. 39–47.
9. IMIELINSKY, T., AND KORTH, H. F., Eds. *Mobile Computing*. Kluwer International Series in Engineering and Computer Science. Kluwer Academic Publishers, 1996.
10. JING, J., HELAL, S., AND ELMAGARMID, A. Client–server computing in mobile environments. *ACM Transactions On Database Systems* (Prelim.Version, 1999).
11. JOSHI, A., WEERAWARANA, S., DRASHANSKY, T., AND HOUSTIS, E. Sciencepad: An intelligent electronic notepad for ubiquitous scientific computing. In *Proc.International Conference on Intelligent Information Management Systems (IASTED'95)* (Washington, USA, December 1995), Purdue University, Dept. Of Computer Science.
12. LEI, H., BLOUNT, M., AND TAIT, C. DataX: an approach to ubiquitous database access. In *Proc. 2nd IEEE Workshop on Mobile Computing Systems and Applications, WMCSA'99* (New Orleans, USA, Feb. 1999).
13. MCDIRMID, S. A distributed virtual machine architecture for mobile java applications. *Handheld Systems 6*, 5 (Sep./Oct. 1998), 37–42.
14. MURER, S., SCHNORF, P., GAMMA, E., AND WEINAND, A. *Eine realistische Applikationsarchitektur f r Multi-Tier Java-basierte Clients in der Praxis.* in: Java in der Praxis. d.Punkt Verlag, Heidelberg, Germany, 1998, ch. 9.
15. RICHARDSON, T., STAFFORD-FRASER, Q., WOOD, K. R., AND HOPPER, A. Virtual network computing. *IEEE Internet Computin 2*, 1 (Jan/Feb 1998), 33–38.
16. ROMAN, M., SINGHAI, A., CARVALHO, D., HESS, C., AND CAMPBELL, R. H. Integrating PDAs into distributed systems: 2k and PalmORB. In *Handheld and Ubiquitous Computing – First International Symposium on Handheld and Ubiquitous Computing (HUC 99)* (Heidelberg, Germany, September 1999), H.-W. Gellersen, Ed., no. 1707 in Lecture Notes in Computer Science, Springer–Verlag.
17. SATYANARAYANAN, M. Fundamental challenges in mobile computing. In *Proc. 14th ACM SIGACT-SIGOPS Symposium on Principles of Distributed Computing (PODC)* (Ottawa, Canada, August 1995), ACM.
18. SATYANARAYANAN, M. Mobile information access. *IEEE Personal Communications 3*, 1 (February 1996).

Mobtel - A Mobile Distributed Telemedical System for Application in the Neuropsychological Therapy

Hendrik Schulze and Klaus Irmscher

Leipzig University, Institute of Computer Science
Chair of Computer Networks and Distributed Systems
Augustusplatz 10-11, D-04109 Leipzig, Germany
{hendrik,irmscher}@informatik.uni-leipzig.de

Abstract. To support patients with brain disturbances the mobile distributed care system named Mobtel is designed, implemented and tested in the daycare clinic for cognitive neurology at Leipzig University. The distributed care system is based on a platform independent implementation using Corba technologies. The mobile device, a palmtop computer, communicates with the stationary care system via bidirectional cellular radio connection. To allow disabled persons the use of the mobile device, an user interface suitable for the patient needs with an integrated emergency call is developed. The base system was developed under the aspect of unreliable connections to the mobile devices. This paper describes the design and function of the system as well as the application conditions in the practical care for patients.

Keywords
mobile distributed computing, Corba, cellular radio networks, palmtop computer, telemedicine, telerehabilitation

1 Introduction

Modern information and communication technologies offer efficient conditions for complex applications in medicine and psychology combining computer techniques with psychological methods, thus allowing telemedical care in the treatment of patients.

This paper describes the design, implementation and use of a distributed care system based on Corba/Java, which uses mobile palmtop computer to support head injured persons in solving real life tasks, by reminding them of essential facts and dates. It is the first time in clinical neuropsychology a bidirectional communication to mobile patient devices via radio telephone connections is used. So it is possible to observe the patients' actions and, if necessary, to react immediately. Experiments with commercial uni-directional pagers showed; the use of paging devices for telerehabilitation purposes is suggestive but the backward channel to receive confirmations about the patient actions is absolute necessary for professional treatment of memory disturbed persons[1].

C. Linnhoff-Popien and H.-G. Hegering (Eds.): USM 2000, LNCS 1890, pp. 176–187, 2000.

Memory disturbances are a frequent outcome of brain damages. Maintenance or enhancement of the patients' life quality often requires an enormous effort of caregivers or family members. We claim, that the use of bidirectional pagers should be superior to conventional cognitive prosthesis. Our device enables the therapist to supervise and manage the actions of brain damaged persons even outside the clinical setting thereby being assisted by the patients' family members.

From the economical point of view time and costs of treatment could be reduced. The patient on the other hand gets an enhancement of autonomy and quality of life. The object-oriented architecture of our care system allows the realization of an extensible, scalable and fault tolerant system. Using generic control and data structures ensures that the system is applicable to a broad class of operation scenarios without any adaptions at source code level. Corba as middleware platform guarantees efficient software development on heterogenous hardware without using proprietary software and allows an easy extension of the system, by adding new server objects or user interfaces for different therapists as well as for family members, which can support the patient.

The patients are furnished with a specific palmtop computer. Because of energy reasons the palmtop is connected only some minutes a day with the care system. The other time it has to work autonomously, but can call the base system in case of emergency every time.

The user interface is adapted to the patients' restricted abilities. To realize an optimal adaption to the patients' needs and to enable an autonomous work of the palmtop a special script oriented specification language MML (Mobtel Markup Language) and a transfer protocol MTP (Mobtel Transfer Protocol) are developed. Besides the development of the technical equipment neuropsychological methods for telemedical care of brain injured patients are developed and evaluated at the daycare clinic of the Leipzig University.

It is suggestive to consider the actual position of the patient, integrating a GPS-module in the palmtop or using information about the current mobile phone cell of the mobile device[1]. With this information the success or failure of patients' actions could be supervised much more effective. But because of the ambiguous legal position in Germany we implemented our system consciously without such features.

To realize this mobile care system the interdisciplinary project Mobtel[2] was founded. The Mobtel project is a cooperation of different partners at Leipzig University (Department of Computer Science / Chair of Computer Networks and Distributed Systems and the daycare clinic for cognitive neurology) together with Max-Planck-Institute of Neuropsychological Research at Leipzig and the RBM electronic-automation GmbH, sponsored by Saxon Ministry of Knowledge and Culture and by Saxon Ministry of Economy and Work.

---

[1] In Germany this service will probably be available summer 2000

2   Architecture

2.1   Requirements of a Mobile Care System

The application of modern information and communication technologies in the rehabilitation of patients with neuropsychological deficits has to take into account the special needs of this group. Memory disturbances are besides attention deficits one of the most common sequels of brain damages. So called prospective memory tasks[2] are very important for the patients' functioning in everyday life. To compensate these deficits external memory aids like calendars or memory books have been used. However, the use of external aids has often failed due to several difficulties inherent in patients' functional deficits[3]. Modern electronic hand-held computer or organizers on the other hand are too complex in design and handling, so the patients are not able to learn the use of such an external electronic device.

Therefore, there is a strong need for an interactive external memory aid which improves the patients' life quality by providing active support in situations where normal function is impaired by disturbed memory or executive functions. Our care system enables the caregiver to survey the activities of a patient so additional support can be provided, if necessary. The patient on the other hand has the opportunity to call for help whenever he doesn't succeed in managing a situation on his own. This bidirectional data exchange is basis of the relatively young research area of telerehabilitation[3].

In this way, the combination of neuropsychological interventions and telematic methods leads to synergetic effects allowing a more effective and better treatment of patients with cognitive deficits.

Main focus of the Mobtel project is the development of a distributed heterogenous system which considers especially the needs of the brain disturbed patients, the unreliability of mobile communication, the limited resources[4] of the mobile device and a heterogenous care region.

So, important parts of the Mobtel project are the development of mobile patient devices adapted to the restricted abilities of the patients, the specification of a language which enables the patient device to work autonomously. Furthermore, it is important to implement a base system, providing the basic services for the care system in the fixed network, which can handle the unreliable connections to the palmtop, which is extensible to new neuropsychological methods, scalable and fault tolerant. Last but not least, it is necessary to create user interfaces for different caregiver classes. Except the mobile device, the system should work on different operation systems to use existing hardware.

---

[2] e.g. the execution of delayed intentions in the future

[3] e.g. the patient may forget to write down an appointment or to look into his/her diary at the right time

[4] especially power supply and communication bandwidth

2.2   System Overview

The complete Mobtel system can be classified into 3 levels. All the different user interfaces can be merged to the user interface level. The base system level contains the whole business logic to manage the system. Last level is the mobile level with the mobile patient devices.

The major requirement, we had to consider during the development of the Mobtel architecture, was the bidirectional communication between the therapist and the patient using mobile telephone technologies. So we had to take into account that there is no 100% reliability to establish a connection every time the system has to communicate. This has two consequences. The mobile patient device has to work independently from the base system and the base system needs a pager proxy object (pager object) for every pager, which stores all necessary information for the pager. During every communication the pager object reads the logfile of the pager and updates its internal state.

Since existing markup and scripting languages like HTML/JavaScript or WML (Wireless Markup Language) and WMLScript [8] [9] are not applicable[5] to our system because they are either too complex or too simple, we developed a special markup language (MML - Mobtel Markup Language), which enables a partial autonomy for the pager, but is not too complex for mobile bandwidths and a simple transfer protocol (MTP - Mobtel Transfer Protocol) on top of TCP, which considers the special features of our architecture.

Hence, the major target of Mobtel is to help patients to solve real live problems, the pager has to display the information that patient needs to solve these tasks. It is important to show only one information at a time, to not confuse the patient. So the basic information unit we consider is the information which fits into the display of the pager. We call it a card or a screen. Analogous to WML a set of linked cards is called a deck. Every task, a patient has to solve, consists of one or more decks. At the mobile level the pager only knows decks and cards but on the base system and user interface level we only consider tasks (refer figure 1). The basic data structure to describe such a task is a graph, where all nodes are screens and the edges are the events which are expected to take place before the next node can be reached. We call such a graph taskplan. Every taskplan must be created by an administrator. But once created, we can derive a task from a taskplan and adapt it to our requirements by changing typical variables or parameters. In this way the complexity of such a taskplan is transparent to the caregiver.

For every activated task a proxy task object is created, which manages the creation of the corresponding MML-description, the transmission to the palmtop and supervises the status of the task on the palmtop by analyzing the pager logfiles. If a critical state is reached the pager object sends a message to the caregiver, using SMS, email or a simple pop-up window.

---

[5] We need a markup language which enables the mobile device to handle several information units at the same time and to switch between them due to their priority.

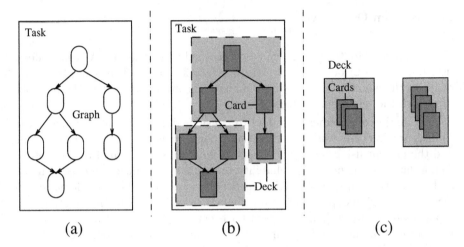

Fig. 1. The representation of a task is different at the several levels of the Mobtel architecture. (a) At user interface level a task, represented by a graph is considered. (b) The base system level transforms the task into decks and cards. (c) At mobile level only decks and cards exist.

Several groups of caregivers can use the system via an individual user interface. So we have interfaces for family members, clinical therapists and system administrators.

2.3   The Mobile Device

The pager should be usable for patients with cognitive deficits, so it must be fault tolerant and very easy to handle. The ergonomic design is very simple, we only have two hardware buttons[6]. All other interactions are performed using the touchscreen. The hardware is a microcomputer based on the Intel Strongarm processor. Input/Output device is a colored touchscreen. With the GSM module a voice or data connection can be established. The voice connection is used for emergency calls to the therapist or to make appointments with a caregiver. The data connection is used to send new tasks to the pager, to update or delete tasks and to receive logfiles from the pager.

Operating system for the pager is Windows CE. On top of the Windows API the pager system software manages and displays the different decks. The problem is that all decks compete for the display. So, the palmtop's system software also has to decide which card is to be seen at a time. This can be handled by using priorities for the decks. The priorities of a deck can change from card to card. To avoid a confusion of the patient, if one deck vanishes from the display and the context changes we lock the display for a deck for a short time (refer figure 2). If a visible card is changed due to an user action or system event the following

---

[6] one button to do an emergency call and one to raise a fixed task for orientation purposes

card will be shown for some time, even if another deck has a higher priority. The locking time can be changed in the MML code of the deck.

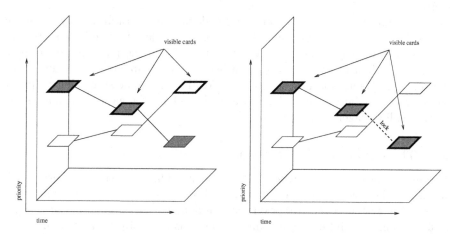

Fig. 2. If a task changes it actual card and decreases its priority a task with a higher priority can get assigned the screen (left). This context change can be prevented by locking the screen for a dedicated time (right).

Major problem in the development of the patient palmtop is the standby time of the device. To ensure a standby time of 12 or more hours the palmtop can use its energy consumptive GSM module only some minutes a day. That's why every communication will be established by the palmtop. If the base system requests a communication to the palmtop a message will be sent using the Short Message Service (SMS) of the cellular telephone provider. The palmtop establishes frequently a connection to the cellular telephone net[7]. If a short-message arrives, requesting a connection, or other reasons[8] for connecting the base system exist the palmtop connects to the base system and establishes a TCP/IP connection using PPP.

2.4   The Base System

Two major requirements influencing the architecture of the base system are the integration of existing hardware[9] and a software technology, which allows a fast and efficient development process. Furthermore, the system must be scalable and extendable to future needs. We chose Corba as middleware and Java as programming language because with this two technologies it is possible to realize a system fulfilling these requirements. So, the base system can be described as a

---

[7] every 30 - 60 minutes

[8] Reasons for connecting the base system could be a critical state of a task, low power or a elapsed interval without communication.

[9] Especially existing workstations in the clinics and private personal computers of patients' family members has to be integrated as terminal.

set of Corba objects distributed to several computers. To store data an object-oriented database is used, which works together with the persistence facilities of Corba.

The connection to the mobile patient devices are established by a special server (pager gateway). This gateway is a Corba object for the base system as well as a socket based server for the palmtop. When the palmtop connects to the gateway, it asks the gateway for a list of new or updated decks and loads down all MML files for these decks. Such MML files can be stored by the pager gateway or they are created dynamically. Therefore, the gateway connects the corresponding pager proxy object.

2.5   The Graphical User Interfaces

The user interfaces are designed as thin clients. This approach has several advantages. The business logic is implemented only once a time in the middle tier, at the base system level. Adaptions can be done without changing the user interfaces. The user interfaces are implemented as Java objects and connect the base system using its Corba interfaces, but if it is necessary other user interface types as Java applets or a web interface using servlets, Java server pages or CGI scripts can be easily implemented.

For different classes of caregivers different user interfaces exists. At the moment there are interfaces for the clinical therapist, family members of the patient and an systemadministrator interface.

3   Realization of the Base System

3.1   The Distributed Model

In general, the implementation of the base system is based on the idea that each real world entity (e.g. patients, mobile devices, tasks) is represented by a proxy object in the base system. These objects are Corba objects and they communicate with each other using their interfaces. Every object is responsible for its real world entity. Additionally, some management objects and Corba services coordinate and simplify the cooperation of the object world. This approach has several advantages. Using UML[10] it is quite easy to switch from the analysis of the system's requirements to the system design and to realize a rapid implementation. Such a modularized model can be easily extended or adapted to future requirements. Using a large number of Corba objects, they can be distributed to several computers to spread the work load and increase the throughput of the base system. With the capabilities of the Portable Object Adapter (POA)[11][7] it is possible to realize a dynamic load balancing over all involved computers. A separation of critical objects (e.g. pager gateway or object database) increases stability of the whole system.

---

[10] Unified Modeling Language

[11] The Portable Object Adapter is specified in the Corba 2.3 specification. First commercial implementations are available since December 1999.

3.2   Main Components of the Architecture

In figure 3 a simplified UML class diagram shows the major objects and their interfaces.

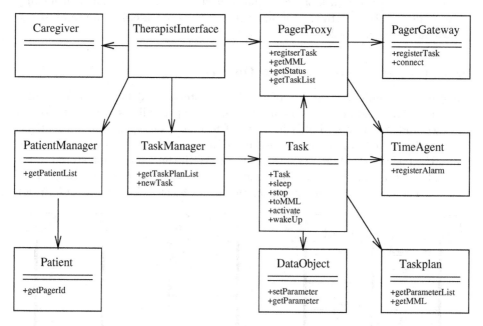

Fig. 3. The relations between the major objects of the base system as UML class diagram.

Pager Object

Every pager object is responsible for one mobile patient device and manages the state of this device. The pager object handles every communication with the palmtop. Since the mobile device is mostly disconnected the pager object stores the newest known state of the palmtop. On the other side, the pager object manages all assigned tasks. So the pager object recognizes two contradictory tasks and refuses one of them or reorganizes the scheduling of the tasks.

Task

The tasks the patients have to solve are represented by task objects. A generic data object and a taskplan object is assigned to every task object. With the data object and the taskplan the task object can create the MML description of itself. The MML description of the task will be commited to the pager object and registered at the pager gateway. If a mobile device connects to the pager gateway, the pager gateway requests all registered MML files from the pager object and transmit them to the palmtop.

At the beginning of every communication between the pager gateway and the mobile device the logfile of the palmtop is transmitted. The logfile entries are evaluated by the pager object, which transmits them to the corresponding task object. Here the task object updates its state. If a task is in a critical state, a message will be sent to the therapist. Using the user interface, a therapist can track the state of a task.

3.3   Cooperation of the Server Objects

A typical scenario for the use of the base system could be the creation of a new task for a patient (refer figure 4). The therapist will use the therapist interface and selects a taskplan in a list of available tasksplans for the patient. The taskmanager creates a new instance of a task object. The task object attaches the taskplan and creates a data object. With the information stored in the taskplan[12] the task can be adapted individually by the therapist to the patients needs. The edited data are stored in the data object[13]. The MML description

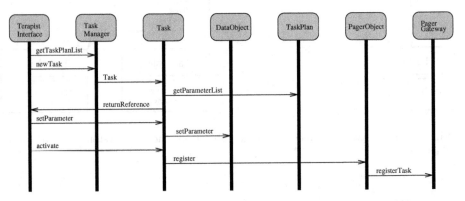

Fig. 4. Sequence diagram for the creation of a new task.

of the task can be created with the data of the data object and the taskplan. Additionally the task calculates the time the patient needs for it and tries to reserve this time at the pager. In this way a caregiver for the patient knows about the patient schedule and if two tasks collide the second task has to start at another time. If a task is registered at the pager object the pager object informs the gateway about the new available task. During the next communication between the patient's palmtop and the base system, the gateway requests the MML description from the pager object. The pager object asks the task object and the task object creates the essential files, which are uploaded to the patient device.

---

[12] Besides the task describing graph, the taskplan contains a table of adaptable data, their data type an valid range.

[13] For example the name of the medicine the patient has to take up differs from patient to patient. It is possible to reuse one taskplan for every reminder to take medicine, if only the different names are stored in the corresponding data object.

3.4   Technical Issues

Although the system can work on a single computer, experiments have shown, that the base system should contain at least 3 computers. The first is the pager gateway which manages the telephone connections. We use a Linux server for this job. Linux supports currently up to 4 ISDN cards in one computer, using the AVM C4 ISDN card with 4 base connections on every card, we can support 32 connections at time.

For stability and performance reasons the database should run exclusive on a server which is connected to the rest of the base system by a fast network[14]. To use the Corba persistence capabilities we use POET, a object oriented database for Java.

At least one computer is needed as server for the base system core. Depending from the number of patients the Corba objects could be distributed to a computer cluster. Since we are using Java 1.2 and Corba[15], we are independent from a special operating system and can support Linux, Windows and Solaris.

4   Telemedicine - Use in Neuropsychological Therapy of Patients with Memory Disturbance

The developed mobile and distributed care system (Mobtel) is tested and evaluated at the daycare clinic for cognitive neurology at Leipzig University. Testpersons are equiped with the bidirectional palmtop. The base system is located in the clinic and is connected with the mobile devices by ISDN and radio telephone connections using the ISDN/GSM gateway of a telephone provider. The stationary care system in the clinic can be extended with further care stations (e.g. home stations) about the Corba bus. Therefore the additional care stations have to establish an ordinary Internet connection.

Besides the functional tests of the care system, the acceptance of the system and especially of the mobile device is tested at patient classes with different mental disturbances. Additionally, new therapy methods or new telerehabilitation scenarios will be developed particularly for the new care system.

Every therapy task must be designed by a programmer in cooperation with the therapist[16], in a way that all probable situations are considered. If the task fails[17] the system has to establish a telephone connection between patient and caregiver to give the therapist the chance to react to the patients actions.

A typical task is the reminder to take up a certain medicine. Medicine used in the treatment of brain injured persons often has to be taken up in very strict intervals. If the patient forgets to take up this medicine the success of the therapy might be critical. Moreover, for the caregiver it is necessary to get a feedback

---

[14] e.g. switched FastEthernet

[15] Inprise VisiBroker

[16] It is planned to implement a graphical tool, which supports the therapist creating a new task, without a programmer or programming knowledge.

[17] A task fails when the patient does not react in a given time or he/her cancels a task.

about success or failure of the actual action. The simplified graph of this task is shown in figure 5.

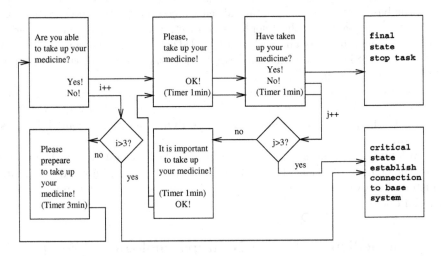

Fig. 5. The simplified graph for the task to take up a medicine.

A more complex task is to lead the patient to a meeting using public transport with a change in between. Such a task starts with a pre-alarm, informing the patient, that he has to prepare mentally and practically for the actual job. When the patient has to leave home, the palmtop will remind him of taking needed things with him, like the keys or money. While it is not important to confirm the pre-alarm, the final alarm with the reminders has to be confirmed. A really critical situation is the moment of changing the tram or the bus because there are a lot of possibilities to fail and the correct state of the patient cannot be tracked in every case. It is impossible to consider all possibilities of such a complex task. Therefore it is important to test which class of brain injured patients can complete such a difficult task.

First serious results of the care system's evaluation will be available in summer 2000. So, first results will be presented at USM2000 conference in Munich.

5   Conclusions

With this solution a telemedical system is provided, that is one of the first systems worldwide to realize telerehabilitation. The use of the bidirectional connection between caregiver and patient is a new quality in psychological therapy and basis of the development of new therapy methods.

In this paper the usability of a distributed system has been shown to realize this complex task using Corba/Java objects. Additionally, solutions to handle the restricted resources of the mobile devices are described.

In future we plan to extend the system for an application in other fields[18]. A migration of the base system to an Enterprise Java Bean (EJB) - based middleware platform is planed as well as the integration of positioning technologies. But major target is to make the system available to interested clinics and patients.

References

1. Kopp, U.A.,Thöne, A.I.T.: Kompensationsstrategien und Selbständigkeit im Alltag bei hirngeschädigten Patienten mit Gedächtniseinbußen. Zeitschrift für Neuropsychologie, 10,1999,pp. 244
2. Irmscher,K. et al.: Mobile Einsatzszenarien von Telemedizin bei der neurologischen Therapie hingeschädigter Patienten mit Gedächtnis- und Exekutivfunktionsstörungen. Research Report. Leipzig University, Dec.1999
3. Rosen, M.J.: Telerehabilitation. Neurorehabilitation,12,1999,pp.11
4. Cole, E.: Cognitive Prosthetics: an overview to a method of treatment. Neurorehabilitation,12,1999,pp.39
5. Gamma,E. et al.: Design Patterns - Elements of Reusable Object-Oriented Software. Addison Wesley, 1995
6. Orfali,R., Harkey,D.: Client/Server Programming with Java and CORBA. Willey&Sons, 1998
7. Object Management Group.: The Common Object Request Broker: Architecture and Specification. Revision 2.3 1998
8. WAP - Forum.: WAP WML: Wireless Application Protocol - Wireless Markup Language Specification Version 1.2, Nov. 1999
9. WAP - Forum.: WMLScript Specification : Wireless Application Protocol - WMLScript Language Specification Version 1.1, Nov. 1999

---

[18] an extension to other patient classes at the one side and complete new applications (e.g. the support of old people) at the other side

Middleware Architectures

Chair: John Vincente, Intel Corporation, USA

Trade-offs in a Secure Jini Service Architecture

Peer Hasselmeyer, Roger Kehr, and Marco Voß

Department of Computer Science,
Darmstadt University of Technology

{peer,mavoss}@ito.tu-darmstadt.de
kehr@informatik.tu-darmstadt.de

Abstract. Jini is an infrastructure built on top of the mobile code facilities of the Java programming language enabling clients and services to spontaneously engage in arbitrary usage scenarios. For a small home or office environment the currently available infrastructure might be adequate, but for mission-critical applications it lacks essential security properties. In the sequel we identify weak points in the Jini architecture and its protocols and propose an extension to the architecture that provides a solution to the identified security problems. We describe the design choices underlying our implementation which aims at maximum compatibility with the existing Jini specifications.

1   Introduction

The Jini connection technology [Wal99,Sun99b] is an innovative and usable technology for building reliable, fault-tolerant distributed applications. It provides an infrastructure that allows clients to find services independent of both party's location. The dynamic nature of locating and using services is one of Jini's major strengths. It is the base for the creation of plug and play devices and services. This works well in one's own home, but already in a small workgroup some problems can arise. While it is usually alright for everybody to access your printer, most people do not want everybody that can access their wireless LAN to take a peek at their latest project data.

This problem becomes even more serious if one wants to use services via an open network like the Internet. Suffice it to say that you want to be sure to give your credit card number only to your favorite online store and not somebody else. Unfortunately, this area is currently untouched by Jini. There are no provisions for data encryption or authentication beyond the abilities of Java 2 and RMI.

The research described in this paper identifies the weak points in the Jini architecture and proposes an extension to the architecture which enables secure lookup of services and trust establishment. The main security concern within the Jini architecture is the use of dynamically downloaded proxies. These provide great flexibility but present a security risk as the client does not know what the code of the proxy is doing. The client can safeguard itself against security breaches with regard to local resources like hard drives or even network connections by supplying a strict security policy. But it has no way of determining what a proxy is doing with supplied data like a credit card number.

The paper describes how this problem can be addressed by requiring all parties involved in a Jini federation (services and clients) to mutually authenticate themselves.

C. Linnhoff-Popien and H.-G. Hegering (Eds.): USM 2000, LNCS 1890, pp. 190–201, 2000.

Furthermore, we introduce the notion of *secure groups* to restrict the visibility of services registered at lookup services and to ease administration of access rights.

Section 2 briefly introduces the Jini connection technology and describes how clients find services and how they interact. Section 3 describes the security properties that we believe to be required in typical scenarios of a future Jini services world. In Section 4 we introduce our extension to the Jini architecture. Our implementation of this extension is described in Section 5. Section 6 discusses an example flow of communication. Relevant work is evaluated in Section 7 and we finally give an outlook in Section 8 on what else has to be done to enable fully secure Jini federations.

2 Component Interaction in Jini

Jini is a Java Application Programming Interface (API) that implements protocols and mechanisms for service registrations and service lookups centered around the so-called Jini *lookup service* [Sun99d]. Jini services are comprised of two components: the Jini *service provider* running on the network node or device offering a particular service, and the *service proxy*, a Java object fetched by clients from a lookup service and executed in the Java virtual machine (JVM) of a client. Both jointly implement the actual service provided. In the sequel we describe the core interactions between components in a Jini service scenario.

Service Registration. Figure 1a shows the relevant protocols for Jini service registrations. Service providers willing to offer their service to potential clients must first find nearby lookup services by means of multicast request messages [Sun99c] sent to the network. Lookup services are required to answer to these requests by opening a TCP-stream to the port and IP-address contained in the original request.

Via this callback the lookup service sends a serialized Java object that implements the well-defined Java interface *ServiceRegistrar*. This serialized object contains the state of the *lookup service proxy* and the so-called *codebase* which is essentially a URL pointing to a Web-server from where the implementation of the proxy in the form of Java bytecode can be downloaded. This bytecode is loaded into the JVM of the service provider and the serialized proxy object is instantiated. Eventually, the service provider uses the *register*-method of the lookup service proxy API to upload its own service proxy augmented with additional service description information to the lookup service.

Service Lookup. Clients obtain service proxies from the lookup service as depicted in Figure 1b. A client first performs the same steps as a service provider to obtain a lookup service proxy from a lookup service. Next, a client invokes the proxy's *lookup*-method to query the lookup service for services it is interested in.

In response to this invocation the service proxy available at the lookup service is transferred to the client. Before the service proxy is de-serialized, its implementation is downloaded to the JVM of the client by means of the codebase attached to the serialized proxy. After the client has instantiated the service proxy in its JVM it uses the proxy's API to invoke methods. It is entirely left open to the implementation of the proxy how it processes these invocations. Some invocations can be completely performed locally in

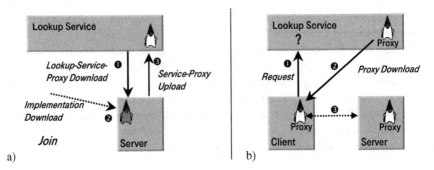

Fig. 1. Jini-Protocols: a) Discovery/Join and b) Lookup

the client's JVM. Others may result in a network communication to the service provider followed by remote computations. Part of the Jini philosophy is not requiring any particular form of communication between a service proxy and its provider. Developers are free to choose any suitable communication channel such as TCP-sockets, Java remote method invocations (RMI), CORBA object invocations, etc.

With the Jini approach, the implementation of a service can be partitioned arbitrarily between the service proxy and the service provider. This feature distinguishes Jini from other comparable service infrastructures. The mobility of Java bytecode is the enabling technology for this approach at the cost of requiring a JVM on both sides, the server and the client.

3   Requirements for Secure Component Interaction

In this section we identify several requirements for a secure component interaction in a Jini environment which have shaped the architecture of our implementation.

Mobile Code Security Issues. If we compare the Jini architecture to "traditional" client-server systems like CORBA or the world-wide Web, we can spot one major difference: in all these systems the client permanently contains the code for communicating with a server. The protocol code is part of the client and therefore part of the client's trusted computing base. If a client needs some kind of security (like authentication or integrity), it can choose to use any protocol that provides the required security properties (e.g. SSL). The Jini approach is fundamentally different. Jini clients do not implement any network protocol at all. They rather rely on the service's proxy object to perform the communication with the server. As mentioned before, proxy objects originate from some (usually untrusted) source on the network. This includes the download and execution of code from that source. Clients do not know what these objects are doing. Studies of the security risks of mobile code (e.g. [RG98]) usually focus on the protection of the execution platform against malicious actions of downloaded code. If we assume that effective protection of the platform can be achieved by the Java sandbox model and appropriate security policies [Gon98], we still have a different concern here: a client does not and cannot know what a proxy object is doing with supplied data. A security approach that is different from those of traditional client/server systems is therefore required. Because the proxy is supplied by its associated service it should know which kind of security is appropriate for its application domain. We therefore trust the proxy to enforce the correct security constraints. By doing this we do not solve the problem of mobile proxies—we shift it to the problem of how to establish trust in proxy objects and, by implication, trust in the service provider that supplied the proxy. In the sequel we describe how this can be achieved.

Proxy Integrity. An obvious thing that is required to establish trust in a proxy object is to ensure its integrity. The object should not be changed on its way from the service (via the lookup service) to the client. As said before, an object consists of the two parts state and code. Both parts' integrity must be ensured. It is therefore necessary to digitally sign the code as well as the state. As we do not want anybody to observe the in-traffic service descriptions, the connections between the lookup service and its clients[1] should be encrypted.

Lookup Service Interaction. Even if we have encrypted communication and authentic objects, we still have to trust the lookup service. Even if a lookup service provides us with untampered objects, it might do so in an unfair manner. Instead of sending us the cheapest service (or whichever we are interested in), it might always only supply its preferred service provider. From a service provider's view even the knowledge of a service's existence might be considered a valuable asset that must be protected. For example, a network operator might have a Jini network management service. The knowledge of its existence might be interesting to competitors. A competitor could find out about that service by simply starting its own lookup service waiting for the service to register itself. It is therefore necessary for a client to trust the lookup service it is talking to. This can be achieved by requiring the lookup service to authenticate itself to its clients.

Now that we trust the infrastructure, it is still possible to have malicious services registered with secure lookup services. We therefore require services to authenticate themselves to the lookup service. Likewise, clients too are required to authenticate themselves to the lookup service. This is an obvious requirement as it is important to make sure that only authorized people access somebody's bank account.

An alternative for the indirect authentication (via the lookup service) would be to shift the authentication to a mutual authentication procedure between each service and client directly. Besides the disadvantage of needing authentication methods in every service interface, trust could only be established *after* the proxy has been downloaded to the client. This is too late as unknown code (e.g. the constructor or the method for performing authentication) is already executed at the client.

Administrative Issues. So far, the described requirements allow us to have trusted proxies. No distinction was made between different services: they all have the same security level. But usually different levels of security are desired. An example are administrators that have access rights for more services than ordinary users. We therefore partitioned

---

[1] From the lookup service's point of view, any communication partner, whether it is an actual Jini service or client, is considered a client.

the services by introducing *secure groups*. Services that have the same access restrictions are put together to form a secure group. Every service registration is associated with one secure group. Clients need appropriate access rights to view and access members of a group. The same holds for services: to prevent them from registering in arbitrary groups, they too must have the appropriate access rights. We therefore introduced two different access rights, namely *register* and *lookup*, which are currently sufficient to model access rights to groups.

Summary. To wrap up this section, we summarize the requirements that our secure Jini architecture has to fulfill:

- signed proxy objects (code and state),
- encrypted communication with lookup services,
- authentication of all participants (lookup services, services, and clients),
- access control to services, and
- limited visibility of service descriptions.

These requirements have guided the development of a secure Jini service architecture.

4   Architecture

Our design was influenced by two objectives. First of all we wanted to preserve compatibility with the existing Jini specifications: legacy clients and services should run without changes. Secondly, it was our aim to keep as much as possible of the dynamic behavior of a Jini federation, although this conflicts with security aspects as we will show later.

Figure 2 illustrates the Jini architecture with our security extensions: additional components are a *certification authority* (CA) and a *capability manager* (CM). Certificates provide for authentication of all participants. Capabilities are used for access control in the lookup service. The capability manager administers the rights for each user.

The only usable solution for the problem of opaque proxies is trust. In a dynamic environment with thousands of services it is impossible for an entity to make a decision about the trustworthiness of each service on its own. In our architecture this process is therefore delegated to the combination of lookup service and capability manager. They are part of the trusted computing base of our architecture.

Secure transfer of the proxy is guaranteed by adding a digital signature to the response message (callback) of the lookup service in the discovery protocol. Service descriptions are kept private by an encrypted connection between lookup service proxy and lookup service.

We have introduced the concept of secure groups in the lookup service. Every access to these groups is controlled by capabilities. A lookup service client must present appropriate capabilities for both registering and looking up services. Through this it is possible to restrict the registration in groups with high security to known services which meet the requirements and to control to whom the service descriptions are passed. Services in other groups are invisible.

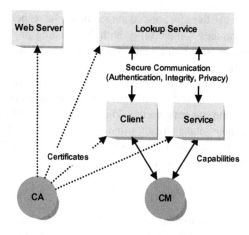

Fig. 2. Secure Jini Architecture

4.1 Certification Authority

Certificates provide for authentication of all participants. They are signed by a well-known certification authority, whose public key is assumed to be known by everyone. A certificate binds an entity's public key to its distinguished name. For authentication an entity proves that it possesses the corresponding private key using a challenge response protocol.

There are four categories of certificates and keys issued by the CA:

1. for signing system classes and LUS proxy code,
2. for the capability manager used to authenticate and sign capabilities,
3. for lookup services used to authenticate and sign LUS proxies, and
4. for clients and services used for authentication.

A signature is rejected if the signer's certificate does not belong to the appropriate category. This ensures that an entity cannot simulate another component without proper authorization. The use of certificates and the administration of the capabilities require some initial configuration. The lookup service additionally uses the capability manager's key to verify the presented capabilities. These administrative requirements obviously reduce the dynamics of a Jini federation in which otherwise arbitrary services and clients can participate without any control restrictions.

4.2 Secure Lookup Service Discovery

Before any interaction occurs, both client and service have to locate a lookup service using the discovery protocols. As a result a participant gets a proxy for the lookup service which performs the actual communication. The proxy is transferred as a serialized object which contains its codebase and its state. It is important to assure that this proxy arrives unmodified and that it is authentic. The signature for the transferred serialized object and the signer's certificate are therefore added at the end of the response message of the lookup service. This guarantees compatibility with the existing protocols because the additional data is ignored by standard clients. The signature can be used to verify the integrity and to identify the signer.

If the proxy classes are unknown, the code will be loaded from the web server indicated by the codebase in the serialized object. Again it has to be ensured that the classes arrive unchanged and are trustworthy. This can be achieved by signed classes using the standard mechanisms Java already provides. Before an entity uses the lookup service proxy it has to verify the signatures of both object and code and has to make sure that the signers are authorized by the CA.

4.3 Lookup Service

In our extended architecture the lookup service is not only the main component in the service discovery process but also the center of the trusted computing base. It has to enforce the capability-based access control mechanism and assure the privacy of the service descriptions. Therefore, the lookup service has to be authentic and the communication with it must be secure.

The lookup service permanently listens for request messages. It is therefore open for denial of service attacks. A message format which supports authentication may be a solution. In this case the lookup service would not even respond unless the request is from an authorized source. We did not evaluate this option because of our goal of compatibility. Practical tests have to show whether this is a real security problem.

4.4 Secure Groups

To simplify the administration of access control and to make a differentiation between secure and less secure services possible we have decided to organize service descriptions in groups. These groups are not to be confused with Jini's group concept for organizing lookup services. We therefore developed an orthogonal concept for the management of services. A client or service needs access rights for a secure group before it is allowed to perform any action on it. Every entity proves its authorization by an appropriate capability.

It is useful to arrange the groups in a hierarchy. An authorization for a group implies the same rights for all subgroups. By this, a number of groups can be united in a simple manner. A group is represented by its name which is denoted like a package name in Java: *group.subgroup.subsubgroup...* For example, we can have the two groups *ito.printers.deskjet* and *ito.printers.lj4000* which contain services for different printers. The right for *ito.printers* permits access to all available print services.

To maintain compatibility with the Jini specifications a special *public* group exists which can be accessed without any permission. Legacy services and clients use this group for registration or lookup.

4.5 Capabilities and the Capability Manager

A client or service proves its authorization to the lookup service through a capability object. A capability is similar to a certificate that contains an entity's name and its access rights. It is signed by a central authority called capability manager. The CM administers a list of names and the associated access rights. Upon request the CM creates a capability object and signs it with its private key. Capabilities allow for offline verification, i.e., the verification can be done even if the CM is not accessible. Like a certificate, a capability is not delegateable and can only be used by an entity which can proof that it is the mentioned subject. Hence, there is no need to protect the communication with the capability manager, although it is definitely necessary to protect the capability manager itself from unauthorized access.

We have implemented capability managers as Jini services. For this purpose a special group has been introduced in which registration is restricted to authorized CM services only, but lookup is open to all users. This is necessary for the bootstrapping process, because an entity must get its capabilities before it can access restricted services.

5   Implementation

The implementation of our security architecture is based on the source code that comes with Sun's reference implementation of Jini (version 1.0). The parts we changed are the implementation of the lookup service and the classes which handle the discovery protocols. Additionally, we have implemented a capability manager as a separate Jini service.

Sun's implementation of the lookup service is called *Reggie* (package *com.sun. jini.reggie*). It consists of two parts: the actual directory service (*RegistrarImpl*) and a proxy object (*RegistrarProxy*). Both communicate via Java's RMI mechanism. We protect the RMI message exchange by tunneling RMI traffic through the SSL protocol. An SSL socket is therefore created instead of the standard socket. SSL has the advantage that besides encrypting the communication it can also be used for authentication of participants. The freely available ITISSL [Pop99] package has been used as implementation of the SSL-API. The lookup service authenticates itself by presenting its certificate in the SSL handshake.

The certificates used by SSL are issued by a certification authority. In an experimental setup the *ca*-tool that comes with ITISSL is sufficient. In a deployment environment a commercial variant should be used. The security of the architecture highly depends on the correct use of certificates.

The functionality of the lookup service is described by the *ServiceRegistrar* interface (package *net.jini.core.lookup*). We added new *lookup* and *register* methods which take the user's capability and a group name as additional parameters. The group name indicates the desired group for registration and lookup. Access rights for this group must be implied by the presented capability. The lookup service otherwise rejects the requested action.

A capability consists of a name and a list of permissions. We use signed objects (*java.security.SignedObject*) for capabilities. A special permission class describes an entity's rights. It is similar in structure to a file permission with the group being the target and *register* or *lookup* being the possible actions. The capability manager is implemented as a Jini service and communicates with its proxy via RMI over SSL.

6   Example Scenario

In this paragraph we describe an example scenario to clarify the communication flow in our extended architecture. Our scenario consists of a service which wants to register itself in the group "secure services" and a client which performs a lookup in this group. We assume that all certificates and capabilities have already been set up and that the capability manager is registered at the LUS in the special group "capability".

Service registration:

1. **Lookup Service Discovery.** The service sends a conventional Unicast Discovery Request message and gets an extended response from the lookup service. This response contains the signature for the lookup service proxy and the signer's certificate. Before the service uses the proxy object, it checks the certificate and the signature. The proxy is rejected if the certificate is not of the appropriate category or the issuer is not a known CA. On deserialization, the code of the proxy object is loaded from a web server. It is only accepted if it has been signed by an entity that has obtained a "class signing" certificate from the CA.
2. **Secure communication/Authentication.** The lookup service proxy establishes a secure communication session between the client and the lookup service with mutual authentication. Communication is stopped if the lookup service cannot present a certificate issued by a trusted CA. The service uses its own certificate for proving its identity.
3. **Capability Manager lookup.** The service calls the LUS proxy's *lookup* method to find an instance of the capability manager. It specifies the group "capability" as parameter. This ensures that only trusted CM services, which are allowed to register in this special group, are returned.
4. **Obtaining Capabilities.** The service asks one of the CMs for its capabilities. The CM consults its database and creates an adequate capability object containing the permissions of this service. The capability is delivered inside a signed object using the CM's private key to guarantee its authenticity.
5. **Registering at the LUS.** The service calls the LUS proxy's *register* method with the desired group "secure services" and its signed capability as additional parameters. The capability is only accepted if the contained name equals the distinguished name presented during the authentication phase (see step 2). The LUS verifies the signature of the capability using the CM's public key and checks if the permission for the specified group is implied. Upon success, the lookup service adds the service description to this group, otherwise it rejects the operation.

Client side service look up: Steps 1 to 4 are the same as above.

5. **Service lookup.** The client calls the LUS proxy's *lookup* method with the group "secure services" and its signed capability as additional parameters. The LUS verifies the capability and checks if the permission for the specified group is implied. Upon success it returns all services of this group which match the given service template.
6. **Service use.** The client selects one service from the result and uses the service proxy for further interaction.

7 Related Work

There are a few research efforts that partly deal with the same area as the work described in this paper. A number of other technologies enabling dynamic service discovery exists. Among those we chose SLP and SDS and take a short look at their security features. Another effort promising to bring security properties to the Jini architecture is the RMI Security Extension.

ICEBERG Service Directory Service. The SDS [CZH+99] is the central service trading component of the ICEBERG project at UC Berkeley. Service providers use the SDS to advertise service descriptions, while clients use the SDS to query for services they are interested in. Services are described with XML [BPSM98] documents that encode different service properties, e.g., service location. SDS has been designed with security properties in mind. All security critical communication is either encrypted or authenticated. Similar to our approach capabilities are issued by a capability manager to allow service providers to register their services with an SDS server.

Service Location Protocol. SLP [VGPK97] is a service trading architecture that enables service providers to register service descriptions with a central component called *directory agent*. Although communication between SLP components is unprotected, SLP offers so-called *authentication blocks* to digitally sign messages to ensure integrity of the transmitted data. SLP does not specify how key distribution should be managed in an SLP environment.

RMI Security Extension. Sun Microsystems is currently working on an extension to RMI that is supposed to allow secure interaction with RMI-based servers including the establishment of trust in downloaded proxies. The specification [Sun99a] is currently in draft status. It allows fine-grained control of different security properties. While the extension is currently only aimed at RMI it is supposed to be possible to use the same methods and interfaces for other middleware architectures as well.

The most interesting part of the specification deals with the establishment of trust in downloaded proxies. The basic method used here is to allow only trusted code to be run. Further security properties (e.g. authentication and encryption) are then guaranteed by the trusted code. Trusted code includes dynamically generated RMI stubs. If a proxy is not an instance of a trusted class, it is asked to present another object which is trusted. The associated server is then asked if it trusts the original object. This method seems to restrict spontaneous networking to RMI-based services.

Furthermore, a few problems that we regard as essential are not addressed. First, objects are instantiated before establishing trust. Malicious code could therefore be executed in the constructor of the proxy. Secondly, the specification is aimed at RMI in general and does not address Jini in particular. Services are therefore still visible to everybody. Different security levels can only be enforced after downloading the service's proxies and depend on their enforcement by every client and server.

8   Conclusion and Future Work

With our approach we believe to have solved the most urging security problems in Jini environments. Clients can safely assume that the service proxies running in their JVM have been properly authenticated to the security infrastructure and have been shipped without loss of integrity. Service providers themselves trust the infrastructure that only clients with the correct capabilities are able to access them. This might be important in those cases where service providers are only interested in the fact that services are accessed by authorized clients only, without exactly knowing the identity of the client. We think that for many application areas the fact that the infrastructure guarantees certain security properties simplifies the development and shipment of services to a significant extent.

While we presented a solution to the problem of secure service registration and lookup, it is important to note that this covers only a part of the Jini architecture. The Jini specifications describe a number of further concepts that were not considered in our research. These concepts are leasing, distributed events, and transactions. We do not know yet what the security concerns are, not to mention how to solve possible risks.

But even in the presented architecture, a few questions are still open. We assume that there is one central CA. In a dynamic environment, a distributed architecture would probably be a more favorable solution. An overview of work in this direction can be found in [Per99].

Despite the obvious advantages of a secure service infrastructure we should not forget that it does not come for free. The drawback is the partial loss of "spontaneity" of client/service interactions which was said to be one of the main advantages of Jini. Plugging devices and services into the network, spontaneously finding these devices via the lookup service, and using them are easily done. Establishing trust relationships in such spontaneous environments seems to be a task that results in a decrease of spontaneity, since prior to actual use administrative processes (e.g. distributing keys) must take place first.

Open is the question whether the trade-off between trust and spontaneity can be avoided by additional means that take the mobility of users and devices into account. We think that mobility is likely to be a driving force for changing service environments. Further work aims at identifying properties and usage models that may facilitate key distribution and granting of capabilities in our architecture.

Acknowledgments. We would like to thank Andreas Zeidler and Prof. A. Buchmann for their valuable comments on an earlier version of this paper.

References

[BPSM98]   Tim Bray, Jean Paoli, and C. M. Sperberg-McQueen. *Extensible Markup Language XML 1.0.* W3C, February 1998. Available at http://www.w3.org/TR/1998/REC-xml-19980210.

[CZH+99]   Steven Czerwinski, Ben Y. Zhao, Todd Hodes, Anthony Joseph, and Randy Katz. An Architecture for a Secure Service Discovery Service. In *Fifth Annual International Conference on Mobile Computing and Networks (MobiCOM '99), Seattle, WA,* August 1999.

[Gon98]   Li Gong. Java Security Architecture (JDK 1.2). Technical report, Sun Microsystems Inc., October 1998.

[Per99]   R. Perlman. An Overview of PKI Trust Models. *IEEE Network*, 13(6):38–43, November 1999.

[Pop99]   A.   Popovici.   ITISSL   -   A   Java   2   Implementation   of   the   SSL   API   based   on   SSLeay/OpenSSL. `http://www-sp.iti.informatik.tu-darmstadt.de/itissl/`, 1999.

[RG98]   A. D. Rubin and D. E. Geer. Mobile Code Security. *IEEE Internet Computing*, 2(6):30–34, November 1998.

[Sun99a]   Sun Microsystems Inc. *Java Remote Method Invocation Security Extension (Early Look Draft 2)*, September 1999.

[Sun99b]   Sun Microsystems Inc. *Jini Architecure Specification – Revision 1.0.1*, November 1999.

[Sun99c]   Sun Microsystems Inc. *Jini Discovery and Join Specification – Revision 1.0.1*, November 1999.

[Sun99d]   Sun Microsystems Inc. *Jini Lookup Service Specification – Revision 1.0.1*, November 1999.

[VGPK97]   J. Veizades, E. Guttman, C. Perkins, and S. Kaplan. Service Location Protocol (SLP). Internet RFC 2165, June 1997.

[Wal99]   Jim Waldo. The Jini Architecture for Network-centric Computing. *Communications of the ACM*, 42(7):76–82, July 1999.

Loadable Smart Proxies and
Native-Code Shipping for CORBA

Rainer Koster and Thorsten Kramp

Distributed Systems Group, Dept. of Computer Science
University of Kaiserslautern, P.O. Box 3049, 67653 Kaiserslautern, Germany
{koster,kramp}@informatik.uni-kl.de

Abstract. Middleware platforms such as CORBA are widely considered as a promising technology path towards a universal service market.
For now, however, no mechanisms are offered for dynamically integrating
service-specific code (so-called *smart proxies*) at the client which is a major prerequisite for the development of generic clients that may connect to
different service implementations offering different quality-of-service guarantees. In this paper, we therefore demonstrate how support for smart
proxies can be integrated within CORBA by means of a native-code shipping service that only relies on the recent *objects-by-value* extension and
portable-interceptors proposal. The feasibility of this approach is shown
by a smart-proxy supported video service.

1   Introduction

Today middleware platforms already play an important role in distributed computing, shielding developers from the particularities of distribution and underlying communication protocols [2,9,10]. Emerging quality-of-service (QoS) requirements, however, can hardly be met while upholding the level of abstraction
provided by RPC and remote object invocations. For tasks such as continuous
media streaming, parameters such as latency and throughput must be carefully
controlled in service-specific ways. Additionally, services are deployed in diverse
environments with largely different resource availability. An ATM network with
resource reservation capabilities, for instance, requires different QoS control than
a best-effort connection via the Internet with large resource fluctuations, and
mobile computing requires different functionality than LAN-based stationary
computing.

   Due to this variety of requirements and environments, one or few protocols built into a middleware platform will prove to be insufficient. Even worse,
the middleware platform might become a stumbling block when service-specific
communication mechanisms with functionality such as bandwidth reservation,
feedback control, and compression are needed. Hence, in CORBA, for instance,
only control and management interfaces for streams are defined [7], while application developers need to implement every protocol required in matching stream
end points.

C. Linnhoff-Popien and H.-G. Hegering (Eds.): USM 2000, LNCS 1890, pp. 202–213, 2000.
© Springer-Verlag Berlin Heidelberg 2000

This particularly is a problem in view of an emerging universal service market, in which ideally a single, "generic" client should be able to connect to different instances of the same service offered from differed providers, with quality of service becoming an important means of distinction among different offers. With current platforms, however, the client has to implement all protocols of all service instances, that is, protocol independence and location transparency are lost. Furthermore, the client developer must know about the internals and low-level details of each service instance, which considerably complicates application development.

As a consequence, we have proposed *smart proxies*[1] that encapsulate any service-specific functionality required at the client side [4]. Smart proxies are loaded from the service dynamically on demand, replacing the traditional client stub while providing the same high-level service interface as if the remote server were co-located with the client. Access to QoS-supporting services then becomes as easy for the client programmer as to a conventional service; all low-level service-specific development efforts are shifted to the service developer, who implements both the server and its smart proxies using whatever protocol functionality and communications patterns are appropriate. Furthermore, transparently to the client, different implementations may be tailored for particular environments while the service interface remains constant (or at least backward compatible).

In this paper, we discuss how passing objects by value (OBV) and portable interceptors can be used to integrate the required support for smart proxies into CORBA. Particularly, a generic code-shipping service for value-type objects, instanced for C++, is presented that allows native-code implementations to be dynamically loaded. In Section 2, the notion of smart proxies is briefly introduced. Section 3 and Section 4 then show how proxy shipping can be built on OBV and how access to even native proxy code can be provided. Afterwards, in Section 5, these mechanisms are illustrated by an example application. Related work is discussed in Section 6, before Section 7 closes the paper with conclusions.

2   Smart Proxies

A *smart proxy* [4] is service-specific code at the client node providing the same interface to a possibly remote server as if the server were local. Unlike generated stubs, however, proxies can encapsulate arbitrary communication and QoS negotiation protocols and patterns for client-server interaction. Furthermore, if smart proxies can be shipped and linked dynamically, the client is free to choose an appropriate service implementation independently of the underlying protocols. During binding establishment, the server then decides which proxy is actually to be installed at the client, taking resource availability both within the client and network environment into account. Then, proxy and server may conduct further

---

[1] Note that these smart proxies differ from those offered by Orbix and TAO as discussed in Section 6.

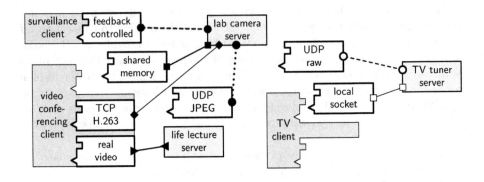

Fig. 1. Exemplified Smart Proxy Usage

QoS negotiation as needed by the application. Moreover with dynamically shipped proxies, an improved communications protocol of an upgraded service can be deployed transparently to the client.

Consider a video service with a standardised control interface including parameter settings such as resolution and frame rate. As shown in Fig. 1, a variety of service implementations may be appropriate depending on the operating environment. If some resource reservation is supported, for instance, the smart proxy can map high-level QoS parameters to low-level reservations in terms of network bandwidth; with best-effort communication only, in contrast, the smart proxy and its server may employ a feedback mechanism to achieve dynamic QoS adaptation. And if bandwidth is scarce, messages can be compressed, while for co-located clients and servers more efficient shared-memory communication might be used. All this functionality, however, is hidden from the client application which is an important prerequisite for a universal service market. Only then, service providers can develop their own sophisticated implementations according to standardised service interfaces that can be dynamically installed at and readily used by any client.

Dynamic loading of smart proxies, of course, effectively requires code shipping from the server to the client, which is significantly simplified if a virtual machine as in Java, for instance, is used for running smart proxies. Proxies then need only to be implemented for the virtual machine instead of for each possible platform in a heterogeneous environment. However, specifically for QoS-constrained services, smart proxies may need to provide good timing predictability and high computational performance and, thus, a virtual-machine approach would be too restrictive, at least for the time being. Yet for platforms that allow dynamic linking of shared libraries at run time, native-code proxies can be built as shared libraries. This approach requires a different proxy version for different client environments and possibly different client languages. Many language implementations, however, provide mechanisms to access libraries in the platform's standard object-code format such as ELF or COFF and, hence, could share the same library code. Developing proxies for each anticipated client environment, however, is still far less effort than re-implementing the same functionality without smart proxies for each client application individually; particularly, since in the latter case not only the service developer must know about the low-level details of the service but also each client developer.

Of course, code shipping in general causes security risks, and with native-code proxies protection is even more difficult than with using a virtual machine. While this problem requires future research, for now, risks may be mitigated by using smart proxies only inside security domains or loading them only with a crytographical signature from trusted servers.

3   CORBA Objects by Value

In contrast to regular, possibly remote, CORBA objects, *value-type objects* as defined in CORBA 2.3 [9] are always local and invoked without ORB mediation. Value-type objects are copied if passed as parameters to regular objects, and the specification of OBV defines how their state is to be marshalled, transmitted, and unmarshalled.

While smart proxies can be implemented as value-type objects, ideally it should be transparent to the client whether it communicates with a value-type proxy object, or directly with a server if, for instance, no appropriate proxy implementation is available or proxies just are not useful in a particular situation. This transparency, however, is not possible if we need to pass the service object as regular CORBA object declared with `interface` and the smart proxy as a `valuetype`. For this case, the OBV specification defines `abstract interface` types which cannot be instantiated but be used as base class for regular interfaces as well as for value types. If an abstract-interface type is used as a formal parameter either an IOR or a value-type object can be passed depending on the actual argument.

```
abstract interface Service {
  // service operations
};
interface Server: Service {};
valuetype Proxy supports Service {};
interface ServerFactory {
  Service bind( ... );
};
```

The IDL above shows how `abstract interface` can be utilised for a proxy-supported service. The actual server as well as the smart proxies implement an abstract service interface and either a proxy or an IOR to the server is passed at binding establishment.

OBV, however, is *not* about shipping the object code in the first place. Only as an optional feature an IOR of a `CodeBase` object might be included in the messages which can be queried for URLs of object implementations. While this extension seems to be useful for and motivated by Java only, implementations of value-type objects in other languages must be present at client and server at compile time.

The OBV extension of the CORBA object model, however, still can serve as a basis for the integration of smart proxies. If we are content with distributing proxy code at compile time, we can simply send proxies as value-type objects during binding establishment. Configuration parameters can be set by the server and are transmitted as part of the proxy state. An approach to add dynamic shipping of proxy code is discussed in the next section.

4   Native-Code Smart Proxies

In this section, we describe how C++ smart proxies can be integrated in CORBA by means of a general code-shipping service for value-type objects. This way, implementation code can be shipped as transparently to the client application as possible while the server provides some information where the proxy code can be accessed.

4.1   Run-Time Linking of Native Code

Even though most languages rely on a standard object-code format (e. g., ELF on LINUX) and most compilers provide some support for calls to system libraries, binding proxies written in a different language than the client application generally remains language-specific. In this case, wrappers may be needed to deal with different calling conventions and argument types, but could be generated automatically from the IDL. For now, we have implemented an infrastructure for one language only. We have chosen C++, because on UNIX-platforms C and C++ are commonly used and CORBA programming in plain C is somewhat more laborious.

The basic prerequisite for dynamically loading native code is the ability to link code at run time. On UNIX platforms, for example, this functionality is available by calling the dynamic-linking loader directly via a programming interface for opening a shared library file and manually resolving all symbols required. This way, pointers to C functions provided by the library can be retrieved. Accessing a C++ implementation of a proxy class is slightly more difficult, because calls to member functions require the this object pointer. Hence, we add a plain C factory function to each proxy library which then is the only symbol that needs to resolved by the linker. These factories return actual C++ objects implemented by the library for which only an abstract base interface must be available.

```
// In the library:
  typedef CORBA::ValueBase* (*generator)();
  extern "C" {
    CORBA::ValueBase* generate() {
      return new Proxy_impl;
    }
  }
```

```
// Library access:
   handle = dlopen(code,RTLD_LAZY);
   ptr = (generator)dlsym(handle,"generate");
   proxy = (*ptr)();
```

4.2 Integration with OBV

As introduced in Section 3, smart proxies should be transparent to the client. That is, an invocation such as

```
service = service_factory->bind(...);
```

could simply return an IOR to a remote service-object, or a local smart-proxy object by value. For value-type objects the ORB demarshals the object state into a newly created instance allocated by an application-provided factory. These *value-type factories* as well as the object implementation are linked to the client application; the former are registered with the ORB during start up. If no factory is registered for some value type, the ORB raises an exception. For smart proxies, this means that their implementation and an appropriate factory must be available at the client *prior to* receiving a proxy value-type object.

An explicit two-way binding process such as

```
orb->register_value_factory(id,
                service_factory->bind_factory(...));
service = service_factory->bind_service(...);
```

could make sure that both are present at the client (see Fig. 2a), yet is not transparent to the client developer.

Alternatively, instead of returning a pointer to the smart-proxy object, a generic helper object per service interface could be introduced in combination with a custom marshaler, as shown in Fig. 2b. In this case, the factory allocates a helper object, while the custom marshaler dynamically loads the required smart-proxy implementation if not already available at the client. Afterwards, the custom marshaler initialises the helper object to delegate service invocations to the actual proxy. Note that the custom marshaler, the helper object, and its factory could be automatically generated from the IDL specification. This way, code shipping becomes transparent for the client at the cost of an additional indirection for each method invocation.

This indirection can be avoided, if the invocation path is intercepted *before* the ORB invokes the value-type factory and, thus, an appropriate factory can registered just in time. While custom marshallers are called only *after* the ORB has requested a new instance from the appropriate factory, the portable-interceptors specification provides a hook for functions that are called between a reply is received by the ORB and the call of any value-type factory relevant to that reply. At that time the missing smart-proxy implementation and its factory can be dynamically loaded and registered as shown in Fig. 2c and discussed in the following section.

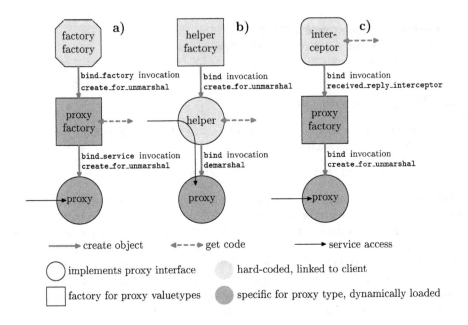

Fig. 2. Design Alternatives for Proxies with OBV

4.3   A Proxy Code-Shipping Service with Portable Interceptors

We have used the *portable interceptors* as proposed to the OMG [8] to build a
service that supports downloading of native code. While we have built this service
to enable smart proxies, it can be used to obtain implementation code of value-
type objects in general. There are three components: Two of them implement
interceptors on the client and the server side, repectively, and a third one acts
as a code repository.

As illustrated in Fig. 3, the `receive_reply` interceptor of the client checks
whether a proxy is being received. If this happens and the corresponding implementation code is not yet available, the interceptor downloads the code from
a repository possibly launched by the server on demand, dynamically links the
code with `dlopen`, creates a value-type factory, and registers it for that type of
proxy; for this, each proxy implementation must be of a different type which is
derived from the abstract service interface. Subsequently, the ORB can create the
proxy and unmarshal its state. All this is transparent to the client application
aside from initialising its shipping-service component.

Two pieces of information are needed by the interceptor to provide this functionality: the repository id of the proxy and the address of an appropriate code
repository. While the former is part of the reply, the latter somehow has to be
communicated by the server. Access to the return value and parameters, however, is only an optional feature of portable interceptors and, hence, there does
not seem to be a portable way of checking for relevant value-type arguments at

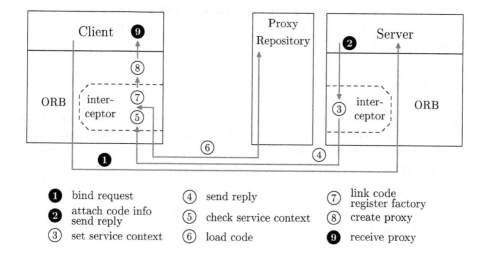

Fig. 3. Binding and Smart-Proxy Shipping

run time. Because of these problems, we send the repository id of the proxies as well as the IOR of the code repository from the server. This information is attached to the reply in a *service context* which is set by a server-side interceptor and read by its client-side correspondent.

For the server application it would be most comfortable if it could simply register code repositories for the value-type objects it may send with the code-shipping service that manages the interceptors. However, also server-side interceptors do not necessarily have access to the parameters of a reply and, thus, cannot check what value-type objects are being sent. Consequently, the server application has to explicitly provide this information for each relevant reply via an **attach** method. That is, before returning a proxy object, the servant notifies the code-shipping service of the proxy's repository id and the code repository's IOR. This information is transferred to the **send_reply** interceptor via the **PICurrent** environment and is sent from there in a service context.

```
typedef sequence<octet> ProxyCode;
interface ProxyRepository {
    ProxyCode get_code(in string RepID);
};
```

Since there is no reason to use an external protocol for the actual code shipping, code repositories are implemented as CORBA objects that encapsulate proxy libraries as a sequence of octets as shown in the IDL description above.

Alternatively to including a repository IOR, the server itself could always be queried for the code. Keeping all code at the server, however, would be less flexible than using one or more separate code repositories. A further alternative is attaching the library code itself to the reply message avoiding an additional invocation. In this case, some effort has to be put into the server side not to send large libraries multiple times and, again, only the server could store the proxy implementations.

5   Example

To demonstrate how smart proxies can be used in CORBA, we have implemented a live-video service providing access to a camera, and a video-conferencing client. Smart proxies were used to provide several communication mechanisms in addition to IIOP. The IDL of the service interface is as follows:

```
abstract interface Video {
    void start(in unsigned short frameRate);
    void stop();
    boolean getFrame(out Frame f, out Time t);
    void close();
};
```

There are five implementations of the service. All of them use CORBA remote object invocations for controlling the transmission, but transmit the actual data differently.

1. The server sends frames to a proxy via UDP. Frames must be fragmented and packet loss must be handled correctly.
2. Video frames are JPEG compressed and also sent via UDP.
3. Proxy and server communicate via TCP/IP.
4. When client and server run on the same node but in different processes, video data can be efficiently passed from server to proxy via shared memory.
5. A server without a proxy communicates directly with its clients and actually transmits the frames in the getFrame calls via IIOP.

The video-conferencing client connects to one or several service implementations and displays the frames received from the respective sources as shown in Fig. 4. In this simple scenario, a server can choose among protocols by simply using information about the network topology and the address of the client.

Servers and client are built with ORBacus 4.0b2 for C++ and run on x86 PCs with Linux 2.2 using a Hauppauge frame-grabber card with a camera as the video source. Fig. 4 displays the frame rates achieved by the respective service implementations demonstrating the different performance characteristics. For the measurements, the client only connects to one video source, either via a 10 Mb/s Ethernet or locally.

Due to the smart proxies, the implemented communication mechanisms with their diverse characteristics are uniformly accessed by the client. More elaborate smart proxies can be used to transparently handle QoS management including QoS mapping and resource reservation as we have demonstrated with the non-CORBA version of this service [4]. Note that with the various communication

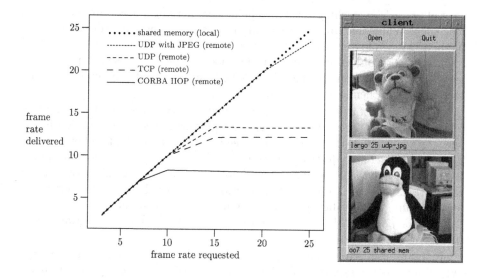

Fig. 4. Frame Rates for Various Service Implementations and Screen Dump

mechanisms being encapsulated in the smart proxies, other clients such as a video surveillance application can also transparently use the service without modification.

6   Related Work

Conceptually, smart proxies are related to fragmented or distributed objects as conceptionally proposed by Makpangou et al. [6] and applied by Globe [14, 15] and AspectIX [3], for instance. These objects are physically distributed and consist of fragments on different nodes. Distribution and inter-fragment communication are hidden from other objects and clients. Globe aims at improving scalability for distributed applications, for instance by providing replication and caching for web documents. AspextIX is extending CORBA to enhance QoS and support for mobile and reconfigurable object fragments. In contrast to the symmetric model of fragments in a distributed object, smart proxies and servers have distinct roles, still similar to the familiar roles of client and server. Hence, the use of smart proxies may be more easily adopted by programmers than the development of services as distributed objects. Moreover, smart proxies require less platform support and even can be built on a standard platform such as CORBA as shown in this paper.

Some CORBA ORBs such as Orbix [1] and TAO [11] also support a kind of smart proxies. They allow application programmers to manually replace the IDL generated stubs with "smarter" ones, which may implement additional functionality such as caching, load balancing, or merging remote invocations for efficiency. While this approach can improve performance, improvements must happen independently of the server and, hence, possibilities are limited by the regular remote object interface. In our model in contrast, smart proxies are server-specific and can particularly benefit from improved communication protocols between them and their servers.

Another way of integrating advanced functionality in proxies at compile time is used in the QuO architecture [5,16]. This platform uses QuO definition languages (QDL) in addition to an IDL for specifying QoS and adaptive behaviour of a service. From these descriptions so called delegates are generated and linked to the client like regular stubs are generated from an IDL. In this way, resource reservation, QoS monitoring, and adaptation can be easily integrated within delegates. Functionality beyond the capabilities of the code generator, however, can only be added to the QDLs as source code, exposing implementation details in the service interface.

In Sun's Jini environment [13,17] proxies also are an important concept. When accessing a service, the client receives sort of a smart proxy from the lookup service. This proxy then handles communication with the server. This mechanism allows devices and services to be dynamically added and removed from the system. Also, proxy and server can choose their own protocol for communicating with each other. The underlying Java and RMI infrastructure [12] provides advantages of security, ease of code shipping, and platform independence, but also incurs the drawbacks of restriction to one language, and the potential performance penalties and unpredictability of a virtual machine.

7   Conclusions

Loadable smart proxies can be used to encapsulate service-dependent client-side code in self-contained modules. The service developer has both ends of a connection under control and may choose the most appropriate communcation mechanisms for a particular service implementation. This way, different network protocols and QoS management functionality can be integrated. These different service implementations are hidden from the client developer, who only accesses a high-level interface defined in IDL. Hence, location transparency can be provided even for services requiring specific functionality on the client node. Moreover, this functionality is available to all client applications using a particular service and need not be re-implemented in each of them, which is an important prerequisite for the formation of a universal service market.

In this paper, we have shown how dynamic loading of native-code proxies can be implemented in CORBA. The mechanism proposed, however, is effectively a generic native-code shipping service for value-type objects. This service does not depend on proprietary ORB extensions but can be used on any CORBA platform supporting OBV and portable interceptors. The implementation of a video service has demonstrated the feasibility and utility of our approach.

Acknowledgements. We are indebted to Marcus Demker for implementing the video service in part. Moreover, we thank the anonymous reviewers for their helpful comments.

References

[1] S. Baker. *CORBA Distributed Objects Using Orbix.* Addison Wesley, 1997.
[2] Microsoft Corp. *Distributed Component Object Model Protocol,* 1998.
[3] F. Hauck, U. Becker, M. Geier, E. Meier, U. Rastofer, and M. Steckermeier. AspectIX, an aspect-oriented and CORBA-compliant ORB architecture. Technical Report TR-I4-98-08, Friedrich-Alexander-University, Erlangen-Nürnberg, September 1988.
[4] R. Koster and T. Kramp. Structuring QoS-supporting services with smart proxies. In *Proceedings of Middleware'00 (IFIP/ACM International Conference on Distributed Systems Platforms and Open Distributed Processing).* Springer Verlag, April 2000.
[5] J. P. Loyall, D. E. Bakken, R. E. Schantz, J. A. Zinky, D. A. Karr, R. Vanegas, and K. R. Anderson. QoS aspect languages and their runtime integration. In *Proceedings of the Fourth Workshop on Languages, Compilers, and Run-time Systems for Scalable Computers (LCR98),* volume 1511 of *Lecture Notes in Computer Science.* Springer Verlag, May 1998.
[6] M. Makpangou, Y. Gourhant, J.-P. Le Narzul, and M. Shapiro. Fragmented objects for distributed abstractions. In T. L. Casavant and M. Singhal, editors, *Readings in Distributed Computing Systems,* pages 170–186. IEEE Computer Society Press, July 1994.
[7] OMG. CORBA telecoms specification. `http://www.omg.org/corba/ctfull.html`, June 1998. formal/98-07-12.
[8] OMG. Portable interceptors revised submission. `http://www.omg.org/cgi-bin/doc?orbos/99-12-02`, 1999. orbos/99-12-02.
[9] OMG. *The Common Object Request Broker: Architecture and Specification (Release 2.3),* June 1999.
[10] The Open Group. *Introduction to OSF DCE 1.2.2,* November 1997.
[11] Kirthika Parameswaran. TAO release information: Smart proxies.`http://www.cs.wustl.edu/ schmidt/ACE_wrappers/TAO/docs/Smart_Proxies.html`, September 1999.
[12] Sun Microsystems. Java remote method invocation specification, October 1998.
[13] Sun Microsystems. Jini architectural overview, 1999. Technical White Paper.
[14] M. van Steen, P. Homburg, and A. S. Tanenbaum. Globe: A wide-area distributed system. *IEEE Concurrency,* pages 70–78, January-March 1999.
[15] M. van Steen, A. S. Tanenbaum, I. Kuz, and H. J. Sips. A scalable middleware solution for advanced wide-area web services. In *Proceedings of Middleware '98 (IFIP International Conference on Distributed Systems Platforms and Open Distributed Processing),* pages 37–53. Springer Verlag, September 1998.
[16] R. Vanegas, J. A. Zinky, J. P. Loyall, D. A. Karr, R. E. Schantz, and D. E. Bakken. QuO's runtime support for quality of service in distributed objects. In *Proceedings of the IFIP International Conference on Distributed Systems Platforms and Open Distributed Processing (Middleware'98).* Springer Verlag, September 1998.
[17] J. Waldo. The Jini architecture for network-centered computing. *Communications of the ACM,* 42(7):76–82, July 1999.

A Middleware Architecture for Scalable, QoS-Aware, and Self-Organizing Global Services[1]

Franz J. Hauck, Erich Meier, Ulrich Becker,
Martin Geier, Uwe Rastofer, and Martin Steckermeier

IMMD 4, Friedrich-Alexander University Erlangen-Nürnberg, Germany

AspectIX@cs.fau.de

Abstract: Globally distributed services need more than location transparency. An implementation of such a service has to scale to millions of users from all over the world. Those users may have different and varying quality-of-service requirements that have to be considered for an appropriate distribution and installation of service components. The service also has to scale to thousands of administrative domains hosting those components. *AspectIX* is a novel middleware architecture which extends CORBA by a partitioned object model. A globally distributed service can be completely encapsulated into a single distributed object which contains not only all necessary components for scalability (e.g., caches and replicas) but also the knowledge for self-organization and distribution of the service. For distribution and installation of components, the service considers object-external policies to achieve administrative scalability.

1. Introduction

The Internet forms a large distributed system and one of its services, the World Wide Web, is probably the largest distributed service that has ever been built. The Web has some anarchic structure with limited flexibility and it is desirable to do better than the Web when it comes to globally distributed services. These services could span the various intranets of large companies or the whole Internet for serving users all over the world. With standard off-the-shelf middleware like CORBA implementations [20] those services can be modelled as distributed objects and be globally accessed using a worldwide unique object identifier. For a client, the service is completely location-transparent, i.e. the client does not need to know where the server object resides. Unfortunately, this does not scale to millions of users from all over the world, because a server object in CORBA can reside only at one place at a time. For geographical and numerical scalability the service has to be built out of multiple components using replication, caching and partitioning of code and data. With using CORBA the globally unique identifier of the service would be lost, because every component had to be implemented by an individual CORBA object with its own identity.

[1] This work was partially funded as project OVEST by the Bavarian Research Foundation, Sun Microsystems Munich, Siemens ATD Erlangen, and 3Soft Erlangen. The IBM Zurich Research Lab granted an IBM Research Award. The project has been funded by the German Research Community, DFG.

C. Linnhoff-Popien and H.-G. Hegering (Eds.): USM 2000, LNCS 1890, pp. 214-229, 2000.
© Springer-Verlag Berlin Heidelberg 2000

Partitioned object models have been adopted, e.g., in the *Globe* [25] and *SOS* [21] research projects. Both systems allow to combine the service components to a single distributed object with a single identity. Regardless where the client resides, it can bind to the distributed object and will get a local component which will become part of the whole service object. Some parts of the object may replicate or cache the object's data whereas others may just serve as stubs connecting to a replica or a caching component. Thus, such systems can encapsulate the components of a scalable distributed service in a single distributed object.

The users of a globally distributed system usually have different quality-of-service requirements when using the service, e.g., one user will heavily use the service and expect a certain throughput whereas another user will only invoke a few query methods and expect up-to-date answers. Neither CORBA nor Globe nor SOS sufficiently support quality of service. In case of a partitioned object model, the QoS requirements have to be considered for selecting an appropriate implementation for the object's local part at the client side, and even for building the complete internal structure of the object.

AspectIX is a novel middleware architecture extending CORBA by a partitioned object model combining the benefits of both worlds. Additionally, it supports a special per-object interface that allows a client to specify QoS requirements on the object's service. A policy-based mechanism encapsulates the decision process, e.g., where to place which part of the distributed object, in the object itself. Even dynamically varying requirements can be handled during run-time, e.g., by transparently replacing the implementation of the local part. The distributed object becomes self-contained and self-organizing. Different objects may have a completely different internal organization, which remains transparent to clients.

As globally distributed services will span over thousands of administrative domains it is necessary to give domain and application administrators some influence on the distribution and instantiation of object parts. Therefore for every *AspectIX* object, administrators can express policies that influence the selection of implementations, the choice of protocols and internal communication channels, etc. Our novel approach thus helps not only to achieve numerical and geographical but also administrative scalability [18].

This paper is organized as follows: Section 2 will identify the demands of globally distributed services. We show how currently available systems can be used to implement such services and uncover the deficiencies of these systems. In Section 3 our own architecture is introduced. Section 4 will compare our approach to other related work as far as it was not already mentioned in Section 2. In Section 5 we will give our conclusions and present our plans for future work.

2. Globally Distributed Services

2.1 Location Transparency

Location transparency means that regardless where the client and the service components reside, the client will be able to easily access the service. The easiest and most transparent way for a client is that the client just gets a location-independent object reference to the service (e.g., from a name service), binds to the service object, and uses the service by invoking methods. The client does not need to care about locations.

CORBA provides location-independent references in form of IORs [20]. The IOR contains at least one contact address of the object for clients, e.g., it contains a so-called IIOP[2]-address. As IIOP is based on TCP/IP, an IIOP address is just an Internet address and a port number, which together are unique on the Internet. The client will get a CORBA stub initialized with the IOR, and this stub will always contact the same server object, the one serving the IIOP address. Alternatively, a so-called implementation repository may be used to serve the IIOP address. It maintains a mapping to the current address of the server object and sends an IIOP location-forward message to the client which will use the returned actual address for subsequent calls. In case of a broken connection, the client will repeat the binding process. Thus, the implementation repository helps to hide the migration of server objects [7].

In both cases there is always one single instance which has a fixed location and cannot be moved without invalidating the IOR, the server object itself or the implementation repository. This single instance is not only a single point of failure but also a bottleneck in case of millions of worldwide users. Thus, CORBA objects cannot scale.

2.2 Scalability

For scalability, we need to structure the service by using replication, caching and partitioning of code and data. In a CORBA environment, our service will consist of multiple CORBA objects implementing replicas, caches and partial services. We would need to install all these objects around the world so that they can cooperate optimally. Now the client has to deal with many object references in order to invoke a method at the service. For hiding that complexity, we could introduce a single mediator which maps a unique service address to the right object references. Unfortunately, such a mediator (e.g., an enhanced implementation repository) will again be a bottleneck and a single point of failure, or has otherwise to be replicated which recursively applies the problem.

Partitioned object models as used by Globe [25] and SOS [21] solve that problem. They allow to combine multiple distributed parts into a single distributed object, which has a single identity. For example in Globe, a client can bind to a so-called *distributed shared object* and will get a *local object*. This local object becomes a part of the distributed shared object. It may replicate or cache the object's data whereas other local objects may just serve as stubs connecting to a replica or cache.

Both, Globe and SOS provide very similar frameworks for building the implementations of replicating and caching *local objects* [26, 12][3]. In the following, we will refer to Globe's framework: Application developers can program a pure nondistributed server object and combine it with layered consistency models [8]. The framework provides all other necessary sub-components of a local object. However, in case of caching it is restricted to the state of the entire object. So, a local cache cannot store semantics-dependent data, e.g., the results of query methods. A

---

[2]IIOP = Internet Inter-ORB Protocol.

[3]SOS's framework was named BOAR.

sophisticated location service delivers the contact information for a newly created local object so that stubs can find replicas and replicas can find each other [24].

Thus, a Globe object can encapsulate the components needed to build a scalable distributed service in a single object. However, it is unclear how the system determines which client gets which available implementation of a local object. If there are multiple available implementations the right choice is crucial for scalability. We believe that it is not feasible to allow the client to decide on that. Instead the local implementation has to conform to the needs of the object and its client.

2.3   Quality of Service

Clients often have different requirements with respect to the quality provided by the service. One client may want to heavily use the service and expects a certain throughput whereas another client may only invoke a few methods and expects up-to-date answers. In a locally distributed environment often a best effort service is enough for the clients, except they have very strict quality-of-service (QoS) requirements, e.g., for transmitting multimedia data. However, if a globally distributed service has no information about the client's expectations, it can only guess what best effort means for that client. Is it more important to achieve good throughput or is it more appropriate to get up-to-date results? An optimum for all of those aspects is not generally possible.

Thinking in terms of a partitioned object model it is even more important to know the clients' requirements because the choice for an implementation of the local part has severe influence on the quality of service that a client perceives. For example, if we choose a local replica we may have up-to-date results but perhaps only poor throughput due to the overhead imposed by the necessary synchronization with the other replicas. Neither Globe nor SOS provide any mechanisms for the client to express quality-of-service requirements.

With the *CORBA Messaging* document [19], the OMG adds some QoS support to CORBA. As CORBA only offers remote method invocation, the requirements are restricted to this communication scheme (e.g., priorities on requests) and cannot deal with general QoS requirements. CORBA extensions like *QuO* [28, 30] and *MAQS* [1, 2] provide interfaces to express quality-of-service requirements, but their implementations focus on QoS characteristics that can be implemented independently of the object's semantics. We believe that this does not help for scalability, e.g, caches cannot be implemented independently of the object semantics.

3. *AspectIX* Middleware Architecture

AspectIX is our novel middleware architecture which extends CORBA by a partitioned object model. First, we explain our CORBA extensions. Then, we will introduce our QoS interface and present how *AspectIX* encapsulates decisions concerning the object's internal structure. Finally, we introduce administrative policies that influence the object's decisions and achieve administrative scalability.

3.1   Partitioned Object Model

In *AspectIX*, a distributed object is partitioned into *fragments* [5]. Clients need a local fragment to invoke methods at a distributed object. Access to a fragment, and to the distributed object respectively, is provided by fragment interfaces connected to a fragment (see Fig. 3.1). When a client binds to a distributed object, the CORBA IOR is evaluated, an implementation for a local fragment is chosen and loaded. Finally, the fragment is connected to its fragment interfaces. Fragment interfaces are automatically derived from CORBA IDL descriptions. As long as the client just binds to an object and invokes methods, the client will not see any differences to CORBA. Standard CORBA objects can be accessed by *AspectIX* objects. Conceptually, for ordinary CORBA objects there is also a local fragment, but it is nothing else but the standard CORBA stub, which is automatically generated. *AspectIX* can also host ordinary CORBA servants.[4]

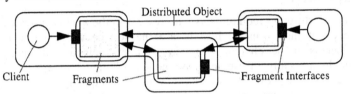

Fig. 3.1 A distributed object with three fragments each placed on a different **host.**

The fragments of a distributed object usually need to communicate. Therefore, *AspectIX* provides so-called communication end points (CEPs), which are similar to sockets but part of *AspectIX*. A fragment can open such a CEP and attach a stack of predefined protocols to it. There are three different kinds of CEPs: connectionless, connection-oriented and RPC-based CEPs. For example, there is a protocol stack GIOP over TCP/IP, which implements IIOP. This stack is used together with an RPC-based CEP to implement standard CORBA stubs and skeletons. However, fragments may also use datagram, stream or multicast communication implemented by various protocols to meet the object's requirements, e.g., to update the state of all replicating fragments. With the *AspectIX* CEPs, fragment developers do not need to use other and nonportable communication mechanisms, e.g., from the operating system. We imagine that an *AspectIX* ORB may download necessary protocol modules on demand from an external repository, but this is beyond the scope of this paper.

Let us consider a simple, global information service that is supposed to implement a parts list for one of a company's products. Using the interface we can enumerate the parts, and for each part number we can query a description string and a price. Some update methods are provided for filling in and correcting the data. First, a developer will describe the interface in CORBA IDL. Then, he will design two different fragment implementations: a server and a stub fragment. The latter is automatically provided by a tool, e.g., an IDL compiler. So far, the design is the same as on a CORBA system. As the developer knows that the service may have millions of users, he has to take care of scalability. Thus, he provides two additional fragment implementations: a replicating and a caching fragment[5]. The caching fragment has the same functionality as the stub fragment, but can store query results in a local cache.

---

[4]This is especially interesting if only some of the application objects need to be truly partitioned, e.g., if a legacy application is ported to *AspectIX*.

[5]Instead of hand-coding the replicating fragment, the replication framework of Globe [26] or BOAR [12] could be used to create it.

Stub and cache fragments can contact either a server or a replica. Replicas are connected by some internal update protocol depending on the chosen consistency model. Object-internal contact addresses are provided by a location service, e.g., the Globe Location Service [24].

3.2   Quality of Service

AspectIX supports a special per-fragment interface that allows the client to specify QoS requirements on the object's service [6]. We adopt the term *aspect* to describe nonfunctional properties of a distributed object, e.g., QoS requirements. But we also consider hints to be aspect configurations of an object , e.g., about the usage pattern of the client. A client can provide aspect configurations on a per-fragment basis, but only for aspects supported by the distributed object. Each aspect configuration has a globally unique name (perhaps maintained by some standards authority). A client can retrieve the names of supported aspects by using the special interface.

In our example, the developer of the information service object chose to support three different aspects: actuality of the returned data, read access characteristics, and lifetime of the object binding. Aspect configurations are represented as objects described in CORBA IDL. The developer of our service may reuse existing specifications, e.g., those described in Fig. 3.2. The *data actuality* aspect can configure how long the returned data can be out of date defined by a maximal age of the data since the last validation. The *access characteristic* can distinguish rare or continuous read access to the object. The *binding lifetime* aspect can be configured for an expected *long* or *short* time that the client wants to keep the local fragment, or the binding to the object respectively. For the sake of brevity, we rather simplified the aspects. However, it is possible to make them as precise as needed by introducing additional attributes.

```
interface DataActuality {
attribute unsigned long maximalAge;// in milliseconds
};

enum AccessPattern { continous, rare };
interface ReadAccessCharacteristic {
                attribute AccessPattern pattern;
};

enum Lifetime { _short, _long };
interface BindingLifetime {
                attribute Lifetime lifetime;
};
```

Fig. 3.2 IDL description of three different aspects.

For setting a configuration, the client can create his own aspect configuration objects and initialize them accordingly. Finally, he will use the distributed object's aspect interface to pass those objects into the local fragment. The fragment then has to fulfill the requirements. Hints can be used to optimize fragment-internal processes.

If the local fragment cannot fulfill the requirement, the aspect configurations become invalid. As soon as the fragment detects that it can fulfill the configurations, they become valid again. These transitions can be signalled to the client via a callback interface. So, the client could try to use another, perhaps less strict, configuration. Additionally, the client can configure how method invocations are handled in case of invalid aspect configurations. The invocations can be blocked as long as the configuration remains invalid (useful when requirements are needed in any case, e.g., communication has to be encrypted). They can raise a run-time exception, signalling the invalid configuration to the client, or they can ignore the invalidity and proceed as usual.

If a fragment detects that it cannot fulfill the requirements it might know another fragment implementation that will do. In this case, the local implementation can be transparently replaced by the other one. In any case, the fragment interfaces and the local aspect configurations remain the same.

3.3   Self-Organization

AspectIX objects should be able to self-organize their internal structure. The internal structure of a service and its development over time should be encapsulated in the object. This urges the object developer to make certain structural decisions inside of fragment implementations. *AspectIX* supports the programmer by asking him first to strictly and carefully separate mechanisms from policies. Mechanisms have to be implemented inside of fragment implementations. Then, the developer has to define decision points at which a certain decision concerning a mechanism has to be made (e.g., "Which protocol shall I use?", "Which fragment implementation shall I load?"). Instead of encoding this decision into the fragment, the developer formulates a decision request and provides policy rules. The decision request is delegated to a decision subsystem provided by *AspectIX*. The central component of this subsystem consists of a policy engine [14]. The policy engine has access to policy rules and all parameters that may influence a decision. These parameters include the requirements set up by the client via aspect configurations and environment conditions of the system. The actual decision is found by the decision engine consulting the policy rules.

We separate two sets of policy rules: developer and default policies. The first set contains rules defining under which conditions the fragments will operate properly. The second set describes rules for a default behavior of the object. The distinction between the two sets has to be carefully made to allow flexible extensions of the policy system as we will see in the next section. For a decision, the policy engine will first consult the developer policies. Those can decide not to make a definitive decision and to delegate the decision to lower prioritized rule sets instead, e.g., to the default policies. When the delegate rule sets made their decision, these decisions can be checked and possibly overwritten by the rule that initiated the delegation.

Policy rules can access the aspect configurations of a client and they can lookup environment variables of the runtime system. Examples are the currently available size of virtual memory or stable storage, and the available network bandwidth. External services, that hide the platform-dependent issues, provide this information to the policy engine. Other external services that may be needed for policy rule evaluation include naming, directory, location and security services (e.g., DNS [15], Globe Location Service [24], and PolicyMaker [3]).

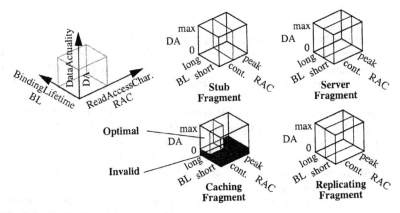

Fig. 3.3 Optimal and invalid aspect configurations for the fragments of a simple information service.

Coming back to our simple information service, we now have four different fragment implementations and three different, supported aspects, of which one is a true QoS requirement. First of all, the developer finds out for which aspect configurations the fragments can work well or cannot work at all. The result for our service is displayed in Fig. 3.3. A stub fragment makes most sense when the client does not use the object continuously. Server and replicating fragment make most sense when their lifetime is not too short. A caching fragment is best suited for continuos usage with data actuality greater than a certain limit. Below that limit the cache would always have to verify returned results. This is not optimal and our developer decided not to allow it, because it implies extra latency. Finally, the cache's lifetime should not be too short.[6]

There are other restrictions that the developer has to set up, e.g., there can be either a single server fragment or several replica fragments. So, the developer has to define how one fragment implementation can be replaced by another. In our case this is easy for most of the possibilities because they do not need any state transfer from old to new fragment implementation. The only exceptions are replacing server and replica fragments by each other, which needs some transfer of state. This is implemented by some internal hand-over interface that both server and replica have to provide.

For an implementation, the developer has to separate mechanisms from policies. For our example we first focus on two decision points and the decision they need:

- Binding of a client to an object: Which fragment implementation should be loaded?
- Replacing the local fragment: Which fragment implementation should be loaded?

The underlying mechanism is the loading of a new fragment implementation. The first decision point is inside of the *AspectIX* middleware, the second inside of a fragment implementation. Both will need the same decision, which is formulated as

---

[6]A careful reader may have noticed that none of the fragments is optimal for continuos usage for a short time, but we could have expected that because such a configuration would be hardly meaningful.

an appropriate decision request to the decision subsystem: `DecisionRequest (needs FragmentType)`

For supporting this decision the developer has to write policy rules. As *AspectIX* aims at providing generic support for policies, we have decided to use a general purpose programming language to formulate policy rules in our prototype. Specific—and thus problem-dependent—policy description languages would limit the expressiveness to their specific problem domain. For the sake of simplicity, we will only use an abstract and more readable representation of policies in this paper. A policy rule consists basically of a signature describing the possible result of a decision (named "provides" clause), a signature describing the dependencies of the rule ("needs" clauses), and the actual rule. The latter is separated into a "decide" clause containing the decision and a "check" clause that can verify and correct a decision returned by a potential delegation.

A policy decision request only consists of a "needs" clause. The policy engine will search for policy rules that generate the desired decision. Their "needs" clauses are satisfied by recursively searching for other policies that provide the needed

```
provides:                           FragmentType
needs:                              FirstFragmentType,
ReplicaAllowed, CacheAllowed
  decide:                  if(  #Fragments  ==  0  )  then
FragmentType            =                    FirstFragmentType
                         else delegate
  check:                 if( (FragmentType == REPLICA &&
ReplicaAllowed          ==           FALSE)            ||
                         (FragmentType    ==   CACHE   &&
CacheAllowed            ==           FALSE)            ||
                         FragmentType == UNKNOWN) then
FragmentType = STUB

  provides:                         FirstFragmentType
  decide:                           delegate
  check:                   if( FirstFragmentType != REPLICA
&&           FirstFragmentType      !=            SERVER     )
                         then FirstFragmentType = SERVER

  provides:                         ReplicaAllowed
  decide:                  ReplicaAllowed = TRUE; delegate
  check:                   if( #Replicas >= MaxReplicas ||
                              #Replicas    ==    0    &&
this.FragmentType        !=                   SERVER     )
                         then ReplicaAllowed = FALSE

  provides:                         CacheAllowed
  decide:                  CacheAllowed = TRUE; delegate
  check:                       if(   aspect(DA.maxAge)      <
MinAgeCache ) then CacheAllowed = FALSE
```

Fig. 3.4 Developer policies for a simple information service.

information. Under-specification and cycles are currently detected and signalled as errors[7]. Over-specification is solved by priorities.

The developer policies describe the capabilities and restrictions of the various fragment types as outlined in Fig. 3.4. The first rule implements the decision requests for a fragment type which is based on the other rules. The second rule is for determining the type of the very first fragment. The third policy rule describes when a replica is allowed. It implements an upper bound for the number of replicas, e.g., imposed by the used consistency model and protocols. The first replica can only be created from a server fragment. The fourth rule takes care that caches are not used when the maximal age required by the client is below a certain limit. To enable the policy engine to give satisfying answers to the decision requests, we have also to provide default policies as outlined in Fig. 3.5. These rules provide a default decision on fragment types. They choose the optimal fragment type for an aspect configuration and are only used when the corresponding developer policy delegates its decision.

So far, the object will start with a server object and clients will bind with a stub or

```
provides:                      FragmentType
needs:                         ReplicaAllowed
decide:                        if(    aspect(BL.lifetime)    ==
_short ) then FragmentType = STUB
                               elsif(    ReplicaAllowed    &&
aspect(RAC.pattern)==rare                                  )
                               then    FragmentType   =   REPLICA
                               else FragmentType = CACHE

provides:                      FirstFragmentType
decide:                        FirstFragmentType = SERVER
```

Fig. 3.5 Default policies for a simple information service.

cache fragment, but the object will never deploy replicating fragments. To extend the objects structural self-organization we assume that in most fragment implementations there is a so-called QoS manager running that constantly monitors certain system conditions and the delivered quality of service. In our example, if the QoS manager detects a high load in form of local invocations, it uses additional decision requests to decide on the creation of new replicas, and initially on replacing the server by the first replica. The decision point and the corresponding decisions are:

- QoS manager detects high load: Shall I create a replica? Where?

The server's QoS manager will request a decision on `ReplicaRequired` and if true the server will replace itself by a replica. The replica's QoS manager will request the same decision and if a new replica is required it requests for an additional `ReplicaLocation` decision. The creation of additional replicas is supported by so-called dwelling services. These are ordinary distributed objects that can be requested to bind to another object at a certain place and to set a certain aspect configuration. With this binding, a local fragment will be created which can be a local replica depending on the `FragmentType` decision. The additional developer and default policies are outlined in Fig. 3.6 and Fig. 3.7.

---

[7]Automatic cycle recovery is subject of current research.

```
provides:              ReplicaRequired
needs:                 ReplicaAllowed
decide:                delegate
check:                 if( ReplicaRequired == TRUE &&
ReplicaAllowed         ==           FALSE            )
                       then ReplicaRequired = FALSE
```

Fig. 3.6 Additional developer policies.

```
provides:              ReplicaRequired
needs:                 LoadTooHigh
decide:                if( LoadTooHigh == TRUE ) then
      ReplicaRequired                =            TRUE
                       else ReplicaRequired = FALSE


provides:              LoadTooHigh
decide:                if( service(SystemLoad) > MaxLoad
      )          then  LoadTooHigh          =       TRUE
                       else LoadTooHigh = FALSE


provides:              ReplicaLocation
decide:                ReplicaLocation    =    service(
      Trader.findNearestDwellingService )
```

Fig. 3.7 Additional default policies.

It is clear that this example is somewhat simplified as otherwise we could not explain

It in this paper. However, our policy system is able to deal with much more complex policy decisions and policy rules as they are necessary in a completely self-organizing globally distributed service. With the definition of developer and default policies, the fragment developer is enabled to separate policies from mechanisms. Decision code is not scattered over the fragment's implementation but collected in form of policy rule sets. This makes the development of fragment implementations much easier and every object instance may encapsulate its own policy decision and rules, which remains transparent to clients.

3.4   Administrative Scalability

The developer alone can not anticipate the optimal service configuration for all possible situations. Thus, we have to introduce further individuals and allow them to use their knowledge for tailoring the service according to their specific needs. To achieve that, we adopt policy concepts that are commonly used in system management [23,13]. We have identified three additional classes of individuals that should be allowed to formulate additional policy rule sets: application administrators, domain administrators and users. As we have adopted role concepts [4] when doing this analysis, we call them *role classes*.

Individuals belonging to the application administrator role class are driven by business goals. They are responsible for the service as a whole and have knowledge about the structure and the characteristics of the data that is processed by the service. Domain administrators have a totally different view. Their influence is limited to their local domain, where they are responsible for all facets of system management. This includes knowledge about the local network topology, available computing resources and security demands. Finally, users should also be enabled to define policies. As it should be avoided that users are required to have some internal knowledge about the distributed service, their influence should normally be limited to the definition of user preferences, i.e. the selection of their favorite text processor or Web browser.

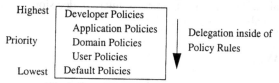

Fig. 3.8   Priority of the policy rule sets.

The role classes define an inherent priority scheme on their rule sets as depicted in Fig. 3.8, e.g., no user is allowed to override domain policies. On the other hand, an application policy is able to delegate decisions to appropriate domain or user policies. Developer policies still own the highest priority within the system whereas default policies can be overridden by any other policy.

```
provides:                          FirstFragmentType
decide:                    FirstFragmentType = REPLICA
```

Fig. 3.9   An exemplary application policy.

```
provides:            ReplicaAllowed
decide:              if(     service(LocalStorage)      >
        MinStorage                                      )
                     then  ReplicaAllowed  =  TRUE  else
        ReplicaAllowed = FALSE
```

Fig. 3.10 An exemplary domain policy.

In our exemplary information service, an application administrator who knows that a large number of users will use this service can decide that the first instantiated fragment should already be a replica. As shown in Fig. 3.9, he can override the default policy FirstFragmentType by an application policy. Similarly, a domain administrator can adapt the service to the local circumstances by requiring a lower limit of available storage for the creation of a replica. He takes advantage of the delegation in the ReplicaAllowed developer policy and defines his own policy rule shown in Fig. 3.10.

When applying these concepts to globally distributed services, the system must be capable of supporting a large number of policy rules. This is achieved by exploiting locality. All individuals belonging to role classes are scattered all over the distributed system and their political standpoints often depend on the administrative domain they belong to. Moreover, not all policies are valid for every distributed service. Thus, the validity of most policies is limited to administrative domains or certain classes of services. With the introduction of *validity annotations* for every rule that can be based on principals, on the type of the distributed services, and on administrative domains, the number of policies can be reduced to the required minimum when making decisions. Validity annotations also allow improvements of the distribution strategies that are applied when a large number of policies have to be distributed within the service. Together with this potential for numerical and geographical scalability [18], a large number of different policies—and therefore a large number of different domains—can be supported. *AspectIX* thus achieves administrative scalability by offering political influence on an object's internal decision processes to a large number of individuals.

4. Related Work

As explained in Section 2, *SOS* and *Globe* use a partitioned object model. In SOS, all intra-object communication is either modelled by so-called channels or by other pre-defined fragmented objects. The *AspectIX* approach of communication end points allows more flexibility (e.g., legacy code can be accessed by standard protocols). Globe and SOS neither consider QoS requirements nor address how a distributed object is organized and maintained. *AspectIX* provides both, QoS requirements in form of aspect configurations and a sophisticated architecture for object-internal decision processing. This allows administrative scalability and flexible, self-organizing objects.

QuO [28, 30] and *MAQS* [1, 2] extend CORBA and support quality-of-service requirements. MAQS can only deal with one-dimensional QoS requirements, whereas *AspectIX* objects can support arbitrary aspect-configuration sets. Both, QuO and MAQS use a local object at the client side to implement the QoS requirements (called delegate or mediator). As this object is only QoS-related but not to the object's semantics it is difficult to integrate functional properties with QoS. This will be necessary if we like to have a client-side local cache to gain performance but less data actuality.

The majority of work within the policy area uses policies as a concept for system management [23, 13]. Much work about the definition of policies [9, 16], policy hierarchies [29], conflict management [11], and the use of roles [4, 10] is available. We used these results as a basis for exploring administrative scalability. The main difference between *AspectIX* and those systems is, that we also integrate the developer into the policy definition process. By supporting the separation of mechanism and policy at a very early stage of the service's software design, we achieve a tighter integration of service design and service management than other approaches.

An IETF workgroup currently defines a policy framework for the management of network systems [27]. They have defined a set of classes, that allow policies to be defined and stored [17] and also employ role concepts to map policies to specific components. The IETF policy framework offers little abstraction for the policy programmer. Due to its concentration on a specific problem domain, it does not provide a generic solution as we do.

5. Conclusion and Future Work

We presented the novel middleware architecture *AspectIX*. Its partitioned object model allows an object developer to partition a single service object into multiple distributed components, which can be deployed for building numerically and geographically scalable distributed services. The *AspectIX* policy subsystem enables a developer to strictly separate mechanisms from policies. The developer has to implement the mechanisms, to identify the decision points and to express the capabilities, restrictions and the default behavior in policy rules. Administrative scalability is achieved by allowing additional administrator and user policies that can influence the object's decision. The policy engine itself can be made scalable as rule sets have some local area of validity and as the relevant rules can be easily found for a decision. Thus, with using *AspectIX* scalable and completely self-organizing, globally distributed objects can be designed and operated.

In this paper we presented only QoS requirements that deal with scalability. In principle, all kinds of requirements can be handled and implemented in multiple fragment implementation. This is subject of further research.

So far, we have multiple prototype implementations validating our concepts: a nondistributed prototype validating the object model and implementing the replacement of local fragments, an implementation of communication end points, and a nondistributed prototype of our policy subsystem that is able to find the appropriate decision with policy rule sets applied. In the near future, we will build an integrated prototype in Java. We are also working on a development environment that will support the developer in designing policy rules and implementing fragments.

References

1. C. R. Becker, K. Geihs: QoS as a competitive advantage for distributed object systems: from enterprise objects to global electronic market. *Proc. of the 3rd Int. Enterprise Distr. Obj. Comp. Conf.*—EDOC (La Jolla, Cal.), 1998.
2. —: Generic QoS specifications for CORBA. *Proc. of the KiVS Conf., Kommunikation in Verteilten Systemen* (Darmstadt, March 1999), Springer, Inform. aktuell, 1999; pp. 184–195.
3. M. Blaze, J. Feigenbaum, J. Lacy: Decentralized trust management. *Proc. of the 1996 Symp. on Security and Privacy*, IEEE, Los Alamitos, Cal., May 1996; pp. 164-173.
4. D. Ferraiolo, R. Kuhn: Role-based access control. *Proc. of the 15th National Comp. Security Conf.*, 1992.
5. F. Hauck, U. Becker, M. Geier, E. Meier, U. Rastofer, M. Steckermeier: AspectIX: A middleware for aspect-oriented programming. *Object-Oriented Technology*, ECOOP'98 Workshop Reader, LNCS 1543, Springer, 1998.
6. —: *The AspectIX approach to quality-of-service integration into CORBA*. Tech. Report TR-I4-99-09, IMMD 4, Univ. Erlangen-Nürnberg, Oct. 1999.
7. M. Henning: Binding, migration, and scalability in CORBA. *Comm. of the ACM* 41(10). ACM, New York, NY. Oct. 1998; pp. 62-71.
8. M. Kermarrec, I. Kuz, M. van Steen, A. S. Tanenbaum: A framework for consistent, replicated Web objects. *Proc. of the 18th Int. Conf. on Distr. Comp. Sys.*—ICDCS (Amsterdam, May 1998).

9. T. Koch, C. Krell, B. Krämer: Policy definition language for automated management of distributed systems. *Proc. of 2nd Int. Workshop on Sys. Mgmt*, IEEE, Toronto, June 1996.

10. E. C. Lupu, M. S. Sloman: Towards a role-based framework for distributed systems management. *J. of Network and Sys. Management* **5**(1), Plenum Press, 1997.

11. —: Conflicts in policy-based distributed systems management. *IEEE Trans. on Softw. Eng.*—Spec. Issue on Inconsistency Management, 1999.

12. M. Makpangou, Y. Gourhant, M. Shapiro: BOAR: a library of fragmented object types for distributed abstractions. *Int. Workshop on Obj. Orientation in Operating Sys.*—I-WOOOS (Palo Alto, Cal., Oct. 1991).

13. M. J. Masullo, S. B. Calo: Policy management: an architecture and approach. *Proc. of IEEE Workshop on Sys. Management*, UCLA, Cal., April 1993.

14. E. Meier, F. Hauck: *Policy-enabled applications*. Tech. Report TR-I4-99-05, IMMD 4, Univ. Erlangen-Nürnberg, July 1999.

15. P.V. Mockapetris: *Domain names—concepts and facilities*. RFC 1034, Nov. 1987.

16. J. D. Moffet: Specification of management policies and discretionary access control. M. S. Sloman (Ed.): *Mgmt. of Distr. Sys. and Comp. Netw.*, Addison-Wesley, 1994, pp. 455–480.

17. Moore, E. Ellesson, J. Strassner: *Policy framework core information model*—Ver. 1 Specification. Internet-Draft, Work in Progress, Jan. 2000.

18. C. Neuman: Scale in distributed systems: T. L. Casavant, M. Singhal (Eds.): *Readings in Distributed Computing Systems*. IEEE Comp. Soc., Los Alamitos, Cal., 1994; pp. 463–489.

19. Object Management Group, OMG: *CORBA Messaging*. OMG Doc. orbos/98-05-05, 1998.

20. —: The Common Object Request Broker: architecture and specification. Rev. 2.3.1, OMG Doc. formal/99-10-07, Oct. 1999.

21. M. Shapiro, Y. Gourhant, S. Habert, L. Mosseri, M. Ruffin, C. Valot: SOS: an object-oriented operating system. *USENIX Comp. Sys.* **2**(4), 1989; pp. 287–337.

22. M. Shapiro: Structure and encapsulation in distributed systems: the proxy principle. *Proc. of the 6th Int. Conf. on Distr. Comp. Sys.*—ICDCS (Cambridge, Mass., May 19-23, 1986), IEEE Comp. Soc.,Wash., DC, 1986; pp 198–205.

23. M. S. Sloman: Policy driven management for distributed systems. *J. of Netw. and Sys. Management* **2**(4), Plenum Press, 1994.

24. M. van Steen, F. Hauck, P. Homburg, A. S. Tanenbaum: Locating objects in wide-area systems. *IEEE Comm. Magazine* **36**(1). Jan. 1998; pp. 104–109.

25. M. van Steen, P. Homburg, A. S. Tanenbaum: Globe—a wide-area distributed system. *IEEE Concurrency*, Jan.–March 1999; pp. 70–78.

26. M. van Steen, A. S. Tanenbaum, I. Kuz, H. J. Sips. A scalable middleware solution for advanced wide-area Web services. *Dist. Sys. Eng.* **6**(1). March 1999; pp. 34–42.

27. M. Stevens, W. Weiss, H. Mahon, B. Moore, J. Strassner, G. Waters, A. Westerinen, J. Wheeler: *Policy Framework*. Internet-Draft, Work in Progress, Sept. 1999.

28. R. Vanegas, J. A. Zinky, J. P. Loyall, D. Karr, R. E. Schantz: QuO's runtime support for quality of service in distributed objects. *Proc. of the Int. Conf. on Distr. Sys. Platforms and ODP, Middleware '98* (The Lake District, UK), Springer, 1998.

29. R. Wies: Using a classification of management policies for policy specification and policy transformation. *Proc. of the IFIP/IEEE Symp. on Integr. Netw. Mgmt.* Santa Barbara, 1995.
30. J. A. Zinky, D. E. Bakken, R. E. Schantz: Architectural support for quality of service for CORBA objects. *Theory and Practice of Object Sys.* **3**(1), 1997.

Service Management

Chair: Bernhard Neumair, DeTeSystem, Munich, Germany

Fuzzy Modeling of Cooperative Service Management

Pradeep Ray [1] and Seyed A. Shahrestani [2]

[1] School of Information Systems Technology and Management
University of New South Wales, Sydney, NSW 2052, Australia
p.ray@unsw.edu.au

[2] School of Mechatronic, Computer, and Electrical Engineering
University of Western Sydney, Nepean, Bldg. X
PO Box 10, Kingswood NSW 2747, Australia
seyed@ieee.org

Abstract. Cooperative service management is concerned with the development, deployment, and operation on network based services involving the cooperation of a number of human/organizational entities. One of the prerequisites for efficient management of these complex systems is related to understanding of the roles of humans and the ways they interact with each other. This paper presents a new methodology for cooperative service management based on Computer Supported Cooperative Work techniques. The methodology is founded on the identification and modeling of human roles and their knowledge regarding their interactions with other people involved. The modeling is based on the notion of fuzzy sets that will readily furnish for the use of linguistic values. This is aimed at unveiling of the deficiencies in the existing collaborative support tools with a view to developing more effective cooperative service applications. The idea has been illustrated with a case study in a large telecom.

1 Introduction

Cooperative service management formalizes the need for cooperation amongst a number of individual and organizational entities to fulfil a collaborative service. The present trend towards downsizing of organizations, and out-sourcing of many aspects of a business, underscores the growing need for cooperative service management. One of the major questions facing the management is how to utilize the emerging Information Technology (IT) tools and techniques to facilitate cooperation to achieve better service levels [5]. The major hindrance to solving this problem is the lack of a mechanism to measure cooperation. This is partly due to the fact that cooperation level is a „fuzzy" concept. It defies any attempt of precise measure and specification.

This paper explores some concepts emerging from the area of Computer Supported Cooperative Work (CSCW) to define a fuzzy framework for the measurement of cooperation levels in order to identify gaps in available support for processes in cooperative service management. The fuzzy logic is used to translate these fuzzy measures into the design of IT solutions for effective service management. Although this framework is applicable in a variety of businesses, for example see [1] and [11],

C. Linnhoff-Popien and H.-G. Hegering (Eds.): USM 2000, LNCS 1890, pp. 232-243, 2000.

this paper illustrates these concepts using a telecommunication network management service.

The remainder of this paper is structured as follows. The next section gives a brief overview of the CSCW methodology for cooperative service management. This is followed by a case study illustration of this methodology through its application to a large telecom organization. This is followed by an illustration of a conceptual framework for systematic analysis of the data gathered from that organization, using awareness levels. This leads to a fuzzy modeling of awareness for cooperative service management. The last section gives the conclusions and outlines future work.

2   Methodology

The aim of Computer Supported Cooperative Work (CSCW) is to facilitate cooperative activity among several interacting groups of people to achieve their common goals [5]. With contributions from diverse areas such as computer science, sociology, psychology, and organizational studies, research approaches in this area widely vary. For example, sociological studies in CSCW pay a great deal of attention to the detail of human interactions whereas computer science strives for abstraction [3]. Most of the reported work in the field of network management has adopted abstraction techniques taken from computer science.

In this paper we use CSCW techniques, analyzing practical scenarios based on concepts, such as roles, interactions, artifacts and tools in a real application environment [13]. We have borrowed some of the concepts from the area of participative design processes of information systems [12]. This analysis involves a top down analysis of the cooperative system under study in the following stages:

• Overall System Study
− The overall „big picture" of the system including the major human roles, activities and the environment.
• Logical Components Identification
− Roles and Tasks: human roles and their major tasks.
− Activities and Interactions: this describes the dynamics of real life processes.
− Tools and Artifacts: some frequently used software, hardware and information structures in the system.
• Process Study
− The study of some sample scenarios in terms of the identified roles and their interactions. This study would reveal certain generic process sequences that have a strong bearing on the efficiency of the process.
• Defining Collaborative Service Requirements
− Repositories: application services using data stores and associated processes.
− Communication Interfaces: mechanisms to access repositories, such as synchronous, asynchronous, remote conference, local meeting etc.
• Analysis
− Matching of scenarios to collaborative services (tools and group communication interfaces)

- Identification of gaps in available collaborative services on the basis of user satisfaction levels
- Analysis of the above information using abstract parameters, such as human role awareness levels. Different human roles can be assigned awareness levels based on the awareness (knowledge) they have about the work, people and organization. This will lead to a conceptual design for a cooperative service management system based on required awareness levels.

The subsequent sections of this paper illustrate our CSCW based methodology in the help-desk based trouble-ticketing environment of a large telecommunication organization.

3   Modeling of Telecommunication Service Management

During the recent past, the abstraction and modeling of network operations and management information/protocols have witnessed substantial progress. Integrated management platforms that can address network and systems tasks in an organization are now commercially available [13]. However, without a group of skilled personnel, the satisfactory operation of a typical enterprise network is not possible. Some recent studies have clearly shown that automation without considering human factors can be counter-productive [14]. Such indications have triggered further research in this area initiated by some leading international telecommunications organizations.

The cooperation amongst experts/operators within and across organizations (e.g. user, software developer, equipment vendor etc) is a prerequisite for solving problems in the management of networked service [6]. The level of cooperation among the people, who take up the various roles needed to achieve a solution, has a significant impact on the level of satisfaction felt by the users of the services. In the general CSCW framework, the term awareness level (AL) is used to correlate with such a measure of human cooperation.

In this respect, it can be noted that in general it maybe advantageous to characterize the awareness levels of any role using the semantic definitions that are actually based on the use of linguistic variables [9]. For instance, a supervisor may characterize a technician by simply stating that „Technician D has a *minimal* awareness level for upgrading link A". Formally, such a characterization can be conveniently modeled through utilization of fuzzy logic and fuzzy modeling. To this end, the calculus of fuzzy logic is used as a means for representing imprecise propositions that are used in a natural language as non-crisp, fuzzy constraints on a variable [15]. Application of fuzzy logic in a network management application is discussed in [8].

4 Results of a Telecom Organization Study

This section illustrates our study based on the methodology described in Section 3. It starts with a description of the management process and major problems in the management environment under study. We then identify various human roles in the process. This is followed by a brief summary of group support systems available in the organization under study. Finally, we present a sample scenario. We studied a number of scenarios to arrive at a summary of requirements for a cooperative network management system [13].

4.1 Management Process

Trouble ticketing is a help-desk based network management application. In this case, management personnel cooperate to manage a problem using various network elements. A customer encountering a problem reports it to the help-desk. The help-desk operator then assigns a trouble ticket to the problem and refers it to an appropriate person who tries to solve the problem. If the technical person is not able to solve problem within some stipulated time, he/she escalates the alarm (i.e. calls the expert) [6].

4.2 Roles and Tasks

A trouble-ticketing environment in a large organization may embrace a large number of roles. Our example scenario, described below, involves Change Management with following human roles:

The *Change Manager* (G) is responsible (on behalf of the telecom organization under study) for successful operation of the given network changes in the given set of user organizations.

The *Technician* (D) at the Network Management Centre is responsible for the technical aspects of this change.

The *Test Coordinator* (C) assists the NMC technician with systems changes and testing in remote locations.

The *Operator* (A) at the Help-Desk is responsible for procedural communication amongst all concerned parties, and updating the repository available for this purpose.

The *User*(s) (U) represent contact persons in the user organizations where the network/systems change is being undertaken.

4.3 Collaborative Services

This telecom organization uses a number of tools and artifacts along with the help-desk systems. T1 to T9 represent different types of management tools (e.g., LAN analyzers, management platform etc) available for supporting these business processes. Group communication mechanisms depend on the nature of the collaborative task [5]. C1 to C9 represent different combinations of communication tools (e.g. email, fax, mobile phone, pager etc) available to support the trouble-ticketing business process.

The described communication mechanisms and collaborative tools/artifacts are indispensable parts for supporting group cooperation amongst network management personnel in the organization under study.

4.4 Example Scenario

In this study, we examined a number of real-life scenarios. These are based on the problems in a trouble-ticketing environment in a large typical organization, as reported by the employees. This section illustrates our study with a process diagram and observations for a typical change management scenario. Each interaction is characterized within brackets with roles and interaction types shown in Fig.1. The scenario is as follows.

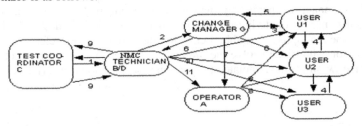

Fig. 1. Process Diagram of the Example Scenario

The existing 2 Mbps Sydney to Perth wide area link needs to be upgraded to a higher version NTU. For this an outage of 30 minutes is required. This involves the following interactions (Fig. 1) amongst the roles defined in the previous section.
1. NMC Technician discusses a suitable time with a remote Test Coordinator
2. NMC Technician/Expert submits the change request with proposed time and user impact statement to Change Manager
3. Change Manager takes up with the affected Users
4. Related Users discuss impact and examine proposed time
5. User resubmits request to Change Manager with possibly an altered schedule
6. Change Manager issues Permit to Work to all concerned
7. Help-Desk Operator is notified by Change Manager before start of the work
8. Help-Desk Operator alerts Users regarding start of work
9. Work coordination between the local and the remote sites
10. Check if OK
11. Help-desk Operator notified of completion of work.

The existing automated tools do not support the majority of the interactions and artifacts. A number of interactions require cooperation of multiple human roles simultaneously. Table 1 describes the available automated support for some of the interactions listed above.

While collaborative tools and communication mechanisms are classified according to the list in Section 4.4 and 4.5, a user satisfaction level is recorded on a scale of zero to ten (10 highest) on the basis of user interviews in the organization under study. We have also recorded what the users believe is the more appropriate communication mechanism. Having recorded the performance of each interaction, it is now necessary to analyze the scenario from the perspective of cooperative service management.

Table 1. Collaborative Service Evaluation

Interaction Number	Tool Used	Communication Mechanism (Now)	Satisfaction Level	Suggested Communication
2	T5 (Change Management)	C5 (Email)	3	C2 (Synchronous)
3	T5	C5, C1 (Face to Face)	3	C2
4 & 5	T5	C10 (Telephone)	3	C2
6	T3 (CISCO Works)	C5	2	C5

5 Cooperation Analysis

5.1 Awareness Model

As shown in Fig. 2, we model all interactions in terms of required and available awareness levels. This is then correlated to user satisfaction levels. If there is a relation between awareness and satisfaction levels, one can arrive at a design specification based on this parameter. Since this is a new experimental model, it is usually necessary to try a number of awareness related parameters, before one or a combination is found useful in the task domain.

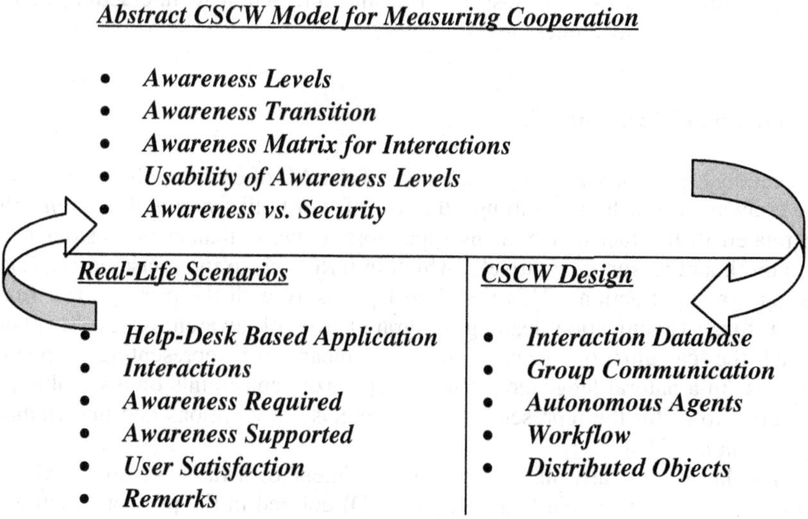

__Abstract CSCW Model for Measuring Cooperation__

- *Awareness Levels*
- *Awareness Transition*
- *Awareness Matrix for Interactions*
- *Usability of Awareness Levels*
- *Awareness vs. Security*

__Real-Life Scenarios__	*__CSCW Design__*
- *Help-Desk Based Application* - *Interactions* - *Awareness Required* - *Awareness Supported* - *User Satisfaction* - *Remarks*	- *Interaction Database* - *Group Communication* - *Autonomous Agents* - *Workflow* - *Distributed Objects*

Fig. 2. Awareness Model

Process knowledge consists of task knowledge and context knowledge. While task knowledge relates to the specification, design and performance of the task, context knowledge relates to the rest of the process knowledge including relationships between various roles, tasks, and the environment of the task. It is possible to characterize role awareness in terms of the required and supported process knowledge for a particular interaction. Some examples are: knowledge of involved employees and their roles in the task, knowledge of other preoccupations of these people within the department/division, knowledge of interrelationship of various tasks in the department/division, and knowledge of other activities of people concerned with the task (external to the organization).

This model is described in more detail in [13]. These are defined by using a parameter called „awareness level". This is likely to be the most important parameter to characterize awareness in an interaction. This is a topic of active research in CSCW [1]. According to this definition, the level of cooperation (in increasing order) in a particular work context can be expressed in terms of several levels of awareness as follows:

- Level 0: knowledge related to the given interaction
- Level 1: level 0 plus knowledge regarding the contact address of people involved in the interaction
- Level 2: level 1 plus knowledge regarding the contact address of all people in the interaction context
- Level 3: level 1 plus knowledge regarding the activities of people involved in the interaction
- Level 4: level 2 plus knowledge regarding the activities of all people involved in the interaction context.

It can be noted that this is an empirical model, and these levels are assigned (in different ways) depending on the type of group situation. For example, required awareness for different members of a group can be different. Since the requirement for this information varies from task to task, and interaction to interaction, people need to keep switching awareness levels.

5.2 Granulation of Awareness Level

From a practical point of view, the assignment of the AL of each role for a given task is more conveniently achieved through the use of words like *minimal* or *high*. This can be related to the fact that humans (operators, experts, managers, customers...) prefer to think and reason qualitatively, which in turn leads to imprecise descriptions, models, and required actions. This fits almost precisely with the principles of fuzzy logic and fuzzy quantization leading to granulation of awareness levels. Zadeh introduced the calculus of fuzzy logic as a means for representing imprecise propositions (in a natural language) as non-crisp, fuzzy constraints on a variable [9]. Fuzzy logic allows for the representation of imprecise descriptions and uncertainties in a logical manner [16].

The granulation basically involves the replacement of awareness level (AL), or constraints, of a particular role (e.g. technician D) defined in the previous section to be of the form

$$AL(D) = a \text{ (where } a \text{ is crisply defined as a member of } \{0, 1, 2, 3, 4\}) \tag{1}$$

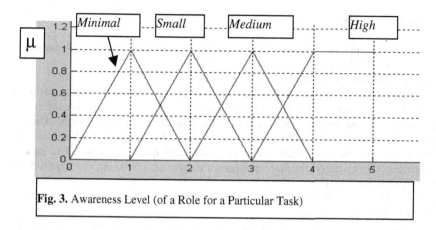

Fig. 3. Awareness Level (of a Role for a Particular Task)

by

$$AL (D) \text{ is } A \tag{2}$$

where A is a fuzzy subset of the universe of the awareness levels of the role. For instance, the technician's lowest awareness level may be represented by

$$AL (D) \text{ is } minimal. \tag{3}$$

Given the semantic definitions that are actually based on the use of linguistic variables this notion of fuzzy logic is obviously more appropriate. In this sense, while $AL (D) = a$ is a particular characterization of the possible values of the technician's awareness level, the fuzzy set A represents a possibility distribution. Now, the possibility of the *linguistic variable* AL (D) is represented by a *linguistic value* as the label of the fuzzy set taking a particular *(numerical) value b* given by

$$Possibility \{AL (D) = b\} = \mu_A (b). \tag{4}$$

The membership function μ shown in Fig. 3, represents the grade of membership of b in *minimal* (as the technician's Awareness Level). Clearly, in comparison to trying to identify each role's levels of awareness as crisp values, this type of representation is more suitable. This is mainly related to the ill-defined (or too complex) nature of the dependencies of these levels and the knowledge required at each level on the variables that actually quantify them (e.g. contact address and activities of other people involved in interaction). Even if for some tasks such dependencies can be defined well enough, it is still advantageous to use linguistic variables to exploit the tolerance for imprecision, allowing for lower solution costs and achieving more intelligent explanations.

5.3 Scenario Analysis

This section presents an analysis of the scenario described in Section 4.4, using the awareness model. The unsatisfactory interactions are:

1. NMC Technician discusses a suitable time with a remote Test Coordinator

- In this case, the manual and hence error-prone method of communication is probably the main source of dissatisfaction. Often the remote test coordinator cannot be contacted because he/she is busy at a customer site, and emails to his/her office go unanswered because he/she hardly has time to read emails. On the other hand, the customer, and the business manager is pressing hard for the change. The lack of appropriate communication mechanisms causes a mismatch between the required and supported awareness levels.

2. NMC Technician submits change request with proposed time and user impact statement to Change Manager.

- The change impact statement requires a considerable amount of context knowledge regarding user configurations. In the absence of an automated facility, the NMC technician is not likely to have the information regarding the User activities and needs. As such, this person shows only a *small* level of awareness with regard to existing artifacts and tools. In order to be effective though, this person should at least possess a *medium* level of awareness. Note that on the basis of crisply defined awareness levels, as in Section 5.1, this is stated as: the NMC Technician is only at level 1 of awareness with existing artifacts (to be effective he/she should be at level 3). Obviously, the use of linguistic variables such as *minimal* and *medium* results in statements, which are closer to human way of thinking. Also it can be noted that appropriate repositories to support information at this level can achieve the required level of awareness.

3. Change Manager takes up with the affected Users.

- While the User need not be at a higher level of awareness, the Change Manager needs to have an adequate level of awareness through appropriate repositories (non-existent in this case). Users are totally unaware of the overall system

4. Related Users discuss impact and examine the proposed time

- For this interaction to be successful, all Users need to have a reasonably high level of awareness about their own system and requirements. The coordinating User knows a little more than the others. This requires adequate group communication mechanisms and repositories to allow for all Users to interact effectively.

5. User resubmits request to Change Manager with possibly an altered schedule

- Due to the lack of adequate level of knowledge, Users may have taken invalid assumptions. The Change Manager is also unable to help in this situation. This can waste substantial amounts of time for all concerned.

6. Change Manager issues Permit to Work to all concerned

- The lack of awareness on the part of Change Manager may lead to missing some parties concerned with the work. Also some Users may not appreciate the need for responding within the stipulated time. All of this may cause substantial damage to the organization's interests.

Table 2 summarizes part of the results for some of the required interactions based on the crisply defined awareness levels defined in Section 5.1. This table shows that many of the interactions have a low user satisfaction level due to the gap between the required and actually supported awareness. We observed this result in all of the scenarios. More research is required to check the validity of this point for all types of organizations. However, this illustrates the process of cooperation analysis.

Table 2. Awareness Matrix for the Scenario

Interaction	Awareness Required	Awareness Supported	User Satisfaction level
2	3-2	1-2	3
3	4-1	3-0	3
4	3-3	1-0	3
5	3-4	1-3	3
6	4-3	3-1	2

An alternative way for characterization of the interactions can be based on fuzzy-based definition of the awareness levels as discussed in Section 5.2. This will provide for the description of the complex systems and interactions using the knowledge and experience of customers, managers, and other involved people in simple English-like rules [7]. The fuzzy-based characterization results in models that are easy to understand, use, and expand even by non-experts. As an example, Table 3 presents the Awareness matrix displayed in Table 2 using linguistic values. While the two tables convey similar information, the fuzzy-based methodology offers significant benefits. In this case, an obvious advantage is related to simplification of modeling process. It can be noted that several automated approaches for classification of dynamic fuzzy models have been developed [4]. In addition, as the fuzzy systems are rule based, the system designer can focus on the actual design process.

Table 3. Awareness Matrix for the Scenario (Granulated Awareness Levels)

Interaction	Awareness Required	Awareness Supported	User Satisfaction level
2	Medium-Small	Small-Medium	3
3	High-Small	Medium-Minimal	3
4	Medium- Medium	Medium-Minimal	3
5	Medium-High	Small-Medium	3
6	High-Medium	Medium- Small	2

The abstract system design specification for the required system boils down to supporting the required awareness levels for every interaction in an activity. This could be realized by having designing appropriate group repositories, appropriate group communication mechanisms and tools. The technologies to implement them use a combination of GroupWare, workflow, intelligent agents, and a distributed object-computing environment. For the sake of brevity, this paper does not discuss the process of system design.

6 Concluding Remarks

This paper has presented a new methodology for successful development of cooperative service management systems. We showed how the classification and modeling of human roles and analysis of some representative scenarios could lead to identification of gaps in the existing collaborative support tools. The methodology is illustrated by its application in a large telecom organization trouble-ticketing process. Our modeling is based on the use of linguistic variables that are interpreted as the labels of some fuzzy sets. This leads to the application of fuzzy logic approaches resulting in granulation and fuzzy quantization.

Future work will involve more research in the validation of this fuzzy framework in various types of organizational processes. While in this paper fuzzy logic approaches are used for modeling of human roles, work is underway to expand them into other aspects of importance in cooperative service management. For instance, based on available people within the organization at various roles with different ALs for a given task, fuzzy inference can be used to identify the combination of people to achieve an optimum solution. This idea can be extended to many service applications in addition to those in network and systems management.

References

1. D. Benech, „Intelligent agents for system management," Proc. Distributed Systems: Operation and management (1996)
2. S. Benford, J. Bowers, L. Fahlen, J. Mariani and T. Rodden, „Supporting Cooperative Work in Virtual Environments", Computer Journal **37** (1994)
3. G. Blair and T. Rodden, „The Challenges of CSCW for Open Distributed Processing," Proc. 2nd International Conference on Open Distributed Processing (ICODP) (1993)
4. S. G. Cao and N. W. Rees, „Identification of dynamic fuzzy models," Fuzzy Sets and Systems **74** (1995)
5. J. Grudin, „Computer Supported Cooperative Work: History and Focus," IEEE Computer Magazine (1994)
6. D. Johnson, „NOC Internal Integrated Trouble Ticket System Functional Specification Wishlist", Internet RFC 1297 (1992)
7. A. Kruse, E. Schwecke, and J. Heinsohn, Uncertainty and Vagueness in Knowledge Based Systems. New York, NY: Springer-Verlag (1991)
8. L. Lewis and G. Dreo, „Extending Trouble Ticket Systems to Fault Diagnostics," IEEE Network Magazine (1993)

9. E. H. Mamdani, „Application of fuzzy logic to approximate reasoning using linguistic synthesis," IEEE Trans. Computers **26** (1977)

10. C. Muller, P. Veitch, E. H. Magill and D. G. Smith, „Emerging AI techniques for network management," Proc. IEEE GLOBECOM '95 (1995)

11. N. Nuansri, T. S. Dillon and S. Singh, „An application of neural network and rule-based system for network management," Proc. 30th Hawaii International Conference on System Sciences (1997)

12. T. Olle, J. Hagelstein, I. MacDonald, C. Rolland, H. Sol, F. Assche and A. Verrijn-Stuart, Information Systems Methodologies: A Framework for Understanding. Addison-Wesley (1991)

13. P. Ray, M. Fry and B. Khasnabish, „A Re-Engineering Methodology for the Cooperative Management Of Enterprise Networks," Journal of Network and Systems Management Special Issue on Enterprise Network Management (1999)

14. P. Sachs, „Transforming Work: Collaboration, Learning, and Design," Communications of the ACM **38** (1995)

15. L. A. Zadeh, „Fuzzy sets," Information and Control **8** (1965)

16. L. A. Zadeh, „The role of fuzzy logic in the management of uncertainty in expert systems," Fuzzy Sets and Systems **11** (1983)

Customer Service Management: An Information Model for Communication Services

Michael Langer and Michael Nerb

Leibniz Supercomputing Center
Barer Str. 21, 80333 Munich, Germany
{langer | nerb}@lrz.de

Abstract. Customer Service Management (CSM) offers a management interface between customer and service provider, which enables customers to individually monitor and control their subscribed services.

In order to model Customer Service Management for communication services, this paper proposes a protocol and technology-independent information model, which incoporates the individual quality of service parameters (QoS parameters) that are specified in customer-specific service level agreements (SLAs), and the logical infrastructure that is used to implement the communication service. The information model is validated for a real-life management environment.

This work has been carried out at the Leibniz Supercomputing Center (LRZ) in Germany as part of a research project that is supervised by the *German Research Network Organization* ("DFN-Verein"), and funded by the Federal Ministry for Education, Science, Research and Technology.

1 Introduction and Motivation

Communication services play a major role in the emerging universal service market: Intranets, Extranets, virtual private networks (VPNs) and the ubiquitous worldwide internet are and depend on communication services. Communication services are enablers for application services such as e-commerce, WWW, mail or news. Depending on the implementation, a communication service can be anything from an OSI layer 1 service to an OSI layer 4 virtual point-to-point connection with an individually specified (and enforced) service quality. In the simplest case, the communication service could be a locigal end-to-end connection with a specific bandwith between two access points; more often, the communication service is a complex VPN that consists of several logical end-to-end connections between many access points. To complicate things, communication services are typically layered on each other (e.g. IP over ATM over SDH).

The resulting service hierarchies illustrate the increasing need for service providers to establish an efficient and effective end-to-end service management, which includes the exchange of service-specific management information over organizational boundaries. Customer Service Management (CSM) [8] introduces concepts and principles to facilitate the exchange of management information between customer and service provider by offering the customer a logical view onto the service management of the service provider.

C. Linnhoff-Popien and H.-G. Hegering (Eds.): USM 2000, LNCS 1890, pp. 244–257, 2000.

In order to provide Customer Service Management for communication services, a protocol and technology-independent information model is needed, which incoporates the individual QoS parameters that are specified in the SLAs and the logical infrastructure that is used to implement the particular communication service. In [9], we introduced an information model suitable for IP communication services. Based on this experience, this paper proposes a **generic information model** for Customer Service Management that is suitable to deal with communication services independent of the position in the service hierarchy and incorporates individual service characteristics.

Section 2 describes the main problems associated with CSM in service hierarchies, identifies requirements that have to be met by the information model and points out, how existing approaches help to address these requirements. Section 3 proposes an information model that provides the neccesary information independent of the position in the service hierarchy. Section 4 discusses a scenario, for which the information model has been used. Section 5 gives a summary and discusses open issues.

2 Problem Analysis

2.1 Scenario

An example of a typical service hierarchy (IP over ATM) that involves several organizations can be found in Fig. 1. A *Carrier* offers a communication service based on ATM PVCs. An *IP-Provider* can use the ATM-PVC service to connect his IP routers, e.g. by means of RFC 1483 [4]. The resulting IP backbone offers an IP communication service, which can be used by an *Application Service Provider* (ASP). The ASP can set up value added services (VAS) on top of the IP communication service, e.g. WWW, email or news, which can be used by *End-Users*. In this scenario, each organization acts in a provider role to the higher layer, and in a customer role to the lower layer.

For the remainder of this paper, we focus on the management issues that result from this service hierarchy: It is very unlikely, that the management systems on each of those layers interoperate, because the management systems differ not only by their vendor (e.g. IBM/Tivoli, HP, CA), but also by the underlying management architecture (e.g. OSI/TMN, Internet, CORBA, Java/WWW, proprietary). Futhermore, the management systems incorporate technology-specific network resource models, as each organization implements an individual network infrastructure in order to manage the specific communication service (ATM and IP).

In this scenario, the goal of Customer Service Management is to mediate between the involved management systems: Each organization that acts in a provider role in Fig. 1 offers necessary management information and functionality to the adjacent organization acting in the customer role. This can be achieved by means of a service-specific CSM (e.g. CSM-ATM, CSM-IP). However, in the

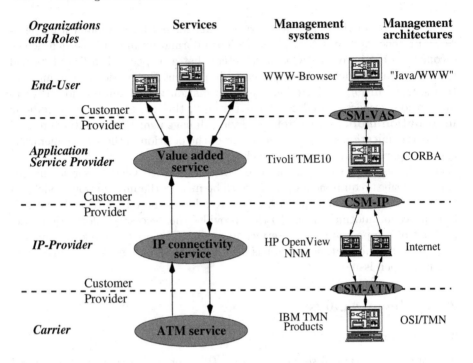

Fig. 1. A typical service hierarchy

context of this paper, we are not looking for an individual information model for
each communication service; instead, we are looking for a generic and abstract
information model that can be applied to a wide range of scenarios (i.e. communication services). Therefore, the following problems have to be addressed:

1. For the customer of a communication service, the knowledge about the resources, that make up the communication infrastructure, is of great importance. For example, the IP-Provider in our scenario needs configuration,
   performance and fault information about all subscribed ATM PVCs. Without this management information he is not able to manage his IP routers
   and subnetworks efficiently.
2. Besides this, the information model must incorporate information about the
   customer-specific SLAs and the contained QoS parameters. Without this information, a customer cannot monitor and control the individual service quality and hence cannot detect QoS violations. For example, the IP-Provider in
   our scenario needs service-specific management information about his subscribed ATM-PVCs from the lower layer in order to provide the IP service
   to the higher layer according to the specified SLAs.
3. The management systems on each layer of the service hierarchy must be
   interoperable with management systems on the lower and higher layer. As
   already pointed out, CSM has to deal with management systems that differ
   not only by vendors but also by the management architectures.

2.2   Requirements

Based on these three problems, the following requirements can be derived:

1. As already mentioned, the knowledge about the resources that make up the communication service, is of great importance for the customer of a communication service. Only by means of the knowledge about these resources and their dependencies, the customer can verify whether the communication service is configured according to his needs and requirements or performance thresholds are exceeded.

    a) For the scope of this paper, the information model only has to incorporate information that is necessary for the customer. For example, inventory details of a particular resource are not relevant for a customer. Instead, the information model must offer a simplified logical view onto the infrastructure as it is perceived by the customer. This shields the customer from the huge amount of managed objects representing the physical and logical resources.

    b) The information model must be applicable on different layers of the service hierarchy, i.e. it must abstract from the details of specific protocols and techniques (such as WDM, SDH, ATM, IP). In particular the information model must be capable of modeling connection-oriented protocols (e.g. ATM) as well as connectionless protocols (e.g. IP).

2. However, the sole knowledge of the logical infrastructure is not sufficient for the customer. In addition, he needs access to service-related management information, i.e. meaningful and aggregated information about the individual service quality. Hence, the information model must reflect the service characteristics of the provided communication services. The individual service characteristics are specified in service level agreements (SLAs) by means of QoS parameters.

3. Finally, CSM has to interoperate with various management systems based on different management architectures. This results in the following interoperability requirements:

    a) The information model must be specified in a description language that can be transferred into the information modeling languages used by the various management architectures (e.g. SNMP-SMI, OSI-GDMO).

    b) The information model has to be mapped onto the different network resource models implemented by the various management architectures. These systems offer the measurable values that are necessary to calculate the service characteristics.

2.3   Related Work

Two areas of related work can be identified from the requirement analysis: *Information modeling of networks* and *QoS modeling*. Due to the various approaches that exist, we cannot discuss all of them in detail here. See [10],[11] and [3] for a good overview over the corresponding areas. As an example of ensuring QoS and in particular service levels across administrative boundaries see [2]. For the remainder of this section, we focus on those approaches that offer concepts and principles that help to solve our problems: G.805 for information modeling of networks and X.641 for QoS modeling.

ITU G.805: The "Generic Functional Architecture of Transport Networks" [6] describes the functional and structural architecture of transport networks in a technology-independent way. G.805 focuses on input/output flows and their bindings within certain processing functions, rather than on physical entities. Hence, G.805 defines abstract architectural components (such as **layer network, subnetwork, link** and **access point**), concepts for **partitioning** and **layering** networks, and **connection supervision techniques**. G.803 [5] and ATM M4 [1], for instance, apply these generic concepts for particular technologies (SDH and ATM) successfully.

G.805 is a very useful source of information for modeling transport networks in a technology-independent way. The "partitioning" and "layering" concepts can be used to decompose and model service hierarchies: Layering allows the hierarchical decomposition of network infrastructures into independent **layer networks**. Partitioning allows the decomposition of a complex layer network infrastructure into independent **subnetworks** (in the same layer network). **Access Points** provide access to subnetworks. However, as the scope of G.805 lies on the identification and definition of architectural components and building blocks, it does not detail the characteristics of the identified building blocks.

ITU X.641: The "Quality of Service Framework" [7] defines terms and concepts to develop or enhance quality of service issues in IT environments. It models **QoS characteristics** as quantifyable aspects of a system and identifies generic QoS characteristics that are of general importance. Further, it introduces concepts to specialize and derive QoS characteristics: **Specialized QoS characteristics** make QoS characteristics more concrete and useable. **Derived QoS characteristics** can be defined as (mathematical) functions of other QoS characteristics. In order to manage the quality of a service, **QoS management functions** are identified, which can be composed of a number of smaller elements, termed **QoS mechanisms**. Finally, the need of **QoS verification** is outlined as the process of comparing the requested QoS characteristics with the observed QoS characteristics.

X.641, although very complex, offers valuable input for modeling quality of service issues of communication services. It provides concepts to model QoS parameters and addresses QoS management aspects such as establishment, monitoring and maintenance of QoS parameters. For our purpose, we adopt some terms and concepts of modeling QoS parameters. The identified generic classes of QoS characteristics are used to derive and specialize network and service characteristics of communication services.

3 A CSM Information Model for Communication Services

The discussion in the previous section pointed out, that existing standards offer valuable concepts and principles that can be used to define a generic information model to be used for Customer Service Management for communication services. Section 3.1 gives an overview of the information model and highlights the concepts used. Sections 3.2 and 3.3 detail the information model.

3.1 Methodology

The basic idea of our approach is to define the information model for Customer Service Management based on the concepts of G.805 and X.641, and extend it by service-level information necessary to meet the requirements identified in section 2.2:

1. The information model must incorporate information about the customer-specific SLAs and the contained QoS parameters. We use some terms and definitions of X.641 and introduce "target QoS parameters" which reflect the individual quality of the communication service as has been negotiated between customer and provider. "Observed QoS parameters" represent the observed quality of the service as it is perceived by the customer when using the service. Furthermore, we add "measurable values", i.e. configuration and performance information about the underlying logical infrastructure, which can be derived from the management systems. According to QoS verification in X.641, we introduce an algorithmic mapping to close the gap between observed QoS parameters and measurable values, which can be described by means of a metric. All negotiated target QoS parameters of a communication service and the associated metrics are speficied in the customer-specific, individual SLA.
2. The information model must be able to model various communication services independent of a specific technology. We introduce a "logical infrastructure" that models the communication service as it is perceived by the customer. We identify generic building blocks of this logical infrastructure and attribute these with measurable values that can be extracted from management systems. Furthermore, we use the "layering" and "partitioning" concepts introduced by G.805 in order to model complex logical infrastructures.
3. We use the Unified Modeling Language (UML) as a graphical notation for the information model. UML provides a common understanding and can be mapped onto the information modeling languages used by different management architectures.

Using UML terminology, the CSM information model for communication services is modeled by two packages: CSMService, which contains information about the SLAs, QoS parameters, metrics and Actions, and CSMNetwork, which contains information about the logical infrastructure, as it is perceived by the customer. Both packages are described in more detail in the following subsections.

3.2   Package "CSMService"

The CSMService package (see Fig. 2) defines managed objects that represent SLAs for communication services as they are negotiated betwen customer and service provider. Service acts as a base class. As we focus on communication services in this paper, we subclass CommunicationService, and refine Guaranteed-

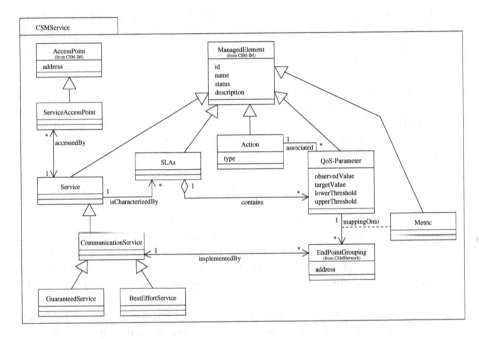

Fig. 2. Package "CSMService"

Service (e.g. ATM-PVC service) and BestEffortService (e.g. IP service). A service can be accessed by a ServiceAccessPoint, a refinement of an abstract superclass AccessPoint. A service is characterized by SLAs. A SLA contains QoS parameters, which are modeled by QoS-Parameter[1]. The QoS-Parameter class is attributed with targetValue and observedValue, which reflect the target and observed QoS parameters. If the thresholds specified in lowerThreshold and upperThreshold are exceeded for a particular QoS parameter, the associated Action is executed. Several QoS-Parameter instances can be associated with one type of Action.

---

[1] The generic QoS characteristic of X.641 can be used to refine QoS-Parameter.

CommunicationServices are implemented by EndPointGroupings. End-
PointGrouping is imported from package CSMNetwork and models the logical
infrastructure that is necessary to implement the communication service. To allow for the mapping of the associated QoS, Metric is introduced, which contains
the algorithmic description of the mapping between the QoS instance and the
associated EndPointGrouping. Service, SLA, Action, QoS-Parameter and
Metric are derived from a generic superclass ManagedElement, which acts as
a common top-level container in the inheritance tree.

3.3   Package "CSMNetwork"

The CSMNetwork package (see Fig. 3) defines managed objects that represent the logical infrastructure that is necessary to implement a communication
service. By means of the classes EndPointGrouping, Link, Node, Network

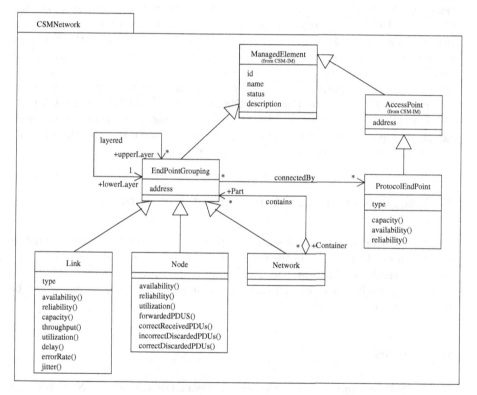

Fig. 3. Package "CSMNetwork"

and ProtocolEndPoint, large, layered networks can be modeled: EndPoint-
Groupings are connected by ProtocolEndPoints, a refinement of the G.805
principle "access point". EndPointGrouping is a base class for the logical building
blocks Link, Node and Network. Link is an abstraction of any kind of virtual
connection (e.g. a physical link, an optical wavelength, a SDH trunk, ATM-VP,

ATM-VC, an IP subnet, ...) and consists of serveral `ProtocolEndPoints` for the purpose of transferring data between them. A `Node` is an abstraction of a network component (e.g. WDM multiplexer, SDH cross-connect, ATM switch or IP router). `Network` models the G.805 principle of "partitioning": By means of the `contains` relationship between `Network` and `EndPointGrouping`, a network can contain `EndPointGroupings`, i.e. the building blocks `Link`, `Node` and `Networks` again. The self-association `layered` of `EndPointGrouping` models the G.805 principle of "layering": `EndPointGroupings` can be layered on `EndPointGroupings` in order to model hierarchies of infrastructures.

The building blocks, especially `Link`, `Node` and `ProtocolEndPoint` provide methods to access the "measurable values" as a function of time. Most of these measurable values are refinements of the derived and specialized characteristics of X.641. For instance, the methods `availability()`, `reliability()`, `capacity()`, `throughput()`, `utilization()`, `delay()`, `errorRate()` and `jitter()` of class `Link` offer access to measurable values that are typical for virtual connections. Furthermore, the `type` attribute indicated the topology and direction (e.g. unidirectional/bidirectional point-to-point or bus, ...). Class `Node` provides access to the typical measurable values of network components by means of the methods `availability()`, `reliability()`, `utilization()`, `forwardedPDUs()`, `correctReceivedPDUs()`, `incorrectDiscardedPDUs()` and `correctDiscardedPDUs()`. Finally, `ProtocolEndPoint` provides methods `capacity`, `availability` and `reliability` for the same reasons; the `type` attribute indicates the protocol used for transmission.

4   Integration in the Management Environment

The information model has been developed within a research project that is supervised by the *German Research Network Organization* ("DFN-Verein"), and funded by the Federal Ministry for Education, Science, Research and Technology. This section outlines the scenario and shows, how the information model can be applied for this scenario.

4.1   Scenario

The DFN-Verein operates a nationwide network (Broadband-WiN, B-WiN), a VPN based on an ATM cross connect infrastructure. Based on the B-WiN, the DFN-Verein offers various services to its customers, in particular an IP communication service, which provides IP connectivity within Germany and to the worldwide internet. The customers of the DFN-Verein are German universities and research organizations; the Leibniz Supercomputing Center (LRZ) is one of those customers.

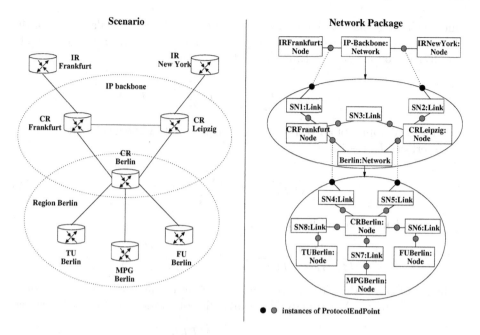

Fig. 4. Modeling the IP infrastructure

The left-hand side of Fig. 4 outlines a simplified view onto the B-WiN[2]: The IP infrastructure consists of an IP backbone that is connected to the US Internet and the European Research Network by means of the international routers (IR) IR New York and IR Frankfurt. The IP backbone and these two routers are linked by two IP subnets, which are visualized by a connecting line between them. The IP backbone consists of three central IP routers (CR) in Berlin, Leipzig and Frankfurt connected by three IP subnets in a ring-like topology. Each CR connects a geographical region to the IP backbone. For example, the three IP edge routers (ER) in the metropolitan area of Berlin (ER TU Berlin, ER MPG Berlin, ER FU Berlin) are connected to the CR Berlin by three IP subnets based on a star topology.

In the B-WiN, no individual SLAs have been negotiated between the DFN-Verein and customers. The DFN-Verein is currently rolling out the successor of the B-WiN, the "Gigabit-WiN" (G-WiN), where customer-specific SLAs are an important issue. For this purpose, the LRZ specified several QoS parameters for the G-WiN, which could be incorporated into the individual SLAs. One of these QoS parameters is the "Availability of the IP backbone".

To demonstrate, how a SLA could look like in the G-WiN, an exemplary SLA is described for the customer LRZ. The target availability for this QoS parameter over a day must be at least 85%; the target availability over a year

---

[2] This scenario details only a subset of all regions, nodes and links in the B-WiN.

must be at least 99,5%. According to the SLA, the observed availability A of the IP backbone in any given time interval $[t, t']$ is calculated from the availability of all n IP routers N_i, $i \in 1..n$ of the IP backbone:

$$A_{IPBackbone}([t, t']) = 1/n * \sum_{i=1}^{n} A_{N_i}([t, t']) \tag{1}$$

The availability of an IP router A_{N_i} is calculated by the availability of all its m interfaces $I_j, j \in 1..m$, :

$$A_{N_i}([t, t']) = 1/m * \sum_{j=1}^{m} A_{I_j}([t, t']) \tag{2}$$

X.641 [7] defines the availability A as

$$A = \frac{MTBF}{MTBF + MTTR} = 100\% - \frac{MTTR}{MTBF + MTTR} \tag{3}$$

where $MTBF$ is the "Mean Time Between Failures" and $MTTR$ is the "Mean Time To Repair". Accordingly, the availability of an interface A_{I_j} is defined as

$$A_{I_j}([t, t']) = 100\% - \frac{MTTR([t, t'])}{t' - t} \tag{4}$$

with $MTBF([t, t']) + MTTR([t, t']) = t' - t$.

Within the SLA, $MTTR$ and $MTBF$ of an interface are mapped onto the reachability from a central management station, which polls the current state of the interfaces of their managed nodes using "ping". The polling results are used to calculate the availability of an interface as follows: $MTTR$ is the time interval, the interface is not reachable from the management station; $MTBF$ is the time interval, the interface is reachable. Finally, the SLA sets the time interval $[t, t']$ to 5 minutes in order to achieve a good compromise between granularity of the reachability information and resulting management traffic. So far, no action is specified in the SLA, when the observed availablility does not meet the target availability of the IP backbone.

4.2   Modeling the Scenario

The right-hand side of Fig. 4 shows, how the CSMNetwork package can be used to model this scenario: Routers are represented by instances of Node, subnetworks are represented by instances of Link. The IP backbone and the region Berlin are modeled using instances of Network. Interfaces are modeled as instances of ProtocolEndPoint, which are connected by Links to Nodes. The Network instance IP backbone contains the Network instance region Berlin and illustrates, how the partitioning concept can be used to decompose a complex IP infrastructure.

In order to add characteristic details of a particular technology or protocol (such as IP in our scenario), the classes of the CSMNetwork package can be refined. For the IP communication service of the B-WiN, this has been done in [9].

To model the described SLA for customer LRZ, one instance of SLA is created for customer LRZ. The SLA instance contains two instances of QoS in order to model the daily target availability and the yearly target availability of the IP backbone: The targetValue attributes are set to 85% and to 99,5% respectively. The observedValue attributes can be calculated by the algorithm (1),(2),(4) described above, which can be specified using the description attribute of class Metric. The measureable values, i.e. the reachability of all interfaces, are provided by the status attribute of class ProtocolEndPoint, inherited from class ManagedElement.

4.3 Prototypical Implementation

In order to provide management information about the IP communication service to the German universities and research organizations, a distributed client/server application based on the "WWW/Java/CORBA" approach has been implemented. Fig. 5 is a screenshot of the Java-GUI. On the left-hand side, the IP infrastructure can be navigated using a hierarchical tree structure. The right-hand side visualizes the same infrastructure using maps, which represent the various regions. Colours indicate the current state of the IP infrastructure. IP subnetworks are attributed with current configuration and performance information such as *capacity* [MBit/s], *throughput* [MBit/s] and *utilization* [%].

The maps are a visual representation of the IP backbone and the various regions (e.g. Berlin). Each map contains regions, IP routers and IP subnets that represent the logical infrastructure for the customer. The reachability information is already implemented and could be used to calculate the observed availability of the IP backbone.

5 Summary and Open Issues

The exchange of management information between customer and service provider is facilitated by means of a service-oriented management interface called "Customer Service Management" (CSM). CSM enables customers to individually monitor and control their subscribed service.

In order to model Customer Service Management for communication services, this paper proposes a protocol and technology-independent information model, which incoporates the individual QoS parameters that are specified in the SLAs and the logical infrastructure that is used to implement the particular communication service.

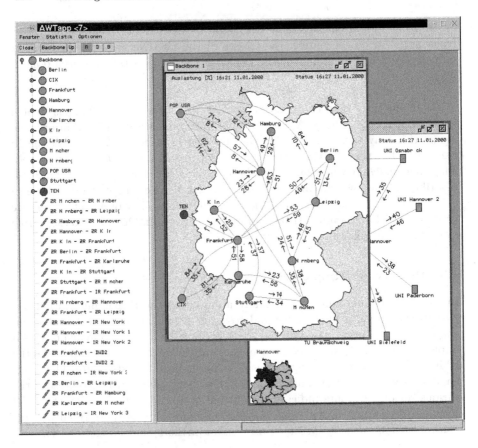

Fig. 5. Customer view of the IP backbone

Using UML as a graphical notation, X.805 concepts of layering and partitioning for describing a logical view onto the network infrastructure, and X.641 terms and concepts for QoS modeling ensures, that the proposed information model is independent of the position in service hierarchies and that it can be applied to a wide range of scenarios.

Beside an IP communication service, we are going to instantiate the information model for other communication services, probably an SDH point-to-point service. Furthermore, we are going to model other QoS parameters using the CSMService package, such as the overall throughput in the IP backbone. The research activities will focus on the mapping techniques that are used to close the gap between observed QoS parameter and measureable values.

Acknowledgments. The authors wish to thank the members of the Munich Network Management (MNM) Team for helpful discussions and valuable comments on previous versions of the paper. The MNM Team, directed by Prof. Dr. Heinz-Gerd Hegering, is a group of researchers of the Munich Universities and the Leibniz Supercomputing Center of the Bavarian Academy of Sciences. Its webserver is located at `http://wwwmnmteam.informatik.uni-muenchen.de`.

References

[1] M4 Interface Requirements and Logical MIB: ATM Network View Version 2. Specification af-nm-0058.001, ATM Forum, May 1999.

[2] P. Bhoj, S. Singhal, and S. Chutani. SLA Management in Federated Environments. *In: Integrated Network Management VI (IM'99), Boston.* May 1999.

[3] P. Ferguson and G. Huston. *Quality of Service - Delivering QoS on the Internet and in Cooperate Networks.* John Wiley and Sons, 1998.

[4] J. Heinanen. Multiprotocol Encapsulation over ATM Adaptation Layer 5. Request for Comments (Standard) RFC 1483, Internet Engineering Task Force, July 1993.

[5] Architecture of Transport Networks based on the Synchronous Digital Hierarchy (SDH). Recommendation G.803, ITU, June 1997.

[6] Generic Functional Architecture of Transport Networks. Recommendation G.805, ITU, November 1995.

[7] ITU-T. OSI Networking and System Aspects - Quality of Service. Recommendation X.641, ITU-T, December 1997.

[8] M. Langer, S. Loidl, and M. Nerb. Customer Service Management: A More Transparent View To Your Subscribed Services. *In: Proceedings of the 9th Annual IFIP/IEEE International Workshop on Distributed Systems: Operations & Management (DSOM'98), Newark.* October 1998.

[9] M. Langer, S. Loidl, and M. Nerb. Customer Service Management: Towards a Management Information Base for an IP Connectivity Service. *In: Proceedings of the 4th IEEE Symposium on Computers and Communications (ISCC'99), Sharm El Sheikh, Red Sea, Egypt.* July 1999.

[10] C.-C. Shen and J.Y. Wei. Network-Level Information Models for Integrated ATM/SONET/WDM Management *In: Proceedings of the 6th Network Operations and Management Symposium (NOMS'98).* February 1998.

[11] Burkhard Stiller. *Quality-of-Service - Dienstgüte in Hochgeschwindigkeitsnetzen.* Internat. Thomson Publ., 1996.

Specification of a Service Management Architecture to Run Distributed and Networked Systems

C. Mayerl, Z. Nochta, M. Müller, M. Schauer, A. Uremovic, and S. Abeck

Cooperation and Management IT Research
Institute for Telematics
University of Karlsruhe (TH)
Zirkel 2, D-76128 Karlsruhe Germany
Phone: +49-721-608-6390, Fax: +49-721-608-4046
email:{mayerl|nochta|abeck}@cooperation-management.de

Abstract. Due to the complexity of running distributed and networked systems, we can recognise a trend of virtual re-centralisation of distributed systems. Since outsourcing IT resources, IT service providers are born. The aim of service providers is to run IT components offering qualified IT services to customers, who specify quality demands as service level agreements (SLAs). Service providers use management tools to assure the quality of IT services and to run IT effectively and efficiently. The management tools available today do not meet all demands of IT service providers fulfilling service level agreements customers. This paper specifies an integrated service management architecture supporting IT service provider to assure the quality of IT services.

Introduction

The migration of IT operators towards IT service providers shifts the focus from IT components to the needs of customers. Customers are interested in IT services and their quality properties, but they are no longer interested in fact whether systems are running on a mainframe machine or a toaster. Buzz words like *IT outsourcing* or *application hosting* describe this trend [Fis99, Pau99]. Service providers have to integrate network, system and application components delivered by developers into a networked system. Examples for components are business and office software running on workstations or mainframes connected by network components like hubs, routers and switches [HAN99]. There are also developers delivering management tools to support an operation of distributed systems [Slo94]. Customers focus on daily needs and choose services offered by providers. They need communication and application services to process business critical information. Customers also need support services in order to use IT services correctly. The quality demands of customers with regard to IT services are specified in service level agreements (SLAs). The aim of a provider is to assure agreed service levels instead of paying penalties. Figure 1 shows a scenario of IT service provision.

C. Linnhoff-Popien and H.-G. Hegering (Eds.): USM 2000, LNCS 1890, pp. 258-269, 2000.

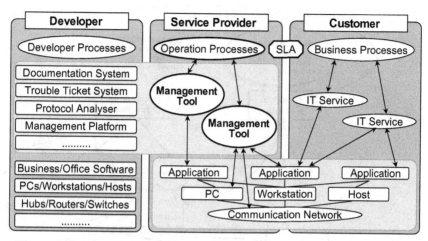

Figure 1: Service level agreement (SLA) between provider and customer

To be effective and efficient, IT service providers use computer based management tools to monitor and control IT components. Although IT management tools like Hewlett Packard Open View, Cabletron Spectrum, Tivoli NetView provide a necessary technical view on distributed components, they do not satisfy the demands of an IT service provider which has to fulfil SLAs [Ghe97]. For example, available management tools do not support co-operation and co-ordination of distributed operation personnel, which is necessary to fulfil quality demands.

Properties of IT Services

For each IT service property customers can specify an individual level determining the fee they have to pay for using that service. There are two kinds of services offered by a service provider, as shown in Figure 2: **Main services** are application and communication products, such as SAP R/3, standard office tools or me-too-products. They comprise functionality provided by network, system and application components implemented as hardware and/or software. When providing services, an integration of used network, system and application components is important. **Support services** are services within, for example, customer management, problem management [CCT95] and change management [CCT98]. They support the use of main services and increase their quality. On the one hand support services can be ordered implicitly, for example by specifying reaction time for a breakdown of SAP R/3 services. On the other hand they can be offered explicitly, for example, help desk service supporting the use of main services [Wal99]. Customers specify properties, such as availability of support teams, reaction and repair times and frozen zones for changes of the system. Figure 2 shows the coherence between the service properties from customers' viewpoint and the underlying technical and organisational resources.

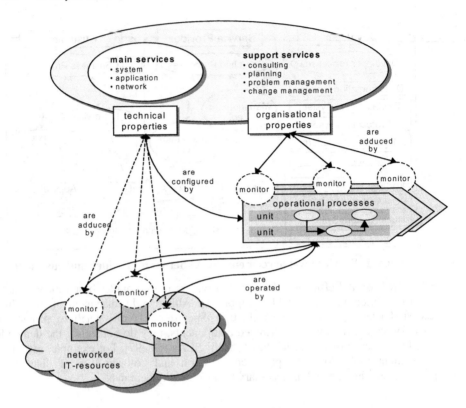

Figure 2: Services and their technical and organisational properties

As mentioned above main services provide technical SLAs adduced by monitored IT resources. Beyond this, technical properties are configured in the context of IT operations management processes. The organisational SLAs of support services are adduced by organisational units executing operational processes. The service model simplifies the quality management of services by structuring and categorising resources and their properties. Within one category a service includes characteristic quality parameters (SLA-parameter) based on IT or organisational resources. Properties of resources define the quality of service as seen from the customers' viewpoint and are the basis of SLAs. A prerequisite for guaranteeing a property of a service is to assure the properties of technical and organisational components. For an evidence of fulfilling SLAs, properties of resources have to be measured and correlated to a service [YKMY96]. Resource properties that cannot be measured and assigned to a service and to an individual customer cannot be assured as a quality of service attribute specified in SLAs.

Main services can cover a range from central data centre operations to desktop services. These services can be differentiated by separate modules.

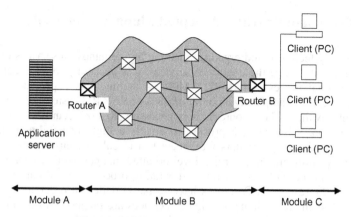

Module A   Module B   Module C

Figure 3: Modules of a main service

Figure 3 explains technical modules of a main service: Module A covers central application components including hardware up to a central router entry point (Router A). Module B contains wide area network (WAN) resources and comprises network resources from the central router (Router A) to an entry point at the local customer's router (Router B). Module C covers resources from the local router up to the desktop equipment on an end-user's desk. Each module has characteristic technical properties within its area of expertise. Technical properties are represented by SLA-parameters, for example availability or response time of an application server, throughput of WAN components, and throughput of local area network (LAN) components. Definition of these SLA-parameters and their measurement checkpoints depends on allocated modules. Important checkpoints are service access points between different modules such as Router A and Router B.

A specification of SLAs for support services can be based on organisational or functional modules [CCT95]. Modules differ from each other by e.g. employee qualification. End-user support provides technical support for registered users, and it is performed by three functional organisation units: first-level support to manage customers' requests, second-level support to solve problems of module A and B professionally, and location support to maintain components in module C. These units handle incoming and outgoing service requests. The first level support acts as a single point of contact for end-users. Important properties of this unit are: Availability of support staff within service hours and resolution time of problems. The second-level support is responsible for the final resolution of service requests which are received from the first-level support. Main tasks of this unit are: solving problems, documenting actions, informing first-level support and documenting the result of actions. SLAs like second-level average problem, request and inquiry resolution time determine the quality of this service. In location support, organisational units deliver onsite support and services to a customer in their local computing environment. There are SLA-parameters, like response times and average resolution time for problems detected in module C.

Specification of Provider Accepted Management Tools

SLAs specify technical and organisational quality demands on services offered by an IT provider. To assure the quality of services, it is necessary to take a closer look at the operational processes [AM97, AM99]. Assuming that a provider guarantees a service level, for example, availability of 98% of SAP R/3 system, it is not enough to run highly available IT resources. It is necessary to use accurate service operation processes, too. An important process to enable a high availability is the problem management process. Providers must react fast to calls by customers and should be able to solve problems in a service level oriented manner, so that guaranteed service levels will not be violated. Therefore, operating processes are often more critical to SLAs than IT resources. Processes have to be modelled in order to understand and implement them. We assume that agreed services are mapped on operation processes and processes realised by process oriented management tools.

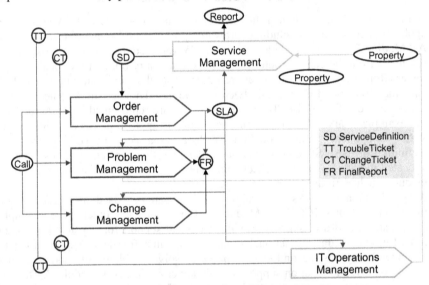

Figure 4: IT operation process model

Figure 4 models the most important operation processes. Service management process defines services and their components, and reports SLAs. Order management process uses the service structure to co-ordinate service levels with customers. SLAs are inputs of all other operation processes. Problem management handles unplanned incidences endangering SLAs [CCT95]. Change management plans and co-ordinates changes on IT resources [CCT98]. IT operations management processes contain tasks to configure, monitor and control components of a networked system.

In order to describe provider demands on management tools, we have introduced an abstraction layer in our modelling scheme which describes demands on tools in an abstract way. We speak of Process Orientated Management tools (POMs) [AM99]. The POM-layer meets the demands of providers as well as those of software developers. A detailed process description and deficiencies identified are used as catalysts to investigate what kind of (tool) support a provider needs to improve the way service is delivered. Hence, consultants and operative staff elaborate in workshops the appropriate data and functionality required to operate efficiently. Depending on the type of support, different POM types can be deployed [MSS99]. In order to improve communication capabilities among process participants, horizontal communication POMs are applied. Horizontal communication can be either directed in terms of pre-defined rules or spontaneously used (non-directed) to get additional information needed to proceed. Besides horizontal communication we propose the use of vertical communication POMs to monitor, control and configure the underlying provider's IT infrastructure. Operative staff can deploy execution POMs if there is a need to compute a result based on input parameters. In principle, POMs encapsulate data and functionality with respect to the context of a process it is used in. It can be described in a pictorial way, such as a form, so it could be used to hold discussions with providers. Described in a object-orientated way, for example, using the Unified Modeling Language (UML), POMs could be used as specification for software developers [Bur97].

Integrated Service Management Architecture

Following methods like PRODEM [MSS99] IT service providers can specify tools to manage a networked system. An investigation of provider demands results in an integrated service management architecture (SMA). This section specifies the most important building blocks of SMA and the relationships between them. Figure 5 shows an overview of SMA.

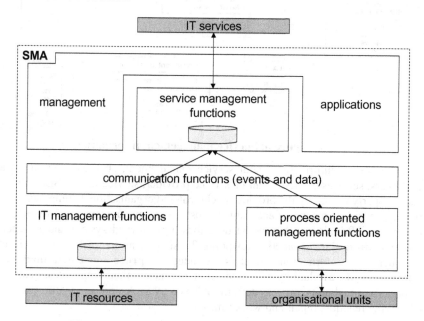

Figure 5: Service Management Architecture (SMA)

SMA integrates IT management functions, process oriented management functions and service management functions. Management relevant information is communicated between building blocks and processed by different management applications. The following sections describe different models as part of SMA extended by process management and service management aspects. These models detail building blocks shown in figure 5.

Information Model

Merely fulfilling SLAs, management information about status and properties of networked components is not enough. Therefore, an existing information model of IT management has to be extended by information about services and customers using services and also information about operation processes and the co-operation of organisational units.

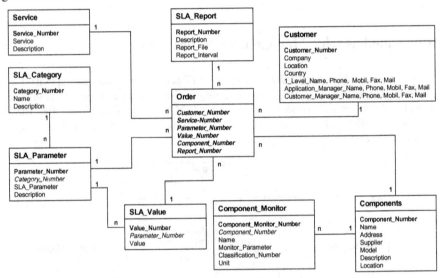

Figure 6: Service management information

Figure 6 shows information about service management, such as information about customers, services offered by an IT service provider, service levels (SLA_Value) for each property agreed by the provider, technical and organisational components as part of a service, measurement algorithms, and parameters to report SLAs (Component_Monitor). This model describes a networked system and its operation processes from the customers' viewpoint. To support an internal view of IT service providers, the information model is extended by **process-oriented management** information like availability of organisational units and their employees, qualification of organisational units, process definition driven by SLAs, process status, time stamps describing reaction, repair and work time etc.

Functional Model

Traditional IT management focuses on the fault, configuration, accounting performance, and security functions of IT resources. In order to meet customers' demands SMA integrates functions of service management to define a new service bundling of technical and organisational modules to a service. SMA also needs functions to manage customers' individual SLAs, to drill down SLAs to properties of components, to monitor technical and organisational components and to correlate measured information to a service. Finally, there must be functions to report and demonstrate the service quality.

Running a networked system effectively and efficiently with regard to SLAs, SMA integrates management functions to guide the execution of operational processes like problem management and change management and to manage involved organisational units. SMA triggers organisational units to act step by step without losing the flexibility to handle undefined exceptions, for example in the context of problem management. This process-oriented management concept is called the guided co-operation concept (GCC) [May98]. GCC describes processes, defines synchronisation points and functions to store, transport and process information. It guarantees also flexibility to handle exceptions. Figure 7 illustrates functions to report SLAs. IT management platforms, such as Tivoli NetView monitor networked systems. Process-oriented management tools e.g. Remedy's Action Request System, and also telecommunication switches including automatic call distribution (ACD) report information about properties of organisational units, such as support teams.

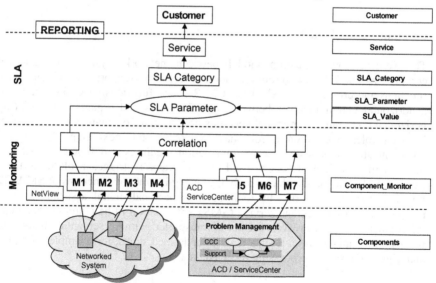

Figure 7: Functions to report SLA fulfilment

Information supplied by monitors depends on technical and organisational components. Therefore the next architecture layer correlates the different monitor information. The correlation can be done by logical rules specifying conditions.

Correlated data can be assigned to service categories described above, to services as well as to customers. Reporting functions support the configuration and illustration of SLA reports.

Organisational Model

IT management standards define roles, such as manager and agents of IT resources. In order to execute operational processes fulfilling SLAs it is necessary to define processes like problem management and change management and their tasks. Roles have to be specified by a service provider to execute tasks of operational processes. Defined roles should co-operate with each other. A role specifies a domain of tasks as part of a process and is occupied by an organisational unit at the execution time of a process. To be more efficient, organisational units need management tools to execute tasks and to co-operate with other units in a co-ordinated way. Service management specifies roles, like customer using services, suppliers of other services, like telecommunication providers, and also internal roles, for example process owners and operational roles. In the context of the problem management process an organisational model defines roles and their co-operation to execute operational processes running a networked system. These roles are: process owner (problem manager), first-level support (help desk or call center), competence centres for module A, B and C (second-level and local support). The co-operation between these roles has to be co-ordinated by defined communication protocols.

Communication Model

The vertical communication model between network, system and application components and roles executing operation processes is supported by IT management functions and protocols like SNMP or CMIP. These functions have to be extended by a horizontal communication between specified roles and organisational units. The horizontal communication model specifies how to transport management information between roles and when a role has to execute the next step. Therefore, the communication model defines communication mediums and functions like phone, mail, email etc. which should be used to co-operate. To trigger a role to do the next step, the SMA interacts with human beings using interaction functions of SMA. These functions can be supported by tools such as personal digital assistants or mobile phones using short message service (SMS). Information to be communicated can be differentiated as data or events. Data is transported without semantic changes to be processed by another role. Events describe a defined status, for example, of a process and trigger a next step processing received data.

Implementation Experiences and Outlook

This section describe a prototype implementing the SMA specified above [Sch00]. Due to heterogeneous networked systems and individual demands on IT service providers, there is no single general-purpose management tool which can support all service providers. SMA integrates different management tools to manage main services and operational processes. Managed objects are: application system (SAP R/3), network (WAN and LAN components), and server (Unix) as well as workstations (Windows NT). These resources comprise a main service with modules A, B and C as described above. We use Tivoli products providing network-, systems- and application- management in order to avoid many integration problems. These management tools collect raw technical data for SLA monitoring and reporting as well as daily system administration purposes. The management tools we used to implement SMA are: Tivoli Distributed Monitoring (DM), Tivoli NetView, and Tivoli Manager for R/3. DM manages end-user systems such as workstations and file servers. Management with DM requires demons running on the local systems which only monitor selected system properties like CPU usage, collect management data and implement a communication interface to management systems. NetView is a comprehensive management tool for heterogeneous devices on distributed networks.

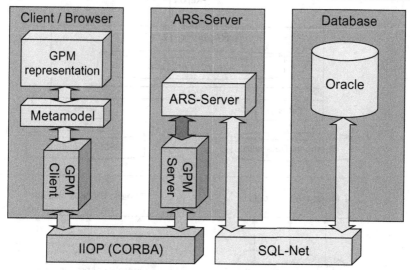

Figure 8: Architecture of the Generic Process Monitor

The Generic Process Monitor (GPM) we implemented monitors processes realised by process-oriented management tools like trouble ticket systems [Ben99, Aug00] such as Remedy ARS (Action Request System). Figure 8 shows the main blocks of the GPM architecture including ARS components. The main goal of GPM is to collect and visualise information about operational processes. GPM is based on CORBA. Central module of GPM is the GPM-server which is responsible for getting information from the monitored process oriented management tool dynamically. The GPM-Client consists of a representation layer to show management data on a web browser and a CORBA client interface. ARS can map IT problem-management processes into so-called forms. ARS is based on a client-server architecture that distributes the forms under predefined rules to according personnel. All information about rules, forms, sequences etc. are stored in a relational database, for example Oracle. In this scenario GPM server uses the open C-API of ARS to monitor the forms. At the moment the GPM prototype monitors ARS.

Transforming raw management data into service- and customer-oriented information is one of the major functions of SMA [MU99]. Customer-oriented information means well defined and formatted reports for high and midlevel management personnel controlling SLA parameters. High-level managers typically need long term reports (e.g. annual reports) to make strategic decisions unlike mid-level managers, who should get short term reports (daily, weekly) to control quality of daily business functions.

In our implementation we use InfoVista providing graphical reports in different formats. InfoVista has a Perl-API that makes it possible to generate reports. Since we use NetView to monitor and administer the network we renounce the network collector functionality of InfoVista. The prototype integrates the reporting functionality of InfoVista into SMA as shown in Figure 9.

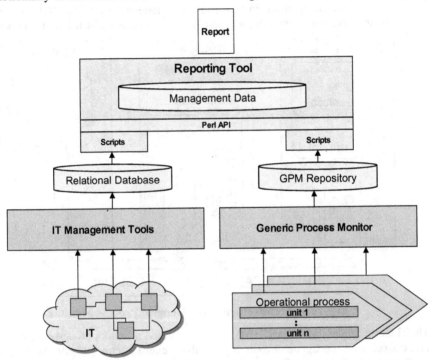

Figure 9: Service level reporting of IT management

The IT management tools together with GPM monitor the networked system and the operational processes. Data collected by GPM are stored in its object-oriented repository. Technical data collected by the Tivoli management tools are stored in a relational database. Presently, the GPM repository includes metadata information collected from ARS. In the future, we will develop a generic repository served by a model engine which is under construction. This engine will enable to convert and store data from other process oriented management tools.

References

[AM97]   Abeck, S.; Mayerl, C., 1997, "Prozeßbeschreibungen als Basis für einen
             qualitätsgesicherten Betrieb von vernetzten Arbeitsplatzrechnern", APS'97,
             Koblenz, Germany.

[AM99]   Abeck, S.; Mayerl, C., 1999, "Modeling IT Operations to Derive Provider
             Accepted Management Tools", IM'99, Boston, USA.

[Aug00]   Augustin, G., 2000, "Generic Process Monitor (GPM)", University of
             Karlsruhe.

[Ben99]   Bender, P., 1999, "Implementation of a Process Monitor using Java and
             CORBA", University of Karlsruhe.

[Bur97]   Burkhardt, R., 1997, "UML – Unified Modeling Language", Addison-Wesley.

[CCT95]   Central Computer and Telecommunications Agency (CCTA), 1995, "Problem
             Management", London.

[CCT98]   Central Computer and Telecommunications Agency (CCTA), 1998, "Change
             Management", London.

[Fis99]   Fischer, J., 1999, "Outsourcing reaches desktop", Computer Zeitung, Volume
             11, Germany.

[Ghe97]   Ghetie, I. G., 1997, "Networks and Systems Management – Platforms Analysis
             and Evaluation", Kluwer Academic Publishers, Boston, London, Dordrecht.

[HAN99]   Hegering, H.-G.; Abeck, S.; Neumair, B., 1999, "Integrated Management of
             Networked Systems", Morgan Kaufmann Publisher.

[May98]   Mayerl, C., 1998, "Process-oriented Approach to Develop Provider Accepted
             Management Tools", EUNICE'98, Munich, Germany.

[MSS99]   Mayerl, C.; Schäfer, A.; Schubert, L., 1999, "PRODEM: Method to Specify
             Service Provider Oriented Management Tools", MobIS'99, Bamberg, Germany.

[MU99]   Müller, M.; Uremovic, A, "Modeling and Implementation of a Service
             Management Environment to Report Service Quality", University of Karlsruhe.

[Pau99]   Paul, M., 1999, "Outsourcing of IT services at universities", Praxis der
             Informationsverarbeitung und Kommunikation, Volume 2, Germany.

[Sch00]   Schauer, Martin, 2000, "Specification of a Service Management Architecture to
             Provide Quality of IT Services", diploma thesis, University of Karlsruhe.

[Slo94]   Sloman, M., 1994, "Distributed Systems Management", Addison-Wesley.

[Wal99]   Wald, E., 1999, "Help Desk Management", MITP.

[YKMY96]   Yemini, S.; Kliger, S.; Mozes, E.; Yemini, Y., 1996, "High Speed and Robust
             Event Correlation", IEEE Communication Magazine.

Mobile Agents and Applications

Chair: Otto Spaniol, RWTH Aachen, Germany

Towards Context-Aware User Modeling

Michael Samulowitz

Corporate Technology
Siemens AG
Otto-Hahn-Ring 6
D-81730 Munich, Germany
Michael.Samulowitz@mchp.siemens.de

Abstract. Research in Ubiquitous and Wearable Computing yielded several types of context-aware applications, dramatically changing the way to interact with computers. Personalizing these applications is a key concern; therefore we investigate ways to apply user modeling to the paradigm of context-aware systems. Our initial work proposes (1) a hierarchy that relates user model data to contextual information, and (2) operations for manipulating the hierarchy. Deploying the operations the hierarchy can act as a substrate for communicating the user's wishes concerning system behavior.

1 Introduction

Context-Aware applications [1] adapt to the context (e.g. location or time) of use. Especially, work in ubiquitous [2] and wearable computing [3,4] substantiates the deployment of context-aware applications (or services). In these settings, the user has increased freedom of mobility. The increase of mobility creates situations where the user's context, such as location of a user and the people and objects around her, is more dynamic. Both wearable and ubiquitous computing have given users the expectation that they can access services whenever and wherever they are [5]. These services should adapt to the wide range of possible user situations. Therefore the concept of context is a useful method, providing means to determine the user's situation, which may be used to tailor the systems behavior accordingly.

Context-aware applications principally aim to improve human-computer interaction by implicitly using context information. A further improvement can be accomplished by *personalizing* these applications. Generally, systems providing personalized applications (or services) are based on a *user model*. A user model contains the system's assumptions about the user, which are utilized to adapt to the user's needs [6].
Here, we want to investigate approaches for user modeling suited to context-aware systems, taking into account their special requirements.

C. Linnhoff-Popien and H.-G. Hegering (Eds.): USM 2000, LNCS 1890, pp. 272-277, 2000.

Basics on Context

The notion of context has significant impact on application design for mobile users, where context is subject to constant change. If context is accessible to applications its possible to dynamically adjust behavior to the current user's context. Prior to discussing context-aware applications and their personalization, it is helpful to provide a definition for context.

Here we render a definition given in [5], which refines and generalizes several definitions that can be found in other sources, e.g. [1,7]:

Context is any information that can be used to characterize the situation of an entity. An entity is a person, place, or object that is considered relevant to the interaction between a user and an application, including the user and applications themselves.

Context information can be categorized in different types of information; certain types of context information are more important than others, particularly considering practical use. These are **location**, **identity**, **activity**, and **time**. These types of context are designated as *primary context*. *Secondary context* types may be derived by given primary context information. For example, given a person's identity (primary context) it may be possible to acquire its phone number (secondary context).

In addition [5] gives a definition for a context-aware system:

A system is context-aware if it uses context to provide relevant information and/or services to the user, where relevancy depends on the user's task.

A rich set of usage scenarios typically enabled by context-aware systems can be found in literature; for example mobile tour guides [8,9], or context-based retrieval applications that gather and store context information and allow later information retrieval based on context information [10].

Basics on User Modeling

User modeling is concerned with how to represent the user's knowledge and interaction within a system to adapt those systems to the needs of users [11]. Work in user modeling is tackled by several research fields, including artificial intelligence, human-computer interaction, psychology and education, which investigate ways to construct, maintain and exploit user models. The following list states general examples where user models obviously enhance usability of applications by embedding user related information:

- Message filtering [12]
- Adaption of user interfaces
- Personalized web pages
- Computer-based training (CBT)

Generally, the following matters are key concerns to user model management: (1) gathering relevant data, (2) appropriate representation schemes, and (3) consistency of user model data. The management of user models is typically done by agents, which constantly monitor user-system interaction, e.g. [15].

2   The Challenge: User Modeling and Context-Awareness

The context-aware computing paradigm helps to improve user-system interaction by implicitly considering contextual information. Personalization deploying user modeling is an another strategy to ease interaction. We propose a way to combine both strategies. Therefore our work aims to develop schemes for user modeling, taking into account contextual information. In particular, we propose a scheme that allows associating user model data to certain context types. For example, we could associate user model data to the user's visited locations (context type: location); hence, it would be possible to design context-aware applications which adapt their behavior to both, the current location and the associated user model data for this place. Besides considering context-awareness our user modeling scheme should regard the fact that a mobile user potentially uses multiple applications; the following list states examples of possibly context-aware applications where user models enhance usability:

- Mobile e-commerce
- Location aware services
- Environment configuration [13]
- Process activation/deactivation in dependence of context [14]

The listed examples clarify the difficulty to introduce a single user model for context-aware systems, because eventual personalization covers several areas of use and there is no common model that fits to all of them. For this reason we propose to separate concerns in user modeling for context-aware systems. This would result in multiple user models each being specialized on a certain context of use. Still there is information common to all of them (or at least to a sub-set) e.g. superior settings regarding security or privacy issues, this information should be propagated to the other user models, in order to attain consistent system behavior.

3   Discussion: A Hierarchy of User Models

As an appropriate modeling scheme we propose a hierarchy of user models in order to organize user-centric data in context-aware systems. In correspondence to the requirements outlined in the previous paragraph the scheme should allow to model data considering context types and common data structures, that may be communicated among different user models.

The initial design for our modeling scheme provides user model **entities**, and **associations** between them. Entities may present the user model data for a certain application, or they may represent user specific data related to context information. Associations relate entities to each other by indicating common data structures between entities, or they are used for assigning user related data to particular context information. The following two examples illustrate the main principles.

Figure 1 states an example for communicating common data structures between user models. The figure shows three user model entities (depicted by circles). The *PeopleFinder* and the *Mobile e-commerce* entity are associated to an entity representing the user's preferred policies regarding security and privacy. Hence, if a user changes these policies, information about this should be propagated to the user model entities associated (PeopleFinder and Mobile e-commerce). If the user selects a "high" privacy level he should neither being locatable nor being annoyed by offers to buy.

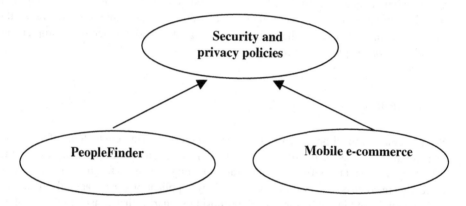

Figure 1. User Models related to each other

Figure 2 depicts another example for distributing user model data on a hierarchy of entities, each entity representing a certain subset of the user model data. In particular, this example focuses on relating user-centric data to context information (location); it takes in account spatial concerns and provides a higher degree of granularity in comparison to the first example. The left side of the figure (Room A) shows the user model data associated to a room; it mainly includes processes which are triggered by certain user actions [14], and references to resources the user normally uses. In this example, the sphere of action of the entities *processes* and *resources* is constrained by location (Room A). If the same user wants to have the same settings ("look & feel") in room B as in room A, he would ask the system to do so. The system would automatically *transfer* all settings related to room A (including the associated entities) to room B. (The set of candidates for transfer operation could be determined by referential integrity constraints.)

Transfer is not always trivial; in the given example it is not sure that room B is equally equipped (e.g. computing resources) as room A is. Hence, this could lead to partial transfer or intelligently adapting functions.

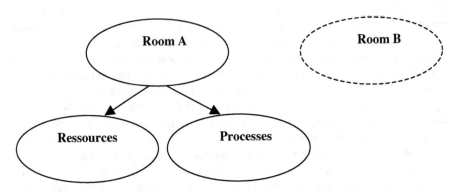

Figure 2. User Model Data and Context

The previous examples introduced two operations on the hierarchy: *propagation* and *transfer*. In order to implement these operations and probably others, we could associate an agent to each of the entities. These agents could co-operatively implement *transfer* and *propagate* operations.

4 Summary

We presented a novel approach to user modeling considering contextual information. Our future work seeks to improve our modeling scheme, especially regarding the following issues: (1) defining a general modeling scheme (for the moment it is basically introduced by examples), (2) how applications can actually evaluate information stored in the hierarchy, (3) proposing scenarios that consider other context types (e.g. activity or time).

References

1. Schilit, B.N., Adams, N.I., Want, R. Context-aware computing applications. Proceedings of the Workshop on Mobile Computing Systems and Applications, pp 85-90. IEEE Computer Society, Santa Cruz, CA, 1994
2. Weiser, M. Some Computer science issues in ubiquitous computing. Communications of the ACM 36, 7 (July 1993), 75-83
3. T. Starner, S. Mann and B. Rhodes The MIT wearable computing web page. http://wearables.www.media.mit.edu/projects/wearables.
4. Abowd, G. D., A. K. Dey, R. Orr, and J. Brotherton, "Context-awareness in Wearable and Ubiquitous Computing," GVE, Technical Report GIT-GVU-97-11, May 1997.
5. Dey, A.K. & Abowd, G.D. Towards a better understanding of context and context-awareness. GVU Technical Report GIT-GVU-99-22, College of Computing, Georgia Institute of Technology, 1999

6. Alfred Kobsa. User modeling and user-adapted interaction. Proceedings of the CHI'94 conference companion on Human factors in computing systems, 1994, 415 – 416

7. Pascoe, J. Adding Generic Contextual Capabilities to Wearable Computers. 2nd International Symposium on Wearable Computers, 146-153, 1998

8. Lancaster University. The Active Badge Tourist Application. Available at http://www.comp.lancs.ac.uk/computing/research/mpg/most/abta_project.html.

9. Abowd, G.D., Atkeson, C.G., Hong, J., Long, S., Kooper, R., and Pinkerton, M. Cyberguide: A Mobile Context-Aware Tour Guide. ACM Wireless Networks 3, 421-433.

10. Rhodes, B. J. The Wearable Remembrance Agent, in Proceedings of the 1st International Symposium on Wearable Computers, ISWC '97 (Cambridge MA, October 1997), IEEE Press, 123-128.

11. M. Brown, Eugene Santos, Sheila B. Banks and Mark E. Oxley. Using explicit requirements and metrics for interface agent user model correction. Proceedings of the second international conference on Autonomous agents , 1998, Pages 1 – 7

12. M. Matthew, C. Schmandt. CLUES: dynamic personalized message filtering. Proceedings of the ACM 1996 conference on Computer supported cooperative work, 1996, pages 113 – 121

13. A. Pentland, "Smart Rooms", Scientific American, April 1993

14. R. Want, A. Hopper, V. Falcao, and J. Gibbons. The active badge location system. ACM Trans. On Info. Sys., vol. 10, no.1, pp. 91-102, January 1992

15. Rob Barrett, Paul P. Maglio and Daniel C. Kellem. How to personalize the Web. Conference Proceedings on Human factors in computing systems, 1997, pages 75 - 82

Context Notification in Mobile Environment to Find the Right Person in Time

Cora Burger

University of Stuttgart, Institute of Parallel and Distributed High-Performance Systems (IPVR),
Breitwiesenstr. 20-22, D-70565 Stuttgart, Germany
E-Mail: caburger@informatik.uni-stuttgart.de

Abstract. People searching for somebody else who is suited for a certain task should not only know about current location and context of this person but also about further characteristics like her capabilities. We propose a solution, that provides added value to existing services for context notification. It can be used in arbitrary networks consisting of mobile devices and stationary computers and is flexible enough for a broad spectrum of application scenarios. Two kinds of filters guarantee the appropriate level of privacy and prevent from information overflow. The prototypical realization is based on IrDA (Infrared Data Association) and a mobile agent infrastructure.

Introduction

Everybody knows the situation of looking around for consultation in a store. Having found a clerk somewhere between shelves, one will recognize that she is already busy with other customers. This problem of unsuccessful trials to find a person suited for a certain task is a very frequent one and wide spread (think e. g., of nurses and medicines in a hospital or of colleagues at office). Besides personal annoyance, it results in lost time and depending on the task in question can have serious consequences.

Mobile devices, phones and sensors bear the potential to overcome this problem and the more general one of handling arbitrary interrelationships between actions of different people most efficiently (see coordination theory in (5)). We start with taking a closer look at the above described scenarios and work out a list of five requirements that must be taken into account by any solution.

Actually, different problems can be involved in the one of finding the right person for a given task: 1. Who is suited at all? 2. Who is suited in the current situation? 3. Where is the suited person?
An answer to the first of these questions can exist, if it is known already who is suited at all. But this knowledge is not sufficient. As long as a clerk is talking to other customers she is not suited to answer questions. The same holds for some colleague who is an expert in a certain area but is currently staying overseas at some conference or has a strict deadline ahead and therefore is not in the right mood for any discussion.

It can be concluded, that a whole set of information about persons and their current environment is needed (requirement 1) and matched against characteristics of the task

C. Linnhoff-Popien and H.-G. Hegering (Eds.): USM 2000, LNCS 1890, pp. 278-283, 2000.
© Springer-Verlag Berlin Heidelberg 2000

to solve the above described problem (requirement 2). Making public this information evolves the next question, the one of privacy issues. People do not want to be observed all the time and not at all by everybody else (requirement 3).

Another point concerns the amount of context information and frequency of notifications at the receiver's side. In the scenario of a store, this information will be queried for and delivered just once. But it can vary in degree of detail. In offices, even the frequency of being disturbed by information about colleagues plays an important role. Thus in either case, it must be possible to restrict information to a useful minimum (requirement 4).

Last but not least, context information can arise in a number of different sources: desktop or mobile devices and sensors. Furthermore, people should have information about others at hand when it is needed. Either of these cases requires integration of mobile devices. But connection to such devices is insecure and subject to frequent interruptions. Nevertheless, people should not miss essential information (requirement 5). Furthermore, information has to be protected against interception and misuse (requirement 3 again).

Current approaches to location and context awareness (e. g., (4), (7), (8)) fail in the scenario of looking for a clerk, because they require a direct identification of the person in question. Furthermore, only privacy issues have been taken into account, but restriction of information overflow was neglected.

Model of Enhanced Notification Service

To properly fulfill requirement 1, the following types of context information are essential
- Identifier, e. g. name,
- role (including capabilities and knowledge),
- location,
- activity and its priority.

With the exception of the identifier, these parameters vary permanently and more or less frequently. Persons can be referenced either directly by identifier or indirectly by some other characteristics. For instance, one is looking for any clerk in a store who is able to inform about a certain product. A more specific question would include further parameters, e. g., a suited clerk staying nearby without talking to anybody else and without being busy elsewhere. For any person referenced somehow, current location is of interest. Furthermore, kind of activity and degree she is currently involved in it are indicators for deciding whether this person can be disrupted or should be left in peace.

Requirement 2 is satisfied by designing an enhanced notification service with proper service elements. Context information is delivered to this service by information producers via the following service element

```
push (own_context, producer_filtering_conditions)
```

By specifying filtering conditions, the producer can determine exactly who is allowed to see which part of her context information. Thus, privacy issues are supported (requirement 3).

For information consumers, two different sets of service elements are offered to get context information about directly or indirectly referenced producers:

```
pull (reference_to_person, current_context, optional:
consumer_filtering_conditions)
subscribe (reference_to_person, context_change_event,
consumer_filtering_conditions) resp. modify, unsubscribe
```

where pull is used for singular queries (e. g. for clerk in store) and subscribe cares for constantly notifying a consumer about context parameters of the producer (e. g. at office). In all cases, the parameter reference_to_person either contains the identifier of the person (direct reference) or some characteristics and optionally selection or preference criteria (indirect reference). Furthermore, the consumer can specify filtering conditions to avoid information overflow (requirement 4).

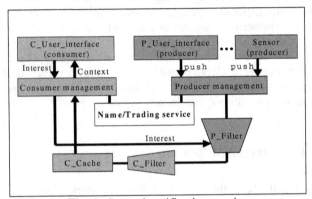

Fig. 1. General notification service

A notification service with functionality as described above must contain components as shown in figure 1. At her user interface, a person in the role of a consumer describes her interest in the form of pull or subscribe with direct or indirect reference to another person. Further treatment of this interest is handled by the corresponding consumer management. In case of direct reference by person's identifier, the relevant producer manager can be found via name service. For indirectly referenced persons by parameters like role, location or activity, a trading service (cf. (6)) has to be used for mapping these characteristics to the most suited producer manager by taking into account selection and preference criteria (requirement 2). For instance, consumer management invokes

```
import (role=clerk_responsible_for_computers,
location=nearest, activity=free)
```

to find someone for consultation on computers in a store.

Depending on the form of interest (pull or subscribe), either an isolated query or a demand for registering is propagated to the P_Filter of the referenced person where it is accepted or rejected depending on the producer's privacy needs. In case of acceptance, filtering conditions contained in the interest result in setting up a corresponding C_Filter. This covers a consumer's interest in a subset of possible context information.

A user in the role of producer addresses the management responsible for her to define criteria for filtering and customize a P_Filter. The producer manager of a person must offer its service to a trader at initiation time, e. g. by

```
export(identifier=Sheila,
role=clerk_responsible_for_computers,
location=callback_location, activity=callback_activity)
```

For an incoming import request the trader asks for current values of location and activity by means of callback methods as specified in export. Whereas for queries and registries of consumers filtering criteria are applied, traders are informed about all values of context information without any restrictions. Privacy issues are preserved nonetheless, because the trading service does deliver mere references of suited producer management to requesting consumer management components.

Current values of context information are either created by the user, some application or some sensor. Via producer manager they are propagated to the corresponding P_Filter that distributes them to all C_Filters of authorized consumers. Depending on its user's interest, a C_Filter either deletes the information or transmits it to the C_Cache. This component is responsible for reliable information transfer to consumer management taking into account the possibility of connection interrupt. That means, information is stored as long as the consumer management is not connected (requirement 5).

It should be noted that because of insecure environment all parties must authenticate and encrypt data before transmitting them (requirement 3).

Implementation

There are several alternatives to implement the notification service as described in the last section. In the following, we present a realization based on an infrastructure for mobile agents. A mobile agent consists of mobile code. While migrating through networks, it is acting almost autonomously. Infrastructures for mobile agents enable life cycle, mobility and communication of agents. Furthermore, they guarantee restricted access to resources and cope with heterogeneity of systems involved.

For instance, the Mole agent system (1) provides an infrastructure for mobile agents written in the programming language JAVA. Its logical structure is defined by locations and two different kinds of agents: system agents and mobile agents. System agents are bound to a certain location and care for secure access to stationary resources. Mobile agents can move between locations to perform their tasks. Communication between agents takes place by means of remote procedure call or messages. Agents can create and start mobile agents.

In (2), a first approach to context notification was presented that was based on the Mole platform. It was restricted to stationary desktop computers and collaborative settings with direct references to other people. In the meantime, this system was extended to be used on handheld devices with Windows CE and connections via IrDA (Infrared Data Association). Furthermore, we introduce the possibility of guest users and indirect references via role to cope with scenarios like the one in a store as well.

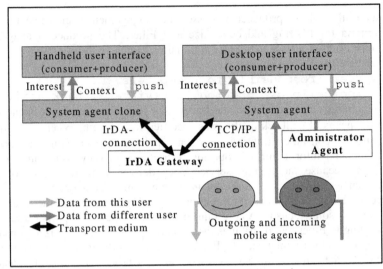

Fig. 2. Notification service in mobile environment

The new architecture is shown in figure 2. It consists of the following components (please refer to (3) for further detail):

- For each user: two different versions of user interface, one for handheld devices and one for desktop devices. They are responsible for presenting context information about other people (consumer part) and for letting users input current context information about themselves (producer part).
- For each user or for the ensemble of guests: system agent in the fixed part of the network, e. g. on desktop device. After registry at the administration agent, it manages interests of its corresponding user interfaces by sending out suited mobile agents to system agents of other users (consumer part), accepts or rejects mobile agents of other users and propagates context information from its user interface to accepted mobile agents according to its filtering criteria (producer part).
- For each pair of users, where one is interested in context information about the other one: mobile agent being created by the system agent in consumer role and transmitting interest and filtering criteria to the system agent in producer role. If the mobile agent is accepted, it filters context information delivered by the foreign system agent and propagates it to its system agent.
- For each user with handheld device: system agent clone to enable configuration of filters and exchange information between user interface on handheld device and system agent of this user via some IrDA gateway.
- On stationary devices being equipped with IrDA-interface: IrDA gateway cares for transmitting data between a system agent clone that is contacting the gateway and the corresponding system agent (or guest system agent).
- Administrator agent, current access point to name service. It is enriched to offer trader functionality also.

Conclusion and Outlook

We have presented a system, that contributes to finding people that must not be known personally but can be referenced by characteristics like their role (requirement 1 and 2). It offers extensive configuration of filtering and security mechanisms to satisfy needs of consumers and producers of context information especially in a mobile environment (requirement 3 to 5).

One of the shortcomings of the current implementation is manual insertion of context information that is rather cumbersome. To avoid this overhead, the user interface of producers can be restricted to assigning priorities to activities and specification of filtering criteria whereas the rest is replaced by suited location services and further services to detect current activity.

As a whole, our notification service for context information increases the probability of finding the right person at right time. It can be extended in several directions. For instance, search for objects can be included and general coordination decisions of people can be facilitated.

References

(1) Baumann, J. et al.: *Mole - Concepts of a Mobile Agent System.* WWW Journal, Special issue on Applications and Techniques of Web Agents, 1998. http://www.informatik.uni-stuttgart.de/ipvr/vs/projekte/ mole.html

(2) Burger, C.: *Team awareness with mobile agents in mobile environments.* Proceedings of the 7th International Conference on Computer Communications and Networks (IC3N'98), IEEE Computer Society, Los Alamitos, October 1998, pp. 45-49

(3) Kramer, A.: *Reachability notification of colleagues by means of mobile devices* (in german). Diploma thesis No. 1777, University of Stuttgart, November 1999

(4) Leonhardt, U.: *Supporting Location-Awareness in Open Distributed Systems.* PhD thesis, University of London, 1998

(5) Malone, T.W. et al.: *What is Coordination Theory and How Can It Help Design Cooperative Work Systems?* CSCW '90 Conference on Computer Supported Cooperative Work, ACM Press, October 1990, pp. 357-370

(6) *ODP Trading Function: Specification.* ISO/IEC IS 13235:1 | Draft Rec . X.950:1 (1997). http://ftp.dstc.edu.au/AU/research_news/odp/trader/trtute/trtute.html

(7) Prinz, W.: *NESSIE: An Awareness Environment for Cooperative Settings.* Proc. 6th European Conference on Computer Supported Cooperative Work ECSCW'99, Kluwer Academic Publishers, Dordrecht, 1999, pp. 391-410

(8) Roussopoulos, M. et al.: *Person-level Routing in the Mobile People Architecture.* Proceedings of the USENIX Symposium on Internet Technologies and Systems, October 1999

Automated Adaptation for Mobile Computing Based on Mobile Agents

Thomas Springer and Alexander Schill

Dresden University of Technology, Department of Computer Science, Institute for System
Architecture, Mommsenstr. 13, D-01062 Dresden, Germany, Tel.: +49 351 463 8261,
Fax.: +49 351 463 8251
{springet, schill}@rn.inf.tu-dresden.de

Abstract. In the last few years the market brought up a big variety of mobile
devices with differing functionality. This development results in an increasing
number of wireless subscribers and in the upcoming demand for a seamless
access to information and services provided by the internet. To support arbitrary
devices in a mobile environment we introduce an approach for adaptation at
application level based on a partitioning model and abstract operations.
Available techniques to support and improve mobile applications are integrated
into a concept with generic and application specific components which adapt
information according to the capabilities of mobile devices, network quality and
user settings. We also describe a multimedia email application for the validation
of our model. The implementation is based on mobile agents providing dynamic
installation, flexible deployment and mobility support.

1 Introduction

One of today's visions in mobile computing is ubiquitous information access [1].
Information (e.g. email, fax and web pages) should be available anywhere at any time.
During the last years the market brought up a big variety of mobile devices with
differing functionality. This development results in an increasing amount of wireless
subscribers and the desire to access information and services provided by the internet.
Unfortunately most of the currently available applications and services for the internet
expect high bandwidth connections and well equipped client devices. WAP [2] is one
approach to overcome this problem but focuses on the characteristics of mobile
phones and does not scale to the extended capabilities of a notebook. For a seamless
integration of arbitrary mobile devices information has to be adapted to their
resources (e.g. memory, display, software, network connections). Moreover users
change between devices (e.g. from PC to PDA) but want to access and handle the
same information. This requires applications which can react very flexibly to changes
in their environment (e.g. changing client devices or network connections) and adapt
to new devices, changing user requirements and individual user needs.

One of the most interesting applications (because it addresses basic user needs) is
reading and writing email. Even mobile phones allow the access to email. But
currently the download of messages via wireless networks or even via a standard
modem is very unsatisfying. Email tools do not allow the selection of certain message

C. Linnhoff-Popien and H.-G. Hegering (Eds.): USM 2000, LNCS 1890, pp. 284-289, 2000.

content or the adaptation of attachments. Especially when only a slow connection is available needless data within a message (e.g. an audio attachment while the device is not audio enabled) should be filtered out automatically. Furthermore large attachments should not be downloaded or compressed before the transfer. Moreover the user should be able to determine what messages he wants to read (e.g. only the messages from certain senders). These examples point out three areas of adaptation: device capabilities, network connection and user preferences. Exceptions (e.g. a user needs to download a large attachment because it contains a map to a location he urgently searches for) should also be handled by the application.

In this paper we introduce a model for automated adaptation of information at application level based on mobile agents to address the requirements of mobile information access. While other approaches focus on special problems like filtering of information [7] or data reduction [6], the aim of our model is to integrate adaptation techniques (e.g. handling of frequent disconnections, varying network quality, low resources on the mobile device and mobility) into a generic approach supporting arbitrary devices. The adaptation is automatically, flexibly deployable and configurable. Section 2 describes an adaptation model with generic and application specific components. We also introduce a concept for the placement of the functionality with relocation of computation between client and server in mind. In section 3 we present a multimedia email application which was prototypically implemented to validate our model and contains most of the functionality described above. The implementation maps the abstract components for adaptation on mobile agents to enable the dynamic installation and placement of adaptation functionality. Section 4 concludes the paper and gives an outlook to future work.

2 Adaptation Model

The model introduces components at application level rather than a system based approach. The distinction of adaptation techniques shown in figure 1[1] was done using two criteria: placement of code and availability of information. For flexible configuration the components are intended to be loosely coupled, i.e. the generic components can be dynamically added and removed at runtime.

For the functionality contained in this partitioning model we have defined abstract operations which can be variably combined to sequences. Each operation gets input data and parameters and produces output data. The algorithms used for adaptation are not determined by the model. Rather the right functionality is selectable from a set of implementations. For instance the queuing operation can be implemented using different strategies (e.g. priorities). The following list of operations is not complete. We only describe the operations used for the implementation of the email application.

---

[1] Details can be found in [3].

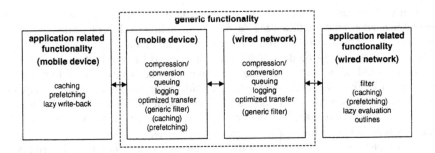

Fig. 1. Placement of adaptation functionality

1. The **Selection** operation checks or selects the input data according to a criterion (e.g. a filter or the content of a data object). One parameter can be the type of the input data to process different data types in different ways (e.g. for conversion).
2. The **Replacement** operation creates a new representation for the input data (e.g. a text description or an outline for an email attachment).
3. The **Composition and Decomposition** operations assemble and disassemble structured data types from and to a sequence of data objects.
4. The **Compression and Conversion** operation enables the adaptation of format and volume of multimedia data specific to the type. For instance a GIF image can be transformed to JPEG with a quality parameter for information loss. Furthermore the color depth and the image size can be reduced. The operation consists of encoding the data, conversions and decoding the data. Thereby the format for encoding and decoding may be different.
5. The **Queuing** operation facilitates the enqueuing and dequeuing of data objects according to the implemented strategy.
6. The **Transfer** operation provides a reliable data transfer optimized for special networks. For example multiple parallel send threads can be used for communication media with high delay times to better exploit the available bandwidth.
7. The **Requirement Determination** operation processes the information of the user and device profile and the actual network quality provided by the environment sensing service and creates a set containing the most restrictive requirements.

Figure 2 shows a possible combination of generic operations. The queuing component enqueues (1) the incoming data objects. If the transfer is possible, one element is dequeued (2). The compression and conversion operation adapts the volume and format of data according to the information provided by the requirement determination operation (3). The transfer operation initiates the dequeuing and controls the transmission of data over the network (4). The incoming data objects are handled according to their data type. Therefore the operations can be used in a generic manner independent from information at application level. The generic components are intended to be used for all applications on a mobile device. The next section describes a sample application and possible implementations of application related operations.

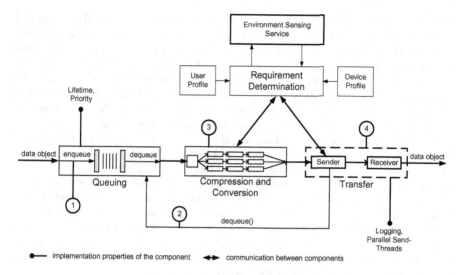

Fig. 2. Generic adaptation components

3 Agent Based Email Application

To validate our adaptation model we have implemented a multimedia email application using mobile agents as components. According to the partitioning model shown in figure 1 the application consists of an email tool (we use Netscape Messenger), two pairs of adaptation components and the mail server.

Configuration. As described in section 1 the application automatically filters and adapts the messages downloaded to the mobile device. The adaptation behavior is configurable. The application related component (email agent) sent to the mail server filters the messages before the transfer over the network. The user can specify two kinds of filters: email header filters (e.g. sender, receiver or subject) and filters for information in the body (e.g. body text or attachment data type and size). The header filters are used for a first selection of messages. Only messages matching at least one header filter are selected for download. If no header filter matches the message is not handled by the email agent but remains on the mail server. The attachment filters are applied before the transfer. Only data types specified in the filter are sent. Furthermore the attachment must not be larger than the threshold assigned to its data type. The generic components are configured independently. Currently the user can specify the data types for compression and the degree of the data loss (in percent). Further enhancements will be rules to convert data objects (e.g. a limited pixel size for images or a maximum number of colors). The user can also transfer a list of headers to the mobile device. What headers the list contains is configurable (e.g. all messages from the account, only new messages, all messages older than x days etc.) From this list the messages for download can be selected manually.

Application. The application is started on the mobile device. The email agent as well as one of the generic components migrate to hosts within the wired network. While the email agent moves to the mail server the generic component migrates to a host near the user and follows him when he moves. The email agent contains information about the mail account, filters and user preferences. At the mail server it asks for messages using the information about the email account. For filtering and transfer of messages the adaptation components shown in figure 3 are used. New messages are selected for download (1) by the evaluation of the headers. Selected messages are decomposed (2) to data objects which are divided (3) into the header, the body text and the attachments for separate handling. For the attachments the filters are applied (4). Attachments removed during the filtering are replaced (5) by another representation (currently a text description is added to the body text). The data objects of the messages are sent to the generic component within the wired network. Before the transfer over the last link to the mobile device data is automatically adapted to the quality of the connection, the resources on the mobile device and user preferences using the requirement determination operation (6). After the transfer to the mobile device the data objects are composed to a MIME message (7) which can be displayed by an arbitrary email tool and the user is notified.

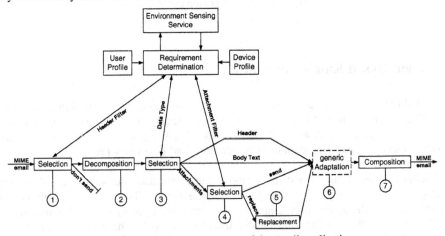

Fig. 3. Adaptation components of the email application

Performance. The implementation is based on Voyager by ObjectSpace [8] and the JDK 1.2 [9]. The communication between agents is based on JavaRMI. With the prototype we have done performance measurements. The test message contains a JPEG image (12204 bytes in high and 4439 bytes in low quality). The transmission of the message containing the high quality image between an Pentium Pro 200 MHz (64 MB RAM, WindowsNT) and a Thinkpad 760D (Pentium 166MHz, 64MB RAM, Windows95) connected via the Xircom Netwave wireless LAN took 809,6 ms with and 774,4 ms without the generic components. For the message containing the low quality image we measured 444,7 ms with and 378,3 ms without the generic components. While the lossy compression of the image (decoding and encoding) needs 135,6 ms in average altogether the transfer time for the message is significantly smaller. The indirection over the generic proxy takes also time but the benefit for disconnection handling and adaptation justifies this effort. For further details see [3].

4 Conclusion and Future Work

In this paper we described a model for automated and flexible adaptation of information according to the available network quality, the capabilities provided by the mobile device and user settings. While other approaches introduced static components and are focussing on special techniques (e.g. filtering of information [7], data reduction [6] or disconnected operations [5]) our concept integrates the techniques into one model and introduces mobile components taking user mobility into account. Because of the partitioning model shown in figure 1 the adaptation functionality can be distributed to where it can be used most efficiently. Moreover the generic components can be used by all applications on a mobile device. Because of the use of mobile agents adaptation components can be dynamically installed at runtime wherever they are needed. This is a big advantage compared to system based concepts with static components (see [4] and [5]). Furthermore the components are loosely coupled, enabling dynamic addition and removing of components (i.e. the generic components). Legacy software can be enhanced with adaptation functionality without changing the existing components. The additional functionality can be added using the proxy approach and client-site agents. Currently we work on the refinement and implementation of the operations described in the adaptation model. Moreover we want to implement further applications to prove the applicability our concepts.

References

1. Weiser, M.: Ubiquitous Computing; www.ubiq.com/hypertext/weiser/UbiHome.html
2. Wireless Application Protocol Forum: WAP White Paper, 1999
3. Schill, A.,Held, A., Ziegert, T., Springer, T.: A Partitioning Model for Applications in Mobile Environments; In Todd Papaioannou and Nelson Minar, editors, Proceedings. Mobile Agents in the Context of Competition and Cooperation (MAC3), a workshop at Autonomous Agents '99, pages 34-41, 1999
4. Schill, A., Kümmel, S., Springer, T., Ziegert, T.: Two Approaches for an Adaptive Multimedia Transfer Service for Mobile Environments; Computers & Graphics, Vol. 23, No. 5, 1999
5. James J. Kistler and M. Satyanarayanan: Disconnected Operation in the Coda File System; ACM Transactions on Computer Systems, 10(1), pp. 3-25, February 1992
6. Fox, A., Steven, D. Gribble, Brewer E.A., Amir, E.: Adapting to Network and Client Variability via On-Demand Dynamic Distillation; Proceedings of the Seventh International Conference on Architectural Support for Programming Languages and Operating Systems, pp. 160-170, October 1-5, 1996
7. Bruce Zenel, Dan Duchamp: A General Purpose Proxy Filtering Mechanism Applied to the Mobile Environment; The Third Annual ACM/IEEE International Conference on Mobile Computing and Networking, 1997 pp. 248-259
8. www.objectspace.com
9. java.sun.com

How to Efficiently Deploy Mobile Agents for an Integrated Management

Steffen Lipperts

Aachen University of Technology, Department of Computer Science (i4)
D-52056 Aachen, Germany
steffen@lipperts.de

Abstract. Along with today's networks, which are gradually converging and setting the field for universal service markets offering value added services to users on a global scale, their requirements are changing fundamentally. It is becoming increasingly important to provide an enabling technology which allows to meet these new requirements. Mobile agents are being discussed as comprising the potential to be such a technology. In order to use mobile agents for an integrated management, however, two problems need to be solved, namely the problem of non-determinism and the problem of competing goals. This paper closely examines performance aspects of mobile agents and evaluates a solution for the two problems which is based on utility theory.

1 Introduction

The years have passed where different kinds of networks, especially in the internet domain, the media, and the telecommunication domains, merely coexisted. Having reached a global scale, networks today are converging in order to provide a uniform platform for all kinds of service provisioning. The management of the individual networks has always been a key issue due to their growing complexity and scale. Now it becomes necessary to provide suitable means for ensuring the availability and reliability of upcoming and converging service markets. The diminishing suitability of current approaches to distributed system and network management with regard to scale and flexibility is becoming more and more apparent and is widely discussed in the literature [1,2]. Accordingly, in October 1999, the Internet Engineering Task Force (IETF) has issued an internet draft (as an update to RFC 2257 [3]), in which it is stated that "This very real need to dynamically extend the management objects..." exists and that "It can become quite cumbersome to configure subagents ... on a particular managed node.". Several approaches have been made or are currently being examined to shape management according to the new requirements.

Some of these approaches aim at extending SNMP to overcome the problems of centralisation and inflexibility, such as the introduction of hierarchies in SNMPv2, Remote Monitoring (RMON), and AgentX. More powerful approaches appeared with the introduction of mobile code, first management by delegation [4], then various

C. Linnhoff-Popien and H.-G. Hegering (Eds.): USM 2000, LNCS 1890, pp. 290–295, 2000.

approaches which deployed mobile agent technology. Several projects are active in this field, either evaluating the suitability of mobile agent for management in general [1,2], or focusing on different aspects, e.g. intelligence [5] and organisation [6] of mobile agents. The main reason for mobile agent deployment is their ability to migrate, which promises to offer added value for distributed systems and service markets through asynchronous, autonomous actions, usually entitled as "disconnected operations", and through the "benefit of locality", i.e. the advantage of a much more efficient local communication, reduced execution times, and reduced network traffic. This, however, is not necessarily always the case, as an overhead is introduced by the migration process. Therefore, by studying the applicability of mobile agents depending on the prerequisites set by the distributed system itself and by the nature of the agents' tasks, this paper addresses a key issue for enabling the deployment of mobile agents in future distributed systems.

The paper is structured as follows. In the next section, two key problems of mobile agent deployment, which so far have been neglected, are pointed out and discussed in detail, together with performance studies which supply evidence for both the existence and the gravity of these problems. The third section illuminates how these problems affect the way mobile agents are to be used – not only for an integrated management – and evaluates a solution for these problems.

2 Performance of Migration

The key feature of mobile agents is their ability to migrate. While this promises several benefits as shown in the introduction, the migration process with its serialisation, transfer, and de-serialisation also introduces an overhead which makes these improvements situation dependent. In order to assess this in detail, measurements have been made to compare the migration process with remote communications. The results are shown in table 1.

The measurements have been made in a local area network. A single agent migration was to be compared to remote CORBA communications, as these are the standard for distributed systems. Two cases were to be distinguished, a migration including a classloading process and another one excluding it. The former is required if an agent arrives at a host it has never visited before and which does not hold the agent's classes prior to its arrival. The latter is given if the classes are already present upon arrival.

Table 1. RPC vs. Migration

1a)

	Time in ms	one migration equals
migration with classloading	1430.1	-
CORBA RPC	0.9	1557
CORBA RPC (100 byte)	1.2	1210
CORBA RPC (1 Kbyte)	3.8	372
CORBA RPC (10 Kbyte)	23.1	62

1b)

	Time in ms	one migration equals
migration without classloading	19.4	-
CORBA RPC	0.9	21
CORBA RPC (100 byte)	1.2	16
CORBA RPC (1 Kbyte)	3.8	5
CORBA RPC (10 Kbyte)	23.1	0.6

As a first result, it can be stated that a migration including classloading is an expensive process, as in the meantime, an awful lot of remote communication can take place, even if the size of the parameters is reasonably large. Yet, one must not forget that in slower (class 2) media, this relation is less extreme, as can be deduced from the results shown in figure 1. Here, it can be seen that a far bigger percentage of a remote communication is affected by the underlying network (marked grey) than with a migration. Consequently, remote communication will perform worse on slow media. Things look even better for the migration process, if no classloading is required (see table 1b). Here, agent migration suddenly becomes very efficient, as in the meantime, only few remote communication can occur and following the migration, the agent will be able to use local communication, which only takes a fraction of a millisecond.

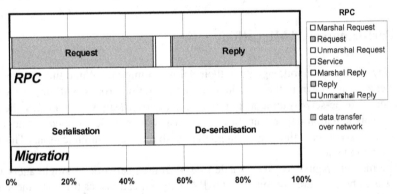

Fig. 1. Percentage of Data Transfer in Entire Process

Taking these results into account, the assumption can be verified that it is situation dependent whether or not an agent migration can provide a performance improvement. Given the results presented above, it can be decided to replace a certain number of remote communications by a migration, taking into account parameters such as

- How many remote communications will be replaced?
- What is the size of their parameters?
- What is the size of the agent?
- Which kind of network is given?

That is, a break-even point can be determined given this information where the migration overhead is compensated by the following local communications. Yet, rather than having reached a solution, here is where the problems start. In most cases, the required information listed above cannot be obtained. Take for example operation that are to complex to calculate their communication costs in reasonable time. Even worse, take non-deterministic operations such as sequential searches or negotiations. In any of these cases, how are the parameters to be determined?

Even under the condition that the required information is given, a decision on the applicability of a migration would be far from perfect if merely the aspect of data transfer and execution time was taken into account. As described in the introduction, mobile agent deployment can offer other benefits which might be just as valuable as a performance improvement, such as improved robustness and availability, reduced error rates, or even required battery power of mobile systems. Picture a case, where not enough communication occurs in order to justify a migration. The link which is used for these communications, however, is not reliable, e.g. a GSM connection in a moving vehicle. Depending on the importance of the process to be executed, improved reliability might be the main target. Moving a mobile agent to the wired network thus might be reasonable after all.

3   A Solution Based on Utility Theory

So far, the necessity for new approaches to management has been pointed out and both the potential and the major problems of mobile agent technology have been discussed, non-determinism and competing goals. In [7], we have presented the outline of a solution for these problems which is based on utility functions. These assign numbers to states in order to express their desirability, thus allowing a ranking of these states. Let $U(S)$ denote such a utility of a state S. Now, let C be the current state an agent is in and A a non-deterministic action with i possible results $Result_i(A)$, i.e. a transition form C to any state in $Result_i(A)$. If for C and for all A, the probabilities P of the results $Result_i(A)$ are given, i.e. $P(Result_i(A)|A, C)$ given for all A and for all i, then for all A, the expected utility EU can be calculated:

$$EU(A|C) = \sum_i P(Result_i(A)|A,C) \cdot U(Result_i(A))x \tag{1}$$

In utility theory, the principle of maximum expected utility (MEU) has been established which denotes that a rational agent should choose an action which maximises the agent's expected utility, i.e. the agent is to maximise the average utility [8]. The algorithm to be followed by a mobile agent thus is as follows (for simplification in pseudo-code):

```
void next_step(){
    determine current status C;
    for all actions Aᵢ {
        for each possible outcome Resultⱼ(Aᵢ) {
            obtain current probability P(Resultⱼ(Aᵢ)|Aᵢ, C);
        }
    }
    maxEU = 0;
```

```
for all possible actions A_i in status C {
    eu = calculate EU(A_i|C);
    if(maxEU < eu)
        maxEU = eu;
    }
    execute action A_i with maxEU;
}
```

Whilst determining the current status is fairly straightforward and can be done by the agent internally, the probability densities of the possible goal states of all actions A_i depend on current system states and thus need to be retrieved from the system, i.e. from suitable system components. A trader or an equivalent component in a distributed platform which is responsible for service procurement can generate this information. Then, given the current state C, the possible actions A_i, and the probabilities of their outcomes, the expected utilities can be calculated and maximised.

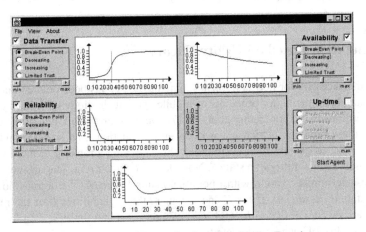

Fig. 2. Tool based Determination of the Utility Function

That is, once the utility functions are given. In [7], we have shown how multiattributive utility functions can be composed by individual utility functions, if a multiplicative form can be determined. Figure 2 shows a tool based definition of such a multiattributive utility function, where the functions for the individual attributes and their respective weights can be specified be the user, leading to an automated composition of the multiattributive utility function.

In order to assess the suitability of the solution presented in this paper, smart mobile agents deploying the utility based behaviour have been implemented and evaluated. A direct comparison has been made with stationary agents and other mobile agents running in the identical environment. The focus has been on the execution times, as these allow a quantitative evaluation of the suitability of the new approach.

Despite the overhead through data transfer, additional calculations, and additional size due to the utility functions carried on their itinerary, the smart agents were able to reduce the execution times as shown in figure 3, always choosing the most effective paradigm, either migration (phase 2) or remote communication (phase 3).

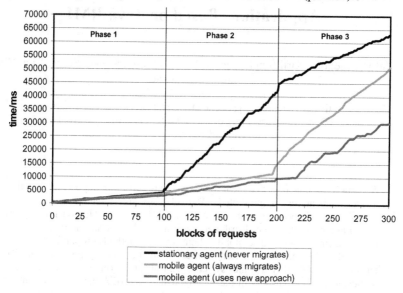

Fig. 3. Comparison of the Different Paradigms

References

1. Bieszczad, A.; Pagurek, B.; White, T.: Mobile Agents for Network Management. In: IEEE Communications Surveys, September 1998
2. Puliafito, A.; Tomarchio, O.: Advanced Network Management Functionalities through the Use of Mobile Software Agents. In: Proceedings of the Third International Workshop on Intelligent Agents for Telecommunication Applications, Stockholm, Sweden, August 1999
3. IETF: Agent Extensibility (AgentX) Protocol Version 1. RFC 2257, January 1998
4. Goldszmidt, G.; Yemini, Y.: Delegated Agents for Network Management. In: IEEE Communications: Management of Heterogeneous Networks, Vol.36, No.3, March 1998
5. Sahai, A.; Morin, C.; Billiart, S.: Intelligent Agents for a Mobile Network Manager (MNM). In: IFIP International Conference on Intelligent Networks and Intelligence in Networks, Chapman & Hall, Paris, France, September 1997
6. White, T.; Bieszczad, A.; Pagurek, B.: Distributed Fault Location in Networks Using Mobile Agents. In: Proceedings of the 3rd International Workshop on Agents in Telecommunications Applications, AgentWorld'98, Paris, France, July 1998
7. Lipperts, S.: On the Efficient Deployment of Mobility in Distributed System Management. In: 3rd International Workshop "Mobility in Databases & Distributed Systems", Greenwich, UK, September 2000
8. Russel, S.; Norvig, P.: Artificial Intelligence – A Modern Approach. Prentice Hall, 1995

This work has been funded by the German Research Council (DFG) under SFB 476 IMPROVE and GRK 185/1-00.

A Scalable Location Aware Service Platform for Mobile Applications Based on Java RMI

Olaf Droegehorn, Kirti Singh-Kurbel, Markus Franz, Roland Sorge, Rita Winkler,
and Klaus David

IHP, Im Technologiepark 25, D-15236 Frankfurt (Oder), Germany
{droegehorn, singh, franz, sorge, rwinkler,
david}@ihp-microelectronics.com

Abstract. In this paper, a generic service platform for supporting location aware applications is presented. The platform is based on Java to be independent of operating systems. We use RMI (Remote Method Invocation) for communication in the distributed system and Jini as an additional tool to offer and find services. The mobile client invokes methods on platform objects via RMI and offers its own remote methods to be used by the platform. To ensure the scalability of the system, central units (platform servers) are replicated in accordance with the deployment scenario. A new mechanism for the hand-over of objects, shared by clients and servers, between platform units is described. We introduce a new concept of objects and auras for efficient support of innovative location aware applications. The platform is also extended for thin clients without a JVM (Java Virtual Machine). A thin client communicates with the platform via a platform gateway using e.g. HTTP.

1. Introduction

For the future success of W-LAN and cellular systems, innovative applications and the underlying middleware platform are important building blocks. Like several other researchers, we believe that location and context based applications have a significant scope in this field of mobile computing [2]. The applications developed and investigated up to now by the research community were basically prototyped applications. On one side these applications demonstrate the potential of taking location and context awareness into account, however, on the other side, it can be seen that these applications are nontrivial to create for two reasons: First, these applications are very complex, they require special skills and knowledge of underlying communication infrastructure. Second, these applications were developed as prototypes and can be used only by few terminals but not with a mass of users.

Location and context aware applications need a common set of functions. To unify the application programming interface for all applications concerning this topic, a universal platform is needed. The platform must be generic in order to be independent of a specific communication network or positioning system. Furthermore, it is important to support a variety of applications, not restricted on a specific business model.

C. Linnhoff-Popien and H.-G. Hegering (Eds.): USM 2000, LNCS 1890, pp. 296-301, 2000.
© Springer-Verlag Berlin Heidelberg 2000

In the literature, several approaches for the design of a service platform have been reported. For example, in [8] a platform called MASE was designed to support mobile users. For this platform, applications like a city guide, mobile multimedia services, etc. were developed. These applications were prototypes and the issues of real world like scalability were not addressed in this project. Furthermore, features like tracking a mobile user and finding local available services were not supported by this platform.

An important aspect of a location aware service platform is keeping track of mobile objects in a scalable way [1]. The Globe project [6, 9, 10] concentrates on the development of an efficient search mechanism for mobile objects. The same issue is addressed by the Nexus project [3, 7].

In this paper, we introduce a platform architecture, which takes care of the basic communication infrastructure required for mobile wireless systems and basic functions required by a location aware application. It is designed to be flexible enough to replicate the platform server as often as necessary in order to fulfil the user requirements concerning the response time of the system. The platform itself is realized in Java RMI/Jini technology in order to be independent of a specific operating system. We introduce a concept of auras. An aura defines a space of interest for an object and can have any dimensions. Auras enable a large number of new services which are not possible by just stating the physical location of an object. Based on the aura concept, the user can register for events such as "object A has entered aura X". The support of thin clients which have limited computational capability is also considered.

The rest of the paper is organized as follows. Section 2 describes the overall architecture of the platform. In section 3, the concept of auras and objects is explained. The support of not Java enabled thin clients is introduced in section 4. Section 5 summarizes the paper and gives an outlook of future work.

2. Service Platform Architecture

Our service platform intends to integrate all functions that are required to support innovative location aware applications. The platform consists of several components responsible for special functions. The platform itself is based on Java RMI/Jini technology in order to be independent of the underlying operating system. Platform server units can be replicated as often as required to fulfil the user requirements concerning the system's response time.

We decided to use Java RMI and not CORBA as the communication mechanism, since CORBA seems to be less suitable for mobile terminals due to the complexity of a CORBA client. Moreover, we are developing the system from the scratch and no legacy systems have to be taken into account. We utilize RMI to transfer Java specific objects between platform servers to avoid the transformation of object types.

The service platform operates at two different locations, one part on the server side and the other on the mobile terminal which is, in our case, the client. The part of the platform, which resides on one or several platform servers implements the desired functionality for each component. The structure of a platform server is shown in Fig. 1.

The location management component deals with location awareness and provides all necessary functions concerning this topic. For example, the application can inquire the location of an object. This object can be a logical element defined by the application, e.g. a service available only at specific locations or just another mobile terminal. To provide these location based functions the platform needs to handle several things. On the first hand it must use multiple databases to store the locations of the desired objects. It is important that this subsystem is implemented very efficiently because this database can be very large for cellular systems.

To get informed about the object's location the platform uses a so called sighting proxy. This proxy gets notifications from an underlying sighting system (location system using e.g. cell ID, some form of triangulation or GPS). This system can be implemented by the network provider or by another service provider.

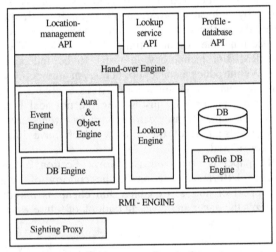

Fig. 1. Architecture of a platform server.

The DB engine has to filter all the sighting notifications in order to reduce the amount of information flow. The DB engine forwards not all sighting updates which it receives from the sighting proxy, but only the first sighting of an object at a particular server and sighting updates for objects on which an event is registered. For example, a user who wants to be notified if he is near a particular moving object, the positions of the objects must be observed. To do this in an efficient way the event engine registers with the DB engine to get all sighting updates for the objects involved in the event. The event engine monitors the positions of the objects and forwards only relevant notifications to other subsystems.

To perform user queries, the engine for auras and objects uses rendering algorithms. The goal is to find out which objects are located in which aura and to determine which auras intersect.

For using a lookup service, the platform supports queries on the Jini lookup system [4, 5]. Users can register their own services with this lookup system or can just use services offered by other devices. The lookup engine at the server side handles the queries and sends appropriate objects to the client.

The profile database is responsible for the support of personalization. Each mobile terminal can give a profile to the platform which contains some common properties of the terminal and the user. For example, security related information can be stored in this profile. Furthermore, the hardware and software capabilities of a specific terminal can be described inside this profile database. All processes which will be handled by the platform in an automatic manner need information about preferences of objects. These preferences are also stored in the profile component. The main engine for this profile database resides on the server and realizes an internal distributed database that is virtually available on each platform server.

To ensure the scalability of our system, the platform unit shown in Fig. 1 is replicated to distribute the workload among a number of servers. The communication between the platform servers is based on hierarchical structures.

The platform must be able to offer the right object references on the right platform server to the mobile client. Because of efficiency reasons not all objects will be available at all locations by definition. The platform has to move several objects from one location to another. This is done in the background by the platform and is not visible to the user or even the platform client. When a client communicates with the platform, the platform chooses the server for the communication with the particular client. For the communication, the server holds remote references of objects residing on the client and vice versa. All the data related to the client (auras, profile, registered events) as well as the remote references of the client's objects are stored at the related platform unit. When the client changes its location and the platform realizes that the client is now in the responsibility range of a new platform unit, a hand-over of the client's remote references and data from the old platform unit to the new one is required. The new platform unit requests the client's data from its neighbored platform units. The old platform unit which holds the data replies by transferring the client's remote references and all other client related data to the new platform unit. The server at the new platform unit registers itself with the client using the clients remote references. The new platform unit overwrites the RMI references of the old platform unit at the client with its own.

The part of the platform running on a client is very small because of the limited computational resources on the wireless terminal. It implements just a proxy for the platform functions which are available on the server side. The application can use well defined API's provided by the components of the platform.

3. Objects and Auras

In the literature, typical approaches concerning location awareness determine just the position of objects or users. This is done by conventional positioning systems or on the basis of the communication infrastructure. That leads in most cases to a model of the real world which deals with mobile terminals and base stations of the wireless system as physical objects and the area around each base station as the space where a mobile terminal can be seen. The main disadvantage of this approach is the dependence of the abstract model inside the service platform on the hardware infrastructure used. If an application designer wants to define objects or areas of interests independent of the used hardware it is mostly impossible to design this model into the service architecture.

For this reason, we propose a very flexible concept of objects and auras. An aura can have any dimensions and defines a space of interest for an object. Each object can have several auras, which are totally independent of each other. An object can be a physical entity like a printer or a mobile terminal. Additionally, we include logical objects in our platform. A service, for example, which is only available in a specific room is a logical object having the aura of this room. For instance, a mobile client can request all objects whose auras overlap with its own aura.

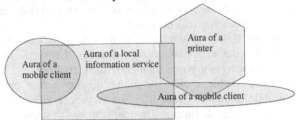

Fig. 2. Aura concept. For each object one or more auras can be defined.

Based on this approach it is the task of rendering algorithms to check if an object or an aura crosses another aura. Which properties these logical objects can have is not specified inside the service platform but in the definition of each application.

With this aura based location aware platform, we are in the position to create a whole range of innovative applications. For example, person A can get informed about the event that person B has approached him by a certain distance (B has entered an aura of A). Upon this, several useful actions can be triggered, like automatic finding of a free meeting room, ordering some coffee, etc.

4. Enhancement for Thin Clients

Since our platform is based on Java and the Java RMI communication mechanism, any client which wants to use a service offered by the platform must have a JVM running on it. Thin terminals like mobile phones or other devices which do not have a JVM cannot use such a service directly. To support such clients, we have extended the infrastructure mentioned in the previous section.

In this enhanced system, we use a mediator which converts messages between a platform server and the thin client. For the platform server side communication, this mediator acts as a regular Java enabled client similar to other mobile clients, which requests objects and services. To communicate with the thin terminal, the mediator uses a common access protocol such as HTTP or WAP. The data received from the platform server are translated into HTML or WML and are sent to the thin client. In this case, the thin client needs only to be able to access the web. It can request HTML pages that meet its service requirements. The mediator is responsible for the correct translation of the messages.

5. Summary and Outlook

In this paper we have introduced a service platform based on JavaRMI/Jini for supporting location and context aware applications for mobile users. Scalability is achieved by replication of server units and a hand-over mechanism for object's references and object related data. The platform can be used for indoor applications as well as for outdoor applications. It is independent of both the operating system as well as the positioning system that provides the location information. An aura concept is used to define regions of interests for the objects used. This enables innovative applications features such as triggering events based on the relative distance of two objects. The platform also provides a lookup service where terminals can offer their services to other people and also can use services offered by other users. Furthermore, the enhancement of the platform for not Java enabled thin clients has been pointed out.

By the end of this year the platform kernel will be implemented. Later, we will develop new location aware applications based on this platform to test its performance and efficiency. These applications will be tested considering a large number of clients. The performance regarding the hand-over of remote references and efficient database searching will be studied with help of field trials and previously performed simulations.

Reference

1. Black A., Artsy, Y.: Implementing Location Independent Invocation. IEEE Trans. On Par. Distr. Syst. Vol. 1 (1), (Jan. 1990) 107-119
2. Brown, P.J., Bovey, J.D., Chen, X.: Context-Aware Applications: From the Laboratory to the Marketplace, IEEE Personal Communications, (October 1997), 58-64
3. Hohl. F., Kubach, U., Leonhardi, A., Schwehm, M., Rothermel, K.: Nexus: An open global infrastructure for spatial-aware applications. Proceedings of the fifth International conference on Mobile Computing and Networking (MobiCom 99), ACM Press (1999)
4. http://developer.java.sun.com/developer/technicalArticles/ConsumerProducts/jinicomm/unity
5. http://jini.org/
6. http://www.cs.vu.nl/~steen/globe/
7 Leonhardi, A., Kubach, U.: An architecture for a distributed universal location service. Proceedings of the European Wireless '99 Conference, Munich, Germany, ITG Fachbericht, VDE Verlag, (1999) 351-355
8. Keller, B., Park, A.S., Meggers, J., Forsgern, G., Kovacs, E., Rosinus, M.: UMTS: A Middleware Architecture and Mobile API Approach. IEEE Personal Communications, (April 1998), 32-38
9. van Steen, M., Hauck, F.J., Homburg, P., Tanenbaum, A.S.: Locating Objects in Wide-Area Systems. IEEE Communication Magazine, (January 1998), 104-109
10. van Steen, M., Tanenbaum, A.S., Kuz, I., Sips, H.J.: A Scalable Middleware Solution for Advanced Wide-Area Web Services. In: Sips. Distributed Systems Engineering, Vol. 6 (1), (March 1999) 34-42

Trends in Data- and Telecommunications

Chair: Sebastian Abeck, University of Karlsruhe, Germany

Design-Aspects for the Integration of CORBA-Based Value Added Services and Intelligent Networks

Frank Imhoff and Marcos dos Santos Rocha

Aachen University of Technology
Department of Computer Science, Informatik 4
Ahornstraße 55, 52056 Aachen, Germany

Abstract: This paper deals with the realisation of Value Added Services known from legacy Telecommunications networks on top of middleware platforms. These legacy services are predominantly based on ITU's Intelligent Network (IN) definitions. Due to the forthcoming network convergence to IP-based networks and the tremendous growth of telecommunications markets these services have to be distributed over a wide range of heterogeneous hardware platforms. Nevertheless, the interconnection to existing circuit-switched networks has to be taken into account. This paper discusses different design aspects for a gateway between CORBA and IN-based services and suggests a dynamic as well as a static approach. Ongoing studies will optimise and evaluate these approaches.

1 Motivation

The technical development and the liberalisation of the telecommunications markets showed that for the operators of predominantly circuit-switched telecommunication networks the provision of *Value Added Services* becomes more and more important. The implementation of such services is difficult. With the introduction of *Intelligent Networks* (IN) somewhat eased the problem but this can not be a solution to satisfy the demand of more and more complex services in the medium-term. *Voice-Data-Integration* and the use of the internet for voice communication (*Voice over IP*, VOIP) requires the introduction of new technologies.

An important aspect during the introduction of new technologies for an efficient implementation of Value Added Services is the independence of the underlying network and hardware platforms. On the one hand this ensures the independence from manufacturers and providers, and on the other hand the internet may be used as transport network [3]. Moreover, potential customers of complex and customised services (e.g. Call Center) want to administer these services themselves, and do not want to invest in expensive, proprietary hardware. Therefore, the use of an object-based software solution such as the Common Object Request Broker Architecture (CORBA) or the Telecommunication Information Network Architecture (TINA) seems inevitable.

2 The CORBA/IN-Gateway

To enable smooth integration of IN-based networks and CORBA the gateway has obviously a key position in the system between these islands. The success of the in

C. Linnhoff-Popien and H.-G. Hegering (Eds.): USM 2000, LNCS 1890, pp. 304–309, 2000.

troduced of CORBA-based Value Added Services depends predominately on the efficiency and functionality of such a gateway [2]. Therefore, to meet the common requirements of existing telecommunications systems such as reliability, scalability, or real-time capabilities become more and more important. First, however the gateway should enable the transparent communication between conventional *Service Switching Points* (SSP) and CORBA based *Service Control Points* (SCP) in both directions.

2.1 Translation Interaction

During the translation interaction, the information which is generated by the translation of the specification, but not transmitted explicitly in the message or the function calls needs to be also taken into account. This could, for example, be a TCAP-message (Transaction Capabilities Application Part) which is only marked by an *operation code* at run-time. The gateway may either statically or dynamically deliver the names of the IDL methods which correspond to this operation code. The timer-values which are allocated to certain operations are another example for the information needed at run-time are. Information such as the allocation of the *Operation Code Function Name* or the coding of the parameters of an operation (ASN.1 tags) can be directly defined and compiled in the code, as well as requested dynamically from a *TcRepository* at run-time. We discuss this important difference in the next sections.

Static vs. Dynamic Gateway

The most important question concerning the design of an IN-CORBA gateway is weather to follow a static or dynamic approach (see Fig. 1).

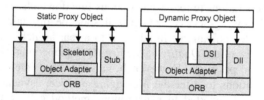

Fig. 1. Static vs. dynamic gateway architecture with integrated proxy

A static gateway implements proxy objects which are defined in their IDL interfaces at compile-time. That is, these objects implement only static interfaces referring to specific protocols, e.g. a variant of INAP. Almost all changes of these protocols lead to a recompilation of the objects. This makes sense if the interaction function is realised in the uppermost layer of INAP, since in this case the gateway only has to be realised for one single protocol. The proxy objects of a dynamic gateway use the functionality of the *Dynamic Skeleton Interface* (DSI) to handle all kinds of function calls. On the other hand the proxies use the *Dynamic Invocation Interface* (DII) in conjunction with the *Interface Repository* to transform an at compile-time unknown INAP message into a CORBA method. Thus, it is possible to create an appropriate call for each function known at runtime, and as a result a transparent communication is still granted. However, the dynamic realisation has its disadvantages. The static gateway knows all the information it needs for the translation at compile time, and allows a much more efficient implementation, because no access to the interface and the TC repositories is necessary, and because additional effort for using the DII and DSI interfaces is required. These access times are difficult to predict. Only an implementation of both the static and the dynamic gateway would allow a realistic comparison. It is to be examined whether a mixed solution (dynamic and static) is of interest.

Translation BER ↔ CORBA-Any
The structure of an INAP message is specified in ASN.1 notation, at runtime they are coded into BER format [8, 9]. The gateway reads (binary) data in ASN.1/BER format and translates them into *CORBA-Any* structures and vice versa. This is realised on a very low level. To implement the dynamic gateway, it seems to be reasonable to use a tree as data structure for the internal encoding and decoding of ASN.1/BER data to reflect the hierarchic structure of the data. This also avoids the low level operations necessary for encoding and decoding of ASN.1/BER data are distributed over the whole program code. This tree structure is used in conjunction with CORBA-*DynAnys*.

Asynchronous Communication and Quality of Service
An operation is called synchronous if no other operations are allowed to be called before it is terminated. TCAP operations are asynchronous, i.e. they do not have the above mentioned limitations. However, for the time being CORBA offers only two function call modules - synchronous and deferred synchronous; the deferred synchronous modules can only be used in connection with the DII.

To convert TCAP operations to real asynchronous function calls, one will need the so called CORBA Messaging-Service, which will soon be officially specified by the OMG (CORBA 3.0 Specification). In addition to a real asynchronous function call, the *Messaging Service* offers *Quality of Service* (QoS) functionality, determining for example timeouts and priorities. However, because it is not intended for a series of CORBA implementations to offer the *Messaging Service*, asynchronous TCAP operations must first be converted to synchronous method calls within the gateway. Thus, an overlap of a given reply time for a method call will not be recognised. Yet, assuming that the present system is fast enough, this should not be a problem.

The Course of the Interaction
We will now explain the typical course of the interaction translation, using an example to show the communication between a legacy *Service Switching Point* (SSP) and a CORBA-based *Service Control Point* (SCP) (see Fig. 2). To simplify, we assume that the gateway objects are already initialised, i.e. the factories for *TcUser* and for the proxy objects have been started and are registered by *TcServiceFinder*. As this is a dynamic gateway, both the Interface Repository and the TcRepository are needed [1]. These are not shown in Fig. 2.

After the SCP has received an InitialDP message, it sends a message to the SSP. This is done through the direct call of the associated function by the proxy. The InitialDP is defined without a return value. If it deals with an operation defining a return value, the proxy will code it in the ASN.1/BER format and passes it to the provider with a *return_result Operation.* Subsequently, the provider sends to the SSP either a Begin-PDU or an End-PDU containing the results. In the above example, the dialogue was initialised from the IN-side. It is foreseeable that the dialogues can also be initiated at the CORBA side, e.g. by the SCP.

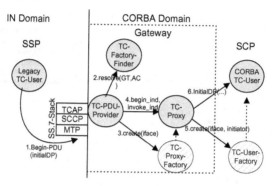

Fig. 2. Example of an interaction: InitialDP

2.2 Integration of the CORBA-Based Application Layer

The interfaces of the CORBA *TcUsers* (see Fig. 2) have been defined in the course of the specification translation. Principally, they could have been implemented directly from the CORBA-based application. Since one could be unwilling to give out for new CORBA applications the interfaces which are defined for an SS.7-based communication, the *TcUser* will become an adapter beforehand. Considering the communication between traditional *Service Switching Function* (SSF) and CORBA-based *Service Control Function* (SCF), it seems to make sense to merge the *TcUser* with the implementation of a CORBA-based *Global Service Logic Program* (GSL). However, whether this can be realised without Threads has to be investigated in more detail.

3 Performance Analysis

First simulations have been done on two PCs (Pentium III 500 MHz, 128 MB RAM) connected over a shared Fast-Ethernet LAN. The first computer was running the simulation manager, the SSP simulators, the *TcPDU* providers, and the *TcFactory Finder.* The remaining objects were running on the second computer. It is important to note that in this first approach each SSP simulator communicates with exactly one *TcPDU* provider creating its own *TcProxy.*

Several simulation runs have been performed to measure the performance of both the dynamic and the static gateway. Additionally, a simulation manager was used to start multiple SSP simulators simultaneously. After an SSP simulator is started, it starts sending *freephone service* (IN-Service "tollfree") requests to the gateway as of *InitialDP* operations encapsulated in TCAP messages. In the next step the gateway translates these messages to CORBA method calls and are forwarded to a SCP simulator. The SCP simulator responds to each *freephone service* request by calling two methods on the *TcProxy*, which translates these method calls in two INAP operations *Connect* and *RequestReportBCSM*. The gateway then sends these operations to the corresponding SSP as a TCAP message. Altogether the gateway translates three INAP operations while handling a *freephone call*.

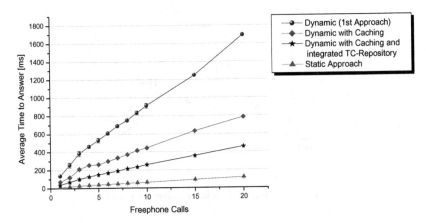

Fig. 3. Static versus dynamic gateway performance including optimisations

Fig. 3 shows that the dynamic translation is much more time consuming than the static one. The reasons for the higher complexity of the dynamic approach can be identified as follows:

- The dynamic marshalling and unmarshalling of CORBA operation parameters and results are very expensive operations. As a CORBA object is not able to implement dynamic and static interfaces at the same time, the *TcProxy* must dynamically unmarshall all the operation parameters and results it receives, even if the signature of some operations is already known at compile-time (e.g. general TCAP message indications).

- The creation of dynamic CORBA invocations is more expensive than using pre-compiled stubs.

- The *Interface Repository* as well as the *TcRepository* may very short become a bottleneck for the gateway. This happens especially if these objects do not use threads, as concurrent requests may always block each other. To reduce the number of accesses to the *Interface Repository*, the *TcProxies* store information about queried interfaces in a cache (see Fig. 3). Another possible approach would be to have the *TcRepository* actually doing the entire translation of INAP operation parameters, results and errors.

- The dynamic construction of data types being unknown at compile-time is a very powerful CORBA feature using the so called *DynAny* (dynamic any) class. Unfortunately, most applications usually do not make use of this class. Especially the translation of long BER encoded ASN.1 "SEQUENCE OF" data sets (e.g. SEQUENCE OF OCTETS) may be very slow.

4 Conclusion and Further Work

As the discussion so far has shown, the higher flexibility of dynamic gateways has its price. Comparing the results with mandatory requirements of telephony systems probably no current CORBA implementation is able to realize complex telecommunications services. For example, 2.0 seconds is the maximum time for the SCP to respond to a message received over the *Common Channel Signaling Network* (CCS) [7]. It takes into account the time it takes the SCP reply to reach the sending node, i.e. the SSP. Yet, future optimizations may enable the use of dynamic gateways described above at least for simple IN-based services.

As the performance of a CORBA application always depends on the Object Request Broker (ORB), it would be interesting to compare the performance of a MICO based gateway to a gateway based on different ORB, for example ORBacus. Nevertheless, the use of threads will improve the overall performance of the gateway. We foresee further performance improvements especially in the dynamic gateway implementation. The key point is the implementation of the *TcRepository*. On the other hand, the static gateway seems to have almost achieved an optimum. Additionally, it would be interesting to analyze the gateway's behavior after distributing the *TcProxies* over several computers and to investigate different load balancing strategies. It seems to be reasonable to combine static and dynamic *TcProxy* objects in one gateway, to get the benefits of both approaches, i.e. flexibility and performance. The integration of both gateway types will be as next step.

5 References

[1] S. Mazumdar, N. Mitra, "Design of a ROS-CORBA Gateway for inter-operable intelligent networking applications", Proceedings of IS&N Conference, Lake Como, Sept. 1997

[2] H.A. Berg, S. Brennan, "CORBA and Intelligent Network Interworking", Proceedings of IS&N'98, 1998

[3] F. Imhoff, A. Küpper: Intelligent Network Functionality in an IP based Environment. In: Fifth International Conference on Information Systems Analysis and Synthesis, Orlando, July/August 1999

[4] Object Management Group, "Interworking between CORBA and Intelligent Networks Systems Request for Proposal ", OMG DTC Document ftp://ftp.omg.org/pub/docs/, 1997

[5] AT&T, IONA Technologies, GMD Fokus, Nortel, Teldec DCU, "Interworking Between CORBA and TC Systems", OMG DTC Document ftp://ftp.omg.org/pub/docs/, 1998

[6] EURESCOM, "CORBA as an Enabling Factor for Migration from IN to TINA: A EURESCOM-P508 Perspective", OMG DTC Document ftp://ftp.omg.org/pub/docs/, 1997

[7] The Open Group, "Inter-domain Management: Specification Translation", Project P509, 1997

[8] S. Mazumdar, N. Mitra, "ROS-to-CORBA Mappings: First Step towards Intelligent Networking using CORBA", Proceedings of the Conference on Intelligence in Services and Networks, Lake Como, Mai 1997.

[9] T. Seth, A. Broscius, C. Huitema, H. P. Lin, "Performance Requirements for TCAP signaling in Internet Telephony", Internet Draft, Internet Engineering Task Force, http://www.ietf.org/draft-ietf-sigtran-tcap-perf-req-00.txt , August 1999

Experiences Building a Service Execution Node for Distributed IN Systems

Menelaos K. Perdikeas, Fotis G. Chatzipapadopoulos, and Iakovos S. Venieris

National Technical University of Athens, 9 Heroon Polytechniou, 157 73 Athens, Greece
[perdikealfhatz]@telecom.ntua.gr, ivenieri@cc.ece.ntua.gr

Abstract. We describe a Distributed Intelligent Network architecture. By laying a distributed processing environment a more flexible mapping between functional and physical entities is afforded. Mobile code can in turn be employed to cater for performance or load balancing considerations as well as to increase the overall flexibility and manageability of the system. Changes in the physical locations of the endpoints of a control relationship can be abstracted to higher layer software by virtue of the location transparency properties of the environment. We report on the development of an experimental implementation and we demonstrate how the aforesaid technologies improved its characteristics.

1 Introduction

The Intelligent Network (IN) approach for providing advanced services to end users aims primarily at minimizing changes in network nodes by locating all service-related (and thus likely to change) functionality in dedicated IN-servers, known as 'Service Control Points' [1,2]. These servers are in a sense external to the core network which in this way needs to comprise only a more or less rudimentary switching functionality (Service Switching Points) and the ability to recognize IN call requests and route them to the specialized service control points. The advent of Mobile Agent and Distributed Object Technologies (MAT and DOT) can help unravel the full IN potential. The IN, being a distributed infrastructure has much to gain from these technologies in terms of flexibility, reduced times to develop, test and deploy new services and an overall architecture that is easier to manage, maintain and extend.

The ACTS MARINE project [3] had the objective to investigate enhancements of IN towards a distributed computational environment, which will model the interactions between IN elements as distributed method invocations and will allow the exchange of Service Logic Programs (SLPs) implemented as mobile agents. IN elements in this context refer to those functional entities that correspond to the endpoints of traditional IN flows as they are described in [4].

For comprehensive descriptions of DOT and MAT see [5,6]. This paper is structured as follows. We first introduce the concept of Distributed IN and provide its rationale. We then describe the architecture of a prototypical implementation. Having employed extensively DOT and MAT in this context we present our experiences and conclude with some thoughts on the applicability of these technologies in this and similar contexts.

C. Linnhoff-Popien and H.-G. Hegering (Eds.): USM 2000, LNCS 1890, pp. 310-317, 2000.
© Springer-Verlag Berlin Heidelberg 2000

2 What is Distributed IN?

In a traditional IN implementation, the Intelligent Network Application Protocol (INAP) information flows are conveyed by means of static peer-to-peer protocols executed at each functional entity. The static nature of the functional entities and of the protocols they employ means that in turn the associations between them are topologically fixed. An IN architecture as defined by [4] is inherently centralised with a small set of service control points and a larger set of service switching points engaged with it in INAP dialogues. The service control points are usually the bottleneck of the entire architecture and their processing capacity and uptime in large extent determine the number of IN calls the entire architecture can handle effectively.

Distributed object technologies can help alleviate that problem by making associations between functional entities less rigid. This is a by-product of the location transparencies that use of DOT introduces in any context.

Once a distributed processing environment has been in place, MAT can in turn be employed to take advantage of object mobility. In MARINE, SLPs are implemented as agents able to migrate to the switch and control its operations locally. This can be justified on performance or load balancing grounds. For instance, having the SLP interact locally with the switch avoids the larger remote communication costs and economizes on network bandwidth. It also relieves a possibly overloaded service control point.

3 The Architecture at Large

Based on the considerations expressed in the previous section, we are augmenting the physical entities of traditional IN with distributed processing and code mobility capabilities. In particular at each computing node that hosts a functional entity, a CORBA ORB and a mobile agent platform are installed. The introduction of CORBA allows a laxer mapping between functional and physical entities, which can in any case change very easily so this mapping is not an intrinsic property of the architecture. In effect, we define a CORBA interface for each endpoint of an INAP information flow and implemented the appropriate CORBA objects for servicing these flows. So, both the Service Control Function (SCF) and the Service Switching Function (SSF) are CORBA objects, peers with each other. Java was used for the implementation of the SCF since the later relied on MAT.

The major physical entities of the system depicted in Figure 1 are:

1. The Service Execution Node (SEN). A workstation hosting – among others – the SCF. A Java-based mobile agent platform (Grasshopper [7]) and a CORBA ORB are installed at the SEN. The SCF agency provides the functionality for SLPs to be introduced, initiated, executed, suspended or withdrawn. The term 'agency' refers to the components that must be installed in a computer node and that provide the necessary runtime environment for mobile agents to execute. SLPs are implemented as mobile agents to take advantage of the mobility characteristics in ways that are described later on in this section. Naturally, not all components of the SCF need be mobile agents. A lot of infrastructure components are stationary agents or simply Java objects having no relationship with MAT except for the fact that they share the same process space. The SCF agency uses the ORB installed at the SEN and so it appears connected on to the CORBA bus of the system. SLP agents in the SEN can migrate to the switch using the agent bus (which is also used when SLPs are initially deployed from a management workstation).

2. The Service Switching and Control Point (SSCP). It hosts a SCF identical with the one at the SEN which caters for SLPs that have migrated locally to the switch. It also hosts the SSF which is for the most part a typical SSF implementation. It is usual for SSFs to be implemented in C++ to respond to stringent performance requirements. Having mobile SLPs implemented in Java communicate with static, C++ code would be a very cumbersome situation if it weren't for CORBA. CORBA's implementation transparency means that language of choice is not important and its location transparency implies that the SSF can behave the same way whether the SLP it is engaged with is locally or remotely located (i.e. located at the SEN's or the SSCP's SCF). Two workstations are shown attached to the switch using bearer signalling. A Broadband Videotelephony and an Interactive Multimedia Retrieval application were installed on each terminal and were used for testing.

3. Finally, there is also the Service Management System node that is used for management, supervision and bootstrapping of the system. The Management System contains the agent repository which hosts a number of service agents (e.g. Interactive Multimedia Retrieval service) that are at bootstrap or reconfiguration time deployed in various agencies of the system. Service agents are originally deployed to the SEN's SCF. The CORBA Naming Service process also appears running in the Management System node but clearly it can run on any other CORBA enabled workstation. The same applies to the Region Registry process which also appears running at that node. The Registry is a Naming Service-like service that is for use within a agent environment and is used in connection with the agent bus.

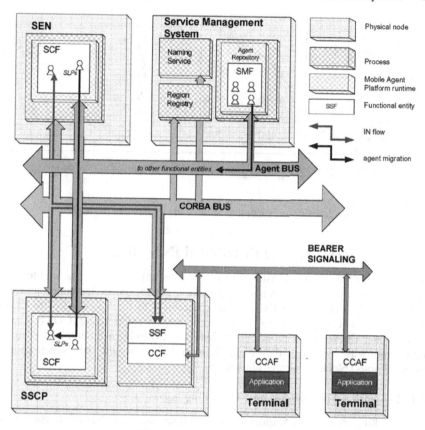

Fig. 1. Reference architecture

With the reference architecture of Figure 1 in mind we can see how automatic reconfiguration of the network's IN flows can take place. Refer to Figure 2 for numbered steps.

Originally all SLPs reside on the SCF located in the SEN and so service provisioning (which involves SLP-switch interaction) occurs between two remotely located physical entities (like in traditional IN). We depict two SSCPs receiving instructions from the same SEN. This corresponds to frame (a) in Figure 2. However, when the load balancing mechanisms of the system detect that a certain service should be served locally (due to either link capacity exceeded or to computational overloading on a node), it uses that deployed service to clone it and create a second prototype. That cloned prototype is then migrated locally to one SSCP (frame (b)) and is used for subsequent sessions to provide services locally. The other SSCP whose load balancing mechanisms presumably did not detect the need for a locally available prototype continues to be served remotely (frame (c)). While the originally deployed prototypes are administered by the Management System, second prototypes' existence is transparent to it. The latter are created and removed by the switch-located SCFs when certain criteria are met. So, at a later point in time we may arrive in a situation where the second SSCP is served locally (i.e. from the SSCP located SCF) and the first one has reverted to remote mode.

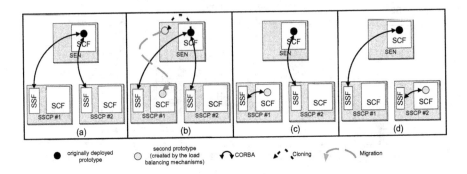

Fig. 2. Automatic reconfiguration of the IN flows of the network

4   Experiences Realising Distributed IN Systems

Reflecting on the design decisions we took while implementing the architecture we described, we can consider as a starting point a typical IN implementation. The first move towards a Distributed IN was the replacement of the SS7 stack with CORBA. This meant that the same IN flows were implemented using CORBA method invocations. The were a number of decisions that had to be taken at this step: the most important was whether the method invocations would be synchronous or asynchronous (blocking or non-blocking).

4.1   Invocation Mechanisms and Threading Issues

Non-blocking method invocations resemble closer the semantics of message passing protocols and thus probably require fewer modifications to existing software. Asynchronous method invocations or message passing mechanisms can be contained within wrapper entities to appear the same to higher layer software. Moreover, since the IN protocol has been defined with message passing mechanisms in mind, asynchronous invocations fit more naturally from a semantic point of view. This is why fewer modifications to existing software are needed after all.

Blocking method invocations are quite different than exchanging messages but they are more natural to use in the context of a distributed processing environment. This is different than saying that they more appropriate with a specific protocol (e.g. INAP) in mind. It is just that, if a distributed processing environment is to provide the illusion of an homogeneous address space, where method invocation are made just as the objects were residing in the same process context, then blocking method calls enhance this view. From a programmatic point of view, the main effect of synchronous method invocations is that they reduce need for threading at sending entities and that the developers don't have to implement synchronisation themselves (because the method calls themselves block until a result can be returned). On the other hand, depending on the architecture and the network of connections between invoking and invoked objects, it may lead to deadlock problems at receiving or intermediate entities where a number of such method invocation chains may pass through.

4.2 Establishing Associations between Objects

Concerning the use of a DOT, another issue we found to be important was the way in which the various CORBA objects of the system (corresponding to the functional entities) would obtain references to each other. Two at least approaches are possible.

One is the use of a simple look-up mechanism where the entities of the system search their peers by means of their names and retrieve an IOR they can then use to directly invoke methods. The Naming Service provides an elegant, standardized and scalable (with federation of Naming Services) solution. Support of nested naming contexts guards against name pollution. Reconfiguring associations is thus readily supported by simply changing the relevant names.

A more structured solution would be to implement a 'configuration server' that would be queried by all CORBA enabled entities of the system. The syntactic form of these queries would be left to the designers of the network to define but it would allow a higher level approach to be implemented, one that would more clearly reflect the idiosyncrasies of the architecture and the roles involved. This server would store in a centralised manner all configuration information about the system facilitating easy monitoring and modifications of these settings.

4.3 Configuring the System

In the MARINE architecture we chose to implemented the Naming Service solution coupled with the use of configuration agents. These agents employ code mobility and are dispatched from a central location to the nodes of the system. One of their uses is to carry configuration settings (e.g. Naming Service names). That reconfigurations should be applicable at all points during the operation of the system and not only at bootstrap time provided the rationale for the use of configuration agents.

In a complex distributed system, one involving many associations between its entities, during bootstrap or reconfiguration time objects can be found to be in invalid states. Catering for such not properly initialized objects can degenerate to a series of ad hoc remedies made on a peer-to-peer basis (e.g. between pairs of communicating objects) and not universally for the entire system. Given that these periods of inconsistent state can be extended (for the time-scales of a telecommunication system) and will occur not only during bootstrap but also during re-configuration or following an erroneous condition, it is easy to lose track of the overall state. A server that centrally stores and administers all configuration information about the system can provide a solution to this problem.

4.4 Applying MAT

Having relied on DOT to provide connectivity between IN functional entities, the next step was to identify ways in which the introduced location transparencies could result in more flexible implementations or even cater for shortcomings of the original centralised approach. Naturally, we considered MAT for this purpose. This presupposed use of Java and installation of special middleware. Since connections between objects were no longer statically defined nor associated with transport protocol addresses, code mobility could be employed to allow a software object to move from one node to another without terminating its associations. Performance optimisations as well as load balancing considerations could justify such a migration.

It is not the objective of this paper to make a general assessment of MAT but we have found that certain conditions hold which warrant the use of mobile code capabilities in the case of distributed IN. First of all, given the intensity of the IN dialogues held for instance between SCF and SSF, performance gains can indeed be expected. Secondly, each SLP is individual in terms of the finite state machines it maintains, the INAP methods it invokes, their parameters, their sequencing. The abstraction of an agent as an autonomous software object thus fits neatly with the concept of a service logic program. We do not believe that alternate ways to transfer control from SCF to SSF are not possible but we hold that the MAT paradigm blends naturally with the abstractions and models of IN and provides a clean cut and intuitively appealing way of doing things. Also, any solution resting on MAT is more dynamic and flexible than changing the logic of the protocols which can be very cumbersome or even unfeasible. Finally, management's ability to reconfigure the network remotely, without interrupting currently executed services makes the case for MAT even stronger. This can for instance be implemented using agents to be dispatched from a management location to a malfunctioning node to locally interact with it in case remote interfaces have not been defined.

With the particular architecture of MARINE in mind, we have found that the ability for an SLP to migrate to the switch and control its operations locally is a very efficient way to respond to an observed pattern of service requests, a congestion or an anticipated failure or maintenance shut down. We also found the mechanism of cloning existing prototypes very helpful all the more so since it was supported directly by the platform we used. We also employed code mobility to dispatch specialised software components to deal with problems or reconfigurations at remote nodes.

5 Conclusions

We have found that CORBA can very reliably substitute message-based protocols like INAP while incurring only mild performance penalties. Furthermore, there is nothing inherent in the paradigm of CORBA that prevents it for operating in even faster ranges, except perhaps its complexity and the larger number of intermediate layers. Those layers comprise for instance facilities for marshalling and unmarshalling that are absent in more rudimentary transport layer protocols. We believe that this is a profitable trade-off and that CORBA's advantages in wrapping legacy code and enhancing code modifiability (along with making it much more compact) for the most cases compensate handsomely. Moreover, development of specialized, real-time ORBs will probably remove performance-premised objections. Furthermore, and while in out prototype we used a private IP network to interconnect the IN physical elements the consortium behind the CORBA specifications has released a framework that enables conveyance of CORBA over a native SS7 protocol stack.

Concerning MAT, the performance of all presently available platforms would have been debilitating for commercial, real-time applications. Two factors contribute to this poor performance: use of Java and the fact that mobile agents in contrast to CORBA objects operate as threads in the context of a much larger and performance bogging entity (the platform providing the runtime environment). It is difficult to make an in-depth analysis comparing the performance of our prototype to that of contemporaneous architectures. This is due to the fact that the benefits accruing from the dynamic distribution characteristics of our approach would be more evidenced in large scale installations. However, an educated guess would probably hold the overall performance of our architecture to be inferior to that of commercial deployments. Nevertheless, and while the focus of our approach is not solely on performance, we believe that there is a clear potential for improvement as this is not due to structural reasons but has to be attributed to the present state of the technologies we used.

Performance or load balancing reasons by themselves should not necessarily lead to the introduction of MAT. However, when the potential for a more efficient environment coexists with the ability to adopt a network design that is more natural for a given context (e.g. agents to implement autonomous SLPs) then MAT is a viable alternative.

References

1. Magedanz, T. and Popescu-Zeletin R. (1996) Intelligent Networks – Basic Technology, Standards and Evolution, International Thomson Computer Press, ISBN: 1-85032-293-7, London, June.
2. Venieris, I.S. and Hussmann H. (eds.) (1998) Intelligent Broadband Networks, John Wiley, ISBN: 0-471-98094-3, Chichester
3. MARINE Project (ACTS AC340), http://www.telecom.ntua.gr/~marine/marine.htm
4. ITU-T Recommendations – Intelligent Network, Series Q.12xx
5. OMG, 'Common Object Request Broker Architecture and Specification', Updated Revision 2.1, November 1997.
6. Menelaos Perdikeas et al., "Mobile agent standards and available platforms", Computer Networks and ISDN systems, Elsevier, Vol 31, pp. 1999-2016
7. http://www.ikv.de/products/grasshopper/index.html

Leasing in a Market for Computing Capacity

Spyros Lalis and Alexandros Karipidis

Computer Science Dept.,
University of Crete, Hellas
{lalis,karipid}@csd.uoc.gr
Institute of Computer Science,
Foundation for Research and Technology, Hellas
{lalis,karipid}@ics.forth.gr

Abstract. One of the challenges in large scale distributed computing is to utilize the thousands of idle personal computers connected to the Internet. In this paper, we present a system that enables users to effortlessly and safely export their machines in a global market of processing capacity. Efficient resource allocation is performed based on statistical machine profiles and leases are used to promote dynamic task placement. We show how leasing, as opposed to static resource allocation, yields a natural renegotiation process through which prioritized computations receive better quality of service and resource providers enjoy bigger profits.

1 Introduction

The growth of the Internet has provided us with the largest network of interconnected computers in history. Many of these systems are often under-utilized, a fact accentuated by the globe's geography since "busy" hours in one time-zone tend to be "idle" hours in another. Distributing computations over the Internet is thus very appealing.

Several issues must be resolved for this to be feasible. Platform heterogeneity must be overcome and security problems arising from the execution of code from untrusted parties must be confronted. In order to register an available machine as part of a computing infrastructure, a corresponding runtime environment must also be downloaded and installed. This not only costs time but also introduces several administration headaches, practically limiting current resource sharing systems. Moreover, in most cases, little is done to make participation attractive to third parties, which we believe is of key importance if such a system is to be widely used.

In this paper we present a platform that addresses these problems, promoting distributed computing over the Internet considerably. In this system, hosts advertise their intention to serve as resource providers in a global market. Clients enter this market to locate machines that are appropriate for their computation. Matchmaking between supply and demand occurs via an economy-based algorithm producing contracts. Contracts have an expiration time, thus are essentially leases of use. In the case that resources are charged for, leasing guarantees

C. Linnhoff-Popien and H.-G. Hegering (Eds.): USM 2000, LNCS 1890, pp. 318–325, 2000.

that profitable contracts will be assigned to resource providers without any intervention on their behalf. With leases it is also possible to place an upper limit to the amount of time prioritized computations can be blocked or experience performance degradation due to other computations with less priority.

2   System Architecture

In order to guarantee cross-platform operability, yet at the same time minimize administration overhead and achieve execution safety for hosts, the system is implemented in Java. Providers connect to the system by pointing a web browser to a given address from which the runtime system is automatically downloaded to their machines as a Java applet. Client applications connect to the system via an application programming interface (API).

Both providers and clients submit orders to a server, specifying their actual and desired machine profile respectively. Hence, they act as sellers and buyers in a market of computing capacity. Given the fact that any machine connected to the Internet can place a sell order, and anyone can use the system API to write applications issuing respective buy orders, a universal market is formed.

An overview of the system's architecture is depicted in Fig. 1. The basic system components are the market server, hosts, the host agent, schedulers, tasks and client applications (or front-ends). The role of and the interactions between these components are briefly discussed in the next subsections.

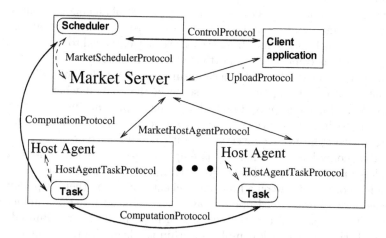

Fig. 1. Overview of architecture

The *Client Application* is a program which needs to perform computations that require considerable processing power. Through the system, it may either distribute a computation across a number of machines or just delegate the execution of an entire computation to a fast idle machine to speed up execution.

The *Market Server* is the meeting place for buyers and sellers of processing power. It collects orders from clients and hosts. Using this information, it then matches buy with sell orders and thus allocates resources.

A *Host* is a machine made available to be used by clients. A host participates in the market through the *Host Agent*, a Java applet. The user visits a URL with a Java enabled web browser and the agent is downloaded to her system. The agent communicates with the market server, takes care of placing orders on behalf of the user and executes tasks assigned to the host. It also provides the market server with the benchmark scores needed for the host's profile.

Computations consist of a *Scheduler* and one or more *Tasks*. The scheduler runs on the market server, placing orders in the market for acquiring machines. New orders can be issued at any time to adapt to changing application requirements or market conditions. When a host is allocated to the scheduler, a task is launched in that machine to assist in completing the computation.

3   Resource Allocation

Host allocation is based on machine profiles. Both hosts (sellers) and clients (buyers) submit orders to the market server, specifying their actual and desired machine profile respectively. The profiles include the mean and variance for a set of benchmarks over key performance characteristics such as integer and floating point arithmetic. Part of a profile is also the host *abort ratio*, which is the ratio of computations killed versus computations initiated on that host (a "kill" is caused when a host abruptly leaves the system in the midst of an ongoing computation). The performance vectors and abort ratio of host machines are automatically produced by the host agents. Profiles can be easily extended to include additional information that could be of importance for host selection.

Further, a credit based [1] mechanism is used for charging. Credit can be translated into anything that makes sense in the context where the system is deployed. Within a non-profit institution, it may represent time units to facilitate quotas or to introduce priorities. Service-oriented organizations could charge clients for using hosts by converting credit to actual currency.

An economy-based mechanism is employed to match the orders issued by providers and application clients. For each match, the market produces a lease, which is a contract between a host and a client containing their respective orders and the price of use agreed upon. Leases are produced using continuous double auction [6]. A lease entitles the client to utilize the host for a limited amount of time. If the client's task completes within the lease duration, then the buyer transfers an amount of credit to the seller as a reward, calculated by multiplying actual duration with the lease's price per second. If the lease duration is not honored, an amount of credit is transfered from the dishonoring party to the other as a compensation.

Since leases have an expiration date, it may not be possible to maintain the same set of hosts allocated to a computation, for its entire duration. In fact, this is highly unlikely to happen if the computation is lengthy, compared to the lease durations specified by the corresponding host providers. Moreover, at some points in time, an application may not be able to get any hosts at all to perform its tasks. As an example, Fig. 2 shows a trading scenario where an application eventually fails to keep the same host due to a price raise. An important consequence is that application schedulers must be able to also deal with (temporary) unavailability of hosts.

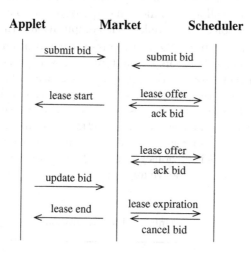

Fig. 2. A trading scenario

The trading protocol is designed to minimize communication between hosts and the market (the number of hosts is expected to be very large). Hosts contact the market only to submit/change their bids while the market communicates with hosts only when their current lease status changes. The interaction between the market and application schedulers is more tight in order to allow for flexible and timely resource negotiation. Essentially, the market notifies schedulers each time a bid can be converted into a contract as well as each time a contract is about to expire. In the former case, the scheduler may either accept or turn down the contract. In the latter case the scheduler may withdraw its bid (as in Fig. 2), leave it unchanged, or update its bid to actively try to re-gain possession of a host. Schedulers may also submit new bids at any point in time.

4   Leasing vs Buying Computing Resources

To illustrate the importance of leasing in an open environment, such as the Internet, we present an experiment conducted using a prototype version of the system. These measurements show how renegotiation affects both the quality of service experienced by clients and the amount of credit collected by providers.

The scenario of the experiment for which the measurements were made is as follows. We let two identical and resource intensive computations, C1 and C2, enter the system under conditions of resource scarcity, i.e. there is not enough capacity to accommodate both computations at the same time. These computations are assigned a different budget for performing their calculations; let Budget(C1) << Budget(C2). Finally, the computation with the lower budget (C1) is given a head start of a few seconds, followed by the other computation (C2). The same scenario is executed twice, one time for an infinite and the other for a limited leasing duration respectively. Leases with no expiration date lead to static resource allocation, meaning that once a resource is allocated to a computation it will not be freed unless the computation terminates.

As it can be inferred from Fig. 3 static resource allocation has a particularly disturbing effect. Since C1 enters the system first, it acquires all resources, and continues to hold them even in the presence of C2, which has a bigger budget. Assuming that budget reflects priority, this implies that a prioritized process is actually blocked by another process of lower priority. Notice that blocking occurs despite the fact that resources are auctioned. While auction mechanisms guarantee price competition they require *all* competitors to be present when the auction takes place. This is obviously impossible in an open system where clients and providers may enter and leave anytime.

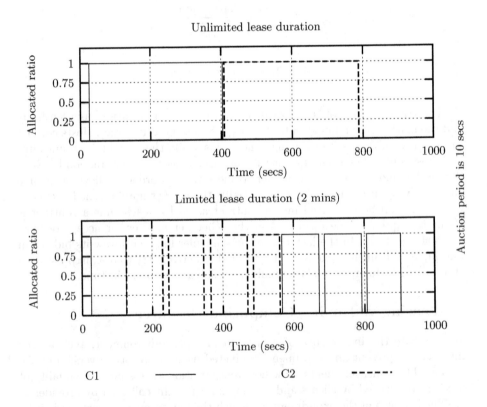

Fig. 3. Allocated resources

This effect is largely eliminated case when resources are leased for a reasonably limited duration. In this case, even though C1 seizes all resources upon entry, these are re-allocated to C2 when the leases expire. Therefore, the total execution time of C2 is only slightly longer than the actual time spent for performing the computation. This is a noticeable difference compared to the first case. Conversely, only when C2 terminates, can C1 reclaim these machines and complete its execution. It can thus be said that leasing compensates for the impossibility of predicting future system traffic in a dynamic system. In other words, leasing is the analog of timesharing within a multiprocess system.

It is worthwhile pointing out another implication of leasing. Even though resource utilization is the same for both cases, providers collect more credits under leasing, as shown in Fig. 4. This is particularly important in a real-life situation were resources are unlikely to be given for free and providers wish to recuperate their costs as quickly as possible. Notably, the increase in provider income does not come at the cost of the low budget computation C1, which allocates resources at the same price yet at a later point in time. It is the computation with the high budget that "pays" more, but always according to its true valuation.

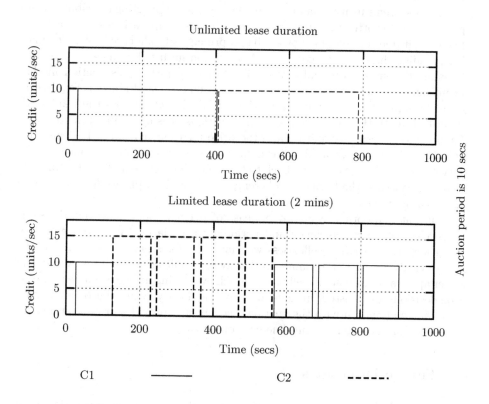

Fig. 4. Provider income

Leases are also practical in cooperative environments. The lease duration allows users to indicate when their hosts are under-utilized. Based on this knowledge, tasks can be placed on hosts that will be idle for enough time, and checkpoints can be accurately scheduled, right before a host becomes unavailable.

5   Related Work

Legion [7], Globus [5] and Condor [8] have mechanisms for describing resource properties and performing matching. These mechanisms were created in order to make it possible to respect local access control policies of hosts and were not oriented towards a market-based approach. None of them uses auctions in order to perform matching of computations to hosts and as a consequence, in order to maximize income in a real market situation, providers would have to constantly monitor the supply and demand for resources and change their offers correspondingly. These systems are also architecture-specific which constrains the market's size and partitions competition. Finally, all require extensive administration which prohibits a low overhead participation in the market.

Other systems using Java have been designed for supporting distributed computations. Charlotte [3], automatically distributes computations over machines. However, it does not employ market-based principles to allocate hosts. The market paradigm has received considerable attention in distributed systems aiming for and efficient resource allocation [4]. Popcorn [9] also uses auction mechanisms but does not provide leasing, which as demonstrated above is required in order to support a dynamic market. The Java Market [2] uses the framework described in [1]. However, it does not use auctions, leasing or an interactive tool for providers to specify and update the price for their machines. It is also not suitable for interactive applications, as source code must be compiled on the server and results are e-mailed back to the client. Therefore it is hard to provide market services in the form of a coherent, user-friendly application which can be installed on a client's desktop.

Currently, no other system offers ease of participation, allocation decisions assistance, economic efficiency and periodic renegotiation. We provide ease of participation through an effortless web interface for sellers. Buyers also participate easily by simply running market-aware applications as they would any other application. Economic efficiency is achieved using auctions whereas allocation decisions are assisted through host profiling. Lastly, renegotiation is enforced and – in combination with the auction mechanism – provides prioritization over a network of heterogenous runtime environments.

6   Future Directions

An issue that we wish to investigate is how the cost of check-pointing (and migrating between hosts) is weighed against the cost of keeping tasks on hosts with degraded performance. It would be interesting to contrast the performance of leasing with checkpoints versus static allocation without checkpoints.

Moreover, we wish to experiment with schedulers capable of recording the performance of previous allocations. Such schedulers can be regarded as the "computational" counterparts of information agents that learn the users' preferences and scan the web for corresponding documents. In our case accumulated information can perhaps be converted into "experience", leading towards more adaptive resource allocation strategies responding to the different requirements of individual applications.

Lastly we would like to look into trading and scalability issues. We are currently considering improvements to the way contract acknowledgment and expiration is handled in order to support a more flexible and efficient re-negotiation process between the market and application schedulers. Also, the current architecture is limited by the market server. A single server could not handle hosts connecting to a truly world-wide version of this service. We intend to overcome this problem by introducing multiple market servers that will allow traffic to be shared among several geographically distributed servers.

References

[1] Y. Amir, B. Awerbuch, and R. S. Borgstrom. A cost-benefit framework for online management of a metacomputing system. In *Proceedings of the First International Conference on Information and Computation Economies*, pages 140–147, October 1998.

[2] Y. Amir, B. Awerbuch, and R. S. Borgstrom. The java market: Transforming the internet into a metacomputer. Technical report, Johns Hopkins University, Center for Networking and Distributed Systems, 1998.

[3] A. Baratloo, M. Karaul, Z. M. Kedem, and P. Wyckoff. Charlotte: Metacomputing on the web. In *Ninth International Conference on Parallel and Distributed Computing Systems*, September 1996.

[4] S. H. Clearwater, editor. *Market-based Control: A Paradigm for Distributed Resource Allocation*. World Scientific, 1995.

[5] I. Foster and C. Kesselman. Globus: A metacomputing infrastructure toolkit. *Intl J. Supercomputer Applications*, 11(2), 1997.

[6] D. Friedman. The double auction market institution: A survey. In D. Friedman and J. Rust, editors, *Proceedings of the Workshop in Double Auction Markets, Theories and Evidence*, June 1991.

[7] A. S. Grimshaw and W. A. Wulf. The legion vision of a worldwide computer. *CACM*, 40(1):39–45, 1997.

[8] R. Raman, M. Livny, and M. Solomon. Matchmaking: Distributed resource management for high throughput computing. In *Proceedings of the Seventh IEEE International Symposium on High Performance Distributed Computing*, July 1998.

[9] O. Regev and N. Nisan. The POPCORN Market – an Online Market for Computational Resources. In *Proceedings of the First International Conference on Information and Computation Economies*, pages 148–157, October 1998.

Virtual Malls for Web Commerce: Observations and Case Study

Anton Nijholt

Centre for Telematics and Information Technology (CTIT)
University of Twente, PO Box 217
7500 AE Enschede, the Netherlands
anijholt@cs.utwente.nl

Abstract In the real world there seem to be essential differences between shops, tourist offices, city halls, theatres and museums. However, when we try to design virtual environments allowing services, transactions, explorations and communication, are these environments really that different? Doesn't the 'virtual' in virtual environments allow us to introduce possibilities for visitors that extend those that are available in each of the mentioned physical environments and that can be become common for each of them? In this paper we survey our research on these issues and our attempt to integrate this research in a virtual environment devoted to the presentation and exploration of theatre information. We try to make clear that the topics we have to deal with do not differ from those that deal with access to commercial environments, museum and educational environments and other service and transaction environments.

1 Introduction

Many distinctions can be made between shopping, going to a theatre performance, visiting an art exhibition in a gallery, going to a museum, asking for information at a tourist office, buying a house and visiting a town hall to arrange a new passport or to register a newly-born child. These distinctions are useful and really make a difference. Nevertheless, we can also distinguish behavior and interactions of the people involved in these activities that is common, rather than distinct. When the activity is not completely routine, people need help and advice. "What else is there to see?", "Do you have similar and cheaper products.", "Is there a Van Gogh painting from the same period?", "Why isn't this allowed?", "Do I have to pay for this?", etc.

In all these utterances the user is making references to information that has not been mentioned or shown explicitly. Generally, this is one of the main obstacles to natural language understanding. However, unlike telephone conversations or menu-based computer-human interaction, in a virtual reality environment we can make an attempt to resolve such references by looking at the 3D context we have designed ourselves. The possibility to match user utterances with both a language model and a visualized context model makes it interesting to explore the embedding of dialogue systems in virtual environments.

In this paper we argue that in virtual reality environments we have the tools both to emphasize and to blur all kinds of distinctions in the natural world. Here we want to

C. Linnhoff-Popien and H.-G. Hegering (Eds.): USM 2000, LNCS 1890, pp. 326-333, 2000.
© Springer-Verlag Berlin Heidelberg 2000

explore similarities in using and visiting virtual environments, rather than differences. However, before doing that, it should be clear that different domains have different audiences; such audiences may require different interaction strategies and such audiences may require different types of help in order to get the information they want, to perform a transaction, to successfully conclude a negotiation or to be able to communicate with other users interested in the same environment. Clearly, accidental meetings may lead to interesting and useful contacts between people and when we design information and transaction systems in virtual worlds, we certainly should take care that such contacts not only remain possible, but also are natural, perhaps more natural than in reality. Nevertheless, we should be aware of the fact that for the majority of people buying a pack of milk from a supermarket, is an act that emotionally is very different from the act of discussing which performance, which art exhibition or which other kinds of cultural events will be visited this evening.

2 What Interactions Are Desired by Visitors?

We take the point of view that despite differences, there are so many similarities for which we need research results that, without neglecting the special needs for the domain of museums, the domain of theatres, the domain of commerce, the domain of (commercial and governmental) information services, etc., we first need to explore similarities rather than differences. Similarities we want to exploit are:

- Visitors need to be able to explore an environment; this requires both visualization of an environment and the available information and the possibility to start dialogues about information, transactions and environment;
- Visitors need to be able to change an environment; changes may differ from changing the number of available tickets for a performance, changing the number of books displayed in a bookshop, changing the color of the furniture in a showroom, becoming a member of the noticeable audience (for a performance, an exhibition or a particular painting) to being able to influence the composition of an exhibition, the lightning during a performance, the behavior of actors during a performance, etc.
- Visitors need to be able to express themselves in their own, natural ways; the environment should be able to detect and interpret the different ways a visitor tries to communicate with the environment. That is, the environment has to understand multimodal user input (keyboard, mouse, language, speech, gestures, touch, eye tracking, facial expressions, body movements, etc,).
- Visitors need help. This may be provided by traditional means (e.g., context-sensitive pop-up windows), but it is more interesting to look at domain agents that know about the environment, that know about the information that is available, and that know about the preferences of a particular visitor. It should be defined how such personal assistants (or butlers) can act, communicate with others, serve their master and decide which private information others can access.
- Visitors should be able to communicate with each other. That is, not only communication with domain agents, but communication with who ever shows interest in the same environment, the information it offers, but much more importantly,

information that is not explicitly available in the environment, but that is available in the shared knowledge of domain agents, visitors and world wide web.

In what follows we don't make a distinction between customers, visitors, users, etc. We present a case study in which we discuss an environment in which we can see and anticipate goal-directed behavior and browsing behavior of people using WWW. These different kinds of behavior follow from the fact that user goals can be more or less definite. In some situations shopping involves stress, in other situations it might be entertainment. The product that is looked for is also important. This shows in the differences between buying the usual pack of milk, the daily newspaper, a pair of shoes, a long awaited book or the ingredients for tonight's dinner. In the latter case, during shopping and depending upon what is available, what special offers there are, what time is available for shopping, etc., the decisions are made and the dinner is composed. Hence, apart from navigating in a physical space (the actual mall, the shop, the web pages shown on the screen), there is navigation in a space with product information and a space containing constraints that need to be considered in order to make decisions. In addition we can talk about a social space in which a buyer operates. A sales person can be part of this social space, but so can other customers or people looking for information. We can talk to them in order to get what we want (direct social navigation) but we can also notice and follow their behavior (indirect social navigation). In a virtual world we can have a social space inhabited by live agents, virtual agents and visitors.

3 What Will Be Influenced by Interaction Characteristics?

Now that we've looked at a virtual environment from the visitor's point of view, we now want to add some observations from the point of view of the environment's owner, the company that wants to sell and wants to make profits, while keeping good relations with its customers. Clearly, offering facilities as mentioned above helps in being a 'good' company. However, there are other aspects, which should be given attention. In particular, the virtual mall owner wants to know about the client's preferences. Not only concerning products, information and advice, but also concerning interaction behavior with the environment, with the domain agents made available in this environment and with other clients visiting this environment. The following, observations, clearly not independent from each other, can be given.

- *Consumer Buying Behavior (CBB)*. There exist several models that describe consumer-buying behavior. In Guttman et al. [2] some of them are related to the use of agent technologies. The main stages that are distinguished are need identification, product brokering, merchant brokering, negotiation, purchase and delivery, and service and evaluation. In particular product and merchant brokering and negotiation are considered to be the agent-centric stages of the models.
- *Trust and security*. Their users will not trust non-secure web systems. However, it is not necessarily the case that technically secure systems will be perceived as trustworthy. The concept of trust in e-commerce systems has been studied by, among others, Soltesz [8]. We adhere to his definition of trust: *The users positive expectations on the e-commerce systems ability to function accordingly to the user intentions expressed through his actions, under conditions of risk*. The paper by Soltesz is interesting because of his avocation of the use of the social psychological

concept of 'action space' in e-commerce research. Action space refers to the possibility of the user to control his environment. Obviously, different tasks and different user groups may require different action spaces. The design of the action space influences the users degree of trust.

- *Commitment.* Trust may be a prerequisite, but it does not necessarily lead to commitment. How can we stimulate the users commitment, his or her sympathy or even love for the system? When we are able to evoke such emotions towards the system, it certainly will help the users willingness to accept (to a certain degree) slow, wrong and non-robust feedback from the system. In a spoken language dialogue system a careful design, anticipating a user's errors and the system's shortcomings, of the prompts of the system is the main non-intimidating tool for achieving commitment.

- *Presence.* 'Presence' (the experience of being in one place or environment, even when one is physically situated in another; see Lombard & Ditton [5]) is an issue in the design of virtual environments that can be very much influenced (using sound, natural interactions, visual effects, etc.). Presence very much influences the user's well being, his or her patience, his or her willingness to buy and explore and to take advice seriously. Causes and effects of presence have been studied in experiments, but the number of parameters involved, e.g., task and user characteristics, makes systematic research difficult.

Among the design issues of 'action space' are: information needed to increase users trust (transparency of the system, who are the owners and trusted third parties, what are the customers rights, which privacy policies are maintained), communication to increase users trust (with company representatives, other users and trusted third parties), which interaction decisions are available (to cancel an order, to delete an electronic trail, etc.) and which information about the system status is available. These issues also influence the commitment the user shows to the system.

Needless to say that for many tasks and activities one may not expect that presence will necessarily enhance performance. On the contrary, presence can be noise which distracts a user from performing a task and which throws away the advantages of individual access from a home PC to, e.g., an information service. There is no need for a virtual waiting queue or the sound of a leaving plane when all we want to know is when the next flight to Amsterdam leaves.

Also in real life an environment may be designed to exploit the 'positive' feelings with respect to the environment, to stimulate trust, commitment and community feeling. In Kooijman [4] a rather comprehensive survey of design concepts for shops and shopping malls can be found. Hardly any attempt has been made to translate such concepts to virtual environments. We expect that in the near future much work will be devoted to the transition of knowledge of design, building, use and user appreciation of physical spaces to knowledge of similar issues in virtual environments.

4 The Case: Twente Virtual Theatre

We discuss a virtual world (Nijholt & Hulstijn [6]) for presenting information and allowing natural interactions about performances, associated artists and groups, availability of tickets, etc., for some existing theatres in the city of Enschede, the

Netherlands. Our virtual theatre[1] has been built according to the design drawings made by the architects of our local theatre. Part of the building has been realized by converting AutoCAD drawings to VRML97. Video recordings and photographs have been used to add 'textures' to walls, floors, etc. Sensor nodes in the virtual environment activate animations (opening doors) or start events (entering a dialogue mode, playing music, moving spotlights, etc.). Visitors can explore the environment of the building, hear the carillon of a nearby church, look at a neighboring pub and movie theatre, etc. and they can enter the theatre and walk around, visit the concert hall, admire the paintings on the walls, go to the balconies and, take a seat in order to get a view of the stage from that particular location. When the performance hall is entered, the lights dim, spotlights are moving over the stage and some music starts playing. Information about today's performances is available on an information board that is automatically updated using information from the database with performances. In addition, as may be expected, visitors may go to the information desk in the theatre, see previews of performances and start a dialogue with an information and transaction agent called 'Karen' (Figure 1). Karen has a 3D animated talking face. On Karen's desk is a monitor on which visitors can see pictures or video previews of performances. Unfortunately, for most performances no video preview is available yet, so we cannot display them for every performance that is in the database.

Fig. 1. Karen at the Information Desk

Domain-dependent tasks are assigned to agents in our environment. It can be useful to visualize such agents using talking faces and animated 3D avatars. From several studies it has become clear that people engage in social behavior toward machines. It is also well known that users respond differently to different 'computer personalities'. It is possible to influence the user's willingness to continue working even if the system's performance does not seem to be adequate. Users can be made to enjoy the interaction and they can be made to perform better, all depending on the way the interface and the interaction strategy have been designed.

---

[1] The system is accessible using the Cosmo Player browser (http://parlevink.cs.utwente.nl)

4.1 An Agent Platform in the Virtual Environment

In the current prototype version of the virtual theatre we have an information and transaction agent, we have a navigation agent and there are some agents under development. An agent platform has been developed in JAVA to allow the definition and creation of intelligent agents. Users can communicate with agents using speech and natural language keyboard input. Any agent can start up other agents and receive and carry out orders of other agents. Questions of users can be communicated to other agents and agents can be informed about each other's internal state. Both the information & transaction agent and the navigation agent are in the platform. But also the information board, presenting today's performances, has been introduced as an agent. And so can other objects in the environment.

4.2   Information, Transaction, and Navigation Services

Karen, the information & transaction agent, allows a natural language dialogue with the system about performances, artists, dates, prices, etc. Karen wants to give information and to sell tickets. Karen is fed from a database that contains all the information about performances in the (existing) theatre.

In our current version of the dialogue system of which Karen is the face user utterances are simplified using a great number of rewrite rules. The resulting simple sentences are parsed. The output can be interpreted as a request of a certain type. System response actions are coded as procedures that need certain arguments. Missing arguments are subsequently asked for. The system is modular, where each 'module' corresponds to a topic in the task domain. For example, a module has to take care of a date a user is referring to (next Wednesday, over two weeks, tomorrow).

Users need help in order to be able to get the information they want. Karen knows about theatre performances and artists and the user knows that she should address Karen in order to get such information. However, when we visualize information (that is, we introduce information boards, posters, doors to rooms containing particular information, embodied agents with particular knowledge, the building and geographically and semantically associated information, etc.), the user expects to get answers that show that the system knows about what the visitor sees and explores and is at least able to initiate a dialogue about the topics the user introduces and to return believable (not necessarily satisfactory) answers. Presently, our navigation agent knows about a geometrically described environment. Where can we find the keyboard, where is Karen, where is the entrance, etc.? When a user addresses the navigation agent with a question that is about performances, the navigation agent makes an attempt to give control to Karen, the information and transaction agent.

4.3 From Environment to Community

Today there are examples of virtual spaces that are visited and inhabited by people sharing common interests. These spaces can represent offices, shops, classrooms, companies, etc. However, it is also possible to design virtual spaces that are devoted to certain themes and are tuned to users (visitors) interested in that theme or to users (visitors) that not necessarily share common (professional, recreational, educational) interests, but share common conditions (driving a car, being in hospital for some period, having the same therapy, belonging to the same political party, etc.).

In the previous subsections we have looked at possibilities for theatre visitors to access information, to communicate with agents designed by the provider of the information system and to explore an environment with the goal to find information or to find possibilities to enter into some transaction. Hence, we have a community of people interested in theatre, in music, in performers, and their environment has been modeled along the lines of an existing theatre. We need to investigate how we can allow communication between users or visitors of this web-based information and transaction system. Users can help each other to find certain information, they can inform each other (especially when they know about the other's interests), they can have conversations about common interests and they can have domain-related collaboration (e.g., in our case, they can decide to perform a certain play where the actors are distributed among different web sites but sharing the same virtual stage).

It is an important question how to integrate the human visitors of our environment with our models of agent interaction, with our models of multi-modal interaction and multi-media presentation, with models of non-verbal agent behavior (associated with verbal behavior) and with models of agent movements. Hardly any research results are available and no experiments have been performed from which we can learn how humans behave in such agent-rich environments. See [7] for the embedding of our environment in a multi-user environment where users can share scenes, can see each other in the environment and can chat with each other about their interests.

5 Conclusions and Future Research

Presently, our agents are not 'believable', i.e., they have very specific and detailed domain knowledge but they are not able to use some common-sense knowledge concerning family, relatives, environment in which they are, etc. Simple questions concerning these issues should be understood, at least in the sense that it becomes possible to recognize them and to generate an utterance that can at least be considered as an attempt to get the dialogue going. Examples are Jennifer, a virtual saleswoman, and Erin, a virtual bartender, both designed by Extempo Systems Inc. [3]. Jennifer, e.g., has detailed knowledge about cars and racing, but questions on family or country music can be dealt with in a believable way. Jennifer has personality, customers feel confident to talk with her and a company that employs Jennifer will build relationships of affection, trust and loyalty with its customers. The information that is elicitated from a customer is stored in marketing and customer databases.

Other issues that need to be studied are user modeling and personalization. Currently, our agents do not employ a model of a user or of user groups. No user model has been programmed in the agent by the user, provided as a knowledge base by a knowledge engineer or obtained and maintained by a learning procedure from the user and customized according to his/her preferences and habits and to the history of interaction with the system. Personalization techniques [1] should be studied and they should be applied to the dynamic generation of presentations in virtual environments and the customization of interaction and presentation styles to different users.

Finally, when considering our specific application domain, we should (now that we have made clear that there are many similarities) study what makes this domain different from others, what properties CBB models for this specific domain have. Similarly, we can look at the usual criteria for selling products via the Internet: technology fit, logistic fit and culture fit. Providing information about cultural events and selling tickets for such events scores high on these 'fitness' scales. There is no need to test the product before buying it, to touch or smell it, to find out how it works and how easy it is to use, etc. Visitors of our theatre will be interested in seeing previews, hearing audio fragments and read additional information about performances, artists and directors, but this is all possible using WWW.

Acknowledgements. I gratefully acknowledge the help of the referees who provided many useful comments on the contents and the presentation of this paper.

References

1. Ardissono, L. & A. Goy. Tailoring the interaction with users in electronic shops. Proc. *7th Conference on User Modeling*. Banff, Canada, Springer-verlag, 35-44, 1999.
2. Guttman, R.H., A.G. Moukas & P. Maes. Agent-mediated electronic commerce: a survey. *Knowledge Engineering Review*, June 1998.
3. Isbister, K. & B. Hayes-Roth. Social implications of using synthetic characters: An examination of a role-specific intelligent agent. KSL Report No. 98-01, January 1998, Department of Computer Science, Stanford University,
4. Kooijman, D. *Machine en theater. Ontwerpconcepten van winkelgebouwen*. Uitgeverij 010, Rotterdam, 1999.
5. Lombard, M. & T. Ditton. At the heart of it all: The concept of presence. *Journal of Mediated Communication* 3, Nr.2, September 1997.
6. Nijholt, A. & J. Hulstijn. Multimodal Interactions with Agents in Virtual Worlds. In *Future Directions for Intelligent Systems and Information Science*, N. Kasabov (ed.), Physica-Verlag: Studies in Fuzziness and Soft Computing, 1999, to appear.
7. Nijholt, A. & H. Hondorp. Towards communicating agents and avatars in virtual worlds. *EUROGRAPHICS 2000*, A. de Sousa & J.C. Torres (eds.), August 2000, to appear.
8. Soltesz, T. Action space as a mean to establish trust in electronic commerce systems. In: A. Paiva (ed.), *Affect in Interactions: Towards a New Generation of Interfaces*. Proceedings workshop of the I3 Annual Meeting *Community of the Future*, Siena, Italy, October 1999.

A QoS Meta Model to Define
a Generic Environment for QoS Management

Jérôme Daniel [1,2], Bruno Traverson [1], and Sylvie Vignes [2]

[1] EDF Division R&D, 1 avenue du Général De Gaulle,
F-92140 Clamart, France
{ Jerome.Daniel, Bruno.Traverson } @der.edf.fr
[2] ENST, 46 rue Barrault,
F-75634 Paris Cedex 13, France
Sylvie.Vignes@enst.fr

Abstract. The management of Quality of Service (QoS) in Information Systems allows their users to request services under certain conditions varying in function of their requirements but also in function of the current capabilities of the computing environment. The kind of the requirements and the notation used to formulate them vary with regards to application area and computing environment used. This paper presents a generic architecture that can manage QoS independently of the QoS domain and of the distributed environment used. We also introduce a QoS meta model (defined with a meta modeling facility – the so-called MOF – standardized by OMG) to exchange QoS models that allows a generic approach for QoS notation. By this way, this QoS management architecture is the first and only one platform which can manage all QoS contract properties (which are guaranty, observation, negotiation and composition) under a generic approach with regards of domain, environment and notation.

1 Introduction

The constant improvement of computers and systems has allowed the definition and the development of high level distributed environments. These environments, which are able to provide very wide functionality to their users, are now more and more used. However, the users are more demanding than in the past, because they do not only want a service but they want to get a service under some conditions (guaranty of response time, proximity constraint, and so on).

These concepts are encompassed in the term: Quality Of Service (QoS). The mechanisms to apply in order to manage QoS are very difficult to define and develop in existing systems. Moreover, several problems are implied by this management as for example the specification of user requirements, but also their observation and guaranty during the application life cycle.

Very often, there are several solutions to manage QoS that are dedicated to a specific domain. For example, some works suggest a QoS management for multimedia

C. Linnhoff-Popien and H.-G. Hegering (Eds.): USM 2000, LNCS 1890, pp. 334-339, 2000.

systems or QoS management for telecommunication systems (where time, jitter, ... are taken into account). But, there is no platform to manage in a generic way all domains of requirements for QoS. The main reason for this, is the difficulty to express in the same notation distinct QoS approaches.

OMG (Object Management Group) defines a meta modelling facility (MOF) [3] that gives numerous advantages as for example the exchange of models via XMI (XML Metadata Interchange) [7] which is a specific XML (eXtended Markup Language) [8] document.

Several application domains have defined their own model to manage QoS with for example a dedicated QoS notation. As we will see in the fourth part of this paper, we have also defined such a model. If we use MOF to create a model of our QoS model (a QoS meta model), we will be able to use XMI to exchange QoS models.

By this way, any QoS notation could be used to express QoS offers and QoS requirements and thus we will also have a generic approach to describe QoS. In conclusion, our platform will be generic with regards to QoS notations.

But is it always possible to transform a QoS model to another one? It is very difficult to provide a definitive answer to this question, but if we have a very wide QoS model that is able to manage any QoS domains, its QoS meta model would be the best candidate for enabling the transformation of one QoS model to this QoS model (because this one is the most complete model).

Moreover, if we use MOF, we will model our QoS model (and by this way our QoS platform and mechanisms). Thus, our technical approach to develop this QoS management architecture will be more efficient and reliable.

At least, with our QoS meta model and MOF capabilities, we will be able to automatically get the IDL interfaces for the QoS model creation and we will be able to maintain a QoS model repository. By this way, it will be easier to lookup for an asked QoS description into the QoS model repository.

This paper is divided in two parts. In the first part, we explain and define our QoS meta model and an example that uses it. In the second part, we expose our generic architecture to manage QoS in distributed environments.

2 A QoS Meta Model

In this part, we describe our QoS meta model. This part is divided in three sections that. The first section explains the needs for a QoS meta model. The second section describes the QoS meta model. Finally, the third section presents the overall QoS management architecture that includes the MOF capabilities.

2.1   The Description of the QoS Meta Model

Note: we are using an UML notation to represent our QoS meta model.

In our model, each functional object is linked to a QoS object. This QoS object contains one QoS offer, and several QoS requirements. A QoS offer is a set of properties where each property can be basic (a simple value and a name), evaluated (requires an external evaluator) or constrained (requires some other QoS objects to be evaluated, this kind of properties is a constraint to some other properties of one or more QoS objects). In the same way, a QoS requirement is a constraint that is applied to a set of properties. The following figure summarises this first subset of the meta model.

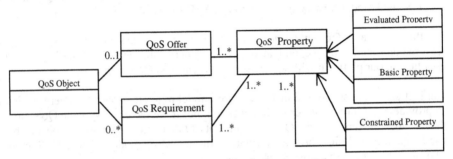

Fig. 1. First subset of the QoS meta model

Two QoS Objects can be linked by a composition (if the first object requires the second one to provide a QoS offer, it means in this case that the first object contains a constrained property on the second object). Moreover, when a QoS contract is established, it contains several QoS objects and more precisely several QoS compositions.

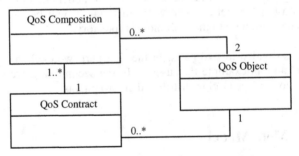

Fig. 2. A QoS contract into the QoS meta model

With these two simple meta models, we have describe all possible links and interactions between QoS Object, thus the QoS meta model is the union of them. To conclude this meta model presentation, let us take a simple example to discover that it corresponds to the QoS meta model.

2.2 A QoS Model Example: A Movie on Demand System

In this example, we distinguish four actors: a user (named foo), a network and two movie servers (A & B). Mr Foo requires a movie with a price and with a good transmission speed.

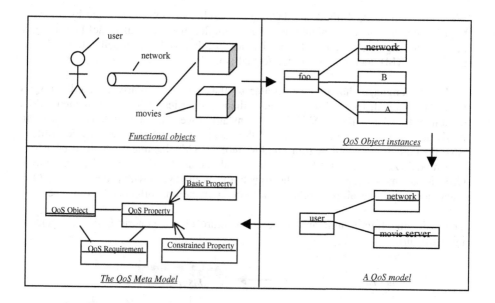

Fig 3. An example of QoS instances, objects, model and meta model

At the left upper corner, the figure illustrates the functional objects which are modelled in QoS by the QoS Objects represented on the right side. These QoS objects are linked by QoS relationships. QoS Objects « A » and « B » are two instances of the same QoS Object.

The corresponding QoS model is shown on the right bottom corner. Here we only have three QoS objects, the user QoS Object (which is only a requirement) and two other QoS objects (network and movie server) which provide QoS offers.

The model can be modelled and the result is illustrated on the left bottom corner. This meta model is compatible with our QoS meta model.

3 A Generic Architecture to Manage QoS in Distributed Environments

Since we have a QoS meta model, we can now use the MOF capabilities to automatically generate a QoS model repository and a DTD for XMI documents.

With XMI and our QoS models DTD, we can exchange QoS models and by this way be independent of QoS notations. For example, we have also defined a QoS description language called « QDL » [Daniel 99] that we have modelled to be able to generate an XMI document from this formalism.

QDL is a language that is very similar to IDL and particularly adapted for QoS notation about distributed objects and their properties. With a dedicated XML document translator like XLST (XML translator) we can automatically translate an XML document to another one. So a QDL description could be expressed with an XMI document that could be translated to another XMI document which respects our QoS model DTD. Then, this QoS notation could be used and managed by our generic QoS management architecture. The translation is always possible because the QoS meta model includes all possibilities for QoS compositions, offers and requirements.

The following figure summarises the architecture of our generic QoS management infrastructure.

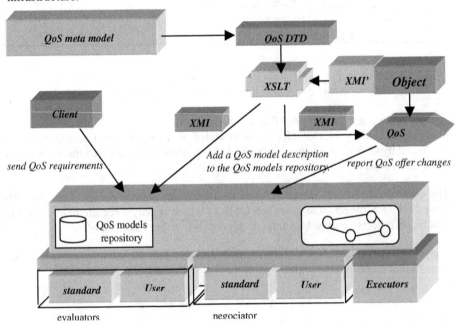

Fig. 4. An overview of the generic QoS management infrastructure

4 Conclusion

In this paper, we have described our approach to manage QoS and our QoS management infrastructure architecture. After that, we have concluded that a QoS model exchange is required to provide a generic QoS management for QoS notations.

This is the reason why we propose to use the MOF (Meta Object Facility) which provides several capabilities and in particular a way to exchange models. Then, we have presented our QoS meta model that can model any QoS model (with compositions, offers and requirements).

At last, we have extended our QoS infrastructure to include the QoS meta model capabilities. This, we can provide a generic QoS management architecture: generic about QoS domain, generic about environment, and generic about QoS notation.

Currently, we are developing such an architecture using Java for CORBA (with JavaORB [2]). The prototype will give us a way to validate our QoS management mechanisms and to observe potential performance problems. Moreover, into component platforms, configuration files and properties are usually expressed with XML. We suggest adding an additional descriptor for QoS (QoS Descriptor) that includes all QoS requirements and offers for the corresponding component. By this way, it will be possible to manage components with our QoS management architecture. So, we envisage applying in future this possibility into a component platform (such as a CORBA component platform or an Enterprise Java Bean platform).

References

1. Daniel, J., Traverson, B., Vignes, S.: Integration of quality of service in distributed object systems. International Conference on Distributed Applications and Information Systems (1999).
2. Distributed Object Group: JavaORB a free CORBA implementation". http:\\dog.exoffice.com.
3. OMG: Meta Object Facility (MOF) version 1.3. OMG Document (July 1999).
4. ISO/IEC: Open Distributed Processing Reference Model, parts 1, 2, 3, 4. ISO/IEC IS 10746-1.. 4 or ITU-T X901..4 (1995).
5. ISO/IEC: Open Distributed Processing Reference Model, Quality of Service. ISO/IEC Working Draft (January 1998).
6. OMG: The Common Object Request Broker Architecture and Specification, Revision 2.3. OMG Document (June 1999).
7. OMG: XMI (XML Meta Data Interchange). http://www.omg.org.
8. W3C: Extensible Markup Language (XML) 1.0. W3C Recommendation 10 Reference : REC-xml-19980210. http://www.w3.org/TR/REC-XML. (February 1998).

Author Index

Lecture Notes in Computer Science

For information about Vols. 1–1825
please contact your bookseller or Springer-Verlag